HOLY GRAIL
ACROSS THE
ATLANTIC

HOLY GRAIL ACROSS THE ATLANTIC

The
Secret History of Canadian
Discovery and Exploration

MICHAEL BRADLEY

With
DEANNA THEILMANN-BEAN

Foreword by John Robert Colombo

For Deanna Theilmann-Bean and Gloria
Shoebridge, but mostly for my son, Jason
Bradley, and for all those . . .

"Who feel the giant agony of the world,
and more, like slaves to poor humanity,
Labour for mortal good . . . "*

*From Keats' The Fall of Hyperion.

Publisher: Anthony Hawke
Designer: Gerard Williams
Printer: Gagné Printing Ltd.
Front Cover Photograph by Bill Brooks

Hounslow Press
A Division of Anthony R. Hawke Limited
124 Parkview Avenue
Willowdale, Ontario, Canada. M2N 3Y5

We gratefully acknowledge the
assistance of the Canada Council
and the Ontario Arts Council.

Printed and bound in Canada.

Acknowledgements

I would like to express my appreciation and gratitude to those individuals and organizations without whom the research of this book could not have been accomplished and presented.

First of all, I would like to thank "Jeanne and John McKay" for informing us of the existence of the apparent castle ruin on their rural property in Nova Scotia, and to express my appreciation for the "carte blanche" they gave us to visit, and investigate, their property even when they were not resident on it. To "Jeanne" and "John" we also owe appreciation for many stimulating hours of conversation about the possible history of their ruins, and their kind offer to leave us the property after their deaths since they had no children of their own (an offer we thought too generous, and refused). "Jeanne" and "John" are pseudonyms I created for this generous and knowledgeable couple, out of respect for their privacy and to attempt to disguise the actual location of the apparent castle ruins.

I would also like to thank the "Special Assistant" of the Nova Scotia Ministry of Culture, Recreation and Fitness, *who requested anonymity,* for material support and personal encouragement in the two-year investigation of the Nova Scotia site and its possible historical connections. Colonel Frank Hofflin, former Canadian Military Attaché to the Federal Republic of Germany, was kind enough to read the first draft of the manuscript and to suggest revisions based on his extensive historical knowledge of the de Bouillon story supported by his fluent knowledge of the French, German, Russian, Italian, Spanish and Polish languages. Colonel Hofflin's stately home in Windsor, Nova Scotia provided, on several occasions, a comfortable environment in which to ponder the incredible. Colonel Hofflin's calm, pipe-smoking insistence that we were on the track of something tangible encouraged us to continue our work when I, for one, was many times on the point of dismissing the whole thing as totally improbable.

Michael Baigent, co-author of the 1982 bestseller, *The Holy Blood and The Holy Grail*, allowed us to reproduce three of his photographs in our book (which are also acknowledged in the text) and inspired us with intriguing comments in his letters. Jonathan Cape Ltd., original publishers of *The Holy Blood and The Holy Grail* permitted us to quote at length from the book, and this helped us to avoid the necessity of referring to many French-language books which have not yet been translated into English, making it easier for English-language readers to delve more deeply, if they wish, into the background of a remarkable story.

I would like to thank the Louvre and the Bibliothèque Nationale in Paris, and the Museum of Antique Art in Rome, for permission to reproduce artistic and archeological material in their collections.

We are grateful to the University of Toronto for permission to reproduce several very early maps of the Canadian Atlantic coast which were traced from originals, or from the best existing sources, by Ganong and published originally in his *Crucial Maps*. Our gratitude is also acknowledged in the text where these illustrations occur. The Champlain Society's permission to reproduce maps and passages from the seven-volume *Works of Samuel de Champlain* is greatly appreciated. The estate of the late Professor Charles Hapgood allowed us to reproduce Hapgood's illustrated analysis of the many inexplicable maps which give support to the argument of this book, and which were originally published in Hapgood's *Maps of the Ancient Sea Kings* by Chilton Books. The estate of the late Frederick J. Pohl allowed us to reproduce maps, and quoted passages, from Pohl's *Prince Henry Sinclair* in which Pohl presented overwhelming evidence that Henry Sinclair, Earl of Orkney, was the same person as the Micmac Indian culture hero called "Gloosscap" (Kuloscap, Kul Skabe, and many other variants). I must also mention here that Frederick Pohl's books, published since 1948, have been an inspiration to me since I was twelve years old. In particular, Pohl's *Lost Discovery* (1952) inspired me to believe that there were still important discoveries to be made to supposedly well-known history, and that basic revisions were required in the "accepted" story of human development. I cannot escape the suspicion that, had Frederick Pohl known of the Arthurian Grail Romances, he would have written *Holy Grail Across The Atlantic* himself.

We are indebted to Pohl's earlier historical detective work which, to a significant degree, provided the key that opened the speculation offered in the following pages. The drawing of the so-called "Newport Tower" was reproduced from Pohl's *Lost Discovery* and also acknowledged in the text where the illustration appears.

I would like to thank The Book Room in Halifax for permission to reproduce their post-card of Oak Island, which gives an aerial view of the island not matched by any other photograph we were able to find. Further, this post-card conveniently notes the places of interest on the island and the famed "Money Pit." We have also reproduced the text on the back of the post-card, which reflects the common view that some pirate, perhaps William Kidd, constructed the "Money Pit" to conceal a treasure. Whereas the evidence offered in this book tends to contradict this view, the post-card summary provides a succinct version of the currently popular belief. I would like to thank Canadian author, D'Arcy O'Connor of Westmount, Quebec, author of *The Money Pit* for permission to reproduce illustrations of the mysterious pit itself and of the more modern tunnels and shafts that have been excavated in an attempt to find the supposed treasure. We also appreciate D'Arcy O'Connor's permission to reproduce several passages from his book. In connection with "The Oak Island Mystery," I would also like to thank David C. Tobias, President of Triton Alliance Ltd., the company presently mounting ultimate attack on the mystery. In correspondence with me he has very kindly outlined the theory behind Triton's expensive assault on the "Money Pit." Triton's working hypothesis about the origin of the pit, and the pirate who deposited the supposed treasure, is not at all at odds with the speculations offered in this book.

Gordon Hardy, trained in aerial photo reconaissance interpretation, tried valiantly but unsuccessfully, to locate existing aerial photographs of "The Cross" and the apparent castle ruins, only to find that the available photos always placed "The Cross" at the edge of the photographic frame where lens distortion prevented any meaningful assessment of ground patterns visible on the films. Keith Atkinson's psychic "reading" of maps of Nova Scotia resulted in an intriguing idea that very early settlements, and possibly locations of buried religious or metallic treasures, might be arranged in the shape of a Maltese Cross with the village I have called "The Cross" at its centre. Only excavation will support the validity of this extremely provocative view of the entire complex, or discard it, but it is a "vision" (if that is the correct psychic term) that might prove to be of importance to organizations like Triton Alliance Ltd. which are apparently focused on just one aspect of a much larger mystery.

British Arthurian expert, Geoffrey Ashe, provided encouragement and inspiration through his correspondence with us, and Granada Publishing gave us permission to reproduce some illustrations from *The Quest for Arthur's Britain* (edited by Geoffrey Ashe) and to quote some passages.

Finally, I would like to thank two people who assisted me "in the field" with the investigations that are the foundation of this book. First, Deanna Theilmann-Bean not only travelled to Nova Scotia with me under difficult circumstances, but also helped to establish a company with me while at the same time never losing her enthusiasm for unravelling the mystery of the castle ruin. Her energy and enthusiasm, and her constant faith that the almost-ephemeral hints and clues were not a chimera, shamed me into continuing research when (I confess) my inclination was to dismiss the thing as implausible and go fishing. From the top of Cadbury Hill in Britain, to the hill top of "The Cross" with its unaccountable ruins, Deanna never faltered in her belief that we were uncovering threads of a hidden historical pattern. Only when I stood beside her on the top of Cape D'Or overlooking the Bay of Fundy, *knowing* that Henry Sinclair had also stood on the very same spot, did I myself become certain that a book was worth writing. Then, I must thank my son, Jason Bradley, for allowing me to share the last months of his childhood with him during 1982-1983, a very real treasure I never hoped to enjoy. Our visits with each other, too infrequent and too brief, sometimes included trips associated with the research of this book. Although I do not think that Jason ever truly believed in the castle ruin, or in the hidden pattern of history it suggested (but was always more interested in pirate gold), his agreement to accompany us on history-related field trips was an incentive to me to continue the research when I otherwise lacked the spirit to do so.

Contents

Foreword/ 7

Author's Forewarning/ 11

Chapter One
The Christmas King of Camelot/ 17

Chapter Two
The Castle at The Cross/ 45

Chapter Three
The Knights of the Temple/ 81

Chapter Four
The Sea-Chieftain/ 113

Chapter Five
Doors/ 149

Chapter Six
The French Connection/ 169

Chapter Seven
Map Memorials/ 199

Chapter Eight
The Shepherds of Arcadia/ 259

Chapter Nine
The Bees of Childeric/ 301

Chapter Ten
The Dynasty in the 20th Century/ 319

Notes/ 361

Selected Bibliography/ 389

An Appreciative Foreword
by John Robert Colombo

When I finished reading this shocking and surprising book what came to mind was the exchange between the writer Tom Wolfe and the media philosopher Marshall McLuhan. After reading his way through McLuhan's books and puzzling his way through McLuhan's aphoristic style, Wolfe asked the following question: "Suppose he's right?" When McLuhan learned of Wolfe's reaction, his response was, "I'd rather be wrong!"

I feel a bit like Wolfe; I am not at all certain that Michael Bradley feels like McLuhan, with his fingers secretly crossed. I sense that Bradley wishes to be right or mostly right in his speculations and his tentatively expressed conclusions. And perhaps he is right . . . in general or in detail.

Phrases other than "shocking and surprising," let me warn the reader, could be used to describe this book. I have in mind such descriptive phrases as "irritating and intelligent," "perverse and penetrating," "tense-making and thought-provoking," "expansive and exasperating," "articulate and argumentative," *ad infinitum.* The book is, in fact, scholarly and showy at the same time. But instead of trying to characterize it in a phrase or two, allow me to make a few general points about this book which you are about to read.

1. *Holy Grail Across The Atlantic* is a contribution to the "secret history" of the world. As such it fits into a class of books, books written to shed light on the dark areas of human history and motivation. The authors of these books go behind the headlines. They set the standard scholarly concerns to one side. They sidestep the received interpretations of history. They find new meaning in old lore. They collect, collate, and conflate information from a great variety of sources in a highly idiosyncratic manner. They revel in assimilation and association and occasionally in argumentation. From the documentation that does exist, they reveal a

cause-and-effect relationship that may well be in effect to this day. Surprisingly the most recent volume in the series of "secret histories" of the world became a bestseller. This is *The Holy Blood and The Holy Grail.* Bradley is indebted to that book and to its trio of authors — Messrs. Baigent, Leigh, and Lincoln — who did so much of their spadework in Europe. Bradley's spadework is done in the New World, as readers will realize when they begin to read his book.

2. *Holy Grail Across The Atlantic* is the most infuriating book ever written about the history of Canada. At least that is my opinion. Although I am not a scholar it will carry some weight with those readers who are familiar with my popular reference books which show that I have examined thousands upon thousands of Canadian books, for I keep referring to them, even quoting from them, in such publications as *Colombo's Canadian Quotations, Canadian Literary Landmarks, Colombo's New Canadian Quotations,* etc. The majority of the books by Canadian authors which I read for research or for pleasure are somewhat predictable. When they are surprising the surprises are few and far between. I seldom come across books that present brand-new ideas or that apply ideas once discredited or deemed heretical in an inspired way. Heated discussions in this country turn on whether or not oral history is creative; whether or not Conrad Black's biography of Duplessis is (*pace* Ramsay Cook) a work of scholarship at all; whether or not Peter C. Newman's books of profiles and company histories are little more than potted biographies and adventure stories; whether or not Farley Mowat is right when he says "the facts keep getting in the way of the truth"; whether or not (going back a bit) Francis Parkman had a right to his principles — now viewed as his prejudices. Are any books that could be described as heretical being written and published in this country these days? My view is that hardly any books being commercially published brave the bonfire, so to speak. Yet here is one that does. It is made conspicuous by the absence of others. The argument the author mounts is certain to infuriate any careful scholars who give it any heed at all; but it is likely to surprise and perhaps delight those creative scholars and general readers who are intrigued by novel ideas that may seem farfetched but are at once traditional and timely, no matter where those notions may have originated.

3. *Holy Grail Across The Atlantic* is an investigation of one of the central motifs of Christian Europe: the numinous notion of the Holy

Grail. As symbol or as substance, the Holy Grail possesses the power to transmit and transform all values. It turns, at least imaginatively, all cultural values into values that are truly civilized because they are deeply expressive of spiritual verities — or, at the very least, expressive of "semi-certainties," to employ the happy term introduced by the French writer Louis Pauwels. In addition to its powers as a transmitter and a trans-former, the Grail possesses the power of movement. Bradley traces its migration from the Middle East, across Europe, to the shores of North America where he located one of its domiciles. Bradley's achievement is the "Canadianization" of the sacred vessel. My feeling is that he should have called his book "The Holy Grail in the New World" to mark its place on our soil. He found, on the trail of the Grail, evidence which suggests that deep significance and a spiritual meaning may be inherent in the history of the New World and of North America in particular and that it was planted here at a very early period of time and that traces of it may still be discerned and uncovered. Whether the evidence is evident or only evidential will have to be decided instance by instance. Still, it is possible to see his book grandly as a study of the motif of the miraculous through the ages or simply as an unlikely and unexpected contribution to the history of the exploration and the colonization of early Canada. Reading it one comes upon an original mind at work on a subject of absorbing interest. Certainly there is a sense of mounting excitement as the author begins to piece together the fragments of the larger whole. The pages devoted to the author's scholarly work are absorbing; but to my mind the most gripping pages are those that are directly expressive of the effect upon him and upon his companion of the realization of the full dimensions and consequences of his scholarly speculations.

4. If I had to characterize Michael Bradley, I would call him a "rehistorian." The function of the historian is not easily defined but one aspect of that function is to "recover" that part of the past that has left "traces." The prehistorian and the revisionist historian have the same concerns. But what is the function of the "rehistorian"? You will not find that word in any dictionary. I have coined it to refer to independent writers, thinkers, researchers, and investigators who offer a radical rein-terpretation of society and history that is based on traces of traces. The level upon which they work may be fine and subtle or crude and dense; but what unites them is that they approach their subject with the spirit of adventure and a sense of reverence for what its revelations might be to the

inquiring mind which approaches it in the light of independent judg-
ment. Great systematizers like Oswald Spengler and Arnold Toynbee are
rehistorians in my sense of the word. So also are Ignatius Donnelly and
Erich von Däniken, Immanuel Velikovsky and Frederick Pohl, Charles
Hapgood and René Guénon, not to mention Messrs. Baigent, Leigh, and
Lincoln. All are rehistorians who place their stock in both scholarship
and speculation. More than the revisionist historian, who merely shifts
the weight of the evidence from one point to another, the rehistorian
redirects the spotlight of inquiry onto the chain of events in an attempt to
reveal hitherto undetected continuities and unsuspected discontinuities.
Michael Bradley is a rehistorian who has found in the Maritimes a radical
reinterpretation of our past in the light of myth, legend, lore, rumour,
innuendo, aside, suggestion, argument, and analysis. His close examination of old maps and documents, not to mention rubble-work in a farmer's
field, has led him and will lead the reader across an ocean of speculation
to a safe harbour at The Cross.

"What we call history is the mess we call life reduced to some order,
pattern and possibly purpose." So wrote G. R. Elton, Regius Professor of
History at Cambridge, in his book *The Practice of History* (1967). He went
on to say that the historian cannot verify; he can only discover and
attempt to explain. He can argue with the facts but he cannot argue them
away. Elton was writing about the historian, of course, but his remarks
apply equally to the rehistorian, to Michael Bradley. The rain of bouquets
and brickbats which could well mark the reception of *Holy Grail Across
The Atlantic* need not bother him or anyone for that matter. All independent thinkers are used to receiving smirks and smiles in unequal measure.
Better to speak and be heard than not to speak at all. Elton also wrote, "It
is not without significance that the one historian among the ancients for
whom no one has a bad word seems to be Asinius Pollio of whose writings
nothing survives."

Author's Forewarning

This book reads very strangely, and I cannot recommend it as entertainment for everyone. It is sincerely offered as nonfiction and as history, but it is, of course, most peculiar history unlike anything you may have encountered in church, school or university.

The history proposed will be offensive to some people. Those who cling to spiritual and occult explanations of human progress may feel that this book diminishes the human spirit, or diminishes the nature of God. Those who are equipped with the normal sort of university education of our time, and who consider themselves liberal-minded and progressive in consequence, will find that the argument presented in this book conflicts with the current neo-Marxist dogma that history is merely human response to easily-identifiable mechanistic forces.

The style of writing may sometimes seem as annoying as the content. I have not always held to the brisk and objective style of communication used by journalists and which is familiar to readers from newspapers, Sunday supplements and magazines, and which many people have come to expect from books. Instead of telling the story from its beginning thousands of years ago, I have told it *as it became revealed to us.* Whereas this method of reporting has permitted a lengthy history to be compressed to reasonable proportions, by allowing me to tap into certain episodes in detail while ignoring others altogether and merely sketching some of the connections with other episodes, this style of reporting has some disadvantages. It demands that our personal experiences, researches and feelings are described to some extent in order to explain why and how we followed certain clues. Some people will find these personal and subjective recollections irritating, will consider them to be irrelevant and unnecessary digressions.

As for any offence offered to the most cherished and most chauvinistic myths of Jews, Moslems and Christians, well, these myths will survive. And I had no malice aforethought.

This book shares some similarity of content with certain French-language books published during the 1950s and 1960s by authors like Gérard de Sède, Pierre Durban, Maurice Magre, Pierre Belperron and Fernand Niel. They really deserve the credit, or blame, for introducing a decidedly bizarre interpretation of Western history into contemporary European thought. Most of these writers have not yet been translated into English and so, while they have had a definite impact on European thinking, even to the point of inspiring a new sort of mass movement that is rapidly gaining adherents in Europe, they are almost unknown to North Americans.

Ten years ago I intended to write a book like this one and pass on, in English, this disturbing French historical research. I hinted at this interest in *The Iceman Inheritance*, published in 1978, where I referred to these French investigators. An encounter with a Nova Scotia mystery between 1982 and 1983 compelled the writing of *Holy Grail Across The Atlantic* now. Happily, the decade-long delay makes the book even more relevant to North Americans than it would have been because of the discovery of the castle in Nova Scotia and the indications of a North American refuge for the Holy Blood.

However, there's no doubt that three British authors — Michael Baigent, Richard Leigh and Henry Lincoln — beat me to the punch in some respects with the 1982 publication of their bestseller, *The Holy Blood and The Holy Grail*. This book was based largely on the research of the French authors referred to, as well as on some original and very interesting contributions by the three Britishers.

The authors of *The Holy Blood and The Holy Grail* did not make any mention of the North American chapters of the Holy Blood's story and these were crucial chapters indeed. Nor did they grasp King Arthur's role in the Grail Saga correctly, in my opinion, and *Holy Grail Across The Atlantic* attempts to return King Arthur to his proper place in history and geography, while emphasizing the North American part of the Holy Blood's tale which has been ignored by the Europeans.

Since the authors of *The Holy Blood and The Holy Grail* synthesized much of the available data from the original French sources, and for the most part did it very well while making some new discoveries of their own, it seemed absurd to pretend that their book did not exist or that

Holy Grail Across The Atlantic owed nothing to it. Therefore, I have referred to *The Holy Blood and the Holy Grail* where necessary instead of always referring to the original sources which would be harder for readers to find. At the same time, while acknowledging the obvious debts, I have also made it clear where I disagree with these authors' conclusions.

Readers have the right to ask whether I actually believe this unorthodox interpretation of Western history. The answer is: "Yes, I really do believe it to be the truth." At least, I believe it to be a much closer approximation of the truth than the history taught in universities. After twenty years of research, and some minor contributions to what might be called "conventional" interpretations of history, I have concluded that the acceptable history of textbooks is inadequate and misleading. While I'm willing to grant that some of the details may be wrong and that some people may have been erroneously consigned to a role in the Great Conspiracy, I have come to believe sincerely that the facts of Western history (such as they are known) argue the presence of an almost-hidden group of people which has molded major patterns of human development, which has managed humanity at crisis points. We have been guided in our progress by a secret organization.

Readers of this book cannot fail to notice that it deals only with what might be called the Western World. If the Holy Grail is a fact, and if it has indeed influenced the course of human progress, then what of the so-called "Third World?" Are we to assume that our brothers and sisters in Africa, Asia and the pre-Columbian Americas were bereft of Grail guidance? Are we to assume that Western Mankind was singled out among humanity to receive the gift of the Grail?

This is, in fact, precisely what the Nazis believed when evolving their ethos of Aryian racial superiority and while attempting to force that racist philosophy upon the whole world. Unfortunately for Nazi doctrine, the facts argue clearly that the power of the Grail has been operative among all peoples. Legend and folklore from Africa, Asia and pre-Columbian America are replete with tales of the first beings who brought culture to humanity and of the subsequent purely human "culture heroes" who refined this original gift with progressive developments. These legends and tales are the Third World's version of the Holy Grail.

Nonetheless, it also seems to be true that the Holy Grail has been woven more intimately into the warp and woof of Western history than it has been in other histories. In Europe, the Holy Grail has inspired fledgling national literatures and, to some degree, molded the culture of chivalry that dominated Europe for several centuries. The motif of the Holy Grail seems to be more prominent in Western mankind's history than elsewhere. The reason for this may not be so flattering to Western humanity.

In 1978 I argued in *The Iceman Inheritance* that Western man has exhibited more aggression than other major groups of humanity. This speculation has subsequently been supported by forensic analysis of Neanderthal-Caucasoid skeletal material (see "Hard Times Among the Neanderthals," *Natural History*, December 1978) and even by a recently-discovered 12-page manuscript of Sigmund Freud (see "Hangups Due to Ice and Id of Byegone Era," *London Observer*, August 6, 1987). If indeed, Western mankind suffers from psychosexual aggressions resulting from glacial evolution, then it may be that those of the Holy Grail have had to labour harder among us. We of the West may have proved more difficult to shepherd toward culture and humane civilization. It may be that we needed the gift of the Holy Grail more acutely than other peoples and it was given more generously to us. For that reason, perhaps, the Holy Grail attained more prominence in our culture.

Michael Bradley
Toronto, Canada
August 1987

"Kyot, the master of high renown,
Found, in confused pagan writing,
The legend which reaches back to the
prime source of all legends."

From *Parzival* by Wolfram von Eschenbach

Chapter One

The Christmas King of Camelot

The story of the Holy Grail apparently began about four thousand years ago and continues to the present day.

The story has been lived through the lives of many people both famous, and obscure, in history. We could begin our tale of the Holy Grail starting with Abraham and Sarah, with Hagar and Mohammed, with Jesus, Joseph of Arimathaea, Mary the Virgin or Mary Magdalene, King Arthur, Clovis and the Merovingian line of Frankish kings, Dagobert II and his surviving son Sigisbert IV, Godfroi de Bouillon and his brother Baudoin. We could start our account with the courage of Esclarmonde de Foix and Jacques de Molay, not to mention the bravery of Joan of Arc and the steady rule of René d'Anjou. We could begin with the desperate Atlantic adventure of "Prince" Henry Sinclair of Rosslyn, in Scotland, patron of refugee Templars, or we could open our account with the explorations of Columbus and Samuel de Champlain.

Or, we could recount the quiet and constant courage of people like Jeanne Mance, de Maisonneuve, Jean-Jacques Olier and de la Dauversière, the founders of Montreal in a hostile wilderness. We could begin with the exploits of Napoleon and his determination not only to destroy the vestiges of feudalism in Europe, but also his commitment to marry one woman in all of Europe, Josephine de Beauharnais.

Or, finally, we could begin the story of the Holy Grail in our own time and work backward to unravel the entire human adventure. We could focus on the people who sat around the conference tables in 1946 at Lake Geneva and thrashed out the details of the Marshall Plan to rebuild war-torn Europe. We would then commence our story with the courage of

Pierre Plantard de Saint-Clair in defiance of his Gestapo torturers, or with Bernard Baruch and Frank Lloyd Wright whom Franklin Delano Roosevelt designated as his personal representatives to Geneva.

We could begin our story of the Holy Grail at almost any time, and with many people, when the course of Western history has been subtly nudged in a new direction or dramatically changed by momentous events. All those mentioned so far apparently had commitment to the Holy Grail.

But I have chosen to begin this book with King Arthur for several reasons. First, his name and legend are known to practically everyone. Second, almost everyone knows that Arthur and his Knights of the Round Table were somehow connected with the Holy Grail, always "questing" for it between deeds of chivalry. Third, until very recently, King Arthur was considered to be mythical and legendary, and of course, the Holy Grail was held to be mythical, legendary and merely mystical along with him.

By starting with King Arthur, we can show that myth and legend are sometimes whispers of real flesh-and-blood history. It is now known that King Arthur really existed. This is accepted by most scholars today because of archeological research undertaken since the 1960s. And, if King Arthur himself really lived, then might not the Holy Grail have existed too?

But there is another, and fourth, reason for beginning this book with King Arthur. He does not come at the genesis, or at the end, of the Holy Grail story.

King Arthur comes about the middle of the long Grail saga. We can therefore work forward, and backward, from King Arthur and get an overview of what the Holy Grail is all about.

Further, King Arthur's time was much like our own in many respects. The known and secure world of Celtic Britain under Roman protection was crumbling with the threat of dramatic change. It was a time of apprehension and uncertainty, just like our own world at the end of the 20th Century when we live under the threats of new technologies with their dangers of nuclear and environmental destruction, and live with the apprehension of increasing population pressure on dwindling resources. Our world is at a crisis point just as Aurthur's was.

King Arthur was a leader who, for a short time, preserved the stability of his world and gave hope to those living in a dying, changing social order. It is said that Arthur will return when he is most needed, that he is "the once and future king", the strong and benevolent ruler to lead humanity from hopeless desperation. His name and memory are proof that hope is never vain, and that alone is an invaluable truth. Perhaps that is why, in our own closing decades of the 20th Century, we witness a recent outpouring of books about King Arthur and the Holy Grail.

Hopefully, this will not be just another book about King Arthur and the Holy Grail. Up to now, all scholarly and popular books about King Arthur and the Holy Grail have dealt only with Europe. This is natural and proper because most of the Grail story took place in Europe and the Middle East.

However, it is my contention that one extremely important chapter in the story of the Holy Grail took place in North America and involved a desperate transatlantic search for a religious haven. I will offer evidence, not proof, that this chapter spanned about four centuries, from 1398 A.D. until about 1750 A.D. Although this is less than ten percent of the whole Grail saga, and has therefore escaped the focus of European writers, it was a crucial chapter in the history of the Holy Grail. If the haven had not been found when it was needed so urgently, the Holy Grail and what it means to humanity would have almost certainly perished.

But the haven was found in North America, the Grail and its meaning survived, and the hope and courage that has sustained Western humanity for four thousand years yet works its magic. Those who braved the unknown Atlantic long before our "history book" explorers, and who established a refuge for the Holy Grail in the wilderness, exhibited no less courage than King Arthur. And they struggled in the face of no lesser desperation.

King Arthur lived between about 470 A.D. and 550 A.D.[1] Traditional accounts of his career insist that he was wounded, but not necessarily mortally, at the Battle of Camlann[2] in the year 542. After the battle, the wounded king was taken to the "Island of Avalon" for the healing of his wounds. It is not known how long he lived after Camlann, but some Welsh stories have him lingering on for a few years as the crippled Fisher King residing in, or near, the Grail Castle.[3]

Although Arthur lived about 1500 years ago, he first emerges into Western literature about 700 years later. By far the most detailed source for the life of Arthur is Geoffrey of Monmouth's *Historia regum Britannae*, or "*History of the Kings of Britain*", which first appeared in 1136. Geoffrey, an Augustinian canon of Saint George at Oxford from the year 1129, continued to revise his *History* for twelve years after he wrote the first version.[4]

Geoffrey claimed that his data for his *History* came from a small book lent to him by Walter, archdeacon of Oxford, who was a book collector and antiquarian. According to Geoffrey and Walter, this little book was written in a "British tongue" and had been obtained from "Brittany". This means that the little book was written in some form of Gaelic and that Geoffrey of Monmouth translated it. And, indeed, Geoffrey never claimed more than that his *History* was basically a translation of this Gaelic book.

Most unfortunately, this Gaelic-language source book has been lost. If it had survived, modern Gaelic scholars could have given us a better translation than Geoffrey was able to manage. Also, Geoffrey had a very incomplete mastery of geography. The result of Geoffrey of Monmouth's work is that it gives King Arthur's life in a plausible gross profile, but the details of people and places are sometimes confused and contradictory. Geoffrey knew the Welsh writer, Caradoc of Llancarvan, who may have offered some translating assistance. The two men certainly had a close working relationship because Geoffrey mentions that Caradoc was writing a continuation of his *History*.

Nonetheless, Caradoc's assistance, although helpful, was not apparently definitive in assuring accuracy of the translation. There are several Gaelic dialects, amounting to languages, and it is known that Caradoc knew only Welsh and Brythonic (Irish). The little book may have been written in some other language or dialect that gave Geoffrey and Caradoc linguistic headaches.[5]

In spite of the obvious linguistic difficulties and geographical blunders, the outline of Arthur's life emerges in the *History* more clearly than in any other literary work. It is the story that popular writers like Mary Stewart have mostly relied on, the story that is familiar to most people when they think of King Arthur, and the story of the Broadway musical, and Hollywood film, *Camelot*.

Ironically for a great king and guardian of the Holy Grail, Arthur was born in sinful circumstances. The High King of Britain, Uther Pendragon, was captivated by the beauty of Ygerne, the wife of the Duke of Cornwall. Uther's passion for Ygerne gave him no rest, and he determined to have her no matter what the consequences. And the consequences could be serious since Cador, the Duke of Cornwall, was one of Uther's most powerful and loyal vassals.

Cador was an old man, but not an old fool, and not only recognized Uther's condition, but also realized the cause of it. Accordingly, the duke secured his young wife in his strongest castle, the stronghold of Tintagel. Uther knew that he could not likely storm Tintagel since the stronghold was built on a sheer sided offshore rock with only a narrow causeway linking it to the mainland. Tintagel could hold off an army, but could not withstand wizardry. In his desperation and urgency, Uther turned to his advisor and magician, Merlin.

The story goes that Merlin, with the aid of his magic arts, transformed Uther into the likeness of Cador and, while Uther's army engaged the real duke on a flimsy pretext, Uther himself made a flying visit to Tintagel disguised as Cador. He was admitted to the otherwise impregnable fortress and lay with Ygerne who, if she suspected anything, gave no indication then or later since her own young passion matched Uther's. That night in April Arthur was conceived. As Geoffrey of Monmouth put it:

> . . . and in such a manner as I tell you was King Arthur conceived in sin that is now the best king in the world.[6]

As fate would have it, however, the Duke Cador was killed in the pretext skirmishing that very night. If Uther had waited just one more day, he could have possessed Ygerne on a slightly more decent basis.

Arthur was born the following December, some say on Christmas Day itself, while other traditions place the birth at the winter solstice (December 21 or 22), the shortest day of the year.[7] The circumstances of his birth had grave repercussions for Arthur. Uther and Ygerne celebrated a rather too-hasty marriage after minimal mourning for the late duke.

Some believed that Arthur was the son of Cador, not Uther, and this compromised his claim to the High Kingship. In a variant tradition, Arthur is presented as the son of Uther Pendragon's brother, Ambrosius (Aurelius Ambrosius), and therefore not a direct claimant to the High Kingship. Whatever the truth of the matter, it seems that Arthur was never accepted as a legitimate king by birth. It was his prowess as a warrior and leader that earned him the title of "king" by courtesy although his only real designation seems to have been *dux bellorum* — a "leader of wars" or "war leader".

The troubles of his time made Arthur's prowess more important than his patrimony. Britain had been a province of Rome for almost 500 years and had enjoyed Roman protection from barbarian invasion. As the Dark Ages migrations of peoples reached its crescendo, Rome stationed, at one point, fully one third of its military power in Britain in an attempt to hold this most remote and vulnerable outpost of the empire. But finally the barbarian pressure all around the empire became too great and Rome sacrificed its westernmost province. Initially, however, the abandonment of Britain came about through British pride and folly.

In 380 A.D. the British legions proclaimed their own general, Maximus, a Spaniard, as Emperor. Maximus forthwith took his legions across the Channel, invaded Europe, and marched on Rome which he took. His success inspired him to attempt a conquest of the eastern part of the Empire in 388 A.D., hubris which was punished by the Eastern Emperor, Theodosius, who inflicted a disastrous defeat on the army of Maximus. Maximus is remembered as "Macsen" in some Celtic legends and it is said that he had a Celtic wife. Many of the later petty kings of Wales traced their lineage back to Macsen.

But the adventure of Maximus had denuded Britian of its trained Roman legions, while the final defeat at the hands of Theodosius guaranteed that the cohesion of the British legions was broken forever. Some survivors returned to Britain, of course, but the real strength of Roman Britain was squandered in the exercise of Macsen's pride.

In 395 A.D. the High King of Ireland, Niall, invaded Britain and sacked Chester and Caerleon. In response to British appeals for help, Rome sent the Imperial general, Stilicho, and an army. These trained soldiers defeated the Irish and sent them packing, but Stilicho's army was withdrawn to Gaul in 405 A.D. as the military situation deteriorated. Thirteen years later, in 418, there was another British appeal for help because of Saxon and Pict invasions. Apparently, another Roman force was sent to Britain in that year because it is mentioned in two sources: the *Anglo Saxon Chronicle* and a history written by a monk named Gildas. In this Roman relieving force there were "unexpected bands of cavalry", according to Gildas. By 425 A.D. this Roman force had been withdrawn, and it was the last of the legions.[8]

Arthur was born into an abandoned Britain, and one at the mercy of constant invasion by Scandinavian Angles, Saxons and Jutes. Various British leaders had attempted, with varying success, to rally the Celts and their remnant of Roman civilization and to oppose the influx of barbarians. Vortigern was one such chieftain, although his use of Saxon mercenary "allies" proved counter-productive. Arthur's immediate forebears, Ambrosius and Uther, achieved some greater, but still limited, success using more purely Romano-British forces.

But the handwriting was on the wall. By the time of Arthur's birth, which most scholars now place around 470 A.D., eventual "Saxon" (as the Britons called the Angles, Saxons and Jutes collectively) inundation of Britain was inevitable.

Arthur is remembered because he held back the barbarian tide for two or three generations. And, under the circumstances, even the dim reflection of sputtering Romano-British civilization seemed like a brilliant jewel in the darkness that was seemingly enveloping the whole world, an "Ancient World" that had existed with some continuity for about three thousand years. People living at the time viewed the barbarian invasions as a world-wide phenomenon that spelled the end of civilization, and perhaps even the end of the world. Against this profound terror and despair, Arthur's limited success was stubbornly remembered as being more glamorous and more chivalrous than the reality doubtless was.

Tradition says that young Arthur won twelve early battles culminating in the great victory of Badon Hill.[9] This 3-day engagement won peace from invasion for a number of years. During the peace, Arthur established the glory of Camelot, the Order of the Knights of the Round Table, and married Guinevere, a Celtic princess whose name ("Gwenhumara") means "white owl".[10]

Military stability did not bring domestic or social peace, however. Tradition has it that Arthur's court at Camelot attracted the flower of chivalry from far and wide. Unfortunately, one of the knights drawn to Camelot was Lancelot who was destined to become not only Arthur's most trusted captain, but also Guinevere's lover.[11] Perhaps, also, the extended peace won at Badon Hill became irksome to Arthur's knights. They yearned for action and adventure, especially the younger ones, and the myth has grown that Arthur invented the "Quest for the Holy Grail" as something of a chivalrous make-work project to absorb his younger knights' hormone energy. If so, this invention proved a dismal failure since what the knights really wanted was blood, strife and the opportunity for rape and pillage.

Perhaps it was inevitable that some of the knights were destined to revolt against the peace of Camelot. Legend insists that Arthur's son, Mordred (or "Medraut"), was the leader of the insurrection.[12] Taking some of the younger Camelot knights with him, Mordred allied himself with Saxons in order to overthrow Arthur's rule.

The battle of Camlann was fought between the forces of Arthur and those of Mordred. According to tradition, it was a bloody draw with Arthur killing Mordred, but being severely wounded himself. Geoffrey of Monmouth says:

> Even the renowned king Arthur himself was wounded deadly and was borne thence to the Island of Avalon for the healing of his wounds, where he gave up the crown to his kinsman, Constantine, son of Cador, in A.D. 542.

This is the story of King Arthur that is familiar to us, and told first by Geoffrey of Monmouth in 1136, allegedly translated from some Gaelic document. It is a good story, but is it a true one?

As early as 1198 William of Newburgh called Geoffrey's life of Arthur " 'fables' and 'fiction' without a grain of truth made up by the early Britons."[13] And, even today "many scholars doubt that Geoffrey's friend passed him a rare book so that he could write from it the life of Arthur."[14]

Nevertheless, in spite of the doubt, there seems to have been *an* Arthur, whatever his rank, station and role, who was active and remembered. "Arthur" is mentioned briefly in a number of Welsh poems, though without the detail that Geoffrey supplied, while another source, the "Nennius compilation" also mentions Arthur. So, Geoffrey of Monmouth is not alone in having some knowledge of an Arthur in the dim British past, but merely unique in supplying such a wealth of detail about his life.

It is certain that there was an Arthur who lived in the first half of the 6th Century and who had some powerful claim to fame, probably military. The reason for this certainty is that after about 550 A.D. a number of Welsh, Scot and Manx princelings were given the name of "Arthur" and they clutter the surviving genealogies.[15] These princes of a warlike society must have been named in honour of someone of recent military renown. The number of "Arthurs" named around this time is even more striking since the name isn't Celtic at all. The Celts rendered it *Arthyr*.

Until the late 1950s most scholars leaned congenially toward the idea that there might have been, and probably was, *an* Arthur active in some military role during the 6th Century, but most scholars were equally derisive of the idea that *the* King Arthur described by Geoffrey of Monmouth ever lived. What changed the "Arthurian Legend" into the "Arthurian Fact" was purely and simply mystical pressure supplied by beatniks (1950s) and hippies (1960s). They descended on the traditional site of Avalon, the modern town of Glastonbury, and turned it into a sort of cult centre. These young mystical immigrants were enthusiastically welcomed by the many assorted British eccentrics who had long since made Glastonbury and environs their home and headquarters.

Why Glastonbury in particular?

The landscape around Glastonbury is part of the answer. Looming above the town is Glastonbury Tor, a tall, conical and step-sided hill that looks thoroughly artificial. Then, just 12 miles away is Cadbury Hill, a tall, flat-topped and step-sided hill that also looks thoroughly artificial. It seemed evident to all who had eyes to see that Glastonbury and the surrounding area had been of special interest to those mysterious people of Ancient Britain who raised barrows, menhirs, stone circles and other artifacts of the megalithic culture. At Glastonbury, they seemed to have molded the earth on a gigantic scale, so it seemed logical to believe that Glastonbury must have been a place of special sanctity to them.[16]

This would have been pagan and pre-Christian sancity. However, Glastonbury has a claim to very special Christian sanctity as well. There's an ancient local tradition that Joseph of Arimathaea came to Glastonbury after the Crucifixion and founded the first church in all of Christendom there. The proof of this is supposedly the famous Glastonbury Thorn. The legend says that when Joseph of Arimathaea arrived in Glastonbury, the place he'd chosen as his haven at the very fringe of Roman civilization and as far as possible from Palestine, he planted his staff in the ground to mark the site of the church he planned to build. This staff took root and began to grow, eventually becoming a large thorn tree.

Although the original Glastonbury Thorn was cut down by a Puritan fanatic in the 1690s, a twig from the original tree was saved and replanted. This, too, has now grown into a respectable thorn tree although it is not necessarily in the exact location of the original one. The trouble with the Glastonbury Thorn is that it does happen to be a species native to Palestine and nowhere else, should not grow in the climate of Glaston-

The famous "Glastonbury Thorn" at Glastonbury Abbey supposedly sprouted from the staff of Joseph of Arimathaea. It is a Palestinian variety of thorn and does bloom approximately at Easter. The original tree was cut down by a Puritan fanatic in the 1600s. The present tree was planted from a salvaged branch of the original one, but the present tree is not necessarily in the same location.

Photo by Michael Bradley.

bury but does, and disconcertingly blooms about the time of Easter every year.[17]

Along with the thorn, Joseph of Arimathaea is supposed to have brought the Holy Grail to Glastonbury too. It supposedly resided there for some time. Then, to top it all off, Glastonbury was once known as Avalon, or more specifically as the "Island of Avalon". Avalon means "apple trees", and the place *was* an island in Roman times, and in Arthur's, because of the low-lying land all around. In Roman times the sea reached all the way to Glastonbury and any tourist can see the Roman-built stone wharfs and breakwater in the lower town. By Arthur's era, the sea itself had receded but had left an extensive system of streams, bogs, meres and small lakes surrounding the "island" which could, however, be reached by a dry land causeway from the northeast. The main highway into Glastonbury today passes over this old causeway.

Megalithic activity replete with legends of fairies and dragons, early Christianity, the Glastonbury Thorn, the Holy Grail, Joseph of Arimathaea and King Arthur's ghost in Avalon all converge on Glastonbury and it is not difficult to see why the town became a mecca for mystical cultists. Today the biggest bookstore in Glastonbury, aptly called The Glastonbury Experience, is crammed with books on Arthurian lore, megalithic civilization, the latent powers of menhirs, ley lines, ordinance survey maps, Druidism and much else mystical and occult.

As the cultists gathered, and talked among themselves, and wrote books and pamphlets for each other to read, Arthur and the Holy Grail naturally passed quickly from historical *possibility* into the realm of mystical and historical *truth*. The cultists chided the established academics for not seeing this mystical reality, and for failing to excavate Cadbury Hill and Glastonbury Tor out of fear of discovering facts that would certainly contradict the conventional view of Western history.

And, in truth, the academics were getting a bit nervous. During the 1950s Mrs. M. Harfield and Mr. J. Steven Cox had patiently collected pottery fragments that had been brought to the surface by ploughing on top of Cadbury Hill. They were not cultists, but quite the opposite, and turned these fragments over to accredited specialists. These experts quickly recognized some pieces as being a type of pottery also found at Tintagel, the traditional and legendary place of Arthur's birth. Also recovered was a fragment of a Merovingian glass bowl, proving that whoever had lived atop Cadbury Hill had had contact with the Frankish

Cadbury Hill, the traditional site of Arthur's Camelot.
Photo by Michael Bradley.

View northwest from the top of Cadbury Hill. Arrow indicates
Glastonbury Tor visible 12 miles away on the horizon.
Photo by Michael Bradley.

culture of Brittany. As our story progresses, this evidence of Arthurian connection with the Merovingians will become suggestive of an important, but hidden, pattern of history.

In 1955, because of oats growing on the top of Cadbury Hill, a pattern of crop marks was photographed from the air that seemed to show outlines of former buildings on the summit. Perhaps I should explain that since the advent of aircraft, crop marks have become important archeological clues. Pilots of early airplanes had often noticed that crops growing on the ground often showed differences in coloration which marked out very definite patterns. Excavation revealed the reason for this and, accidentally, turned up archeological sites of significance. The different coloration of the plants represented different nutritional values in the soil. Organic debris in the soil caused plants to grow more lushly and more greenly, while stone remains offered less of nutritional value. A crop of oats, say, growing over ruins of former wooden and stone structures would show distinct patterns of rich green where the wooden walls had decomposed, but would show an equally distinct pattern of pale green over stone walls. Crop marks in regular and geometric patterns had become an accepted sign of former occupation and construction.

The pottery shards and the piece of Merovingian glass, plus the distinct crop marks photographed in 1955, began to convince established archeologists that Cadbury Hill would be worth investigation. "Responding in November 1959 to a proposal for excavations, Dr. (Ralegh C.) Radford gave the inevitable answer that, without a sum of money running into thousands of pounds, the site seemed too big to handle."[18]

Dr. Ralegh Radford had formerly been President of the Royal Archeological Institute, and he was a leading figure in British archeology. His interest in Cadbury Hill, and any possibility of authenticating King Arthur, ensured eventual financial support. In order to get the money for excavation, Radford and others formed the Camelot Research Committee in June 1965. Radford was Chairman and co-founder, the well known British author, Geoffrey Ashe, was Secretary, and Sir Mortimer Wheeler accepted the Presidency. The Camelot Research Committee boasted representation on its Board from: the Society of Antiquaries; the Society for Medieval Archeology; the Somerset Archeological Society; the Honourable Society of the Knights of the Round Table; the Pendragon Society; the Prehistoric Society; the Society for the Promotion of Roman

Studies; the University of Bristol; and the Board of Celtic Studies of the University of Wales.

With such an august Executive and wide-spectrum Board, the Camelot Research Committee launched its "Quest for Camelot" fund-raising drive in late 1965. Money was supplied by the BBC, newspapers, private donors and universities. Excavations began in July 1966 and have continued ever since.

Evidence for the existence of an "Arthurian Age" at Cadbury Hill came almost immediately, during the excavations of 1966 and 1967. Although nothing was found on Cadbury Hill that absolutely proved the existence of *the* King Arthur, or absolutely identified the place as Arthur's Camelot, these conclusions were almost inescapable because of mutual support of local legend and archeological finds. As Geoffrey Ashe, Secretary of the Camelot Research Committee, put it:

> Cadbury Castle around the year 500 must have been more than a mere refuge. The Saxons were nowhere within many miles. The conclusion is inescapable that it was the fortress of a great military leader, a man in a unique position, with special responsibilites and a unique temper of mind . . . Nothing has emerged to show what his name was, and we shall be lucky indeed if it ever does. But the question of the name is hardly more than a quibble. The lord of Cadbury was a person as much like Arthur as makes no matter: a person living on a site traditionally picked out as his home, in the traditional period, with resources on the traditional scale, playing at least part of the traditional role; a person big enough for the legends to have gathered around him.

Goeffrey Ashe put the supposed "Romanization" of Arthurian Britain into the perspective compelled by excavation results:

> The dark-age rampart shows no Roman influence whatever. While 'towered Camelot' may well have been a reality, the towers were wooden look-out posts appropriate to Cymbeline rather than Caesar. The *dux bellorum* defended — no doubt consciously and proudly — what Britain retained of the Imperial heritage. He may have done it in virtue of some Imperial title. But he did it as a Briton.

The flat top of Cadbury Hill encompasses 18 acres and only a bare third of this area has so far been excavated by archeologists. Yet, every square foot of turf has yielded some evidence of an Arthurian Age settlement. If, indeed, the entire 18 acres was built upon, and occupied, during the Arthurian period, Cadbury Hill is more than large enough to accommodate legendary descriptions of Camelot. It would have been a huge and populous fortress, about four times the size of Tintagel.

Purely military researches of people like Geoffrey Ashe and R. G. Collingwood, one of the contributors to the *Oxford History of England*, support the popular and traditional picture of Arthur as a leader of heavy cavalry whose strategy was to sally forth with a picked corps to support any remote British princeling who might be threatened. There is some evidence that Arthur's only official title, *dux bellorum*, was a borrowed whisper from Roman times and that his cavalry was copied along Late Roman plans for the defence of Britain.

In the late empire, Roman generals in charge of provincial defence held the rank of *dux* ("leader") or *comes*. These are the original forms of "duke" and "count" in later medieval terminology. Collingwood notes that under a Roman defensive scheme drawn up for the Western Empire in the early 400s, Britain was allotted a *Comes Britannarium*, or "Count of Britain", who had a roving cavalry command with a mandate to protect the coast from Scotland to the Channel with six cavalry units.

By the early 400s, Rome had developed two different sorts of heavy cavalry. The *cataphracti* of the Eastern Empire were heavily armoured bowmen and were used against the mounted bowmen coming from the steppes of Russia. The lengthy survival of the Eastern Empire and Byzantium up until 1453 A.D. is attributed in no small measure to the effectiveness of these mounted and armoured archers.[19]

In the West, though, another sort of cavalry was used since the barbarians themselves had no horsemen and fought on foot with axe, sword, mace and spear. Western Roman cavalry were called *clibanarii*. They were armoured in chain mail, carried a long and heavy lance for their initial charge, and used the Roman long sword, the *spatha*, from the saddle to cut down fleeing barbarians. *Clibanarii* were the original template for the later medieval knight.

Therefore, under the Late Roman defensive plan, the *Comes Britannarium* supposedly had six units of *clibanarii* to speed to points of barbarian landings on the coast, break up the barbarian beachheads by lance charge, and drive the barbarians into the sea with the *spatha*. Like many Roman military plans of the early 400s, it is likely that this one existed only on paper. Otherwise, surely, some source such as the *Anglo Saxon*

3rd Century A.D. graffito of a Roman *clibanarius*.

Chronicle or Gildas would have mentioned the exploits of this *Comes Britannarium*. In the Roman campaign of 418-425 A.D., Gildas did mention "unexpected bands of cavalry", but nothing so grand as the paper plan of the *Comes Britannarium*.

Nonetheless, these "unexpected bands of cavalry" would have been Late Roman *clibanarii*, and there is nothing implausible in the idea that abandoned Romano-Celtic chieftains knew of the Roman plan and did their best to implement it. There's nothing at all implausible about the idea that Arthur's success was due to the fact that he refined and perfected the old Roman cavalry plan and even borrowed a Roman cavalry title when the High Kingship was denied to him.

This is all very plausible, but there is no proof for any of it. Yet it certainly fits the traditional legend of Arthur well. And, although there is no proof that legendary King Arthur was the lord of Cadbury Hill, as local traditions insist, such a site *would have been* perfectly suited to a commander of *clibanarii* defending western England. Cadbury Hill is tall enough to be in line of sight communication with Glastonbury Tor 12 miles to the northwest, and in line of sight communication with other flat-topped hill forts. Fire beacons from other hill forts in Somerset could be seen directly, or relayed, to Glastonbury Tor and Cadbury Hill. Warning of an attack on the borders, and the location of it, could come within minutes to the lord of Cadbury Hill. His heavy cavalry could respond quickly to support a threatened princeling on any border. Furthermore, the 18-acre expanse of Cadbury Hill offered ample room for stables and for the safe nightly quartering of numerous horses which would forage by day at the base of the hill on the lush grass of the Vale of Avalon.

If he was a commander of *clibanarii* in southwestern England, King Arthur of tradition almost had to have been lord of Cadbury Hill. As the peasants insisted through generations of folk memory, Cadbury Hill was very likely the site of Arthur's Camelot.

However, it is only natural that someone of Arthur's stature would be claimed by other regions of Great Britain. In her 1986 book, *King Arthur*, linguist Norma Lorre Goodrich claims that Arthur's Camelot was modern Carlisle and his area of activity was Scotland and northern England, not the southwest. She further claims that Arthur could not have been a leader of heavy cavalry primarily, but instead defended his realm by ships based on the Clyde. Further, she maintains that linguistic evidence points to the Isle of Man, not to Glastonbury, as the legendary Avalon.

Goodrich's linguistic contentions may well be true and I am in no position to argue them. Besides, even with the Cadbury Hill finds, no one is in a position to say where Camelot was and where Arthur ruled because there is not even any absolute proof of his existence. But one non-linguistic criticism can be levelled against Goodrich's work. She maintains that an island chieftain cannot defend his realm by cavalry, but only by controlling the surrounding sea. In support of this idea she quotes Sir Halford J. Mackinder's *Britain and the British Seas* to the effect that "the defence of Britain rests fundamentally upon the theory implied in the command of the sea."

Mackinder's statement is true enough . . . *provided that one is concerned with defending a Britain that has not yet been invaded.* Arthur was not in that enviable strategic and tactical situation. Arthur's Britain had long been invaded, and even settled, by Angles, Saxons and Jutes. In fact, by Arthur's time, Celtic Britons held actually only about half of the British Isles. Eastern Britain, from Scotland to the Channel, was already in

Scandinavian hands. These parts, the entire eastern shore, were called the "Saxon Shore".[20]

Arthur had no opportunity to defend an unviolated Britain merely threatened with seaborne invasion. Invasion and settlement by the barbarians had long been a fact. King Arthur could hope only to prevent Saxon expansion into new inland regions of Britain and to oppose any fresh landings on coasts still held by Celts. He could do this with cavalry, not with a navy, as the Romans had realized long before.

Although I am in no position to dispute Goodrich's linguistic evidence since, as she says, she is master of "more than twenty ancient and medieval languages", I do offer the opinion that her military notions have little to do with strategical or tactical reality. Arthur is better placed on Cadbury Hill, and the presence there of himself and his heirs may have something to do with the fact that the Saxons did not conquer Somerset until 250 years after Arthur's death. Ironically, Goodrich uses the Saxon-free Somerset as an argument about why King Arthur could not have been headquartered there!

However, it is true, as Goodrich claims, that Arthur's first twelve legendary battles, culminating in the great victory of Badon Hill, do seem to have taken place near the Scottish border. Goodrich and some other scholars consider that these battles are too far from Cadbury Hill to have been fought by a southwestern *dux bellorum* and so conclude that King Arthur must have been a north English or Scottish personality. But it seems to me that these experts may be grossly underrating the mobility and radius of action of trained cavalry. None of Arthur's twelve initial battles were more than 400 miles from Glastonbury, and he had a superb network of still-usable Roman roads to exploit. The old Roman Empire was some 3000 miles in east-to-west extent and was held by cavalry much like Arthur's. Macsen thought nothing of crossing the Channel, invading France and conquering Rome a century before Arthur. And the bulk of Macsen's army would have been infantry.[21] Why should Arthur then, a leader of cavalry, balk at fighting a battle on the borders 400 miles from his headquarters? In fact, from a purely military point of view it makes good sense to engage the enemy as early as possible and as far from your heartland as possible. Not only will less of your own territory and people be despoiled by the enemy before the battle is joined, but in the event of defeat you have a large loyal area through which to retreat and where there is some chance of rallying forces for another attempt to confront the enemy.

I have dealt with Goodrich's *King Arthur* at some length because it is one of the most recent books on the subject and because the author is an established expert, in the purely academic sense, and not an amateur enthusiast like Geoffrey Ashe. In gross injustice, in addition, her academic colleagues have praised her book as being "the first" definitive work which "authenticates" Arthur as a real historical personage. In a sense, the emergence of *King Arthur* with all of its curious notions is a good sign and an inevitable one. It simply means that King Arthur has become respectable enough to interest an accredited academic, and Goodrich's book begins that seemingly inevitable process whereby scholars appropriate to themselves a subject really discovered and made respectable by amateurs.

Sandwiched between Goodrich's pedantries, irrelevancies and amusing military theories are snippets of value which serve to make the Arthurian story somewhat less mythical and more plausible. She suggests, for instance, that the famous Round Table was born of a linguistic mistake in translation. Goodrich points out that various romances have different numbers of knights sitting at this "Round Table". Layamon, a translator and adapter of Geoffrey of Monmouth, stated that this Round Table had been made in Cornwall and could accommodate 1600 knights! As Goodrich points out, this is a little unlikely and is an impossible carpenter's nightmare. Instead, she suggests that this "Round Table" was a mistake in translating and understanding the Latin word *rotunda*, a round building of stone. The knights of Arthur's retinue would have met in this building, which was open to the sky, and did not sit around a table of any sort. One immediately thinks of Stonehenge as the Arthurian "Round Table".

Strangely enough, for all the linguistic minutae she brings to her book, Goodrich has little to say about the Holy Grail. Yet, in a way, the Holy Grail is the most important aspect of the legendary King Arthur's life. It was, somehow, infinitely precious, and he was guardian of it. In fact, guarding the Holy Grail was King Arthur's principal spiritual mission in all the romances, fully equal to, if not actually superior to, his secular mission to protect Britain from Saxons.

Of the Holy Grail, Goodrich merely concludes:

> After long reflection, doubtless, each of our twelfth-and-thirteenth century authors, some of whom had received the benefit of advice and religious counsel from fellow scholars in their own congregation

at home and abroad, made his own decision as to what the "graal" or Holy Grail really was. Some called it a cup or chalice; some thought it was a platter, or a monstrance, or a brilliant gemstone. All associated it with dazzling white light and with a secret ceremony involving both men and women in the hidden Grail Castle in the presence of the immobile, wounded Grail King.

So much for the Holy Grail in the view of linguist Norma Lorre Goodrich, author of *King Arthur*. She follows the popular and common belief that the Holy Grail was the "cup of the Last Supper", the same vessel (in tradition) which Joseph of Arimathaea held aloft to catch the blood of Jesus when the Centurion, Longinius, pierced Christ's side with a spear. This cup or chalice was the Holy Grail that Joseph of Arimathaea brought with him to Glastonbury according to local legend. Or, as another variant, the Holy Grail might be the platter on which the head of John the Baptist was borne by Salome. In any event, this mysterious Holy Grail was a vessel of some sort to hold the holy blood, in some romances the font of all good things, which only the pure of heart might behold.

Another linguist, the Frenchman Jean-Michel Angebert, has studied the matter more deeply and can offer some insights into what this Holy Grail might be. The Holy Grail first appeared in Western literature with the romance of Chrétien de Troyes.[22] Other troubadours in France took up the theme and also referred to the Grail in their own Arthurian romances.

These troubadours all spelled "Grail" as "graal", and the Holy Grail was, for them, *San Graal*. Jean-Michel Angebert points out that *graal* is something of an artificial and concocted word. It seems to be a composite of the Latin *gradual*, meaning a prayer book; of the Provençal French word *grasale*, meaning a chalice or vase; and of the Arabic *al go'ral*, meaning "something inscribed upon". Provençal French in which most of the troubadour romances were written was a language heavily influenced by Arabic from Moorish Spain across the Pyrenees.[23]

So, it seems that the troubadour composers of the Arthurian romances went to some length to *invent* a word, graal, with several alternative meanings. Possibly they invented this strange word in order to make a pun. San Graal, in pronunciation, approximates the modern French "sang real" . . . which means *blood royal*. In an era when royalty and kingship were believed to emanate from divine dispensation, another meaning for *San Graal* would be "holy blood".

Therefore we face a paradox which leads us far from the idea of the Holy Grail as a mere cup or chalice (or platter). The Holy Grail not only *held* the holy blood, the Holy Grail *was* the holy blood. This is not really so obscure and there's a simple answer to the apparent difficulty.

The Holy Grail was not any sort of physical vessel, whether cup, chalice or platter. The Holy Grail was a lineage, pedigree or bloodline *of people*. This lineage was coyly referred to as a "cup" because it was the living vessel in which the holy blood was held and preserved. And in using this pun based on an artificial word, the troubadours were attempting to disguise a monstrous religious heresy from the Inquisitors of the Roman Church.

Although the true nature of the Holy Grail was a secret that had to be disguised by puns and allusions, and was a secret revealed only to those who had proven their purity of heart and staunchness of character, I think there is enough circumstantial evidence to establish the Holy Grail as a fact of Western history. There is an intriguing pattern of history to suggest that four thousand years of human adventure in the West have been largely molded, and certainly influenced, by a very special bloodline of people. They are apparently still living, and still working.

The Holy Grail is not an inanimate object, but is a living reality. The troubadours were careful in coining their artificial word to describe, and disguise, this human truth. The special lineage was a *graduale*, or prayer book, because it represented hope for the attainment of human progress; the bloodline was also a *grasale*, or vase, because it held the promise of human progress and guidance; the holy blood was also *al go'ral*, "something inscribed upon", because it is a genealogy containing the names of the most illustrious heroes and heroines of Western history.

I hasten to assure the reader that this interpretation of the Holy Grail as a lineage of people is not merely my own. Aside from the linguistic contributions of Jean-Michel Angebert in unravelling the component parts of that artificial word *graal*, we will discover that the troubadours themselves used extended and complex poetic allusions making it clear that the Holy Grail was a succession of people related to each other. Wolfram von Eschenbach, the Bavarian troubadour (or "minnesinger" to use the correct Germanic analog), whose Grail Romance *Parzival* is perhaps the greatest literary product of the medieval period in the opinion of not a few scholars, states frankly that men and women issued from the Holy Grail to become leaders of communities. Other troubadours likewise associate children with the Holy Grail and emphasize that it is a thing that can renew and perpetuate itself.

If the Holy Grail is a bloodline, what relationship does King Arthur have to it?

The truth of the matter is that the authors of the Grail Romances seemed uncertain themselves. King Arthur is always portrayed as related to the Holy Grail lineage, but somewhat distantly related. He is a protector of the Holy Grail, but not really a part of it himself.

This situation, in a curious way, parallels Arthur's situation in Geoffrey of Monmouth's History. Arthur is not a really legitimate "king," he's somehow removed from the truly royal succession, but his prowess commands respect and recognition. He becomes the "King of Britain" by acclaim rather than by proper succession. Arthur is a somewhat shadowy figure, not only in Geoffrey's History appearing in 1136, but also in the spate of Arthurian Romances written by Chrétien de Troyes, Robert de Boron, Wolfram von Eschenbach and other troubadours between 1190 and 1220.

And here may be the place to mention a distinct difference between Geoffrey of Monmouth's History and the somewhat later Arthurian romances. Of all the so-called Arthurian literary material, Geoffrey's is not only the first, but it is unique in dealing principally with the life of King Arthur himself and unique because Geoffrey nowhere mentions the Holy Grail. All of the later Arthurian romances deal principally with Arthur's successors and the Holy Grail, leaving Arthur himself as a great, but remote, personality in the background.

There is a reason for this which will become clear as the argument of this book progresses, but can be stated now even though the facts which make it all understandable have not yet been presented. Simply put, Geoffrey's History was written during the 1130s when the dynasty of Godfroi de Bouillon still securely held the Kingdom of Jerusalem, but all of the Grail Romances were written after 1187 A.D. when the dynasty of Godfroi de Bouillon lost the Kingdom of Jerusalem.

The significance of this will become clear later, but it is enough to say that, with the de Bouillon's loss of the Kingdom of Jerusalem, a history and eulogy of the ancient Holy Grail, the bloodline itself, became important. Therefore the troubadours writing in the wake of the de Bouillon defeat concentrated on those personalities around Arthur who truly represented the Grail lineage.

Therefore, the troubadours focused on Gawain, Lancelot, Percival and Galahad and upon the "Quest for the Holy Grail". But, while they did this, they were also confused about the epoch when the Arthurian drama took place and they disagree about which people were central to the Grail lineage. We should remember that the troubadours of circa 1200 were writing about events that happened some 700 years before their own time. It is natural that there would be some disagreement and uncertainty.

But one thing was agreed upon by all the troubadours: the true Holy Grail lineage derived from Joseph of Arimathaea. Gawain, Percival and Galahad were a legitimate part of this lineage, but King Arthur, great though he was, was not.

At this point, I can only ask the reader to bear with me while trusting that all of this will eventually make some sense, but it is actually quite simple. The Holy Grail that Joseph of Arimathaea brought with him to Glastonbury according to popular tradition was not an *object*, but was a very special *person*. The children of this individual married into the Romano-Celtic royalty and nobility. By the time of King Arthur, some 400-odd years after Joseph of Arimathaea, many of the Romano-Celtic ruling houses boasted blood relationship to this special individual and, through her, to Joseph of Arimathaea. Some had a more direct relationship than others, of course, and it may be that King Arthur *almost* had the most direct claim of any . . . except for the nagging doubts about whether his father was Uther or Cador.

The Provençal troubadours were concerned mostly with Arthur's successors and with the Holy Grail because, after the Battle of Camlann and the wounding of Arthur, the Grail lineage of Joseph of Arimathaea was evacuated from England to France. It was probably Percival who brought the holy blood into France. That is why Percival (or "Parzival") takes such a prominent place in the French-authored Grail Romances.

*   *   *

In early February 1983, Deanna Theilmann-Bean and I took a quick week-long trip to Britain. Obviously, at that season our objective was not pleasure, but business. Back home in Kentville, Nova Scotia we had rather miraculously been able to establish a boat building company with unusual goals. We were not designing and making boats for the recreational market. We designed and built boats intended for poor village fishermen in developing nations, and we worked in association with the Canadian International Development Agency.

This unlikely business had been inspired by my interests in primitive and non-Western naval architecture, voyaging and navigation, and, perhaps, by ill-advised encouragement on the part of colleagues at the Centre for African Studies at Dalhousie University in Halifax where I had been a part-time lecturer. My researches had led me to believe that primitive and non-Western principles of boat building, if rendered in modern materials, might result in seaworthy fishing boats that were inexpensive enough for impoverished village fishermen in the Third World. Needless to say, I had no illusions about actually making money doing this kind of thing. Neither did Deanna when she cast her lot with me. But we thought we could scrabble a bare living from it, in Nova Scotia, while I kept a promise to my son.

In all the world, there appeared to be only three other companies committed to the same philosophy and goal. Although we were all technically "competitors" in the aid and development business, we all realized that the "market" was so huge, and the urgency so desperate, that nothing much would be harmed by sharing information, design innovations and ideas. As it happened, all three of these companies were located in Britain, where they worked in association with the British version of CIDA, the Overseas Development Agency or ODA. In early February 1983 we received cordial invitations to visit all three and there seemed to be a real possibility that one of my designs might be chosen for manufacture under license in Britain.

Our week was hectic with meetings at Impex Southern, Fairey Alday Marine and Gifford Technology, not to mention the Overseas Development Agency.

As a "designer" and supposed expert on primitive boats of all sorts, I viewed with interest and admiration the Third World fishing boats being built by "Giff" Gifford in Southampton. Giff had laboured for years to perfect and evolve his catamaran fishing boats used in India and Sri Lanka and, although he had support from the ODA and several humanistic Peers of the Realm, Gifford and his wife, like Deanna and myself, worked definitely for satisfaction and commitment, not for comfort. That much was obvious from Gifford's Southampton establishment. The marvel was that he and his design team had gradually evolved the catamaran so that not one square inch of precious plywood was wasted. It was design perfection I could never hope to attain myself. Yet, after discussions and consultations, Giff adopted our crab-claw lateen sailing rig for his cata-marans as being more efficient than the traditional "oro" sailing rig of Sri Lanka.

As President of our little company, Deanna probed and parried congenially with the Chief Executive Officer of Fairey Alday Marine, also in Southampton, concerning the conditions of licensed manufacture of our 32-foot fishing boat. While Deanna conducted her high-level nego-tiations, I wandered around the Fairey Alday factory looking at the latest creations of one of the world's best marine designers. Tantalizingly, I saw the hull of Britain's America's Cup contender under construction and wondered idly how much the New York Yacht Club might pay for a photograph ... Unfortunately, my "guide/guard" in the Fairey Alday factory had already politely relieved me of my camera.

Our last business meeting was held over an informal lunch at Gifford Technology, with much goodwill and equal amounts of dark British ale. We had a day remaining until our low-cost week-long excursion flight re-turned to Canada and, as soon as we'd finished lunch and had said cordial goodbyes, we jumped into our rented Chevette and headed for the A303.

Like so many people of our uncertain time, Deanna and I each have one foot in two different worlds. There's the mundane world of business and making a living, and there's the world in which, it seems, something intangible is working to lend sense and purpose to the human story.

Some people choose to call this other reality "spirituality", or "the occult", "mysticism", or "religion". Deanna and I both tended to suspect the existence of another reality, although we probably shaped it in our minds a bit differently than most people.

I had been studying the Grail Romances for almost ten years and I had been forced to conclude that a great human truth lay purposefully concealed within the apparently frivolous poetry of the troubadours.

In fact, I had come to agree with Wolfram von Eschenbach when he wrote in *Parzival*:

> Kyot, the master of high renown,
> Found, in confused pagan writing,
> The legend which reaches back to the
> prime source of all legends.

I had been compelled to the conclusion that "spirituality", "the occult", "mysticism" and "religion" — even "witchcraft" — were but garbled and distorted inklings of *one* awesome and secret human and historical truth. At least one of the troubadours, Wolfram von Eschenbach, knew "the legend which reaches back to the prime source of all legends" although he did not reveal it entirely. Nor will The Great Legend be fully told in this book, although I suspect its profile and hinted at it in 1978 with the publication of *The Iceman Inheritance*.

But, with a day of free time, Deanna and I determined to visit a focal point where one chapter of The Great Legend had been played out. So, after lunch at Gifford Technology in Southampton, we took the A303 highway to South Cadbury.

We arrived at the foot of Cadbury Hill in the early evening of a blustery February day. A storm was raging off Land's End, a danger to shipping the car's radio informed us, and the gale whipped Cadbury Hill with cold rain while grey clouds writhed across the sky. The weather was enough to keep local Arthurian enthusiasts off the hill, but it posed only mild discomfort to newly arrived Canadians like Deanna and me, and we had Camelot to ourselves.

It was something of a struggle to get to the top of Cadbury Hill since the rain had turned the only path into a rivulet of mud, but eventually we made it and walked on the grassy 18-acre meadow that passes for the summit of the flat-topped hill. In the fading light we could make out scars in the turf that marked the spots of 1982 archeological excavations. I recounted to Deanna what I knew of the Camelot discoveries.

Ostensibly, we had come to Cadbury Hill to confirm what seemed obvious from a study of ordnance survey maps: that Cadbury Hill was in line of sight communication across the Vale of Avalon with Glastonbury Tor and other hill forts in Somerset. This was confirmed quickly enough. Even in the darkening evening we could see the mysterious conical shape of the Tor on the horizon 12 miles northwest, and the lights of Glastonbury itself below the Tor. Shepton Mallet and Frome to the north, Warminster to the northeast, and Shaftesbury to the southeast all glimmered in the distance. Cadbury Hill seemed surrounded by distant village lights as if a huge necklace of diamonds had been coiled around it. Once, we knew, a jewel blazed on the top of Cadbury Hill, the central diadem of Celtic Britain. Camelot. But now it was extinguished. There is no modern habitation of any sort on Cadbury Hill. Only the meadow with its secrets nestled below turf.

Once we'd verified the maps there was really no reason to linger, but we stayed for a few minutes in spite of the chill and the wind driven rain. We both wanted to get the *feel* of the place, but there was nothing mystical about our desire.

Although Deanna is British by birth, she had never visited a hill fort. I was born in Alabama, had spent all of my life in North America, and consequently had had no opportunity to visit a real, verified hill fort either. And it was vital for us to get an idea of what a true hill fortress looked like, and felt like.

It was vital to us because, back home in Nova Scotia, we had been invited to visit, and officially asked to investigate, something very similar to Cadbury Hill.

Chapter Two

The Castle at The Cross

About a year before we climbed Cadbury Hill and Glastonbury Tor we found ourselves atop another summit. This time, it was a hill top in Nova Scotia.

It was a bitterly cold January evening in 1982 that we first saw the castle ruins at The Cross.[1] The biting wind off the Atlantic chilled us to the bone, but it also swept the snow from parts of the hill top. It was possible to make out the walls in the fading light. Ruined walls, rather, that made patterns of stone on the ground. They meandered over the hill, and snaked away to become lost in the distance, the darkness and the flurries of driven snow. At places, the patterns formed angles on the ground, the corners, apparently, of a large building that had once perched on this flat-topped mini-mountain in mid-peninsular Nova Scotia. I examined these angles with interest. They seemed to have obvious buttresses. They had once been rubblework masonry. It was an architectural style characteristic of late 14th Century Norse and North Scottish constructions.

Rubblework architecture is no more or less than what the name means and what you'd imagine from it. Walls are constructed by the simple expedient of piling stones on top of each other. Naturally, the builders took care to choose rocks with irregularities, and took care to place adjoining rocks so that their irregularities would fit into each other and form a bond of sorts. Rubblework is obviously a technique used by primitive builders, or builders in a hurry with no better solution to hand. Whenever possible, rubblework builders tried to use flat pieces of stone, such as might be found in definitely stratified limestone and sandstone

45

formations. But sometimes they were forced to use whatever was available, and this might mean roughly rounded stones from a river valley which had been rolled and ground by water action into more or less spherical shapes. Naturally, rubblework walls tend to be both very thick (up to three feet thick for a small cottage) and very low, usually not more than about six feet high. Rubblework corners are especially vulnerable to gradual "degeneration" as stones are worked loose by the wind or by encounters with farm animals, passers-by or wagons and agricultural implements dealing glancing blows. As a rule, therefore, the corners of rubblework constructions are "reinforced" or "padded" by adding a mound of extra stones leaning up against the corners of the building. These extra mounds of stone at the corners are "buttresses."

Rubblework sometimes incorporates mortar as a better bonding agent than the mere friction of rocky imperfections locking against each other. With mortar, rubblework walls can be thinner and higher. Rubblework columns can even be contrived with mortar as a bonding agent.

Naturally, rubblework has long since been supplanted by more modern ways of building. Nonetheless, rubblework cottages are still inhabited all over Europe and the British Isles, but particularly on the Outer Hebrides, the Orkney and Shetland island groups around Scotland. I have illustrated dry wall rubblework (no mortar) with a photograph taken from Hammond Innes' *Sea and Islands*. This is a cottage on South Uist in the Outer Hebrides west of Scotland. This photo gives a very good idea of typical North Scots and Scandinavian rubblework, and may be very much as the ruins at The Cross appeared at one time.

From what we could see of the apparent ruins at The Cross, the rubblework structure which had once stood on the hill top was much, much larger than any cottage. In fact, the walls snaking away into the blizzard seemed to have once been palisades of castle proportions.

The remains of a castle were about the last thing we expected to find in the middle of Nova Scotia.

The winter night came early, and with it came increasing cold. We tore ourselves reluctantly from the fascinating, but now almost invisible patterns on the ground, and made our way toward the house where cheery yellow light splashed from the rear windows onto the streaming and drifting snow.

Deanna sadly stated the obvious: that if the morning's forecast was correct we weren't likely to see any more of the ruined walls until spring.

Black house on Uist in the Outer Hebrides.
Photo by Hammond Innes.

This was the first heavy snow of a winter that had been holding off until now. The winter was likely to make up for its leniency. Snow could be expected to follow snow, building on tonight's blizzard, until the spring thaw.

We took refuge in the farm-style kitchen around a hot wood stove while John and Jeanne McKay revived us with cups of steaming coffee.[2]

We'd learned about the castle ruins because of Jeanne's letter. She'd bought a copy of my latest book, *The Black Discovery of America*.[3] It was about evidence that the black West Africans may have first crossed the Atlantic Ocean to the New World. But, as general background, I also wrote about the known Norse, Irish, Celtiberian and North African traditions of navigation on the Atlantic. Jeanne had read this with interest, thinking that maybe I might be able to help her where no one else had paid much attention. She had uncovered the stone patterns in her back yard ten years before while starting a garden in their new home. She had immediately informed the Nova Sctoia Museum, but the two investigators who had travelled down from Halifax had not seemed much

Apparent ruins on the McKay property at The Cross. External walls of the alleged "castle" extend onto neighbouring properties of the hill top village.

Photo by Michael Bradley.

interested. The walls were "either French or Indian", they had told Jeanne, and they'd just shrugged their shoulders and had driven back to Halifax.

This wasn't good enough for her. She knew well enough that there was no record of precolonial stone construction techniques among the Micmac Indians of Nova Scotia. A little research showed no record of any Acadian French settlement in the area. The earliest colonial survey showed these walls as already existing long before the first British settlers actually arrived in the early 1800s.

Then who had built these walls? When? And how and when had they become ruins? What sort of building had originally stood there?

Using the resources available to them, Jeanne and John McKay began a decade of research, but Jeanne's interest supplied the greater part of their motivation. They gradually reconstructed the history of the place to their own satisfaction. The tale that Jeanne came up with bore little relation to history in standard textbooks.

She became convinced that the place had an ancient history, and had been visited by Europeans before the birth of Christ. Later, the Norse had come. They built a city on the mid-peninsular hill top. Jeanne connected her ruined walls with the lost city of Norumbega. After Columbus, but still long before any known European settlement at the present village, the old Norse site of Norumbega had served as a refuge for Stuart princes. Gold to finance Stuart intrigues and doomed military adventures had come from the local area, from the gold-rich sand and gravel of the Gold River.

No one at the Nova Scotia Museum or at Dalhousie University took her reconstructed history seriously.

But after reading *The Black Discovery of America* and learning of my research into pre-Columbian transatlantic voyages, she thought that I might at least come to look at the place. She wrote a long letter in care of my Toronto publisher. It was duly forwarded and eventually arrived in Halifax.

We read it. Many times. We were both fascinated and dismayed. We discussed whether or not to answer the letter. Jeanne McKay had written much more than an historical sketch and a description of the ruins. She'd also revealed to us her own personal connection with ruins. She herself was not only a Stuart pretender, but was also related to Eric the Red and Marco Polo. And Magellan. She'd known about the place before immigrating to Canada and Nova Scotia. There were tales and whispers in her family about some "secret history" and an overseas refuge. It had once been ruled by "a cruel queen".

We were fascinated if there were genuine pre-Columbian ruins on Jeanne's property.

We'd received her letter before Christmas, but with the holidays we didn't call to arrange a visit until well after New Year's Day. We didn't know what to expect.

On that cold and windy evening we saw the ruined walls, at least, they looked like ruined walls.

And while we sipped coffee as close to the wood stove as possible, we tried to assess our host and hostess between bouts of shivering. Both Jeanne and John bore our scrutiny pleasantly enough, obviously well aware of our wariness and misgivings.

John, a swarthy Welshman, was a chemist by profession and a professor. He'd taught at Acadia University in Wolfville, about 40 miles away on the Fundy coast, but at some point the long distance commuting had proved too much and he'd accepted a position teaching senior high school in the village. This, however, was coming to an end because of local unease relating to Jeanne. John had taken a position with a private company in Labrador City. The McKays would be leaving the village.

Jeanne was one of those tiny, frail and completely indestructible Englishwomen. She'd obviously been a beauty in her youth, and traces lingered, although she'd aged greatly since a serious accident some time before. Nothing, however, could dim the brightness of her eyes, the sharpness of her wit, and the truly wide learning that graced her conversation. Jeanne McKay wore eccentricity like a badge of honour.

Interspersed with a discussion that displayed Jeanne's almost frightening knowledge of history, she cheerfully informed us that they had to leave the village, and John had to find work elsewhere, because the locals believed her to be a witch.

And while accurately recounting some extremely obscure aspects of European exploration, she would digress to fill us in on the "real story" which, most often, involved some economic or military machinations of her family, which is to say, a lineage of nobility ranging back through the Stuarts to the kings of the Norse.

After we'd warmed sufficiently, we politely asked to see the artifacts that John and Jeanne had recovered from the site after a decade of gardening. They explained that they had never attempted any sort of excavation because they were amateurs. They'd always been trying to convince someone at the museum or the universities to undertake a professional archeological excavation of the place, and they had not wanted to disturb the site with ignorant delvings.

Only once, their curiosity had gotten the better of them. They wanted to know how far down into the ground the walls went. John had chosen a place at random and had dug down four feet. He didn't reach the bottom of the wall, the foundation. But the stones did get larger, he said, and instead of the walls remaining rubblework, some of the larger stones were squared and fitted together. We were shown photographs of this hole and John belly-deep in it beside the uncovered wall. The lower courses of stone were, indeed, roughly squared and fitted, unlike the sort of "rock-cottage" construction higher up.

This had been the only purposeful dig into the ruins themselves, but during a decade of dedicated gardening, John and Jeanne had uncovered some curious items.

Left – Portions of flaked flint knife blade allegedly found in the apparent ruins on the McKay property at The Cross.

Right – Part of an iron or steel dagger-blade segment allegedly found in the apparent ruins of The Cross.

Photo by Michael Bradley.

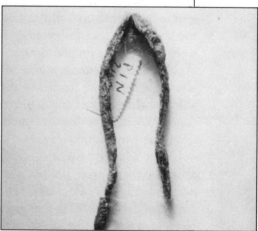

Left – Portion of what appears to be the point of a 14th Century sword.

Right – Metal pin or "fibula" recovered from the alleged castle site at The Cross, Nova Scotia. This artifact is similar to Celtic fibulae in use between about 400 B.C. and 600 A.D., but identification has not been confirmed by an archeologist.

Photo by Michael Bradley.

There was a portion of a flaked stone knife. It looked Celtic, such as the later Celts made in imitation of Neolithic originals as late as the Julian conquest of Gaul.[4] Along with that, we were shown a photograph of what Jeanne called "the Herm", a roughly man-shaped stone that stood on the property. We'd seen it outside, but covered with snow. The photograph showed it much better in brilliant summer sunshine. Yes, it could possibly be Celtic of a style known as "petromantic".[5]

About this time, Jeanne informed us that she really wasn't a witch, at all events, she wasn't a *bad* witch. She had no truck with black magic, but only with white magic. The only spells she tried to cast were for good and beneficial purposes. Sadly, the villagers could not apparently understand the differences among witches.

John showed us the metal objects that had been recovered. A sort of pin, or "fibula", much corroded. A portion of a "swordblade" which, John agreed, could equally be from some sort of agricultural implement. A portion of a finer and narrower "dagger blade" which did look like just that.

Jeanne had collected a number of curious wooden objects. They were small (3 inches long) wooden cones, slightly curved. One and all were split at the narrow end, while some showed evidence of cord wrapping at the larger end. Jeanne explained that these had puzzled her until she'd seen, from Europe (in photographs), museum examples of medieval gold-working tools. These cones were, she said, small vises for holding fine gold bits while they were shaped by the smith. Further, they were obviously able to hold a ring of any diameter at some point along the expanding cone. According to Jeanne, these cones would have been fixed into a sturdy table top in simple holes.

The gold itself had come, of course, from the source of the Gold River about 500 yards from the hill top site. The lode must be underground nearby, but in any case the Gold River washed quantities of it out of the ground and it collected in the river's bed of sand and gravel. It only had to be panned out. This gold, after being worked crudely at the castle, was transported down to Oak Island where it was kept safely in the famous "Money Pit" until enough had accumulated to justify a shipment. Then, a ship belonging to one of her ancestors, the de Hopes, would fetch it back to Europe. It helped to finance military ventures of people like Bonnie Prince Charlie.

John showed us a government geological map of the area which indicated minerals discovered and claims staked. The symbol "Au" (gold) was frequent around the headwaters of the Gold River. We could look down into the valley from the front windows. John told us about the gold rush of the 1890s in the village. Enough gold was extracted to make a few fortunes, not many. Even downstream, in Mahone Bay at "the Ovens", the river deposited enough gold there so that in the 1870s there was a gold rush twenty-five miles away. A few fortunes were made. The Nova Scotia government has erected an historical plaque marking the event.[6]

Jeanne explained that there had been a lot more gold in the old days. When the castle stood on the hill. But the Stuarts and their agents, the de Hopes, had taken most of it long before the 1870s and 1890s. Now, only a few nuggets might be left. It was probably scarce even when Inigo Jones, her ancestor, had come to design and build a mansion within the castle walls. Did we know that there was a three-year period in Inigo Jones' life that was not accounted for? Well, he was here, raising a mansion for a Stuart princeling.

We made motions to leave, having seen, and heard, enough. Before saying our good-byes, we asked what John and Jeanne expected of us. John said he just wanted us to see the place and the artifacts and to tell them what we thought about it all.

Jeanne snapped that the obvious thing to do would be to convince some official organization to undertake proper excavations, plus get busy arranging for a reputable lab to undertake radio-carbon dating of a wood cone. And she slapped one of them into my palm. *She* didn't need a radio-carbon date because she knew the age already, but it would be necessary for experts to accept the site. The gold was taken out between 1400 and 1680 A.D., and the cones would date from that period. The de Hopes had done the mining, or at all events had done the shipping, and they could be traced back to the Red Headed Earl who, of course, was Eric the Red, through Lief's children. Did we know that the de Hope coat of arms was "three gold coins from over the sea"?

On the way back to Halifax, Deanna and I tried to digest all this. The blizzard made it a long drive, but we did not have nearly enough time to make sense of it all.

Altogether, the ruins appeared to me, at least, to be generally similar in type of construction and style to the famous Newport Tower in Newport, Rhode Island. And, in mentioning this Newport Tower I am introducing a controversy that will crop up throughout this book. First,

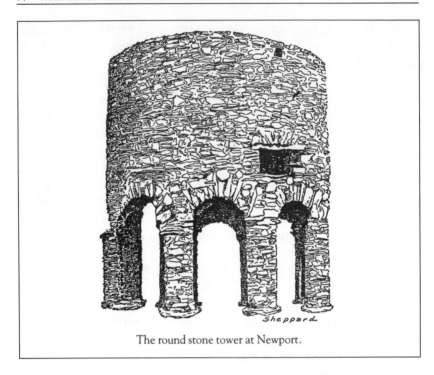

The round stone tower at Newport.

something must be said about the Newport Tower specifically and then something must be said about the numerous other pre-Columbian, but apparently European, structures that allegedly exist in New England.

The Newport Tower presently stands in the town of Newport and any tourist can view it. The problem with this structure is that it was apparently standing before Newport was founded in 1639. It is a round stone rubblework tower supported by eight columns. It incorporated mortar in its construction. In architectural style, it is late 13th Century Scandinavian. With its round section and eight columns, it closely resembles various North European churches: notably Great Hedinge Church in Denmark, St. Olaf's Church at Tønsberg in Norway, and the Church of the Holy Sepulchre at Cambridge, England.

The earliest undeniable colonial reference to the tower is in a deed for a cemetery dated February 28, 1677. It is called "a stone mill". In his will of December 24, 1677, Governor Benedict Arnold of the Rhode Island Colony referred to it as "my stone built windmill."

However, there is persuasive evidence that this structure was referred to in earlier documents. At one time, Sir Edmund Plowden was given letters patent to found the "Province of New Albion" which was granted land including "all that entire island, near the Continent or Terra Firma of North Virginia, called the Isle of Plowden, or Long Island . . . and forty leagues square of the adjoining continent . . . all and singular islands and isles, floating or to float, and being in the sea, within ten leagues of the shore of the said region." In short, the land grant to the proposed "Province of New Albion" included Rhode Island and the site of Newport. Having got the letters patent, the Plowden Company made a survey of the region, and in due course published, in 1632, a document called "The Commodities of the Island Called Manati, or Long Isle Within the Continent of Virginia". This document was something of a prospectus to tempt potential colonists. It listed the good things *to be found* in the territory. Among these existing commodities were: deer, vines, turkeys, chestnuts, various kinds of fish, "spring waters as good as small beere", and a good sandbank on which to dry codfish "60 miles to the northwards". All of the things listed were existing commodities of the land. But an interesting reference occurs in the section dealing with trade with the Indians and protection against them: Section 27 of the "Commodities" states that "30 idle men as souldiers or gent be resident in a rownd stone towre and by tornes to trade with the savages and keep their ordinance and armes neate." The very next section of the "Commodities" (Section 28) again deals with trade and protection vis à vis the Indians and states a pledge of the Plowden Company:

> The Partners are willing to mentaine the governor & 2 men to wayte on him & a Seward and a factor and his man theise to be att the chardge of the Adventurors and 25 souldiers and 25 marriners to trucke and trafficke by torne with the savages, and never above ten of them abroad at once in a pinnace planqued against arrowes.

All this has interesting implications. The "rownd stone towre" is listed as an already existing commodity of the region, not a planned structure to be built. This is clear because, if the tower was something to be constructed in the future, why specify that it be "rownd" when a square tower would be easier to build? Then, why specify it to be of stone when a small ship planked against arrows was deemed to be sufficient protection against Indians?

Then, sometime between 1629 and 1634, a young man named

William Wood made a map of the east side of Narraganset Bay and found evidence of some former European settlement at the present site of Newport. Woods's map was published in a document called "New England's Prospect" in 1635. On his map he entered the existing Plymouth, Massachusetts as "New Plymouth" and called the future site of Newport "Old Plymouth" although there was no known colonial settlement there at the time and this was four years before the founding of Newport.

All this suggests strongly that the Newport Tower was in existence long before the founding of the town in 1639, and perhaps there were other ruins, too, that Wood noted on his survey but which were covered by the colonial building of Newport.

What has muddled the issue about the Newport Tower are the colonial documents of 1677 that refer to it as a windmill. It was certainly *used* as the foundation for a windmill, but that doesn't prove that it was originally *built* as a windmill. In fact, Hjalmar Holand among others has shown that the "rownd" tower is, in fact, out of round and that colonials converted it into a windmill foundation only with considerable difficulty by adding a wooden deck, which was truly circular, to the top of the tower. Holand also pointed out that the windows in the tower, though unnecessary for a windmill, are perfectly sited to overlook the water approaches visible from the tower's location.

In spite of the style of architecture, the references predating the establishment of Newport, the placement of the windows and the 13th Century style of chimney flue, conventional historians are loath to admit that the tower may have been made by unknown Europeans who preceded the known colonists. However, there is yet another indication that the Newport Tower must have been built prior to the accepted colonial periods. It seems to have been built using a measurement known as the Icelandic *fet*.[7] The details of this argument must be banished to a footnote as they may bore most readers, but the objective conclusion must be that the Newport Tower was built by someone using Scandinavian units of measure and Scandinavian architectural style. This does not necessarily mean that the Newport Tower was built by "Vikings", as we will see.

In addition to the Newport Tower, there are alleged to be many hundreds of precolonial, but still European, structures throughout New England. Some of these appear to be Norse in nature, while others appear clearly to be "Celtic" of various periods. All of these alleged precolonial European structures are hotly denied by the more conservative establishment scholars. Yet, the interested reader can see photographs of some fairly dramatic and Celtic-looking rubblework structures in Dr. Barry Fell's *Saga America* and *America B.C.* as well as in Salvatore Michael Trento's *The Search for Lost America*.

The problem with all this evidence is not the evidence itself, but the attitudes attaching to it on both sides of the controversy. There's little doubt that some people on the "pro" side have made exaggerated claims for piles of stone and have concocted dubious translations from "inscriptions" that are more likely weather-marks or plow-marks on field stones. On the other hand, some of the ruins are definitely man-made and rather obviously predate any known colonial settlement. No one has yet taken a dispassionate and truly professional archeological approach to these alleged ruins in New England, just as no one has taken the ruins at The Cross seriously.

When that is finally done, my feeling is that many if not most of the supposed ruins will be shown to be natural formations resulting from glacial action, but that some of them will be confirmed as real artifacts of precolonial and pre-Columbian European visitation of North America's Atlantic seaboard. Evidence of real and extensive settlement, as opposed to mere visitation, may also come to light. It may also come to pass, after some dispassionate and professional investigation, that several different eras of European visitation or settlement are revealed by excavation. Although I am not an archeologist, it appears that the mystery of The Cross is connected with the mysterious (alleged) sites in New England.

The most important question was simple. *Was there really a precolonial ruin of some sort on the village hill top?*

We couldn't say for certain. The stone patterns in the ground had gradually been uncovered by the McKays' gardening efforts over the years. They looked like paths at ground level. Paths composed of football-and-fist-sized rocks. Between the rocks was a quantity of fine sand, possibly the remains of bad quality mortar. The French had experienced trouble making good quality mortar in Nova Scotia, too, and much of the mortar of Louisbourg had similarly been "leached" away to leave only fine sand. Maybe the builders on this hill top had run into the same problem.

These paths formed patterns that *looked* like the outlines of buildings. The corners had apparent buttresses. The "ruined walls", if that's what they really were, ran under existing buildings on the McKay property and appeared again on the other side. These buildings pre-dated the McKay occupation of the property. It wasn't likely that John and Jeanne had made these ruins. Then, too, the apparent walls ran off the McKay property to an unknown extent and onto neighbouring properties in the village. Jeanne had not been able to investigate this because of her uneasy status in the village, but as far as possible Jeanne had looked around. The walls seemed to indicate a roughly 5-sided palisade of large extent with smaller buildings placed inside the main enclosure. Jeanne called it a castle.

One characteristic of the ruins did interest me a lot. At a few points, large boulders had been incorporated in the "walls". Perhaps these boulders were already on the hill top and it was easier to make the walls incorporate them than to move them. But the practice of amalgamating large boulders into a castle wall is rather primitive. It is not Late Medieval or Renaissance in character, except, perhaps, on the fringes of Europe in places like Scandinavia or North Scotland and the Isles. Otherwise, there are not characteristic examples of this in the more cosmopolitan parts of Britain and the continent much after about 1200 A.D. Some Saxon and Norman churches in Britain do have large and irregular boulders imbedded in the walls up to about the 13th Century, but not often afterwards. This detail suggested to me, along with the general rubblework type of construction, that the ruin could be Norse or North Scots dating to the 13th Century or earlier, but perhaps even to the end of the 14th Century if the builders were concerned only with making a rough "keep" or glorified hill-fort.

Something with stone walls, or at least with a stone foundation, had been built on the hill top. The ruins could have been the remains of a 19th Century colonial farm complex, but the inclusion of several large boulders in the patterns and the rather irregular shapes of the patterns seemed to rule out a colonial origin.

The "artifacts" proved nothing conclusively. The flaked knife blade could have been Micmac. Then, too, both John and Jeanne hailed from the British Isles and both had been collectors of Celtic and Roman objects. "The Herm" could be a boulder fragment that just happened to have "shoulders" and a squarish blob-like "head". There were scratches on this object that might have been Celtic symbols, or even an Ogham inscription, as Jeanne insisted. But these scratches, if they were man-made, were weathered too much to make out more than vague shapes.

As for the iron objects, all could be bits and pieces from colonial farm or household implements. There was no way of telling without a metallurgical analysis, and perhaps not even then.

The little wooden "bent cones" were interesting. Jeanne had found a number of them. She had identified them to her own satisfaction, but I had no clue what they might be. Jeanne was right. A radio-carbon analysis of them would be helpful.

As for the history that Jeanne had constructed about the place, well, it seemed far-fetched. And it was personal. It was too easy to imagine the whole thing to be something dreamed up by a lonely, transplanted Englishwoman whose eccentricities and education alienated her from her neighbours. A tale yeilding identity, a feeling of superiority and belonging.

Yet . . .

The Stuarts were intimately connected with the early history of Nova Scotia. They were originally Scottish and had much contact, both friendly and otherwise, with the Norse who controlled much of Scotland and the Isles from the 8th to the 13th Centuries. The Stuarts did spend an inordinate amount of gold, and they must have got it somewhere. The Gold River does flow from the "castle" down to the Atlantic at Mahone Bay. And, what's more, at the mouth of the Gold River is the most famous Nova Scotia mystery of all, the inexplicable Money Pit on Oak Island. It is about 17 miles from the inland "castle site". And the Gold River did once supply fair quantities of the precious metal, as its name suggests. The gold rushes of the 1870s and 1890s are a fact.

Could all of this be coincidence? Yes, it could be. But it could also hint at a hidden pattern of historical relationships. Jeanne McKay had done a great deal of research. She could see this suggestive string of coincidences as clearly as anyone else who bothered to ponder them. All she had to do was to construct a secret sort of history conforming to the coincidences, and all she had to do was claim Stuart descent in order to be a part of it all.

The coincidences were real enough, and the "secret" history might even be plausible. Only Jeanne's connection with it need be purely wishful thinking.

Yet, what was a woman like her doing in the middle of Nova Scotia? And was it true, as both Jeanne and John insisted, that they had searched for this place purposefully?

Pros and cons like this were argued back and forth on the long drive back to Halifax. We soon realized that we couldn't assess the plausibility of any of it. Our problem was sheer ignorance of Nova Scotia history.

Both of us were interlopers in Nova Scotia, and immigrants to Canada. Deanna had been born in Great Britain, and I in the southern United States. We had met each other, and had ended up in Halifax, through a rather unlikely and unhappy chain of events. My marriage had broken up, my wife elected to return to her native Halifax. She relocated our son, Jason, with her. If I wanted to maintain a relationship with him, and I did, then I had to relocate to Halifax as well.

Deanna had spent most of her time in Toronto, as I had since coming to Canada, and it was there that we ran into each other after my marital break-up during one of my trips back to deal with publishers. One thing led to another and Deanna threw in her lot with me. We both relocated to Halifax. But neither of us knew much about Nova Scotia. I found out quickly enough, however, that it was difficult to make a living there as a writer, being so far from major markets. And Deanna discovered that there were much more limited opportunities for employment in her field of operations management.

In order to make a living, therefore, so that I could plan to spend two years near Jason to help ease him over a difficult time of transition, we formed our own business. After the publication of *The Black Discovery of America* I put writing on the back burner and we turned our energies toward the design and manufacture of simple fishing boats intended for village fishermen in developing nations. We'd been in Halifax about nine months when we received Jeanne's letter, and we'd been too busy to learn much about the early history of the place, while we learned too much about the present economic realities in the Maritimes.

Although I had written books about exploration, history and anthropology, my first love was somewhat ancient history and primitive navigation. Whereas I knew a fair bit about Egyptians, Polynesians and very early voyages in the Atlantic and Pacific, my knowledge sort of petered out with the Norse as far as European history was concerned, except for matters dealing directly with navigation techniques.

Deanna, although well-travelled in Europe and even in the Far East, had always been primarily a business person, not an historian.

We were therefore both unequipped to deal with John and Jeanne, their "history" and their absurd castle ruin in the middle of Nova Scotia. It might have seemed best to have dumped our problem in the lap of the

Nova Scotia Museum, or maybe in the lap of the History Department at Dalhousie University, both of which are in Halifax.

But both of these institutions had already been unresponsive to Jeanne's overtures and, we suspected, might have been over-exposed to Jeanne's eccentricities. Besides, we were fascinated with the ruins and Jeanne had contacted us. We therefore decided to do what we could ourselves, but it was a case of starting from scratch about Nova Scotia. Whereas we had a lot of ground to cover, our ignorance gave us one advantage: we began and ended our research without preconceptions. Maybe we had another advantage. Since we had no academic noses to keep clean, we didn't shy away from conclusions that might be unacceptable.

But where to start?

Jeanne had mentioned that some very early maps of Nova Scotia referred to a "refuge" in the neighborhood of Chester on Mahone Bay. Further, she hinted that some of these early maps showed rather strange illustrations for the coast of Nova Scotia. If this much could be confirmed, then maybe we could place more faith in some of Jeanne's other historical pronouncements.

A brief consultation with Ganong's *Crucial Maps* confirmed Jeanne's assertion about the "refuge" and about the curious symbols. We found some things that Jeanne had not mentioned, such as place-names that seemed to spell out cryptic sentences or messages, references to a settlement and a "lord" who had "labourers".

All of these maps dated from long before the first known European settlement of any part of mainland Nova Scotia. It seemed evident that some of the early cartographers were in on a secret that has been concealed from later historians.

These "Map Memorials" will be dealt with fully in a later chapter because at this point not enough pieces of the puzzle have been put in place so that their full significance can be appreciated. We are not dealing only with an apparent secret settlement, but with a secret settlement of possibly unbelievable importance.

In addition to the map confirmations, we discovered something else entirely. It is something that John and Jeanne had not told us about. Later discussions demonstrated that they had always been wholly ignorant of it.

I have mentioned our boat-building business. In early 1982 we needed fabrication facilities due to a completely unexpected marketing success.

The Nova Scotia government was prepared to help us with equipment purchase and with subsidized rent if we would locate our business outside of Halifax-Dartmouth and set up in some lesser centre where unemployment was a problem. We began scouting around. We didn't want to get too far from Halifax, partly for purely business reasons and partly because I wanted to stay relatively close in order to keep seeing Jason every week.

We ultimately selected Kentville, about 65 miles from Halifax on the Fundy coast. It had a provincially-operated "incubator mall" for fledgling businesses featuring space enough for our modest requirements and low rent. While enquiring about zoning and tax regulations at the Kentville Town Hall, I happened to glance at the old map decorating the township's office.

I immediately noticed an Oak Island. It was at the mouth of the Gaspereau River. As soon as our business was finished, Deanna and I drove the few miles to this Oak Island. We discovered that it was an island no longer. We were informed that Depression dyke-building had made this Oak Island a part of the mainland in an effort to reclaim several thousand acres of fertile land from the Fundy tides. But it had been an island before the 1930s. With binoculars we could see the oaks still growing on the "Oak Island" which was now the tip of a dyked-in peninsula.

I somehow knew what I would find even before I unfolded our well-creased road map on Nova Scotia. It had to be.

I have stressed that the village with the "castle" is in the middle of Nova Scotia. It is, in fact, on the watershed between Atlantic-bound rivers and Fundy-bound rivers. The Gold River leads from it to enter the Atlantic at the town of Chester on Mahone Bay. And the famous Oak Island of "Money Pit" fame is just off the mouth of the Gold River.

The Gaspereau River flows from this same watershed, but it flows westward into the Bay of Fundy. And at its mouth is another Oak Island.

But that is not all. If you stand on *either* Oak Island and look toward the mainland, you will see the mouth of the river *to your right*. Follow the river to its source and you'll end up at the "castle".

And is it merely another coincidence that "oak" in Celtic is *duir*, meaning both "right" and "door"?

Something had always been bothering me about a "secret refuge" in Nova Scotia. How could anyone be sure of finding it?

I knew something about early navigation. Medieval captains could

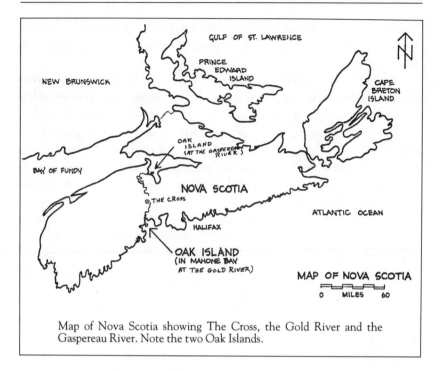

Map of Nova Scotia showing The Cross, the Gold River and the Gaspereau River. Note the two Oak Islands.

not tell their longitude (position east or west) with any certainty at all. They were forced to make the crudest, and sometimes the wildest, of guesses.

The situation was a bit better about latitude, the position north or south of the equator. In the northern hemisphere, at least, the navigator could measure the height of the pole star above the horizon in degrees and that would give him his latitude within a quarter of a degree, assuming that his measurement was accurate.

It seldom was. It is hard to take an accurate angular measure from a small ship at sea because of the wave motion. Even modern yachtsmen with modern sextants experience some difficulty and it takes a fair amount of practice to obtain accurate measures. The medieval sailor didn't have a sextant, but a cumbersome ancestor of it called a backstaff. Many didn't even have that. They estimated the altitude of the pole star above the horizon by the number of "hands" and "fingers" that would fill the distance. A backstaff was a little better.

Errors of 3 or 4 degrees were common in determining, or "estimating", latitude. Since a degree works out to about 60 miles on the earth's surface, it was easy for a navigator to be a couple of hundred miles north or south of where he wanted to be, or where he thought he was. Sometimes much more.

Nevertheless, because accurate latitude could be determined, after a fashion, and accurate longitude could not, mariners adopted the principle called "latitude sailing" in order to grope toward desired landfalls. The idea of latitude sailing is simple in the extreme. The navigator sailed immediately north or south until he reached the same latitude of the place he sought, then he sailed either east or west, trying his best to maintain the proper latitude, until he arrived at (or more usually, nearby) his planned destination.

But Nova Scotia presented special problems for a navigator using latitude sailing across the Atlantic. Assuming that the planned destination was a "secret refuge" about the latitude of Mahone Bay, his problems were compounded. Nova Scotia does not lie on a north-south line, but more nearly on an east-west axis. And, through an accident of geography, Mahone Bay, the entrance to the Bay of Fundy, Passamaquoddy Bay all happen to lie on about the same latitude, at least given the margin of error in early navigation. Further, within this margin of error, the mouth of the Gaspereau River is also on virtually the same latitude.

The medieval mariner bound for the "secret refuge" from Europe would try to keep to about $44\frac{1}{2}$ degrees north latitude. He might get lucky, make a landfall somewhere on the Atlantic coast of Nova Scotia, and merely have to sail north or south a short distance until he entered Mahone Bay, sighted the Oak Island and found the river leading up to the settlement.

But what if he wasn't so lucky? He might easily get too far to the south because of navigational error. He might sail past the southwest point of Nova Scotia and find himself off the Atlantic seaboard of New England instead of Nova Scotia. Then, if he tried to correct matters by sailing north to the proper latitude of the "refuge", he would find himself in the Bay of Fundy with the entire peninsula of Nova Scotia between him and his target landfall on the Atlantic side at Mahone Bay. He'd become hopelessly muddled. And, in fact, mariners were confused about the geography around Nova Scotia, and about the fact that three large bays seemed to have the same latitude even though they were all on the same ocean. Many early maps of the area reflect this puzzlement about the Bay of Fundy, Mahone Bay and Passaquamoddy Bay.

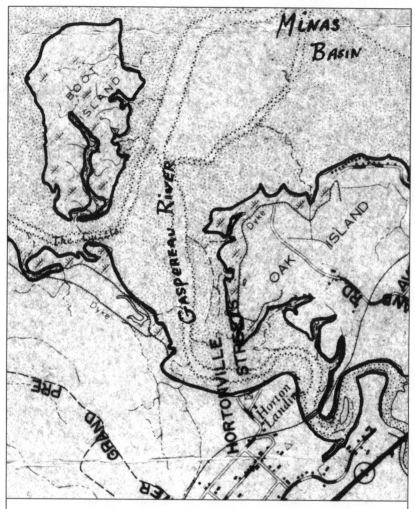

Portion of the official map of King's County, Nova Scotia showing the "Fundy" Oak Island in Minas Basin off the mouth of the Gaspereau River. Although this land is still referred to as Oak Island, and is labelled as such on this map, it is no longer a true island. Depression dyke-building filled in the tidal region between the island and the shore, making Oak Island now the tip of a peninsula.

Although roads lead onto the "island", we were never able to make an appointment with local farmers in order to see whether this old Oak Island had rubblework constructions on it similar to the structures at The Cross and on the more famous Oak Island in Mahone Bay.

Some navigational aid had to be established on the Bay of Fundy so that even if a navigator sailed past the preferred landfall on the Atlantic, he could still find his way to the "refuge" by sailing north into the Bay of Fundy. It looks as though this was done. The Oak Island off the Gaspereau River marks a "door" to the inland settlement, assuming there was one, just as the famous Oak Island marks the river-door on the Atlantic side.

Some sort of navigational landmark such as this would have been essential. Aside from error in determining latitude, there was also the fact that the pole star was not always visible in any case. Nova Scotia fogs are notorious, and so is overcast weather. A ship's latitude would be, at best, just approximate when nearing Nova Scotia and any regular and convenient navigation to any hypothetical "secret refuge" demanded a landmark on the Fundy side as well as on the Atlantic side.

The two Oak Islands, both off mouths of rivers leading inland to the "castle", certainly provide the necessary navigational aids. They still do. The question is whether these two Oak Islands are just coincidental, or whether they are man-made artifacts.

The famous Oak Island in Mahone Bay is the only one of some 350 islands in the bay to have any oaks on it. The reason is simple. Acorns don't float.

Similarly, the Oak Island in the Bay of Fundy is the only island in that body of water to have any oaks growing on it.

The presence of oaks on these offshore islands was noted by settlers and surveyors and was reason enough to name them "Oak Island" as a means of distinction. The name they retain to this day.

If acorns don't float, then how did oaks come to be growing on these islands? We could only conclude that they must have been planted purposefully. And long before the earliest known settlers in the area. They would form a unique and self-perpetuating navigational aid. Since "oak" (duir) in Celtic also means "door" and is associated with right-handedness, it would be the perfect signpost for any "secret refuge". This sort of thing was, in fact, the kind of cryptic pun so dear to the Celtic heart. On the other hand, the existence of oaks growing on an inshore island might not be noted by any casual mariner who might happen to make a landfall, particularly when so many oaks grew on the mainland behind. It was a detail that would not give the secret away to anyone not already in on it.

In checking old records we found that Samuel Champlain was struck by the artificial-looking nature of the oak groves when he explored the Bay of Fundy in the 1600s. He noted that they were planted as if for the pleasure of man.[8] And Champlain is supposed to have been the first known European explorer of the region. Who planted the oak signposts?

We couldn't attribute the oaks on these islands to natural coincidence. Nor could we believe that the geographic positions of these two islands were coincidental. It just seemed too much to believe that the only two "oak" islands in either bay just happened to be off mouths of rivers that led to the "castle" site inland. And too much to believe that, in each case, the rivers just happened to be "to the right" by accident, given the meaning of the word "oak" in Celtic.

It seemed to be stretching coincidence too far.

But if the situation wasn't coincidence, then it pointed strongly to something of very great significance. Although there is a partly artificial construction on the Atlantic Oak Island, the famous "Money Pit", it would not seem to be *the* secret. The Atlantic Oak Island, like the Fundy one, were signposts for two separate rivers leading inland to the same place. The river-doors marked by the two Oak Islands strongly suggested that "the secret", whatever it was, could only be found inland, where the rivers led, and it was just there, almost at the source of the two rivers on a mid-peninsular hill top, that Jeanne McKay claimed to have discovered her castle ruins.

For me, the discovery of two Oak Islands in such a geographical relationship very nearly proved that something significant and concealed from history was located in mid-peninsular Nova Scotia. I was all the more convinced of this because of my knowledge of early navigational problems and of early Celtic lore. The two Oak Islands meant something.

Something else kept bothering me. It was the Celtic penchant for sometimes communicating in allusion which often had several levels of meaning. The Celtic word for "oak" (*duir*) not only meant "door" and "right-handedness". It also meant "royalty", or even "divinity", and in any case these words once meant the same thing.

Were the oaks telling a story on several levels? Were they a message that the rivers were a doorway to an inland refuge of royalty? From what I knew of Celtic poetic language, the oaks might well be saying even more than this.[9]

*   *   *

Our discovery that there had once been a Fundy Oak Island in a sort of geographical mirror-image of the Atlantic one all but convinced us that Jeanne McKay's "castle" could be a reality.

And it was this discovery that all but convinced the Special Assistant to Nova Scotia's Minister of Culture, Recreation and Fitness. Like us, he could just not believe that such an exact and complex coincidence could be accidental.

One afternoon in late winter, Deanna and I sat in this Special Assistant's office at the top of one of the new towers of downtown Halifax. We had dropped off a great mass of material a couple of days earlier. The Special Assistant, and the Minister, had studied all of it. We were summoned for a face-to-face meeting.

The meeting with the Special Assistant went on all afternoon. We went over all the site photographs, the photographs of artifacts, the photocopies of old maps showing strange symbols and suggestive place-names, new topographical maps which showed the geographic relation-ship between the inland "castle" and the two Oak Islands. And, not least in importance, we discussed the Atlantic Oak Island of "Money Pit" fame in Mahone Bay. Our topic was not the "Money Pit" itself, but the reference to the "walls" which appeared on the earliest colonial surveys of the island and which could not be attributed to any early farmer. These walls were shown not only on the late 18th Century survey maps, but also on the modern "Pirate Charts" sold to tourists who visited the island. Naturally, the things were called "pirate walls", although hard work and permanent constructions were not normally characteristics of pirates. Who had built these walls? When?

Oak Island, like the rest of Nova Scotia, was still covered with snow. We had not yet had a chance to visit it, but these walls were high on our list of priorities. We were prepared to bet pretty heavily that they would turn out to be the same sort of rubblework construction as allegedly existed on the hill top some 17 miles inland up the Gold River.

Some carbon dating had been done on planks retrieved from the "Money Pit" on Oak Island. The resulting dates had interested us very much, and they interested the Special Assistant. The radio-carbon dates only occasionally matched the proper "pirate era" of the 17th and early 18th Centuries. Some were several centuries earlier.

If these dates were accurate, and if the walls and "Money Pit" on Oak Island were somehow involved with the "castle" ruins at The Cross, then we had at least one time frame for some of the European activity that had taken place in Nova Scotia. The only trouble was, this activity had been going on long before the textbooks said that Nova Scotia was discovered by Europeans.

Along with the supporting material, we'd submitted an outline of known European history that could be correlated with Jeanne's "castle". It made startling reading, and it wasn't too different from the history that Jeanne had concocted from her ten years of research. We were acutely and uncomfortably aware of this as the Special Assistant cross-examined us. We were as honest and as objective as we could be in our replies, both in our many grave reservations and in our general enthusiasm.

We'd already covered a lot of research ground. The picture seemed clear enough, and we didn't hold back with the Special Assistant. We'd been forced to conclude that Nova Scotia, and probably also a lot of the New England Atlantic seaboard, had been known from the earliest times of what might be called European "civilization". This knowledge had been passed on to selected people through the course of many, many centuries, and right up until the so-called "Age of Discovery" when Europeans "supposedly" discovered Nova Scotia and the rest of the Americas. In fact, we'd come to suspect that some early accounts by explorers like Samuel Champlain were a purposeful attempt to disguise the fact that Nova Scotia and parts of North America had been well-known to some people for a very long time. In short, the knowledge was disguised and hidden, the property of a few. We laid all this on the Special Assistant.

And the purpose of it all?

We didn't hold back on that, either. As far as we could tell, the purpose of keeping transatlantic discoveries secret had varied during different phases of European history. At first, the secret seemed merely to be an economic one. Later, the knowledge of new lands across the Atlantic was kept secret for religious reasons. The place was used as a refuge, and perhaps it had also been, for a time, the safe repository of a momentous religious truth.

Just as we had assessed John and Jeanne McKay in their farm-style kitchen a few months before, so the Special Assistant to the Minister of Culture, Recreation and Fitness of Nova Scotia was clearly sizing us up now in his downtown office eyrie. We realized all too well that it would be easier to dismiss us as crackpots. The story we suggested was stranger than

Nova Scotia   **Department of Culture Recreation & Fitness**

Post Office Box 864
Halifax, Nova Scotia B3J 2V2
(902) 424-7512

Mr. Michael Bradley
Post Office Box 306
Kentville, Nova Scotia
B4N 3X1

Dear Mr. Bradley:

This will acknowledge your letter of ██████ and the material included in it. Thank you very much for this and for the photographs. I will take the liberty of sharing it with ██████████, Deputy Minister, and with ██████████, Regional Representative of this department for the South Shore region.

Early in July I prepared a summary report on the matter for ██████████████████, our Minister. I asked him to consider certain aspects of the overall situation and give me additional directions. As he has been away until today there was no opportunity to discuss it. Until his assistance is received I will not be able to undertake any public efforts involving the department.

Sincerely,

Director of Cultural Affairs

AB/ab

On this and the following two pages are photocopies of correspondence from the Nova Scotia government with deletions of dates, names and location of the site.

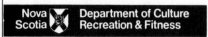

Nova Scotia **Department of Culture Recreation & Fitness**

Post Office Box 864
Halifax, Nova Scotia B3J 2V2
(902) 424-7512

Mr. Michael Bradley
Post Office Box 306
Kentville, Nova Scotia
B4N 3X1

Dear Mr. Bradley:

Thank you for the recent interesting letters about the ▆▆▆▆▆ site in ▆▆▆▆▆▆

As I indicated to ▆▆▆▆▆▆▆▆▆ the Department will pay for ▆▆▆ ▆▆▆▆▆▆▆▆▆▆▆▆▆▆▆▆ The invoice for this should come to me.

I am intrigued by the last paragraph of your August 13 letter. Of course I would be prepared to hear more about this in a private situation. Would you like me to meet you at your office in the Kentville area?

Sincerely,

▆▆▆▆▆▆▆▆

Director of Cultural Affairs

AB/ab

Revd. ▆▆▆▆▆

Department of Culture Recreation & Fitness

Post Office Box 864
Halifax, Nova Scotia B3J 2V2
(902) 424-7512

Mr. Michael Bradley
Post Office Box 306
Kentville, Nova Scotia
B4N 3X1

Dear Mr. Bradley:

Enclosed in this envelope is one wooden artifact provided to me on
loan by ▮▮▮▮▮▮▮▮▮▮▮▮▮▮▮▮▮

This item is being placed in your hands for scientific investigation.
At the conclusion of this I would ask that a copy of any report be
sent to me, and also that the artifact if still intact be returned.

Sincerely,

Director of Cultural Affairs

AB/ab

encl.

anything claimed by Jeanne McKay, although the outlines were similar in a general way. I had therefore taken the precaution of submitting copies of my nonfiction books along with the other material. Some of these books were on accredited history courses, and even at Dalhousie University. Others had been course-adopted in the States. While being an author is not in itself a guarantee of sanity, and sometimes even the reverse, we hoped that these books would be regarded as credentials of a sort. Something to gain us the hearing that Jeanne McKay had been denied.

The Special Assistant asked us whether, in our opinion, there was enough evidence to warrant an archeological excavation of the McKay site.

We answered that there was, without doubt, in our opinion.

But I quickly added that, to me, an immediate archeological dig on the McKay property wasn't the real issue. The relevant question was: where to excavate? The stone patterns on Jeanne's property ran off onto neighboring plots. The entire hill top might well be an archeological site, and we had no guarantee that the most significant part of it was on Jeanne's little piece of the hill. Then, there might be other sites nearby. If the Oak Island constructions were somehow connected with Jeanne's "castle", then there might be other constructions along the course of the Gold River from The Cross to the Atlantic. For that matter, there could be sites along the Gaspereau River from the "castle" at The Cross down to the Fundy Oak Island, and very possibly on *that* Oak Island as well, just as there were walls on the Atlantic one. In our budding suspicions, both islands had been outposts to protect the inland site from surprise visits. Both should have constructions of some sort.

The Special Assistant asked my advice about what should be done and, for what it was worth, I gave it. The entire swath of Nova Scotia along the course of the Gold River and the Gaspereau River should be subjected to aerial photography *in the summer* when crop marks might reveal patterns of unsuspected human habitation. The hill top at The Cross should be subjected to the same aerial attentions, but with two flights at different times of day so that shadows might enhance the patterns on the ground. Differing shadow-patterns could be studied and might yield a reasonable idea of the extent of the ruins and, maybe, even some clue as to the most important parts of the site.

While all this aerial photography was going on, other things could be looked into. We could visit the Atlantic Oak Island to see first-hand if the walls there were like the ones of the "castle". We could visit the end of the peninsula that had once been the Fundy Oak Island to see if there was anything immediately obvious there in the way of old stonework. We could continue our historical research to see if any known history could be tied in with the Nova Scotia sites, or if there were any "hinted" or plausible connections since we did not expect to find any explicit references.

Then there was the matter of the "holy well" on Jeanne's property. She insisted that it was just within what had once been the "castle" walls. It never went dry even though it was on the crest of the hill, even when other wells in the area ran dry in the summer. The local fire department used it as an unfailing source of water. According to Jeanne, this well was shown as already existing on the earliest colonial survey prior to settlement, and, according to her, the local Micmac Indians considered this well to be "holy" or "special" in some way. The water should be analysed, and the Micmac legends should be checked out as far as possible.

And why was the village called "The Cross" long before there were any colonial roads in the area and, therefore, long before any justifiable reference to a "crossroads" of any kind? And why were Micmac quill boxes *from this area* often decorated with a cross motif?

If some of this research could be done along with the aerial photography, then everyone might have a better idea of what confronted us. The best places for archeological excavation might suggest themselves so that digs could be undertaken with the least possible disruption for the local inhabitants of The Cross and other villages along the rivers.

And it was this point, we had long ago realized, that must be of major concern to the Special Assistant and the government in general. It could also account for the villagers' hostile stance toward Jeanne McKay.

Nova Scotia legislation provides for strict protection of confirmed historical sites of importance. Archeological excavation would at the very least inconvenience the residents of The Cross. It could end up evicting them if a site of great historical significance was confirmed on their hill top. Even short of outright eviction by provincial expropriation of property, land values would plummet if a genuine site was confirmed because severe restrictions on sale, land usage and new construction would be imposed.

Only someone like Jeanne McKay would relish seeing something like this come to pass, and only someone like her was willing to make economic sacrifices for the sake of some old ruins. Her constant claims that there was a site of importance at The Cross were a very real threat to the villagers. This explained not only the villagers' accusations against her, and their ridicule of her, but also the government's justifiable caution. It was easier to ignore the stone patterns on Jeanne's property.

Yet they could not be ignored, not when supported by the geographical and historical patterns that existed.

We had presented the Special Assistant with a pretty irony, and the fact that we had "gone over the head" of the proper channels assured him that we appreciated the irony, and the difficulty of the Ministry's position. We should have gone first to the Nova Scotia Museum, which was under the Ministry of Education, or to any one of the many universities that were likewise connected with the Ministry of Education but we had not.

If our historical reconstruction was at all valid, then the site at The Cross and the others associated with it might turn out to be of overwhelming historical relevance. Enough to justify excavating the entire hill top, enough to justify a reconstruction of the ruins. Enough, perhaps, to warrant dislocation of other villagers in other places.

For the site at The Cross might well turn out to be *the first European settlement in the New World*. It would require major revision of our ideas, for just being the first European settlement in the Americas would not be its primary claim to fame. It might turn out to be a site of central importance to modern religion and, in the entire context of history, *have a claim to sanctity rivalling Jerusalem or Mecca*.

If our suspicions had any foundation in fact, and if the site at The Cross was genuine and from what we had come to believe it might be, then it presented explosive and controversial problems. It was at once much too big, and far too delicate, to be handled "through channels". Something had to be done, but the first steps had to be taken without any indication of official, government interest or involvement. There could be no anxious confrontation between the villagers of The Cross and an "authorized" excavation team from the Nova Scotia Museum. Not only would that lead to complaints because of fears of expropriation and economic loss, which would quickly become a political football in an election year, but scholars heartened by any show of official interest might put two and two together pretty quickly. The anxiety and confrontation would rapidly expand. The repercussions couldn't be foreseen, but it was certain that they would be great.

Apparently the Special Assistant assessed us favourably. It seemed that our advice had something to recommend it.

He asked us if we would continue what research we could and *report directly to the Ministry*. To him, personally. We could tell Jeanne and John what we learned. The Ministry would arrange for the aerial photography to be carrried out as suggested. The Ministry would pay for analysis of the well water, and for the survey of the stone patterns visible on the McKay property if we would arrange everything as private citizens. And discreetly.

The Nova Scotia Museum would not be informed about our investigation, the Ministry's promised aerial photography, or the survey of the McKay site and the analysis of the well water that we were to organize. If things tended to confirm the need for archeological excavations, and if evidence pointed to the best places for digs, then the Ministry would order the excavations to be undertaken by the Nova Scotia Museum as required. We could be involved in any such digs if we wished, and would be guaranteed access to all data.

But.

We were asked not to publish anything about the site for two years, unless it was cleared with the Ministry first. After two years I could publish anything I liked, but, if the Ministry was referred to, it was free to deny anything and everything whatsoever.

We agreed to co-operate with the Ministry as outlined. This involved doing only what we were doing already, when time allowed, except that the Ministry would pay for the survey and analysis that should be done and that we couldn't afford to commission ourselves. The two-year ban on publication was not serious since I was far from being able to write anything based on the research we'd done so far, and I felt it would be many months before any writing would be justified.

But on the way down in the elevator we both imagined that we could hear Jeanne McKay's snorts of disgust and impatience.

There was to be no immediate and official archeological dig on her property. The Ministry had bought two years of silence about her "castle" for very little. There was no guarantee that the promised aerial photography would really be done, and no guarantee that we would ever see the photographs if any were taken.

While Jeanne might be right to sniff with displeasure, as we easily imagined her doing, we learned from the Special Assistant that she had always been wrong about one thing.

Her alleged "castle" had always been taken seriously. Both the Special Assistant and the Minister himself had known about it before we had submitted our material. The Special Assistant had let us know, in so many words, that the powers that be at the Nova Scotia Museum didn't really think that the ruins "were either French or Indian" as Jeanne had been told. We were given to understand that Jeanne's "castle" had long been a problem that was best ignored. To illustrate how seriously the Ministry regarded this possible site, the Special Assistant told us that the promised aerial photography would be done by an out-of-province firm in Ontario in order to conceal any hint of official interest from local Nova Scotians.

On the long drive back to our new home in Kentville, we ignored Jeanne McKays' imaginary expressions of disgust about what we'd been able to accomplish at government levels. The Ministry had at least promised some action, while we were in no position to force the government to do anything. And further, what I had said to the Special Assistant was true, however much Jeanne might not like it: if there was a genuine archeological site at The Cross, there was no guarantee that the most significant part of it was on her property. Given the possible repercussions in this particular case, a professional archeological excavation would be unwise until more was known about the place and about the entire complex of things that seemed to be associated with it.

On the drive back to Kentville, Deanna and I first got the feeling that we've had many times since. It was a conviction that the hill top at The Cross would somehow never get investigated by accredited archeologists, the conviction that, in high places, there was the agreement that some things should never be officially admitted.

At that time, we didn't know how high the stakes were. We gradually found out. And our first feelings were confirmed. More than a year later, after we had at last amassed enough data to write an account, we gave the resulting manuscript to a former high-level military advisor to the Canadian Government. Colonel Frank Hofflin was formerly Canada's military attaché to the Federal Republic of Germany. He wasn't surprised at the contents. He knew the story already, and said that everyone at appropriately high levels in Europe and North America knew it too. He advised us not to publish any of it.

And this is as good a place as any to complete the story of what has happened with the apparent castle ruin up to the time of publication of this book. Although this book covers our researches of 1982-1983, I called our old friend, the Special Assistant, by telephone on the late morning of Wednesday, June 24, 1987. He was still a Special Assistant and still doing the same job as he was back in 1982-1983 when we were active in Nova Scotia.

First, he confirmed what I feared. The promised aerial photography had never been done. Air photography of the entire swath of Nova Scotia between Chester on the Atlantic side on Mahone Bay and the mouth of the Gaspereau River on the Bay of Fundy side of the peninsula might have revealed additional evidence of ruins so that an assessment of the whole situation might have been easier. But, although the Special Assistant himself advocated the aerial photography, there was, as he put it "no interest in spending the money in the higher levels of the Nova Scotia government."

Then, since we had drifted out of touch with Jeanne and John McKay in the intervening four years, the Special Assistant filled us in on Jeanne's latest efforts to have her beloved, alleged, castle site given the attention it deserved. Being residents of Labrador and Newfoundland since leaving The Cross, Jeanne wrote to the Federal Minister of Transport, that flamboyant MP from Newfoundland, John Crosbie. He, in turn, wrote to the government of Nova Scotia on behalf of his constituent requesting some statement about the site. According to the Special Assistant, Crosbie's request was answered by the Nova Scotia Museum which is under the Ministry of Education, not the Ministry (or Department) of Culture, Recreation and Fitness. Crosbie received the same answer that Jeanne McKay had gotten from the Museum more that a decade previously. The ruins were "either French or Indian and dated from the 17th Century at the earliest", and were consequently of no interest to the Museum.

This reply has presumably been passed on to Jeanne McKay by Crosbie. I can almost hear the imprecations from far-away Labrador City . . .

Our Special Assistant is one of the few officials of any level of the Nova Scotia government to have actually bothered to visit The Cross and to have seen the apparent ruins with his own eyes. His comments to me over the phone on June 24, 1987 must therefore carry some weight. Knowing as well as I do, and as Jeanne McKay herself knows, that there's no record of Acadian French settlement or construction in The Cross in the 17th Century, and knowing as we all do that the native Micmac Indians of Nova Scotia did not indulge in stonework of castle proportions, our Special Assistant stated: "As a rank amateur in matters of archeology, I nonetheless feel that there are unanswered questions about this site. If I were a minister I would see that the site received proper investigation."

As for the role of the Nova Scotia Museum in all of this, after emphasizing (again) that the Museum is under a different Ministry, the Special Assistant said: "I have never been satisfied that the Museum follows investigations as far as both common sense and the dictates of scholarship require. I believe this to be the case not only about the apparent ruins at The Cross, but also in several other and non-related matters that have come to my attention."

And that is the state of affairs up to 1987. I claim to be nothing more than a rank amateur in matters of archeology, just like the Special Assistant. Nonetheless, like him, I have seen these apparent ruins for myself. My feeling is that there is something unusual on the hill top of The Cross, something that *looks* like the ruins of a once-substantial rubblework structure . . . but which might, under expert investigation, prove to be nothing more mysterious than a unique deposition of glacial detritus. I don't know. I am in no position to identify or assess these intriguing deposits of stone.

But I am in a position to say that an equally intriguing pattern of circumstantial evidence on old maps, about almost-forgotten voyages, and concerning ancient religious secrets and conflicts seemingly converge on the hill top of The Cross in an almost uncanny way. The presentation of this pattern of circumstantial evidence, not any claim to the presentation of proof, is what the remainder of *Holy Grail Across The Atlantic* is all about. Ours is a detective story with the *corpus delecti* still awaiting excavation.

Chapter Three

The Knights of the Temple

By the end of the 11th Century the Christian crusaders had wrested much of the Holy Land from the Islamic Saracens and, in the year 1099 A.D., a rather obscure French nobleman by the name of Godfroi de Bouillon was offered the Kingdom of Jerusalem by "an anonymous conclave"[1] of clerics and secular leaders. The ascension of de Bouillon's line to the throne of Jerusalem has somewhat puzzled later historians. It apparently bothered no one at the time, and it seems that de Bouillon, at least, knew what was going to happen before he left Europe on the Crusade. He gave up his lands and titles in Europe. He allied himself and the fortunes of his House to Palestine. The newly-created Kingdom of Jerusalem was accounted equal to the most illustrious European royalty.

Nineteen years later, the second King of Jerusalem, Baudoin, established the famous Order of the Temple, better known as the "Knights Templar".

The Knights Templar have loomed more mysteriously in history than even the curious elevation of Godfroi de Bouillon to the throne of Jerusalem.

At first, there were only nine knights of the Temple and for nine years no other recruits were admitted. The mandate of these knights was to protect pilgrims on all the roads of the Holy Land. Aside from the fact that their numbers were wholly inadequate to perform such a task, there is no record of the Knights Templar actually protecting any pilgrims in Palestine.[2]

Yet within a very short time the new Order had gained enormous prestige in Europe. Saint Bernard spoke highly of the Templars and a papal decree made them answerable only to the pope and independent of all secular authority.

Although individual knights of the Order were sworn to poverty and to a strict code of behaviour drafted by Saint Bernard himself, the Knights Templar immediately began to amass great wealth. And almost as quickly individual Templars, at least, began to acquire a reputation for overbearing arrogance that conflicted with their supposed code of behaviour. "To drink like a Templar" became a common expression. Sir Walter Scott portrays them as bullies.

"According to tradition, their quarters were built on the foundations of the ancient Temple of Solomon, and from this the fledgling Order derived its name".[3] Some writers have suggested that the Templars were not established to protect pilgrims in the Holy Land, but to form an elite guard for the Kings of Jerusalem, and to be a fighting arm of that mysterious power that Godfroi's line apparently wielded. It has also been supposed that the Templars' almost instant wealth derived from some treasure that might have been discovered in the Temple of Solomon.

Whatever the truth of such speculations, it is undeniable that the Knights Templar very quickly accumulated financial resources that enabled them to become the bankers of their age.[4] They built protected warehouses all over Europe in which merchants could store their goods in safety. They loaned money and they revived the ancient practice of issuing and honouring letters of credit, cheques, so that merchants could avoid carrying large amounts of bulky and tempting money around with them. Whether or not the Templars did much for pilgrim traffic in the Holy Land, it is certain that they encouraged the growth of trade and commerce in Europe.

Scholars are not usually agreed on anything, but one thing in which *almost* all historians are agreed is that the rise of the merchant class in Europe was the beginning of the end of the feudal system. This puts the Templars in an ironic position. They were the idealized apex of chivalry, the unique ideal of feudalism. Yet their banking and warehousing activities were not only far removed from appropriate "knightly" activities, but assisted the growth of a non-feudal class which eventually undermined feudalism itself.

Feudalism was an agricultural social structure based on the control of land. Trade and commerce, however, are essentially urban activities and largely unconnected with the control of land and an organization based on agriculture. The rise of the merchant class in Europe also marked the rise of the cities. The revival of trade and commerce spelled the end of the "Dark Ages" and the start of the Renaissance and the modern world.

Because the Templars were independent of all secular authority, they could pursue their banking and warehousing throughout Europe, irrespective of the wishes of the local noble who thought he controlled things. The Templars betrayed the very class they supposedly represented, at least in an economic and political sense.

The Templars could not have been ignorant of this. The dukes and counts ... and kings ... who complained about them saw the situation clearly enough. It is difficult not to conclude that the Templars were somehow intended to fulfill this role. Perhaps Templar recruits were required to give up all their worldly possessions and titles, not as a religious concession to humility, but as a more practical measure designed to prevent "conflict of interest". As nobles and knights themselves, the possessions and titles of potential Templar recruits were feudal, and involved control of land. By giving up such titles and possessions, Templars not only became unorthodox within the scheme of feudal chivalry as a knightly organization, but could individually work without too many second thoughts to undermine their own class.

The Templars did not ignore the possibilities of sea-borne trade. They had their own fleet, based in La Rochelle. Maritime activities of the Templars have an important bearing on later events.[5]

But in spite of these mundane, and even inappropriate, fiscal pursuits, the Order had an aura of mystery and sanctity about it that has never been adequately explained. Wolfram von Eschenbach, a Bavarian poet-knight and author of *Parzival*, makes the Templars guardians of the Holy Grail.

Certainly, among their contemporaries, the Templars were believed to be custodians of some great treasure, or of some momentous secret, that subtly altered the orthodoxy of their professed Christianity. Although they were zealous warriors on the battlefields of the Holy Land against geopolitical foes of de Bouillon's clan, they apparently also at the same time established peaceful contact with both Jewish and Moslem savants in Palestine and in Moorish Spain.[6]

In addition to being unorthodox in an economic and political sense in Europe, they were also apparently unorthodox in matters of religion. It was not long before the initial aura of sanctity was transformed, among the already financially disgruntled nobility, into suspicions of heresy.

It seems that the Templars may also have been involved in financing the astonishing and short-lived phenomenon of Gothic cathedral-building. It may be only a coincidence, but it is nonetheless a fact, that the brief profusion of Gothic-style "Notre Dames" were constructed only during the two centuries of Templar ascendency. Gothic architecture, except for mock-antique constructions, disappeared with the Templars. Just as the origin of Templar wealth is a mystery, the financing of huge cathedrals by small towns remains an enigma.

Some investigators, such as Louis Charpentier, maintain that Gothic architecture contained secret messages in stone, keys to ancient religious and spiritual knowledge. And there is some evidence to suggest that the "Our Lady" of the Gothic cathedrals was not the Virgin Mary, but another Mary.[7]

In the year 1187 A.D., after less than a century of Christian rule, Jerusalem and much of the Holy Land was recovered by the Moslems. The dynasty established by Godfroi de Bouillon lost much of its prestige along with its throne. And along with the loss of its "geopolitical power base", Godfroi's line lost its security. The Templars, whose fortunes and *raison d'etre* were closely tied to the fortunes and curious power of de Bouillon's line, began to be regarded with less tolerance by both secular leaders and the Papacy.

But the first blow was struck against de Bouillon's family and supporters, not directly against the Templars. Their turn would come later.

Godfroi de Bouillon had sprung from an obscure bloodline which arose in the south of France. In the Pyrenees. During the 10th to 12th Centuries this area in the south of present-day France was the centre of a unique culture. It was unique in several ways. First of all, compared to most of Europe at the time, the civilization of Languedoc and Provence was advanced in the arts and sciences. There was much contact with the neighboring Moors across the Pyrenees, and much contact with the Jewish savants who lived among these Moors. Noble French families in the south inter-married across the Pyrenees.

The civilization in the south of France was advanced in terms of trade and economics, again because of close contact with the Moors who controlled much of the Mediterranean and all of the trade routes to the Far East. Languedoc and Provence were wealthy in relation to the rest of feudal Europe.

But the most profound way in which this southern French civilization differed from the rest of Europe was religious. It does not seem as if this civilization was really "Christian" at all in the way that term was understood then and is understood now. Or, if the civilization was Christian, its religion was a heresy.

The religion was called "Catharism" or the "Albigensian heresy" after the town of Albi which was a particular centre of this aberrant religion.

It is difficult to tell what Catharism really was, because all the accounts of it come from enemies of the religion. The Cathars themselves, and their own writings, were systematically destroyed by the victorious Roman Church.

At the "grassroots" or "village level" of participation, Catharism seems to have been vaguely Christian, or at least molded on the Christian model. There were Cathar churches operating in competition with Catholic ones. By about 1200 A.D., most of the population of Languedoc and Provence patronized Cathar churches in preference to Catholic ones. There were Roman churches in southern France where a Mass had not been said in several generations.

On the simplest level, the popularity of Catharism is easy to explain. The Roman clergy was corrupt and suffered by comparison with the Cathar "parfaits" or "perfected ones" who passed for Cathar clergy. Indeed, Saint Bernard, who travelled to Languedoc to preach against these heretics in 1145 A.D., was impressed by them: "No sermons are more Christian than theirs, and their morals are pure"[8], he wrote.

By "Christian", the good saint must have meant *Christian in spirit*, because the Albigensians certainly were not Christian *in dogma* according to the tenets of the Roman Church. Indeed, there are some who suspect that Saint Bernard was extremely impressed with the Cathars and became one, in secret.

Cathar "Christianity" rejected the idea of the death and crucifixion of Jesus. Catharism seems to have rejected the propriety of this sacrifice, and perhaps even the notion of salvation, as these concepts were understood by Roman Catholics of the 13th Century and modern Christians of all sects nowadays. Instead, the Cathars stressed the reality of "living love" and the still-existing living legacy of love bequeathed by Jesus as *one, and perhaps the latest, manifestation of God's boundless love*. It seems as though some of the Cathars, and certainly some of the higher-ranking Templars, were able to accept Mohammed within this context, not as a living example of God's love incarnate as Jesus was viewed, but as a legitimate messenger speaking and writing about God's love.

As "Christians", these Cathers therefore rejected the cross, the Roman Catholic "crucifix", as a proper symbol to focus meditation upon, or worship of, the love that Christ was and remained. Instead, one important Cather symbol was the dove.[9] It represented for them then, as it does for us today, the idea of "peace" or, more accurately the more subtle concept of "grace", that state of being *in* God's love. After the first crusades, when European Cathers in the entourage of Godfroi de Bouillon established some contact with the Sufi mystics of Islam, the symbolism of the dove sometimes became linked iconographically with the Islamic mystical idea of *baraka*, which also means "grace" and with the idea that a person could be a "vessel of grace". And, like the very similar "pun" that brought the Grail into existence, the Sufi concept of baraka, "vessel of grace", was often depicted in Arabic calligraphy as a stylized ship with strokes of Arabic characters drawn as oars propelling the vessel. Indeed, this concept of a "vessel of grace", and the Arabic word *baraka*, evolved into the word *bark* that signifies a small ship in most European sea-faring languages. In some instances, the Cather dove flying with its wing outstretched was rendered in an artistic motif very similar to the stylized ship meaning *baraka* in Sufi calligraphy, with the feathers of the dove and the oars of the vessel alike representing the flight and freedom of the soul.

This is certainly no place to go into Cather symbolism in any great detail, but some aspects have to be mentioned because they have relevance to our story. Another common Cathar symbol was the serpent or dragon. This probably represented the much-maligned "Serpent of Wisdom" in the Biblical Garden of Eden. The Cathars apparently believed that love without knowledge was a potential hazard to the individual and to others around him. Unguided, ignorant love could be a menace and, from the Cathar point of view, the truth of this perspective was self-evident in the behaviour of their enemies, the followers of the Pope and the practitioners of the Inquisition. In the name of love and Christ, the Inquisition of the Roman church justified hideous cruelties inflicted on an estimated three million human beings between 1200 A.D. and 1800 A.D.

Therefore the Cathars venerated knowledge, or wisdom, and symbolized it through the serpent or dragon. The Cathars were therefore *gnostics* (from the Greek *gnosis*="knowledge"). Readers of this book cannot fail to note the dragon symbolism that runs through the whole story of the Grail. King Arthur's banner was the Red Dragon of Wales. Arthur's father was Uther Pendragon — or "Uther, the Chief Dragon". The coat of arms of Henry Sinclair, whom we will meet shortly, was very aptly a dragon bearing the burden of a royal crown around its neck. Samuel Champlain, who has an important role in our story, wrote of a mysterious patron named "Mondragon".

These Cathar symbols became important after the Albigensian Crusade and the dispersal of Cathar heretics and Templars. Obliged to profess outward orthodoxy, but secretly preserving their heresy and knowledge, the underground heretics or far-flung refugees had to devise some means of recognizing each other. The heretical families therefore often adopted names based on Cathar symbols as a means of mutual recognition. Often, these names were not merely symbolic "Doves" or "Dragons", but more complicated allusions to these symbols in the interest of greater security.

Family names based on secret Cathar symbolism crop up repeatedly, as we shall see, in the story of transatlantic voyages of discovery and exploration. Christopher Columbus is a Latinization of the Italian "Colon"="Dove", and there is evidence that Columbus was a member of that Cathar-Islamic-Jewish amalgam that crystallized around the de Bouillon power complex in the Pyrenees and the Albigensian heresy that could, and did, bind together the intellectuals of the three great Western religions. Champlain writes in his journals that his first mentor, the man who helped him to become a credible exlorer, was one "Don Coloma" (the Spanish analog for "Dove"). There are ample reasons for suspecting that these names are more than mere coincidence.

And further, when we read of an obscure Englishman who adopts the name of Francis Drake (from the Latin draco=dragon), is a pirate specializing in predation upon Spanish Catholic treasure armadas, is knighted by the Queen for his services, and the English Crown seems to be financially involved in his freebooting adventures ... well, we may suspect that something besides mere piracy was going on.

Sir Francis Drake has, indeed, some peripheral relevance to our construct because the President of Triton Alliance, David Tobias, told me that the latest research indicates that the Oak Island treasure (if there was one) may well have been booty gleaned by Drake's second or third campaign against the Spanish Main. And further, Tobias' research hints that if there ever was an Oak Island treasure, and if it was recovered by its putative "owners", the date of recovery may have been between 1602 and 1605 and, as we shall see later in this book, this date of possible treasure recovery points intriguingly to a man whose first mentor was a "Dove" and whose ongoing court patron was "Mondragon."

This digression into Cathar symbolism has been unavoidably longer than intended, but it is extremely suggestive within the context of the speculative history offered in this book. I can only ask the reader to file this information away in memory for now, trusting that the significance of it all will suggest itself in the following pages.

For now, back to the Cathers.

In addition to "non-Christian" symbolism, the Cathers were unorthodox in another important respect. They repudiated the idea of priests as intermediaires between God and man. The Albigensians had no priests.

Instead, the Cathars had religious, or "spiritual" leaders. These were called "parfaits" or, in Latin, *perfecti*... which means "perfects" or "perfected" ones. These people were vowed to honesty, poverty, chastity and, apparently, vegetarianism. And they practised it. Where the Catholic priests were corrupt, the Cathar *perfecti* were not. Thus, by example, Catharism attracted the majority of the population of southern France.

In another departure from Roman practice, the Cathar "perfects" could be both men and women. In fact, by about 1200 A.D., there were more women *parfaits* than men.

At the higher levels of initiation it has been disputed that the Cathars were Christian at all.[10] Runciman says that they were Buddhists[11], while others insist that they were Sufis[12], that they only used "Christian" words, phrases an parables to ease communication with the simple peasants who had been exposed to Christianity for generations. It is certain that the Cathar *parfaits* approximate our idea of a "guru" or a "teacher" more than our idea of a priest, but apparently without the negative connotations that "guru" and "teacher" have recently acquired due to the proliferation of questionable sorts who have climbed on the consciousness bandwagon.

Again, although it is difficult to tell from our perspective, the Albigensians may have also somehow accommodated the "Old Religion of Europe" which was based largely on fertility, seasonal changes and "control of natural forces" through *wicca*, or "witchcraft". Our ideas about witchcraft are so garbled that this is dangerous ground, but there did seem to be a "fertility component" in the Cathar scheme of things. How this can square with the "chastity" practised, and seemingly strictly, by the *parfaits* is anybody's guess.

But there were supposedly "courts of love" operating in the castles of Pyrenees nobility. It is hard to say what went on in these "courts of love".[12] The inquisitors of the Roman Church hinted darkly of orgies, but maybe this is a slander. These "courts of love" may have been only meetings presided over by Carthar *parfaits* in which the tenet of "living love" was expressed. Early Christian "love meetings" were similarly misconstrued as being carnal in nature when, as we know, the early Christians were a dour sort of ascetic. The Christian orgies suspected by the Romans were, maybe, wishful thinking. The orgies suspected of the Cathars may have been another excuse for destroying them.

Whatever they were, something emerged from these "courts of love" that survived to change Europe. Poetry. Knight-poets composed and sang ballads celebrating *amor courtoise*. This is usually translated as "courtly love", but is better rendered as "gentle love", and it was a profound departure from the normal male-female relations in the rest of feudal Europe. "Courtly love" expressed a respect for women which was un-heard-of elsewhere, and introduced the novel notion that a man and a woman could have a spiritual and personal relationship that was more than sheer reproduction.[13]

The knight-poets, or troubadours, of Provence and Languedoc composed long romances based on this sort of theme. It was a literary form that quickly captivated what passed for the "intelligensia" of Europe, which is to say, the nobility. The romances of the troubadours combined the existing feudal system with chivalry, a revolutionary idea that a true knight bore an obligation to serve and protect in accordance with the dictates of "gentle love". In short, the knight had a "higher loyalty" than mere loyalty to his feudal master.

How far this went in practice is hard to say. Maybe not far. It is known that women in southern France did have, technically, a higher legal staus than in the rest of Europe.[14] A number of women held fiefs at the time of the Albigensian Crusade. And there were even famous women military leaders like Esclarmonde de Foix, who controlled the last Cathar stronghold.

In addition to all of these departures from European society elsewhere, the Cathar civilization of southern France was supposed to have another distinction. It was believed that they possessed some great treasure, or some great secret, of a religious sort. The exact nature of the Cathar secret has been much debated, but the knowledgeable *minnesinger*, Wolfram von Eschenbach makes no bones about it. In his romance, *Parzival*, von Eschenbach states clearly that the Templar-guarded Holy Grail reposed in the castle of "Munsalvaesch", which most scholars agree was the Cathar citadel of Montségur.[15]

Of all of these departures from European orthodoxy, perhaps the truly fatal one was wealth. The prosperous civilization of southern France excited the greed of the northern French barons. So long as Godfroi de Bouillon's line held a kingdom in the Holy Land . . . perhaps one should say *The* Kingdom, since it was Jerusalem . . . the prestige (plus the swords of the Templars) protected Godfroi's descendants and his "constituency" in the Pyrenees. But when Jerusalum was lost, hostile forces rapidly converged on Languedoc and Provence. Wealth, probably, was the major motivator, but Cathar and Templar heresies were the pretexts.

In 1209 A.D., northern armies invaded the south in response to the Pope's call for a Crusade against the Albigensian heretics. This was only 22 years after Godfroi's clan lost Jerusalem.

A protracted war of unparalleled ferocity raged for a third of a century until the last Cathar stronghold, Montségur, fell in March of 1244. The Cathars were crushed. The heretics, the *parfaits*, died at flaming stakes or on the torture-racks of the victors. The Roman Church invented the Inquisition at this time, to interrogate the Cathars by particularly hideous means, and the object of the Inquisition was not only to find the depth of their unorthodoxy, but to find the location of their secret. But the victors did not find the treasure of the Albigensians, whatever it was. Tradition says that it was taken out of doomed Montségur by four knights a few days before the citadel fell.[16] None of the tormented *parfaits* revealed where it had been taken, and it is said that those who could still speak after the tortures of the Inquisition sang as they burned at their stakes. The soul of Esclarmonde de Foix ascended from the smoke in the form of a dove so it is said.

For a time, their sheer power . . . military, political and economic . . . prevented any overt moves against the Templars, even though many had participated in the defence of southern France and even though many had died at Montségur. But on Friday, October 13, 1307, King Philippe of France ordered simultaneous raids on Templar castles, priories and warehouses in his domain. Agian, Templar wealth and a desire to break their power was the motivation, their various unorthodoxies the excuse. By 1312, King Philippe had pressured Pope Clement V into disbanding the Templars. In 1314, the last Grand Master of the Knights Templar, Jacques de Molay, was roasted to death over a slow fire by order of king and pope.

Templar wealth eluded the king. In addition to their own reputed treasure, it was widely believed that the Cathar treasure or secret had been passed on to the Templars after the fall of Montségur. If so, the last Grand Master refused to reveal its location during his long agony.

The Templar fleet put to sea from its port of La Rochelle a few hours before King Philippe's dawn raids of October 13, 1307. It has never been heard from since. It is a reasonable conjecture that this fleet carried the Templar treasures to safety, and perhaps the treasure of the Cathars as well.

The Templars who survived King Philippe's sudden strike against the Order dispersed to various countries outside of France. They were welcomed in many places. It is known that some fled to Scotland where they found refuge at Rosslyn, the family seat of the powerful Saint-Clairs.[17]

Others fled to Portugal.

When the pope officially disbanded the Order in 1312 A.D., those Templars in Scotland, Germany, Scandinavia and other corners of Europe went underground. Some joined the Teutonic Knights and fought in Eastern Europe against the Mongols and Tartars. Others apparently formed secret societies which continued whatever concealed doctrine the Templars may have had. It has been asserted by a number of scholars that the Freemasons, the Rosicrucians and the Illuminati of Bavaria were offshoots of the Knights Templar. And just as with the Templars of old, members of these new Orders often found positions in high places where they could influence policy and protect their secrets, whatever they were. It is likely, too, that these "neo-Templars", if we can call them that, had some influence in the development of Protestantism. Even the Cathars are supposed by some authorities to have been "proto-Protestants".

But in Portugal, when Clement V disbanded the Templars, they did not go underground. They merely changed their name. They became the Order of the Knights of Christ, and again, they found favour in high places. Prince Henry of Portugal, who would earn the appellation "The Navigator" because of the voyages of discovery he sponsored, was a Grand Master of the Knights of Christ.

And what survived of this "great adventure", whatever it was?

What was the legacy of de Bouillon's dynastic ambitions? Of the Templars' supposed sanctity and mysterious prestige? Of the Cathars' supposed treasure and religious secret?

It appeared that little survived except for a body of "courtly love" troubadour poetry and romances on the one hand, and a few Templar-inspired cults on the other.

As for the poetry and romances, they lived on. The knight-poets wove their romances of chivalry around the story of the Holy Grail and Arthur's Camelot, *but why they did so has never been explained.* Their stories inspired other writers, in succeeding generations, to create yet other versions of the Arthurian Theme. It is a legacy of literature that has endured until today. Mary Stewart's multi-volume best-selling story of the life of Merlin is one example, the successful musical and film, *Camelot*, is another. Why should these southern French troubadours have leaned so heavily on the story of an obscure British *dux bellorum*? How did they even learn about him?

And the Templar-inspired secret societies have also endured to the present day. The Masons, and the Rosicrucians, are still with us. And all profess to know a secret truth. We take this with a grain of salt and endure the Shriners' Parades. We express gratitude for Shriner contributions to hospitals. We may be a bit puzzled at their wealth, but shrug and explain it away by assuming that they're wealthy businessmen. But why would wealthy businessmen, and therefore presumably relatively intelligent and responsible ones, be attracted to such nonsense? Might there not be a whisper of something else to it all, something concealed from the rest of us?

It appeared that nothing survived except the literature and the cults.

But appearances are deceptive.

*   *   *

What on earth was going on for 200-odd years? From the time Godfroi de Bouillon became King of Jerusalem until the time of the final Templar dispersion?

What were all these "secrets" . . . the secret of Godfroi de Bouillon's power and elevation to kingship, the secret treasures of the Templars and Cathars?

As it happens, about the only "non-ancient" period of history that ever interested me very much was this 200-odd year period. During the late 1950s and early 1960s there was a spate of books published about this period. They were almost all written and published in France.

Many of them seemed to hint that something extremely important had happened. That a "turning point" in human histroy had somehow happened, but that the significance of it had escaped the notice of establishment historians. I was impressed by this torrent of books and by the vehemence of their authors, and I had been studying the Grail Romances of people like Wolfram von Eschenbach. I wasn't concerned with literature, but with the facts the troubadours seemed to be trying to communicate. It seemed to me that there was something more to the Cathars, troubadours and Templars than met the eye. In 1978 I wrote in *The Iceman Inheritance*:

> We may not agree with historian Maurice Magre that the Albigensian crusade was the greatest single turning point in the religious history of Mankind. But it was an important turning point for *something*. If North American writers have not been so sensitive to this turning point, European writers have been. In recent years the spate of European-published books on Catharism and the Albigensian crusade has been nothing short of astonishing. We have *Actualité du catharisme* by Pierre Durban, *La croisade contre les albigeois et l'union du Languedoc a la France* by Pierre Belperron, *Le Sang de Toulouse* and *La trésor des albigeois* and many others, most published since 1960 and untranslated into English.[18]

And further, after a long and detailed argument based on sociology and anthropology, I again referred to Maurice Magre . . .

> If the evidence and argument presented in this essay are valid, then we must disagree with Magre, not because he said too much, but because he may have said too little. The war against the Albigensians may have been the greatest single turning point, not in the *religious* history, but in the *entire* history of Mankind.[19]

At the time I dared not say more, even though it was possible to suspect what had gone on. At that time, too, I was hungry for academic and "establishment" acceptance and I bowed to caution in the presentation of what was supposed to be a biological and "scientific" theory. My discretion was rewarded. The theory as presented so cautiously in *The Iceman Inheritance* was indeed supported by top anthropologists. Lectures and seminars about it were held at a number of universities in the U.S. and Canada. I was asked to speak on an educational radio series with Nobel laureate, Konrad Lorenz, and with Dr. Hazel Henderson of the Princeton Institute for Alternative Futures. *The Iceman Inheritance* was bought for mass-market paperback reprint in the U.S. and Canada.

I mention all this to demonstrate the rewards awaiting the academic, or would-be academic, who tells some of the truth in acceptable "scientific" jargon, but who prudently refrains from telling the whole truth!

This truth has been "unravelling", to use Watergate terminology, for several decades in Europe, particularly in France. It is just now coming to the attention of the English-speaking world, and more particularly to the attention of North American readers, with the recent publication of a bestselling book entitled *The Holy Blood and The Holy Grail* in 1982.

But no one has had the courage to write about what seems to the whole truth. The three British authors of *The Holy Blood and The Holy Grail* skirted cautiously around it, just as I shunned it out of caution in *The Iceman Inheritance* four years earlier.

So, throwing caution to the winds, what did happen during those 200-odd years?

It seems as though a unique lineage of humanity was almost, but not quite, *re-established* on earth. This same dynasty had occupied other thrones, in many times and in many places. Scions of the dynasty had ruled before, and some still do. But the importance of those 200-odd years was that this lineage had a chance of rising to extreme prominence *at a time that was on the brink of becoming "the modern world"*. Had the dynasty been successful, our world would have been much different. Perhaps much better.

But the dynastry failed. Its enemies closed in. It was defeated and driven undergound.

The long process of rebirth and re-establishment began with the fall of Montségur and the dispersion of the Templars. They are nothing if not persistent. They had "started again" many times.

Before we can understand exactly what this lineage is, we must follow their efforts, their triumphs and their defeats, because *this struggle is what they are, their "reason for being", their purpose.*

More than troubadour romances and esoteric cults survived from the wreck of Godfroi de Bouillon's bid for power. Even in defeat, and during the desperate business of reconstruction as hunted refugees, de Bouillon's dynasty and its faithful guardians molded much of our own modern world. They inspired the "Age of Discovery" and have been behind our progress since then.

Leaving aside, for a moment, the matter of the more mysterious Templar secrets and the more esoteric religious treasures supposedly possessed by Cathar and Albigensian, might it be possible to come to grips with the identity of somewhat more mundane secret treasures held by these people?

It is more than possible, because similar secret treasures have come into the hands of modern experts.

The Templars had been involved in trade and commerce. On land, they built protected warehouses and indulged in banking. But the Templars also had a fleet of ships, and it is likely that they were also engaged in maritime trade. The prime requirement for maritime commerce, after seaworthy ships, is accurate charts. Sea captains had to be able to find their way from port to port while avoiding hazard.

Not long after the Templar dispersal, very accurate and inexplicable sea-charts began to appear all over Europe. These maps, called *portolans* (thought to be derived from "port to land"), were far superior to the Ptolemaic maps studied by academic ecclesiastics in the monasteries and fledgling universities. Most of the *portolans* covered the area of the Mediterranean and the European Atlantic coast. They covered the areas crucial to European sea-commerce.[20]

The earliest dated portolan chart is the Opicinis de Canestris map of the Mediterranean of 1335 A.D. It demonstrates that maps of inexplicable accuracy began to appear in Europe less than 25 years after King Philippe's surprise raids against the Templars and the papal elimination of the Order under Clement V. It is not altogether implausible to suggest that so long as the Templars existed as an official Order, they kept these maps to themselves to aid their own commerce. De Bouillon established the Templars and, had his Kingdom of Jerusalem survived, its economic well-being would have depended upon trade, not upon agriculture. Palestine was as arid in the 12th Century as today. And, just as it is today, Palestine is a crossroads of three continents: Europe, Asia and Africa. A natural centre of commerce . . . and conflict . . . between continental powers.

The eventual importance of commerce in the economic life of the Kingdom of Palestine must have been immediately obvious to Godfroi and the later rulers of the dynasty. If the Templars were guardians of de Bouillon's line, one of their prime duties must have been to safeguard information that could control trade on both land and sea.

Even after the fall of Jerusalem, and the "regrouping" of the family in Provence and Languedoc, the Templars must have still played this role until the surrender of the last Cathar stronghold in 1244 A.D. Wealth characterized the civilization of southern France, and it was wealth derived in large measure from trade. As the real "power centre" of what might be called "the de Bouillon complex", it is unlikely that the Templars would have neglected the well-being of Languedoc and Provence. They did not, as is clear. Cathar wealth prompted the war against them, their heresies merely provided the moral excuse.

It is likely that even after the fall of the last Cathar fortress, the Templars would have kept their geographic knowledge to themselves for the sake of de Bouillon survivors. So long as they remained a cohesive force, and so long as they remained a recognized Order under the Papacy, the Templars represented a core of strength around which the "de Bouillon complex", whatever it was, might regroup and begin re-establishment.

But with the dawn raids of 1307 and the final dissolution of 1312, the "jig was up" as far as any rapid reconstruction was concerned. The Templar core was destroyed. Recouping the de Bouillon fortunes would be a long business. A policy decision was apparently made. Since the treasure of geographical knowledge *relating to European lands and waters* was of limited use to the surviving Templars and refugee de Bouillons, the precious charts would be released to the "general public" to assist mercantile development. Characteristically, just as they'd done on land, the assistance was made available at the "grassroots" and practical level, not on any ecclesiastical or academic one. Just as they had constructed warehouses and invented banking for practical merchants on land in the 13th Century, the Templars apparently leaked the valuable charts to practical seamen in the 14th Century.

The Opinicus de Canestris portolan chart of 1335 is one of many that has survived to the present day. There were obviously several hundred in circulation at the time. The surviving portolans show so many similarities, and such inexplicable accuracy, that modern scholars are of the

The Ibn Ben Zara Portolan chart.

opinion that there must have been only a few original maps, perhaps only one, from which hundreds of copies were made. Nordenskiöld believed that there was only one original.

Professor Charles Hapgood of Keene State Teacher's College in New Hampshire studied portolan charts for many years. He arranged to have his mathematical analysis checked by the Cartographic Section of the U.S. Air Force's Strategic Air Command (8th Reconnaissance Technical Squadron).

He discovered what Nordenskiöld had asserted half a century earlier, that the portolans were extremely accurate charts of the Mediterranean and the European Atlantic coast. In some cases, their errors were less than modern highway maps (but not less than modern Admiralty charts). This is true of the de Canestris portolan of 1335 as of later ones. I have not represented the de Canestris chart because it does not reproduce well. The original is pretty faded. Further, it would be disconcerting to modern eyes. Fanciful faces of kings and queens are made to fill the land masses and it looks, at first glance, to be a typical work of medieval imagination. But actual measurements taken from landmark to landmark reveal it to be, for all its confusing artwork, accurate to within about a degree (60 miles) over the extent of territory covered by the chart, about 3000 miles.

Much better as a portolan illustration is the Ibn Ben Zara map of 1487. Hapgood says of it:

> I had been attracted to a study of this portolan because it seemed definitely superior to all other portolan charts I had seen in the fineness of its delineation of the details of the coasts. As I examined the details in comparison with modern maps, I was amazed to see that no islet, however small, seemed too small to be noted . . .
>
> The grid worked out for the map revealed, indeed, a most amazing accuracy so far as the relative latitudes and longitudes were concerned. Total longitude between Gibraltar and the Sea of Azov was accurate to half a degree.[21]

This is an error of 30 miles over a total distance of 3000. It is better accuracy than can be claimed by modern road maps.

For the most part, establishment scholars have ignored the portolans and the problems they present. I know this well from my lectures on navigation and voyaging. Scholars stubbornly keep on misleading students of history that the best geographical knowledge available during the early Renaissance came from the Ptolemaic school of Alexandria. This is stated as a fact in all universities I've visited and has now been canonized as Gospel by the *Time-Life* "definitive" volume on exploration and the *"Age of Discovery"*. But it is false. One has only to pick a portolan chart of the Mediterranean at random and compare it with one of the Ptolemaic charts of the Mediterranean. The portolan will be accurate, the Ptolemaic map will show great distortion due to academic ignorance of geography.

But Claudius Ptolemy was an academic, working in what might be called a "university" environment in Alexandria. Maybe that's why modern professors must believe that he and his geography represented the apex of knowledge available at the time. It was simply not true. While Ptolemy and his scholars tried to make sense of their distorted world, any reasonably successful ship captain in Alexandria had, squirreled away in his sea-chest, a chart showing a very accurate world. I thought it would be a good idea to include a Ptolemaic sea-chart here so that anyone can see that the portolans were a lot better . . .   Ptolemy, of course, never

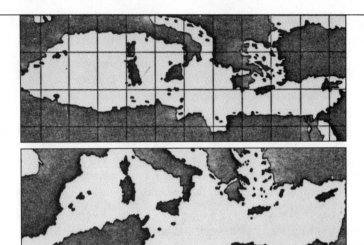

Comparison of Ptolemy's Map of the Mediterranean (top) with the Dulcert Portolano of 1339 (bottom).

The portolan looks almost modern, whereas the Ptolemaic chart shows great distortion. The accuracy of the portolans remains a mystery. It is thought that they came from the Middle East.

apparently bothered to check the waterfront for geographical knowledge. Nor did his scholarly successors. What could ship captains possibly know about geography?

But some charity can be extended to contemporary professors. It is understandable, if not excusable, that the portolans have been purposefully ignored.

They exist, but they should not. Their accuracy is simply inexplicable. They are a mystery. They are a key to a door that no one really wants to open. One of many keys jangling.

I mentioned before that neither sailors in the Ancient World nor sailors in the Renaissance could determine their longitude, their position east or west of any given point. This seems to be a fact. There is no evidence that longitude could be determined at sea before the invention of the chronometer in the 18th Century. This victory was the result of keen competition among clockmakers and the incentive of a great prize offered by the British Admiralty.

On land, there was one theoretical way of determining longitude. It could be used by savants with proper equipment, proper almanacs and plenty of time. I quote from Hapgood who explains this method:

> The only known method of ascertaining longitude in Columbus' day was by timing an eclipse. Regiomontanus's *Ephemerides* and Zacuto's *Almanac Perpetuum* gave the predicted hours of total eclipse at Nuremberg and Salamanca respectively, and if you compared those with the observed hour of eclipse wherever you were, and multiplied by 15 to convert time into arc (1 hour of time = 15 degrees of longitude) there was your longitude west of the almanac maker's meridian. Sounds simple enough, but Columbus, with two opportunities (1494 and 1503) muffed both, as did almost everyone else for a century.[22]

Admiral Morison, a pretty fair navigator himself, who became interested in the historical comedy of navigation errors, writes:

> At Mexico City in 1541 a mighty effort was made by the intelligensia to find the longitude of the place by timing two eclipses of the moon. The imposing result was 8 hours 2 minutes and 32 seconds west of Toledo (= 120 degrees and 32 minutes west of Toledo) but the correct difference between the two places is 95 degrees and 12 minutes, so the Mexican savants made an error of 25½ degrees, or 1450 miles! Even as late as the 18th Century, Père Labat, the earliest writer to my knowledge to give the position of Hispaniola correctly, adds this caveat: "I only report the longitude to warn the reader that nothing is more uncertain, and that no method used up to the present to find longitude has produced anything fixed and certain."[23]

Even if all this navigator's jargon seems foreign, and even if the mathematical principles are unfamiliar, my point must be clear enough by now: nobody could determine longitude until the 1770s.

If that is the case, and it was the case, then how are the medieval portolans so accurate in their east-west measurements? How could a portolan dating from the 1300s have an error of only 60 miles in 3000 when measurements made 200 years later with the best instruments resulted in an error of 1450 miles in 4500? The earlier portolan was more accurate by several factors.

How could this be? Who made such accurate measurements that were impossible until much later? When were such accurate measurements of the earth made?

And the answer is that nobody knows. The portolans just exist. Their accuracy cannot be explained. That is why they are carefully, and stubbornly, ignored in history courses and why Ptolemy is discussed instead by professors of history and geography.

If we cannot truly "explain" the portolan charts, we can account for them in a rather cowardly way by saying simply "they came from the Middle East". This doesn't really answer any questions, but it postpones the nastier ones for a little while and it tells us how the Templars could have gotten hold of such maps. The problem concerning who . . . or what . . . created these maps will be left until much later.

Is there any proof that the Templars actually obtained such maps in the Holy Land and that they came into the possession of the Kings of Jerusalem?

No, there is no absolute proof of this, but there is evidence suggesting that it is likely. The evidence is simply that modern scholars have stumbled across similar maps in Middle Eastern archives, while it is known that the Templars sacked many such archives when taking cities from the Saracens.

In 1929 a map of inexplicable accuracy was accidently discovered in the old Imperial Palace in Constantinople. It was painted on parchment. It had been made by Piri Ibn Haji Memmed, better known as Piri Re'is, who had been a one-time pirate and the scourge of the Turkish Navy. Apparently on the principle that "if you can't beat 'em join 'em" the Sultan decided to make Piri Re'is an Admiral in the hope that the old pirate would become respectable. The newly-discovered map caused quite a stir and was the subject of both intense scholarly examination and excited popular press stories *because it showed the American continents very accurately.* More accurately, in fact, than any map drawn until 200 years later. American Secretary of State of the time, Henry Stimson, began a flurry of correspondence with Turkish authorities that lasted during much of the early 1930s. He requested detailed searches for other old maps that might have been forgotten in the archives. The Turks conducted a careful search, but no other maps were discovered.

But similar maps had been found before, in the 1860s, though they had not caused as much press coverage. One of them is the Hadji Ahmed world map. I have reproduced these two maps, the Piri one and the Hadji Ahmed one, to show how accurate and "modern" they look. Just look at the geography, not the artwork.

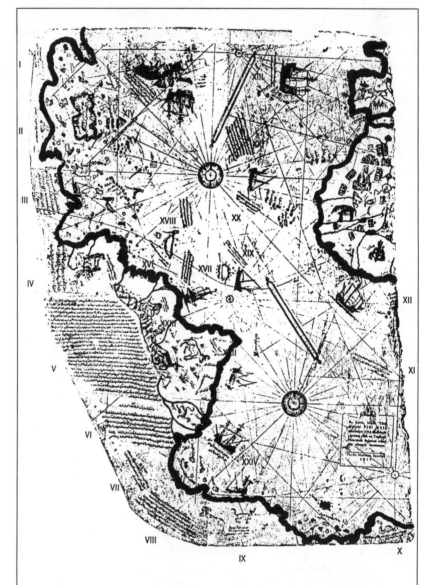

Surviving fragment of the Piri Re'is Map discovered in 1929 in the archives in Constantinople. To the left is the American continent. Compare Piri Re'is American geography with the shape of the American continent derived by Equidistant Projection based on Cairo (next two pages). Coastal outlines emphasized by Author.

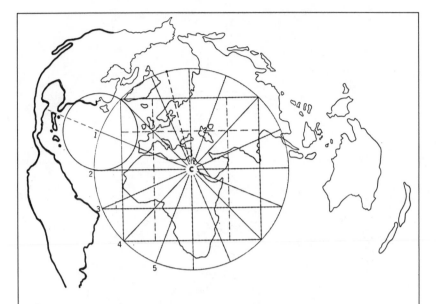

The Piri Re' is shape of North America and South America imposed on an "Azimuthal Equidistant Projection" of the world. This is not really as difficult as it sounds! *Azimuth* is an Arabic astronomical and navigational term meaning the angular distance between the horizon and the observer's zenith. *Zenith* is another Arabic astronomical and navigational term meaning a point directly over the observer's head. Therefore, in "Azimuthal Equidistant Projection" simply pretend that you're suspended high above some convenient point on earth and that the horizon is equally distant from you all around. Then, pretend that, somehow, the surface of the *whole earth* has been miraculously split open and spread flat so that you can see even land masses that were on the other side of the earth. The most convenient point for doing this happens to be directly above the Great Pyramid near Cairo in Egypt. The reason for this is that the Great Pyramid happens to be located at the centre of the earth's land masses and the earth's surface can be "split and flattened" with the least distortion if viewed from this point. If you are successful in imagining this projection, you will immediately see that the costline of North and South America of the Piri Re' is map, which I have emphasized to make it clearer, is remarkably similar to the same coastline shown in a modern Strategic Air Command "Azimuthal Equidistant Projection" of the world. It is this similarity of the Piri Re' is map and modern ones that raise the question of how the Piri Re' is projection appears on a map drawn in 1519, but based on even earlier ones. At some time in the past was the earth surveyed from space? Whatever the answer, experts have concluded that the Piri Re' is map must have been based on aerial photography of some sort to present so accurate a representation of the American coast as seen from a great distance.

Modern U.S. Air Force Equidistant Projection map of the world centered "near Cairo" (i.e. centered on the Great Pyramid). Note that the shape of the American continent is almost identical with the geography of the Piri Re' is Map.

Both maps had been recovered from archives in the Middle East by modern investigators. There must have been many more such maps a thousand years ago, filed away in the libraries of the many Moslem cities taken by the Templars. There can hardly be any doubt that the Templars came into the possession of charts like these. And they would constitute a treasure in themselves to any kingdom dependent upon trade and commerce for its economic survival.

After the dispersion of the Templars, the European portions of such maps were of little use to the surviving knights of the Order and to the refugee survivors of the de Bouillon clan. Their enemies were victorious in Europe and they could not indulge openly in military, political or economic activities. Not in Europe. So perhaps the "policy decision" was made to leak these maps out to the practical seamen who could use them to make maritime trade easier, less hazardous and more certain and frequent. It was another nail driven into the coffin of feudalism.

But what about the *non-European* portions of the maps? Both the Hadji Ahmed map and the Piri Re'is map show the Americas with incredible accuracy.

And the Americas represented a haven from Europe. At least, from the point of view of the surviving Templars who were still guardians of the de Bouillons, the strange new lands shown on the edges of such maps would have held the hope of a refuge. And the de Bouillons were in desperate need of a refuge for themselves and for their secret that the Roman Church sought so avidly and with such cruelty.

The new lands on the edges of the old maps represented hope in what must have been the darkest hour in the long history of the lineage.

If these lands really existed.

But if the European and Mediterranean portions of the maps had proved accurate, why should the rest of the maps be any less accurate?

There was only one way to find out. Explore. Verify that the new lands existed. Establish a refuge.

Many of the Templars fled to Portugal, while others fled to Scotland. Is it mere coincidence that voyages of exploration on the Atlantic almost immediately set out from these two places? Is it mere coincidence that Prince Henry "The Navigator", who began Portugal's and Europe's "Age of Discovery" was the Grand Master of the Knights of Christ, the new Portuguese name for the old Knights Templar?

There is absolutely no doubt that the royalty of Portugal possessed

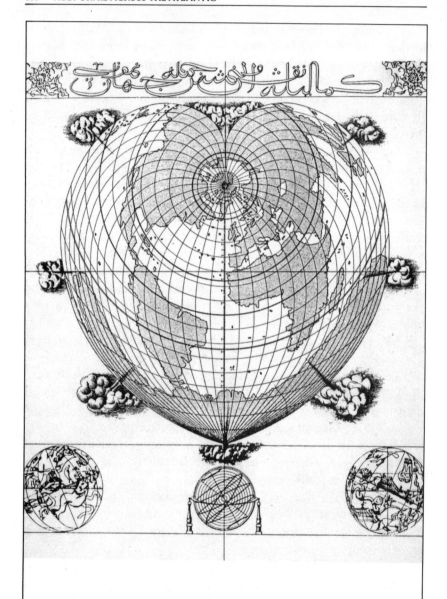

Another Middle Eastern map of inexplicable accuracy, the Hadji Ahmed map of 1559. There is no Bering Strait between North America and Asia, but instead a large land area. This corresponds to the actual size of the "Bering Land Bridge" during the last Ice Age, but modern scholars did not know this until 1958.

maps already showing geographical facts that would be "discovered". The maps showed geography very literally "at the ends of the earth" before the supposed "discoverers" ever arrived to confirm the truth of the charts. One of Magellan's officers wrote about the historic voyage to "discover" the passage at the tip of South America. Pigafetta, a navigator, says:

> The sentiments of every person in the fleet were that it (the "Straits of Magellan") had no issue in the west; and nothing but the confidence they had in the superior knowledge of the commander could have induced them to prosecute the research. But this great man, as skilful as he was courageous, know that he was to seek for a passage through an obscure strait: this strait he had seen laid down on a chart of Martin de Boheme, a most excellent cosmographer, which was in the possession of the King of Portugal.[24]

And that about says it all. Magellan's "discovery" was already shown on a chart. He was sent to confirm it. He did. The chart was accurate. The "Strait of Magellan" is at the tip of South America and connects the Atlantic with the Pacific. Who originally drew this chart that Martin de Boheme copied?

That may well never be answered. But how did it get to Portugal and where did it come from? *That* can be conjectured with a high degree of probable accuracy. The chart probably came from the Middle East, and was probably similar to the maps of Piri Re'is and Hadji Ahmed (which shows the "Straits of Magellan"). It had probably been discovered by Templars in the Holy Land and brough to Portugal after the Order was crushed in France.

This is not an isolated example. The southern tip of Africa, the Cape of Good Hope as Diaz called it when he "discovered" it, had already been shown to him on a chart drawn by Fra Mauro.

And what did Columbus know?

Navigational historian, Frederick Pohl, writes:

> We cannot see all that was in Columbus' mind, but it is obvious that when he set sail on August 3 he had some knowledge that he had not publicized about the Atlantic Ocean but that was vital to his success.[25]

We don't know all that was in Columbus' mind, but we know some of it. He insisted to the scholars of the Spanish examining commission that he "might find some very beneficial island or continent" some "750 leagues" (about 3000 miles) to the westward. He did exactly that, and at exactly that distance westward. Is that mere coincidence? Or did Columbus, too, come into possession of a chart? This is more than likely. Columbus married the daughter of Perestrello, one of the more minor Portuguese heroes of the "Age of Discovery", but nonetheless a captain with access to the geographical treasures in the royal archives. Perestrello may not have seen charts showing America with his own eyes, but he would have heard rumours of them from his captain colleagues. Perhaps even detailed descriptions of lands and distances.

It is known that Columbus had a map of some sort because it is mentioned in his log. A few days before sighting land, Columbus held a conference with the captains of the *Niña* (Alonso Pinzón) and *Pinta* (Vincente Yañez Pinzón) aboard his flagship, the *Santa Maria*. The subject under discussion was whether to change course *according to their map* and according to the overflights of land-seeking birds. They did change course and sighted land eight days later. Many have speculated on this map, where it came from and what it might have shown. In *The Black Discovery of America* (recently re-released as *Dawn Voyage*), I suggested that this map might have been drawn by Perestrello, the father-in-law of Columbus. Perestrello had apparently sailed as far south as Cape Verde. It is written in Omari's *Masalik-al-absad* that at least one Emperor of Mali (and probably a second emperor as well) had sent expeditions out into the Atlantic and had discovered the trade winds and the North Equatorial Current. These expeditions would likely have sailed from the Senegal and Gambia rivers which flank Cape Verde. They allegedly took place sometime between 1325 to 1350. I speculated that Perestrello had taken African slaves from Cape Verde, since all Portuguese voyages south were also slaving operations, and that he had learned of land to the west from these captured Africans. There is little doubt that the Malians reached the New World in the early 14th Century, while other Africans had crossed much earlier. It seems reasonable to suppose that Perestrello documented African information on maps in his journal. These were given to Columbus by Dona Moniz Perestrello, the widowed wife of the Portuguese captain. This is still a reasonable conjecture. But it is also possible that Columbus had one or more maps similar to those of Piri Re'is and Hadji Ahmed. If so, as Hapgood points out, Columbus would not have understood the mathematical projections employed in these maps, but he could have worked out a rough scale from portions of Europe he recognized and gotten at least a rough idea of distance and direction to land.

Columbus knew something. We will probably never know exactly how much. Or how he found out about it. But is it mere coincidence that his flag-ship, the famous *Santa Maria*, bore *Templar crosses* on her sails when Columbus set sail from Palos? Is it mere coincidence that his voyage was financed, not by the sale of Isabella's jewellery as so commonly thought, but by a mysterious consortium of wealthy men which included Jews and other heretics?[26] And is it only coincidence that Columbus weighed anchor on August 3, 1492 just a few hours before the deadline for all Jews to be out of Spain?

We will recall that the "de Bouillon complex" in southern France had close connections with the Jewish and Moslem savants of Moorish Spain. As did the Templars. It seems significant that the Moors were finally expelled from Spain only in 1492, the year of Columbus' voyage. Did he take some of the mixed Cathar-Jewish-Moslem-Templar refugees with him? Was *that* why the venture was financed by "heretical" money?

Perhaps. One thing is certain. Columbus, with three ships and ninety crewmen, set sail without a Catholic priest. Is this not strange considering it was an expedition of "Their Most Catholic Majesties"?

In general, the entire "Age of Discovery" exhibits a curious characteristic. The early explorers show inordinate representation by heretics, Protestants and other sorts of religious dissidents and/or refugees from Roman Catholicism. We shall meet with this phenomenon again in the north. *And, inexplicably, these dissidents and heretics often sailed with charters granted by supposedly orthodox Catholic monarchs.* And, in some cases, by undoubtedly orthodox ones who were, simultaneously, conducting religious wars of great ferocity against co-religionaries of the explorers themselves.

In fact, it can be said that the entire early exploration and colonization of the Americas bears the unmistakable stamp of a religious refugee movement.

The "Pilgrim Fathers" of American history are too familiar to need much elaboration. They were Protestants fleeing from religious oppression.

But recent research has shown a similar phenomenon elsewhere. Many of the "Spanish" discoverers and conquistadors turn out to have been a mixture of Cathar-Jewish-Moslem refugees from Andalusia, the

Pyrenees fringe area again, after the region was finally acquired by Catholic royalty from the Moors in 1492.

In the north, we find Protestants, like de Monts, prominent among explorers and colonizers for the Catholic king of France. And religious wars raged at the time.

What was going on beneath the blanket of history?

It seems simple enough. Although the Cathars and the Templars had been crushed, and although the de Bouillons were underground, they still somehow wielded some sort of power that the Catholic establishment feared. And, in spite of the persecutions, this power steadily drew supporters. In short, whatever the "de Bouillon complex" represented, it could not be completely eradicated. It could only be pushed out of sight, pushed underground, so that orthodoxy "appeared to be served". But not really. There was some sort of secret, and it gave some sort of power.

Enough, perhaps, to negotiate (or "blackmail"?) a deal with the Roman Church and various Catholic monarchs. It must have gone something like this: the heretics would, as far as possible, simply leave Europe; they would pay for the exploration of the new lands, take a rather small percentage of any profits of exploitation while leaving the lion's share to the European monarch. The heretics would represent the politics or nationality of their country of origin. *But, in return, they would be granted a measure of religious tolerance in the new lands.* It was agreed by both parties that it would be "business as usual" in Europe itself, which meant continued ferocious religious wars, the heretics not being willing to change, and the Church wanting uniform orthodoxy and absolute control. And, as both parties realized, *all* the dissidents and heretics couldn't emigrate. There were too many. The stay-at-homes who couldn't, or wouldn't, leave would just continue to slug it out with the Inquisition.

There seem to have been local variations of the deal. In some places, and at some times, the heretics apparently agreed to maintain "outward and visible" orthodoxy or, at least, to keep a "low profile".

It must be understood that there was no mercy or goodwill in this compromise. It was a sort of situation that developed as the result of a balance of power. A "Mexican stand-off". Both parties would manipulate things as best they could for their factions.

In south of Europe, things did not go so well for the "de Bouillon complex". The monarchies of Spain and Portugal became well and truly Catholic. The Church gained control of these countries with a grip that is only now beginning to slacken. And the Church gained a foothold, and then virtual control, in the overseas colonies of these countries. The Inquisition raged in tropical America, just as it did in Europe. In fact, some of the Cathar-Jewish-Moslem refugees who had once fled from Andalusia to Mexico as "Spanish" conquistadors after 1492, later found themselves in trouble with the inquisition, again, in Mexico itself. Many died at flaming stakes (again) or on the torture-racks of the victors (again). Those who were not prepared to recant their secret Cathar, or Jewish or Moslem tenets fled further. Into the southwestern U.S. And they remained what they always had been, whether in Andalusia or on the coastal plains of France or in North Africa. Herdsmen. As they had been also in Mexico. They began the cowboy tradition of the southwestern U.S.[27]

As "cow-pokes", they continued to "poke" cows with the long poles still used in Spain, France and North Africa to herd cattle. The same long poles which, in times of war, were the lances of the Pyrenees Cathar-Jewish-Moslem knight-herdsman levies that fought beside the Templars for the lineage of Godfroi de Bouillon. In time, they adopted Catholicism peacefully, along with the American Indian lariat, but they were still called "cow-pokes", even when Anglo-Saxon Protestants from the northeast adopted the trade. They are familiar to us. From endless episodes of *Bonanza* and *Gunsmoke*. Just as familiar as King Arthur, from the film and musical of *Camelot*.

And in the north?

The "de Bouillon complex" fared better. The Church never gained the same sort of authority in the north as it did in the tropics. Not even in the French possessions of North America. There was never any Inquisition in the north.

Except.

Wicca suffered. Witchcraft. The women suffered. Not much, as similar things are accounted in Europe, but they suffered. *Wicca*, the old fertility religion of Europe, may have been somehow incorporated in the Cathar beliefs of southern France and was destroyed by the Inquisitors. Disguised, even among refugees, it apparently got transplanted to the New World, where, ironically, it was just as ruthlessly persecuted by the spiritual descendants of the Cathars, the Massachusetts Puritans. But it did not suffer much, as things were accounted in Europe. Some 3 *million* women died in Europe, as witches, so it has been estimated, between 1244 A.D. and 1750 A.D.

Barely a score died for witchcraft in America. Yet, it should be noted, *wicca* has been the most persecuted religion on a "per capita" basis, not Judaeism.[28]

But, at least, the Inquisition and the intolerance did not rage in North America as it did in Europe and in the tropics of America.

If "Prince Henry the Navigator" of Portugal was an agent of the underground, then it must be said that he failed to establish a secure refuge for those he was charged to protect. The Roman Church appropriated all of his geographical discoveries and the Roman Church was the enemy in the long struggle, now 1500 years long, that had been going on beneath the blanket of history.

Another "Prince" Henry had been more successful. He was not a legitimate Prince. It was a title bestowed out of courtesy, in recognition of what he achieved.

It is known that the Templars fled to Scotland, too, after the dissolution of 1312, and it is known that some found refuge among the Saint-Clairs of Rosslyn in Midlothian. There is a Templar cemetery there. In the year 1345 a son was born to this lord of Rosslyn. The boy's name was Henry.

He, too, became "a navigator", although his story is almost unknown. He voyaged upon the Atlantic. He discovered lands across the ocean. And it is recorded that he founded a city across the ocean, and stayed there until the founding was done, at the peril of his own House. He returned to Scotland just in time to die in the defence of his domain in the Orkney Islands.

There is no longer any doubt that the land he discovered must have been Nova Scotia. And it is recorded that he founded a city there. Where? Why? No one knows. If legends of Nova Scotia's Micmac Indians are to be given credence, then it seems inevitable that Henry Sinclair[29] stood on the hill top of The Cross. Are the apparent ruins at The Cross the remains of Henry Sinclair's lost settlement? There can be no way to answer this question definitively without professional investigation of the hill top site. But it is at least suggestive that the ruins of The Cross appear to be Norse-North Scottish rubblework appropriate to Sinclair's era.

Chapter Four

The Sea Chieftain

Sir John Bernard Burke, in his *Vicissitudes of Families and Other Essays*, wrote:

> The vicissitudes of great families forms a curious chapter in the general history of mankind . . . The interest attaching to individual fortunes excites more human sympathy than the fate of kingdoms. But such details are not on the surface. They must be dug up from buried documents, disinterred and the dust swept off . . . Greatness (in a family) is built up by well-directed energy . . . There is little stability in the highest gifts of fortune. Family trees, like all other trees, must eventually perish. The most lasting houses have their seasons: their spring, summer sunshine glare, wane, decline and death . . . No family in Europe beneath the rank of royalty boasts a higher antiquity, a nobler illustration, or a more romantic interest than that of St. Clair.[1]

In a similar eulogy, the Reverend J.B. Craven noted in his *History of the Church in Orkney*:

> We have many families of ancient descent in Scotland, but it may be questioned if any of these families has produced such a roll of eminent men as that of St. Clair . . . Although the actual possession of the Earldom of Orkney by the noble family of St. Clair lasted for less than one hundred years, the time of their rule appears to have been the most successful and prosperous in the History of the northern diocese. The nobility, refinement, justice and kindly manners of that family appear in all its traditional history.[2]

No, the Saint Clairs were never elevated to a throne and the status of royalty, but, like several other families, including the houses of Boulogne and Angoulême and Razès, faithfully served for centuries as knights errant to succeeding generations of what seems to be Western humanity's most illustrious bloodline and, as we shall discover in later chapters, some descendants of these same noble houses still appear to fulfill this role up to the present day. Further, when this bloodline seems to wane in vitality, new infusions of human potency seem to be drawn from the genetic resources of these "almost royal" families.

Of all of the heroes who have emerged from these faithful houses over thousands of years to become paladins in the West's most noble cause, few deserve greater praise than "Prince" Henry Sinclair, the first Earl of Orkney to come from the St. Clair, or Sinclair, family.

His achievement needs to be put into a perspective.

King Arthur worked to hold back the barbarian invasions at the close of the Roman civilization in the West. It is not too much of an exaggeration to say that, had it not been for him, the conversion of northern Europe to Christianity would have been delayed by several centuries at least. It is even possible that some of the northern barbarians might never have accepted Christianity at all. This means that northern Europe would have come much more slowly to "civilization" because the Christian Church represented all that remained of Roman culture. Arthur not only gained time for the barbarians to become somewhat civilized, his example assisted in their eventual conversion. Arthur, as a warrior-hero who was Christian, inspired a respect for Christianity among warrior-barbarians.

This appears to have been Arthur's intended role, and he appears to have been partly successful at playing it. Yet, even if Arthur had failed completely, all would not have been lost. In Italy itself, in southern France, and along the major rivers of southern Europe, Christianity and "civilization" were in a position of some security. About the time that Arthur was born, around 470 A.D., the Church took steps to ally itself with a much more powerful temporal power complex than Arthur represented. This "power complex" was located in France where it could not be cut off by barbarian invasion as insular Britain could be, and was. This French connection was the core of the bloodline in the dark times after the fall of Rome. For all of Arthur's heroism, and for all of the legends he and his companions inspired, the entire Arthurian effort was a peripheral action. A rear guard skirmish. It did not really matter whether

Arthur succeeded or not. If he failed, then the same pattern of history would still have been unfolded, it just would have unfolded more slowly.

In a later chapter we will look at this French "power complex" that was established at the same time as Arthur's birth and which has apparently influenced the mainstream pattern behind Western history.

Godfroi de Bouillon's adventure appears, in retrospect, to have been a premature bid for geopolitical power at the watershed between the feudal world and the modern one. It failed, and plunged the bloodline into what was the most desperate predicament in its long history. The power of the Roman Church was under-estimated, and the power of the feudal backlash. De Bouillon's "power base" in the Pyrenees and southern France was crushed with relative ease, the Cathars destroyed, the Templars dispersed.

The need for a refuge was real, and desperate. Exploratory efforts were launched from several Templar refuges to find this urgently required haven. In the south, in Portugal, Prince Henry "The Navigator" may have failed in his primary objective. He discovered new lands, but the Roman Church appropriated his discoveries and instituted the Inquisition there. The same thing happened with Columbus sailing for Spain. Whatever his original and secret motives, and whatever the magnitude of his discoveries, he appears to have failed as well. The tropical Americas that Columbus opened up did not become any sort of refuge for whatever "neo-Templar" underground he may have represented. Heresies and secret doctrines were quickly wiped out by the Inquisition in tropical America.

Unsafe and hunted in Europe, and with hopeful havens appropriated by a merciless enemy, the Grail Dynasty was in very real danger of perishing altogether. And it might have.

Except that "Prince" Henry in the far north did not fail. He found and established a transatlantic settlement that his namesake in Portugal failed to find and establish. Because of Henry Sinclair, the bloodline may have survived the Inquisition in a secure haven across the Atlantic, to await the dawning of a more modern, and more tolerant age.

It is only within the last 30 years that Henry Sinclair has begun to take his place even on the "warp and woof" of establishment history, as a recognized and major explorer and no more. His secret role has not been suspected even by the man responsible for bringing Henry Sinclair's exploratory achievements into the realm of popular knowledge.

The man who disinterred Henry Sinclair is American historian and author, Frederick Pohl. This chapter relies heavily upon Pohl's book, *Prince Henry Sinclair*.[3]

Pohl, almost single-handedly, has popularized an episode of history formerly known only to a few specialists. And it is an important episode because it involves nothing less than the European discovery of America a century before Columbus *and the establishment of a European colony on the American continent at the same time.*

The original account of Henry Sinclair's voyage is recorded in a document long known to historians called *The Zeno Narrative*. For many years *The Zeno Narrative* was regarded as a "boastful claim of Venetian discovery" of America before Columbus, but recent study has established the authenticity of the document. This is not the place to chronicle all of the scholarly wrangling concerning *The Zeno Narrative* because Pohl covers it fully in his book which is available in any large North American library. It is necessary only to note that the *Encyclopaedia Britannica*, the *Encyclopedia Americana*, the Nova Scotia Museum and most other authorities now accept the reality of the voyage.[4] As will become apparent, details in this document could not have been imagined or invented because they accurately reflect the geography of Nova Scotia and nowhere else. And this geography was unknown to "establishment" historians, geographers and explorers when *The Zeno Narrative* was first published in 1558.

More important and conclusive for modern scholars is the fact that *The Zeno Narrative* includes a map, called "The Zeno Map of the North", and this shows Henry Sinclair's discoveries and the location of the city he founded across the Atlantic.

But this map is inexplicable. It is like the Piri Re'is map and the Hadji Ahmed map. It shows things that it shouldn't. Things that were unknown until three or four centuries after Henry Sinclair lived. And it is drawn on a complicated and mathematical type of polar projection that was not supposedly "invented" until four centuries later. "The Zeno Map of the North" presents the same difficulties that the portolans present. It probably came from the same source, the Middle East.

It may be reasonable to speculate that the original Middle Eastern source map for "The Zeno Map of the North" was taken to Rosslyn in Scotland by refugee Templars. There is no doubt that Rosslyn of the

Sinclairs was a Templar haven. The Authors of *The Holy Blood and The Holy Grail* write:

> ... we encountered repeated references to the Sinclair family — Scottish branch of the Norman Saint-Clair/Gisors family. Their domain at Rosslyn was only a few miles from the former Scottish headquarters of the Knights Templar, and the chapel at Rosslyn — built between 1446 and 1486 — has long been associated with both Freemasonry and the Rose-Croix. In a charter believed to date from 1601, moreover, the Sinclairs are recognized as 'hereditary Grand Masters of Scottish Masonry'. This is the earliest specific Masonic document on record.[5]

This is, admittedly, the slimmest of justifications for the important speculation of this book. On the other hand, it cannot be denied that Rosslyn Castle was, in local legend, associated with secret documents and hidden "holy" treasures.

Father Richard Augustine Hay, author of *Genealogy of the Sainteclaires of Rosslynn*, wrote in 1835 that the charter room of Rosslyn castle had "many secrets to tell" before many of its records were destroyed by fire.[6] Hay had had access to this library before the fire, but he chose not to reveal these alleged secrets in his book. In a similar vein, James Jackson told in his book, *Historical Tales of Roslin Castle from the invasion of Edward I of England to the Death of Mary, Queen of Scots*, that precious manuscripts of documents were supposedly hidden in a sealed room in the cellar of the castle. Jackson states that an attempt to find these manuscripts was made by "General Count Poli, an Italian descendant of the prevost of Roslin Castle, who came in 1834 with an ancient volume" which supposedly contained the key to finding this cellar vault[7]. Whether or not Poli found anything is not known. Jackson also quotes Sir Walter Scott, who seemed to know about Rosslyn's secrets:

> From the inner edge of the outer door,
> At thirty feet of old Scotch measure,
> The passage there, that's made secure,
> Leads to the holy Roslin treasure.

So, it is not unjustifiable to speculate that maps and charts originating from the Middle East may have been brought to the castle by refugee Templars. If any credence is to be given to Sir Walter Scott, we may even suppose that Rosslyn guarded a holy treasure. Perhaps this, too, like the

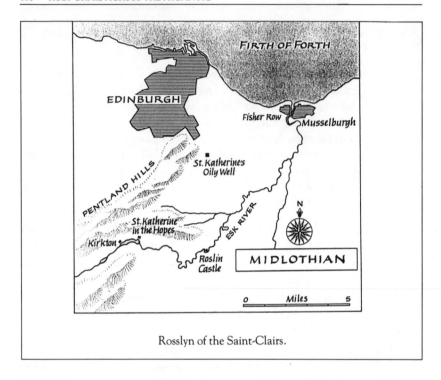

Rosslyn of the Saint-Clairs.

supposed Cathar treasure, was brought to the Sinclair family seat by fleeing Templars.

Henry was born in 1345, about a generation after the Templar dispersal, into a family that had always been special paladins of de Bouillon's dynasty. Henry's ancestor and namesake, Henri de Saint-Clair, fought beside Godfroi de Bouillon at the taking of Jerusalem. Several Saint-Clairs became Templars themselves. The Sinclair lands were a Templar centre. What was more natural than that Rosslyn of the Sinclairs would become a Tempar refuge? And what more natural than that the noble and powerful Sinclairs would have become leaders of "neo-Templar" secret societies like the Freemasons and the Rosicrucians?

It was probably inevitable. And it was just as probable, too, that secret maps from the Middle East, or copies, might have ended up at Rosslyn. It was a certainty that the burden of verifying the lands shown on the edges of such maps, of finding the haven so desperately needed, would have fallen on the shoulders of the Sinclair heirs because Sinclairs had always been knights-errant for de Bouillon's line.

The problem was that the Sinclairs of the 14th Century were landlubbers, like most of their colleagues in the agriculturally-based Norman feudal aristocracy. The Sinclairs had hardly completed the task of securing their landholding in Scotland, and of building up some agricultural security in the typical feudal manner, when they were required to undertake oceanic explorations.

Nor was the Sinclair holding in Midlothian ever really secure. Aside from squabbles with other Norman nobility, which eventually led them into conflict with the King of England, the Sinclair lands were never safe from the Scandinavians. Although the Scandinavians of the 14th Century could no longer be called "Vikings", they claimed much of what the Vikings had originally conquered, and this included some of modern Scotland. But this Viking-Scandinavian association cut two ways. Through a complicated series of feudal inter-marriages and documents, Henry Sinclair was born heir not only to Rosslyn, but also to the Earldom of Orkney. This earldom included the Shetland Islands as well as the Orkneys.

These territories were owned by the King of Norway. In the confusing and purely familial pattern of the Middle Ages, Henry Sinclair held Rosslyn as a vassal of the Kings of England and Scotland, but held Orkney as a vassal of the King of Norway. Henry thus had holdings which offered much potential for future conflicts of interest.

But, in becoming Earl of Orkney, Henry Sinclair became the first Sinclair to become a sea-chieftain. His island earldom demanded a navy in order to control it, and demanded an emphasis on shipping if its wealth was to be exploited. The most valuable resource of his new earldom was a fishing indusry that brought in much more income than Rosslyn. And it also attracted the attentions of pirates and other Norman, and Scandinavian, feudal competitors

The Norwegian king "gave" Henry Sinclair the earldom to be held in fief, but it was, at first, something of a backhanded compliment. Although the Orkney and Shetland islands were owned and claimed by Norway, they had been independent in practice for some years. As the new Earl of Orkney, Henry's job was to regain control of the independent islanders. This entailed a mixture of warfare and diplomacy over almost 20 years. Henry proved exceedingly adept at both. By the time he could call himself Earl of Orkney in fact as well as in title, he really had become a sea-chieftain with an effective navy and with a good knowledge of

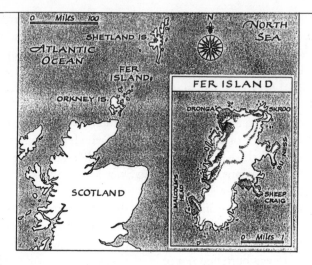

The Orkney and Shetland island groups north of Scotland which comprised Henry's Earldom of Orkney in the late 1300s. Claimed by Norway, Henry held his earldom as a vassal of the King of Norway, while holding other territories as a vassal of the Scottish king. Fer Island, between the Shetland and Orkney groups is where Henry Sinclair met Nicolo Zeno in 1391 A.D.

maritime matters. And he'd become as much "Norse" as Norman-French.

This cultural transformation was most important. From his Viking-descended island subjects Sinclair not only obtained a corps of experienced sailors, he also adopted their sturdy little ships that had evolved to cope with North Atlantic conditions. These ships were themselves descendants of Viking long ships and trading *knorrs*.

Which brings us to the matter of the Viking voyages. Earl Henry was a prominent noble of Norway after his investiture as Lord of the Isles. It is known that he made several journeys to Norway to be present at important state occasions. And, being a sea-lord and in close contact with the royal court in Norway, he could not have failed to hear of the Norse sagas of transatlantic exploration. In Henry's time, in the 14th Century, these sagas were just being written down in Latin and formed the nucleus of Scandinavian native literature. Everyone was talking about them in 14th Century Scandinavia, and especially the nobility who claimed descent from the earlier Viking adventurers.

Most of the sagas were written first in Iceland from still-current verbal accounts preserved by descendants on the spot. The resulting books were quickly copied for dissemination in Norway. Among these were *Erics Saga Rauda* ("The Saga of Eric the Red"), the *Hauksbók* and the *Flateyjarbók*. All dealt with the Viking explorers of Greenland and America, and all were being avidly read by the Scandinavian nobility.[8]

Not only that, but trade was still maintained between Norway and the old Viking colony in Greenland.[9] Henry Sinclair must have learned much about the lands across the North Atlantic which had been seen and explored by Lief Ericsson, Thorfinn Karlsefni, Thorall and other Northmen about 350 years earlier.

In short, in addition to sailors and ships, his Norse subjects and noble associates provided him with confirmation that there *was* land across the Atlantic to the west, just like the Templar maps showed. Not too different from the lands shown on the "Zeno Map of the North".

By 1390, Henry's fleet numbered 13 ships: two undecked oared galleys of Mediterranean type useful for manoeuvering in the narrow channels of the Orkney and Shetland island groups (and a favoured labyrinth for pirates and discontented island smugglers); one decked longship for battle, based on the old Viking lines; and ten decked sailing barks suitable for oceanic patrols around the island groups.[10]

If he had the ships, the sailors and the confirmation of land to the west, there were still two things that Henry lacked before he could undertake any mission to locate and establish a transatlantic refuge.

He needed cannons and he needed navigational expertise.

It was not enough just to locate and establish a refuge. It was also necessary to establish a secure European base from which frequent voyages could be undertaken to the haven. Henry Sinclair had the islands as a base, but only cannon could make them secure. Cannon had been used for the first time in Europe in 1346 at the Battle of Crecy.[11] By 1381, cannon had been adapted for shipboard use by Carlo Zeno of Venice, at the Battle of Chioggia against the Genoese.[12] But, as an obscure lord of a remote island earldom in the far north, Henry had no apparent access to these advanced Mediterranean innovations in the use of shipboard cannon.

Likewise, although Henry had a good supply of practical seamen, he had no apparent access to the advanced navigational theories and mapmaking skills being developed in Italy, and above all in Venice.

By one of the most unlikely coincidences in history, *if it was a coincidence*, Henry obtained the expertise he needed from the two people in the Western world who could best supply it.

In 1391 a Venetian ship entered the Orkney earldom.[13] Aboard was Nicolo Zeno, brother of Carlo Zeno who had pioneered the use of cannon for Venice at the Battle of Chioggia. After spending some time with Sinclair, Nicolo Zeno wrote home to Venice and instructed his brother, Antonio, to join him in the Orkneys. Nicolo and Antonio Zeno together supplied the expertise that Henry lacked. They knew how to forge the new lightweight cannon for shipboard use, and they were familiar with the latest navigational theories and cartographic skills. They stayed in the service of Sinclair until death.[14]

This in itself is remarkable. These Venetians were definitely not nobodies. They were brothers of the most illustrious Venetian hero of the day, Carlo "The Lion" of Venice. They were among the foremost maritime experts of the time. Yet, somehow, they turn up in the far north just when needed *and they stay there*. Instead of returning to honours and comfort in Venice as scions of a very wealthy and powerful family, Nicolo and Antonio remained in the semi-barbaric earldom of Orkney with Sinclair.

The Zeno Narrative consists of the letters that Nicolo and Antonio wrote to their borther, Carlo, back home in Venice. These letters were arranged and edited by a Zeno descendant and finally published in 1558.

The Zeno expertise in cannon-making and in general marine matters proved sufficient so that the Sinclairs were able to hold on to the island stepping-stones for almost a century. This entailed throwing back several invasion attempts and pirate raids. We must conclude that the Venetian cannons served their purpose in making the European "staging area" secure.

Then comes the transatlantic voyage itself. *The Zeno Narrative* makes no mention of secret maps or of Norse traditions. Instead, a fisherman's tale of land to the west is offered as the reason why Henry Sinclair decided to discover new lands across the ocean . . .

> This nobleman (Sinclair) is therefore resolved to send forth with a fleet toward those parts, and there are so many who desire to join in the expedition on account of the novelty and strangeness of the thing that I think we shall be very strongly appointed without any public expense at all.

The Arms of the Earl of Orkney. These arms are taken from the *Amorial de Gelre*, 1369-88, an early heraldic work now in the Bibliothèque Royale, Brussels, and are almost certainly those of Henry Sinclair.

These arms represent a dragon bearing the burden of a crown around its neck. This creature may not seem much like our idea of a dragon, but our conception of a dragon as a reptilian-like giant lizard with claws and (sometimes) wings is actually fairly recent and is due to Oriental depictions of dragons dating from the mid 17th Century. The dragon shown here is actually the original kind of dragon as conceived by the Celts and Scandinavians from the remote past until the medieval period. The Scandinavians called dragons Great "Orms" (Worms) and saw them as segmented creatures of great size which lived mainly in the water. The Scots called dragons "*Afrancs*" or "Water Horses" and, like the Scandinavians, conceived them as a sort of giant worm or eel which had a horse's head. In addition to calling them "Water Horses", the Celts sometimes called dragons "Horse Eels". This dragon depicted on Sinclair's coat-of-arms is, in fact, what people claim to have seen in Loch Ness! And this artistic rendition may be taken as a "real", rather than stylized, dragon representation. This coat-of-arms has relevance to the secret history offered in this book. If the dragon is symbolic of wisdom, then Sinclair's coat-of-arms is a message: The Sinclairs, because of their secret knowledge, bear the burden of the true royalty or "Holy Blood" represented by the crown.

I set sail with a considerable number of vessels and men, but had not the chief command, as I had expected to have, for Sinclair went in his own person.

Our great preparations for the voyage to Estotiland were begun in an unlucky hour; for exactly three days before our departure, the fisherman died who was to have been our guide: nevertheless, Sinclair would not give up the enterprise, but in lieu of the deceased fisherman, took some sailors who had come out with him from the island.

Steering westwards, we sighted some islands subject to Frislanda, and passing certain shoals, came to Ledovo, where we stayed seven days to refresh ourselves and furnish the fleet with necessaries. Departing thence, we arrived on the first of April at the island of Ilofe; and as the wind was full in our favour, pushed on. But not long thereafter, when on the open ocean, there arose so great a storm that for eight days we were continuously in toil, and driven we knew not where, and a considerable number of vessels were lost to each other. At length, when the storm abated, we gathered together the scattered vessels, and sailing with a prosperous wind, we sighted land on the west.

Steering straight for it, we reached a quiet and safe harbour, in which we saw a very large number of armed people, who came running, prepared to defend the island. Sinclair now caused his men to make signs of peace to them, and they sent ten men to us who could speak ten languages, but we could understand none of them, except one who was from Iceland.

Being brought before our Prince and asked what was the name of the island, and what people inhabited it, and who was the governor, he answered that the island was called Icaria, and that all the kings there were called Icari, after the first king, who was the son of Daedalus, King of Scotland.

Daedalus conquered that island, left his son there for king, and gave them those laws that they retain to the present time. After that, when going to sail farther, he was drowned in a great tempest; and in memory of his death that sea was called to this day the Icarian Sea, and the kings of the island were called Icari. They were content with the state which God had given them, and would neither alter their laws nor admit any stranger.

They therefore requested our Prince not to attempt to interfere with their laws, which they had received from that king of worthy memory, and observed up to the present time; that the attempt

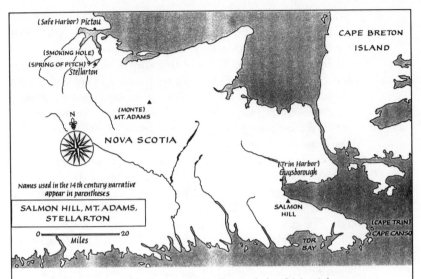

Burning open pitch deposits at Stellarton behind Mt. Adams were responsible for the "burning hill" Sinclair's explorers first thought they saw. The description confirms Cape Canso as the area of landfall on June 2, 1398.

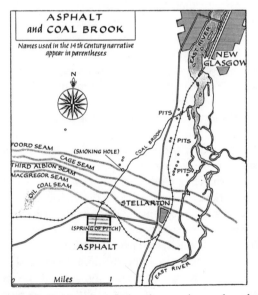

Small circles labelled "pits" are faults where coal seams have burned in historic times in the Stellarton deposits.

would lead to his own destruction, for they were all prepared to die rather than relax in any way the use of those laws. Nevertheless, that we might not think that they altogether refused intercourse with other men, they ended by saying that they would willingly receive one of our people, and give him an honourable position among them, if only for the sake of learning our language and gaining information as to our customs, in the same way as they had already received those ten other persons from ten different countries, who had come into their island.

To all this our Prince made no reply, beyond inquiring where there was a good harbour, and making signs that he intended to depart.

Accordingly, sailing round about the island, he put in with all his fleet in full sail, into a harbour which he found on the eastern side. The sailors went ashore to take in wood and water, which they did as quickly as they could, for fear that they might be attacked by the islanders and not without reason, for the inhabitants made signals to their neighbors by fire and smoke, and taking their arms, the others coming to their aid, they all came running down to the seaside upon our men with bows and arrows, so that many were slain and several wounded. Although we made signs of peace to them, it was of no use, for their rage increased more and more, as though they were fighting for their own very existence.

Being thus compelled to depart, we sailed along in a great circuit about the island, being always followed on the hill tops and along the seacoasts by a great number of armed men. At length, doubling the north cape of the island, we came upon many shoals, amongst which we were for 10 days in continual danger of losing our whole fleet, but fortunately all that time the weather was very fine. All the way till we came to the east cape we saw the inhabitants still on the hill tops and by the sea coast, howling and shooting at us from a distance to show their animosity towards us.

We therefore resolved to put into some safe harbour, and see if we might once again speak with the Icelander; but we failed in our object; for the people more like beasts than men, stood constantly prepared to beat us back if we should attempt to come on land. Wherefore, Sinclair, seeing he could do nothing, and that if we were to persevere in this attempt, the fleet would fall short of provisions, took his departure with a fair wind and sailed 6 days to the westwards; but the winds afterwards shifting to the southwest, and the sea becoming rough, we sailed 4 days with the wind aft, and finally sighted land.

Probable forms of north European ships in the late 1300s. The kind of vessels in which Sinclair's voyage was probably made.

As the sea ran high and we did not know what country it was, we were afraid at first to approach it, but by God's blessing the wind lulled, and then there came on a great calm. Some of the crew pulled ashore and soon returned with great joy with news that they found an excellent country and a still better harbour. We brought our barks and our boats to land, and on entering an excellent harbour, we saw in the distance a great hill that poured forth smoke, which gave us hope that we should find some inhabitants in the island. Neither would Sinclair rest, though it was a great way off, without sending 100 soldiers to explore the country, and bring us an account of what sort of people the inhabitants were.

Meanwhile, we took in a store of wood and water, and caught a considerable quantity of fish and sea fowl. We also found such an abundance of birds' eggs that our men, who were half famished, ate of them to repletion.

While were were at anchor there, the month of June came in, and the air in the island was mild and pleasant beyond description; but as we saw nobody, we began to suspect that this pleasant place was uninhabited. To the harbour we gave the name of Trin, and the headland which stretched out into the sea was called Cape Trin.

After eight days the 100 soldiers returned, and brought word that they had been through the island and up to the hill, and that the smoke was a natural thing proceeding from a great fire in the bottom of the hill, and that there was a spring from which issued a certain substance like pitch, which ran into the sea, and that thereabouts dwelt a great many people half wild, and living in caves. They were of small stature and very timid. They reported also there was a large river, and a very good and safe harbour.

When Sinclair heard this, and noticed the wholesome and pure atmosphere, fertile soil, good rivers, and so many other conveniences, he conceived the idea of founding a settlement. But his people, fatigued, began to murmur, and say they wished to return to their homes for winter was not far off, and if they allowed it once to set in, they would not be able to get away before the following summer. He therefore retained only boats propelled by oars, and such of his people as were willing to stay, and sent the rest away in ships, appointing me, against my will, to be their captain.

Having no choice, therefore, I departed, and sailed 20 days to the eastwards without sight of any land; then, turning my course towards the southeast, in 5 days I sighted on land, and found myself on the island of Neome and knowing the country, I perceived I was past Iceland; and as the inhabitants were subject to Sinclair, I took in fresh stores and sailed in 3 days to Frisland, where the people, who thought they had lost their Prince, in consequence of his long absence on the voyage we had made, received us with a hearty welcome . . . Concerning those things that you desire to know of me, as to the people and their habits, the animals, and the countries adjoining, I have written about it all in a separate book, which please God, I shall bring with me. In it I have described the country, the monstrous fishes, the customs and laws of Frisland, of Iceland, of Shetland, the Kingdom of Norway, Estotiland and Drogio; and lastly, I have written . . . the life and exploits of Sinclair, a Prince as worthy of immortal memory as any that ever lived, for his great bravery and remarkable goodness.[15]

And that is what *The Zeno Narrative* says about the transatlantic voyage. The "I" in the narrative is Antonio, for Nicolo had perished some years earlier in the service of Sinclair.

Antonio gives no date for this voyage, but it must have taken place sometime between 1396 and 1400 because of other facts known about Sinclair. Henry Sinclair had returned home by August of 1400 because European records state . . .

Henry Sainclaire was advertised of ane armie of Southerns that came to invade the Orchade Isles, who resisting them with his forces, through his too great negligence and contempt for their forces, left breathless, by blows battered so fast upon him, that no man was able to resist . . . was sclane thair crowellie be his innimis.[16]

This "armie of Southerns" was probably a minor military probe associated with the invasion of Scotland by England's King Henry IV in August, 1400. If Henry Sinclair was "slain cruelly by his enemies" in this campaign, his transatlantic voyage must have been earlier.

It is accepted now that the second "island" where Henry Sinclair stayed for the winter is Nova Scotia. The first to recognize this was Dr. William H. Hobbs, a geologist at the University of Michigan.[17] In 1951 he pointed out that the only open pitch deposits anywhere near the northeastern coast of North America were at Pictou and Stellarton in Nova Scotia. With that clue, other details of the narrative immediately fell into place, confirming Nova Scotia as the place where Sinclair stayed to found his settlement. Stellarton, Nova Scotia is the only location in

North America that satisfies *The Zeno Narrative's* description: "the smoke was a natural thing proceeding from a great fire in the bottom of the hill, and that there was a spring from which issued a certain substance like pitch, which ran into the sea."

The pitch deposits of Stellarton in Pictou county do run into the tidal river which also provides an excellent harbour, as the narrative insists. The native Micmac Indians of Nova Scotia called Stellarton-Pictou "that place where the water is ever strangely moving because of the rising of the bubbles" . . . moving bubbles of gases from underground pitch and coal deposits. In early pioneer days, miners' wives would ignite the bubbles rising from Pictou Harbour and make "natural gas" elements for boiling water. The pitch deposits around Stellarton have burned out of control in historical times, and faults in the coal seams argue that similar fires must have burned before the Europeans came. And, only around Stellarton did the Micmacs live in the numerous caves. Elsewhere, they lived in bark wigwams. The faults in the Stellarton coal seams provided convenient shelters.

Working backwards from this clue, Frederick Pohl realized that Mount Adams must have been the "great hill that poured forth smoke" of the narrative, because Mount Adams is in a direct line with the Stellarton pitch deposits *if viewed from Guysborough Harbour*. The headland that stretched eastwards could then only be Cape Canso. The geography of Nova Scotia fitted the descriptions of the narrative like a glove.

Ingeniously, Frederick Pohl saw a way of dating the expedition because of a statement about naming the harbour "Trin". Since it was often the practice of Christian explorers to give discoveries names from the religious calender, Pohl thought that "Trin" might refer to Trinity Sunday, the 8th Sunday after Easter. But as Easter is a moveable feast, so is Trinity Sunday. Pohl obtained dates for past Trinity Sundays from the Vatican Library and from the almanac of Augustus de Morgan. These dates were:

> June 6, 1395
> May 28, 1396
> June 17, 1397
> June 2, 1398
> May 25, 1399
> June 13, 1400

The Zeno Narrative says that the fleet was at anchor as the month of June came in and states, as an apparently logical conclusion, that the harbour and cape were named Trin immediately thereafter. Pohl saw that the only date that worked was June 2, 1398 . . . the fleet came to anchor on Saturday, June 1 when "the month of June came in" and the names were given the next day, Trinity Sunday, June 2, 1398.

And this date, 1398, is accepted as the year of Henry Sinclair's visit to Nova Scotia.

Antonio Zeno explained that Sinclair sent the fleet away and re-tained only rowing boats and those people who cared to face the winter with him. He spent at least one winter in Nova Scotia, but he could have spent two. *The Zeno Narrative* doesn't say and we have only the laconic record of his death in 1400.

Antonio neglects to say a lot in his letters, while a lot more can be read between the lines of the little that he does say. We are never told, explicitly, how far westward this land was from "Frislanda" which is what Antonio calls the Orkney group. He doesn't give the total days of westward sailing on the outbound voyage, though he must have kept a record. On the return voyage he specifies 28 days, but is careful to omit details of navigation in his letter. Presumably, Antonio would have given the navigational specifics to brother Carlo only in person, verbally. The exact location of Sinclair's discovery would remain a secret not com-mitted to writing.

Antonio says that Sinclair "conceived the idea of founding a settle-ment" and, apparently, stayed behind to do just that. If so, we can be sure that Sinclair kept the necessary provisions, tools, materials and personnel to do it. And to make a ship for the return voyage. Certainly, he would have kept a smith and a forge, and enough iron to make nails and other building necessities. He would have kept a good deal of weaponry, maybe even some of his Venetian cannon, and a number of men-at-arms. Although he was assured that the local inhabitants were of "small stature" and "very timid", the inhabitants of the first island, which was not so far away, had proved decidedly aggressive.

There's no reason to assume that Sinclair founded his settlement in the Stellarton-Pictou area. That was just the first over-land discovery made. Sinclair had the entire summer to explore the new land. He could have founded his settlement anywhere on the "island". What did he do after Antonio and the fleet left? And, was Sinclair just as happy that only a few chosen companions elected to remain with him? Where *did* he found his settlement? And how many people ever knew of its exact location in the New World?

These questions would seem impossible to answer, for Antonio's knowledge appears to end with the return of the fleet to Frislanda.

*   *   *

We might never have known the answers to some of these questions had it not been for the ingenuity of Frederick Pohl and his tireless historical detective work.

Pohl first pointed out that there *was* a record of what Sinclair did in Nova Scotia after Antonio Zeno left with the fleet. It is an Indian record, a sort of living legacy of Sinclair's visit. That record is the body of Micmac legends about the culture hero called Glooscap.

Other scholars before Pohl had concluded that the Glooscap legends referred to visits by early Europeans, but Pohl was the first to identify Glooscap as Henry Sinclair. Pohl was able to make a list of 17 specific similarities between Glooscap and Sinclair, including the fact that they each had three daughters. It seems significant that the Micmacs say they first met Glooscap at Pictou:

> Glooscap was the first,
> First and greatest,
> To come into our land —
> Into Nova Scotia . . .
> When the Master left Ukakumkuk,
> Called by the English Newfoundland,
> He went to Pictook or Pictou,
> Which means the rising of bubbles,
> Because at that place the water is
> Ever strangely moving.
> There he found an Indian village
> A town of a hundred wigwams.[18]

It seems reasonable that Sinclair would have transferred his people who had elected to remain with him to the place scouted out by the 100 soldiers. He certainly would not have stayed on the open Atlantic coast with only rowing boats. Such craft were good only for exploring inland waters, protected waters. Such waters stretch away from the excellent river-harbour of Stellarton-Pictou. Then, Sinclair wanted to find out about the country and the only way to do this was to open communication with the inhabitants. As Antonio tells us, the first landfall on the Atlantic at Trin was not inhabited. Sinclair had to go where the people were. Pictou.

Frederick Pohl traces the movements of Glooscap in great detail in his book, *Prince Henry Sinclair*. Glooscap stayed among the Micmacs only for part of one summer, over one winter, and he left them the next summer, but he made a great impression on the Indians during this short time:

> Glooscap being a handsome
> And very stately warrior
> With the air of a great chief,
> Was greatly admired by all,
> Especially by the women,
> So that everyone felt honoured
> Whose wigwam he deigned to enter.[18] (same source)

> He read the thoughts of men
> As though they were strings of wampum —
> Seeing deep into every heart.[19]

> He was ever a boon companion
> And a right valiant smoker.
> In all the world no man was
> Who loved a well-filled pipe
> Of good and fragrant tobacco
> So heartily as he.[19] (same source)

But aside from impressing the Micmacs with his smoking, and charming Micmac ladies with his visits to welcoming wigwams, the Indians were primarily impressed with Glooscap's tireless explorations of the country. Before winter set in, the Micmac legends record that he crossed the Nova Scotia peninsula to the Atlantic and returned to the Bay of Fundy.

Frederick Pohl, trying to reconstruct Glooscap's explorations in *Prince Henry Sinclair* suggests that Glooscap crossed over to the Atlantic by first paddling southwest along the Fundy shore to the site of modern Digby. From Digby, he followed the Fundy shore to modern Annapolis where he discovered the mouth of the Lequille stream. Following this as far as possible by canoe, "a short but rugged portage" would have brought the exploratory party to the Liverpool Head Lake, a long lake system

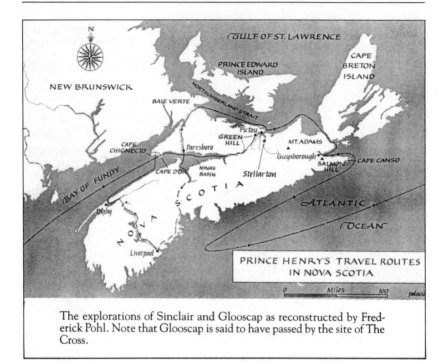

The explorations of Sinclair and Glooscap as reconstructed by Frederick Pohl. Note that Glooscap is said to have passed by the site of The Cross.

running across the peninsula and drained by the Mersey River which empties into the Atlantic at the site of present-day Liverpool, Nova Scotia. Except for that one rugged portage, the route was all water and easily managed by canoe. Pohl's intimate knowledge of Nova Scotia is revealed by this suggestion of route. It is the easiest way *across the widest part* of the Nova Scotia peninsula.

But I think Pohl, having made this ingenious suggestion, then committed a trivial error in supposing that Glooscap/Sinclair would have returned by the same route. Surely, any explorer would want to see as much of the country as possible, and would therefore use two different routes, to cross to the Atlantic and return to Fundy. Since the Lequille-lake-Mersey River route crossed at the widest point, surely it is not unjustifiable to speculate that Glooscap/Sinclair would also want to cross the peninsula at its narrowest point? That would give him a very good idea of the general width of the peninsula. This shortest route across the peninsula is the Gold-Gaspereau river route and, if he used it, Glooscap/Sinclair *must* have stood on top of the hill at The Cross. I've therefore

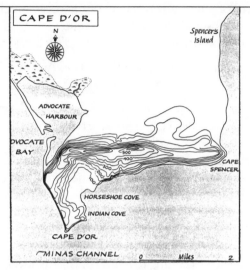

Map of "Owokun," Glooscap's winter home on the Cape D'Or promontory. Champlain called the place "Port of Mines" from which the present Minas Basin received its name.

Looking down on the existing lighthouse from on top of Cape D'Or. The turbulence in the water is a tidal rip formed by the two cubic miles of Minas Basin water emptying past Cape D'Or every 12 hours, and filling every 12 hours. It is the most spectacular tidal rip on the Bay of Fundy which has the highest tides in the world.

Photo by Michael Bradley.

taken the liberty of altering Pohl's map of Glooscap/Sinclair's explorations to show a peninsular crossing by both routes.

It is said that Glooscap wintered on Cape D'Or in the Bay of Fundy.

> He remained all winter near Cape D'Or, And that place still bears
> the name of his wigwam — "Owokun".[20]

"Owokun" means "where the deep sea dashes" and, sure enough, at the foot of Cape D'Or is the most impressive tidal race in the whole Bay of Fundy. And this is saying something for the Bay of Fundy has the highest tides in the world, and boasts many tidal races. But the one at Cape D'Or is the most spectacular because twice a day the entire Minas Basin drains and fills through a channel only 6 miles wide. Cape D'Or projects into this channel like a spear.

In choosing this site for his winter wigwam, Glooscap indeed revealed himself to be a "stately warrior" with the "air of a great chief", and one with European strategic training to boot. For the tip of Cape D'Or is not only picturesque, it commands a view of the entire length of the Bay of Fundy. Glooscap could see any unwelcome intruder long before they could arrive at Owokun. He could flee along any of the waterways that he could see from Cape D'Or. But, if Glooscap elected to fight, the steep promontory of Cape D'Or was easily defended by few against many.

Glooscap and his men were busy over the winter, for in the spring he unveiled his "stone canoe". Glooscap's canoe was "stone" because men could walk on the top of it as on a small island and, like a small island, it seemed to have trees growing on it. This is rather obviously a European decked ship. Glooscap gave a farewell feast before he sailed away. He "invited all to a parting banquet"

> By the great lake Minas shore
> On the silver waters' edge.
> And when the feast was over,
> Entered his great canoe
> And sailed away over the water,
> The shining waves of Minas.[21]

And, in memory of this parting, the Micmacs traditionally chanted:

> Nemajeeck, numeedich.[22]

This, as Frederick Pohl noted, sounds like the words of an old Norse sea-chanty sung when weighing anchor.

Nu mo jag, nu mo deg.[23]

There is, of course, no absolute proof that Glooscap was Henry Sinclair. Although most scholars believe that the Glooscap legends reflect "the encroachment of the Europeans", most also believe that the traditions refer to Europeans who came after John Cabot in 1497. But there is an interesting circumstance that argues against this. According to the Micmacs, Glooscap taught them how to fish with nets.

> Before he came they knew not
> How to make nets.[24]

Archeological excavations in Abanaki[25] Indian middens have shown that stone weights for fishing nets date back to about 1400 A.D. and that they appeared very suddenly. This date is suggestive and, of course, teaching the Indians to use nets would have been a natural past-time for Sinclair's Orkney and Shetland fishermen-sailors. They themselves would have fished with nets for winter provisions, and the Indians would have observed this.

The Micmac language is a strange one to European ears. There is no sound for "r" in the Micmac tongue and "l" substitutes. There are other peculiarities of pronunciation. "Jesus Christ" in Micmac becomes "Sasoo Gool" because of their difficulty in uttering certain sounds and refusal to end words with certain consonants.

Pohl has suggested that "Glooscap" may be an attempt to say "Jarl Henry" in Micmac. Sinclair was, of course, a Norwegian "Jarl" (the original form of "earl"), and the Indians may have heard his men referring to him by title. Again, a usual form of address in medieval Europe was to refer to the noble's holding. Sinclair's earldom of Orkney was then called "Orchadie" and Sinclair would have been called "Orchadie" by some of his men, as readers of Shakespeare will appreciate. This name, too, seems to be reflected in Micmac place-names, *but only along the routes where Glooscap is said to have travelled.* Particularly along rivers. This is the familiar Nova Scotian suffix "acadie" applied to things like the Shubenacadie River, and many other features of the province. Is this *acadie* a Micmac version of "Orchadie" as Sinclair was undoubtedly called on occasion? Was it applied to places where Sinclair travelled?

This seems at least plausible. It is an explanation for one of the more minor mysteries of history and geography. Nova Scotia was first known as

"Acadia" or as "Arcadia". It has been conjectured that this name may have derived from that *acadie* suffix that occurs so often in Micmac place-names. And it may. But there is also another possible origin, though one also linked to Sinclair by another route. It is possible that Henry Sinclair, like many explorers before and after him, named his new discovery after his familiar home. Since his earldom was "Orchadie", he may have called the new lands by the same name when he returned home and drew maps. This may have been gradually corrupted into "Arcadia" or "Acadia" among other and later mapmakers privy to Sinclair's discoveries.

There's another reason why Sinclair might have chosen this name for his new lands. There was an "Arcadia" in the world of ancient myth. It was a haven (as we shall see), but better known as a land of fertility and pleasant climate. Antonio Zeno stressed that Sinclair was impressed with "the wholesome and pure atmposhere, fertile soil, good rivers, and so many other conveniences". The new land was, truly, an "Arcadia" and a much better one than the rather barren and windswept "Orchadia" of the earldom. It would have been a good choice of name. It may be then that Sinclair's voyage is remembered on both European maps and in Micmac memory by the same words remembered for the same reasons by completely separate people. A rather remarkable coincidence.

*   *   *

From our new location in Kentville all of "Glooscap country" lay very literally at our feet. We made our home in the nearby town of New Minas which, as the name suggests, is on the Minas Basin. We lived in a mobile home park on a hill above and behind the town and we looked down on "the shining waves of Minas". In clear view from our front window was the peninsula on the other side of the basin which terminated in Glooscap's Cape D'Or.

Not only was our new location best for our business, but it rather uncannily fitted into the investigations we'd promised to pursue for the Ministry of Culture, Recreation and Fitness. Not only were we in the midst of Glooscap country, but we were only about 25 miles by highway from The Cross, a highway that followed, for the most part, the Gas-pereau River which passed not 3 miles from our living room. From the same front window, by craning our necks a bit, we could see the Oak Island (the Fundy one) at the mouth of the Gaspereau.

After work on long summer days, and some weekends, we had spare time to follow up our investigations "on location". Not infrequently, our research was combined with picnic outings with Jason and fishing along the Gaspereau River.

It was easy to follow in Glooscap's footsteps. In fact, by car it was unavoidable. One of the major tourist highways in the area is called "The Glooscap Trail." In the summertime, in the tourist season, it seems that every second road-side snack bar is called the "Glooscap Take-Out" and about every third souvenir shop is called "Glooscap Handicrafts". Many of the small towns around the Minas Basin have "Glooscap Festivals."

Whereas it is now accepted that Henry Sinclair voyaged to Nova Scotia in 1398, no one quite knows what to do with the historical repercussions. John Cabot is still honoured as the "first discoverer" whose name we know for certain. Another tourist highway is called "The Cabot Trail." Although there is ample evidence that Glooscap must have been Henry Sinclair, Nova Scotians seem reluctant to abandon their image of Glooscap as a Micmac warrior. On signs advertising all the snack bars and souvenir shops, he's invariably shown with an Indian feathered headdress (and sometimes a Plains Indian headdress borrowed from the Sioux on television). At Glooscap Festivals, the little towns construct giant effigies of the Micmac warrior. Some are pretty horrible.

Deanna and I frequently drove through all of the Glooscap memorabilia on our way to Cape D'Or. We went in search of the archeological site sought by Frederick Pohl from 1957 to 1960.[26] If Sinclair had indeed wintered on Cape D'Or with a fairly large number of Europeans, then surely there would be some evidence? Pohl looked for it with funds supplied by the Kermit Fischer Foundation and with scientists from the University of Maine. They found no definitive proof, but they did find several rectangular house sites on the promontory. The most promising site had been half-obliterated by a road. No artifacts of Sinclair's period were recovered, but the house sites themselves were suggestive of some sort of European occupation before any known colonial settlement.

In any case, a colonial settlement on Cape D'Or would make no sense, for the same reason there is no settlement on the Cape today. The promontory is rocky and high. There is no expanse of land that can be farmed and no pasturage for more than a few sheep or cows. It is a superb lookout, an easily defended winter headquarters for strangers in a strange land. And that's about all. Within this context, the rectangular house sites take on some significance.

Giant Glooscap effigy being prepared for the tourist season in Parrs-
boro, Nova Scotia.

Photo by Michael Bradley.

We frequently stood on top of Cape D'Or trying to see it as Sinclair would have seen it. The peculiar geography of Nova Scotia was spread out below from horizon to horizon. The puzzle of the Bay of Fundy (as it appears on many early maps) is immediately apparent to anyone from the top of Cape D'Or. You can see down the entire length of Fundy to where the end of Nova Scotia curves eastward toward the Atlantic. There can be no confusion about the distribution of land and water from atop Cape D'Or, just as there can be great confusion about geography for anyone approaching from the Atlantic. If Sinclair had ever stood on top of the Cape, and if he had crossed the peninsula twice as Glooscap probably did, then he knew enough about Nova Scotia to plan a refuge that could not be found unless someone knew where, and how, to find it.

Such a refuge would not be on top of Cape D'Or itself. For all of its advantages as a lookout, Cape D'Or is too exposed and too obvious a landmark and landfall for anyone sailing up the Bay of Fundy either by accident or design.

The ideal refuge would be inland, in the middle of the peninsula, with a lookout to either side. One on the Atlantic side, and one on the Fundy side. Inhabitants of the refuge would get ample warning of any intrusion from either coast. A simple smoke signal could be seen inland from either coast, *providing the refuge was located at the narrowest point of the Nova Scotia peninsula*. Providing that such a refuge was located on the hill top of The Cross. If Glooscap had ever travelled this narrowest trans-peninsular route, he would surely have appreciated the strategic position of The Cross, just as he appreciated the strategic view from Owokun.

I wondered if Glooscap had, in fact, wintered at Owokun as the Micmacs insisted. Certainly, he wintered there *part* of the time, and certainly *some* men wintered there *all* of the time. But had Sinclair and *all* of his men spent *all* of their time on Cape D'Or during the winter of 1398-1399? I began to suspect that Sinclair could well have taken some of his men inland in order to construct his settlement while others stayed at Owokun to serve as lookouts and to construct the ship that would take at least some of them back to Europe.

Antonio Zeno said that Sinclair intended to found a settlement. There is no evidence of a settlement on Cape D'Or. For reasons already stated, it wouldn't be a good spot for a settlement anyway. The best place for a settlement would be in the middle of the peninsula, where Jeanne McKay claimed to have found castle ruins.[27]

Could Sinclair have divided his force, leaving some at Owokun and taking the rest to start a rude settlement inland? This could obviously have happened, and the Micmacs would not necessarily have known about it immediately in order to connect the inland site with Glooscap. These Indians were relatively immobile in the winter because the river-routes were closed to them by ice. If Glooscap was at Owokun in the fall, and was there in the spring, the Micmacs would assume that he'd stayed there all winter. But the legends do not specifically say anything about what Glooscap did in the winter.

A party of determined Europeans could very well have left Owokun, spent the winter constructing a crude settlement at The Cross, and Sinclair could have returned in the spring to appear back at Owokun with his marvellous "stone canoe" when the Indians became mobile again after the spring thaw.

This could have happened . . . but did it? And surely the Indians would sooner or later have discovered any European settlement at The Cross. Just as surely, they would have woven any such settlement into their legends?

Is there any evidence that there was a settlement, and that the Indians knew about it?

There is a hint, no more. On one of his travels, Glooscap was supposed to have met the "Sorceress of the Atlantic" at some point along the peninsular river-crossing. We do not know who this female personage was, or where she resided for certain. We only know that Glooscap "met" her at some point in the peninsula. It is slim enough grounds for speculation, but speculate we must.

There are too many possibilities. First, the Indians regarded Glooscap specifically as someone who "came and went" with a few companions. They might not have connected people who stayed behind with Glooscap at all. The legends were handed down orally for hundreds of years before being recorded by scholars. A distinction may have been made from the beginning, or may have crept in over generations, be-tween the specific Glooscap and a few companions who "came and went" and those of Sinclair's party who remained in a settlement inland. The settlers might not have entered into the Glooscap cycle of legends, but into some other body of tradition.

Then, there's the fact that the Micmacs were essentially coastal people. Their means of livelihood and transportation were evolved around Nova Scotia's navigable waterways. Although they hunted, their primary occupation was fishing and gathering of clams. Their main mode of transport was by canoe. Although they knew the principal rivers leading inland, and had a good idea of the geography of the province, they didn't live further inland than rivers were navigable. Neither the Gold River nor the Gaspereau is navigable, even for a canoe, very far. They are useful as routes leading inland, but not as navigable waterways.

Few Micmacs could ever have lived in the mid-peninsular region around The Cross before modern colonial times. Then, the mere mention of a "Sorceress of the Atlantic" near such a region suggests some sort of reason for avoiding the place, a supernatural or "tabooed" location which might better be left alone. Maybe that's why we get no details about this "Sorceress" beyond the bare fact of her existence.

One can easily imagine that, *if Sinclair did establish a refuge settlement*, a "taboo" would be a useful mechanism to keep the local Indians away, to keep them vague about the nature of the settlement. After several hundred years of transmission, the Glooscap legends retain only a grain of truth. Perhaps Glooscap didn't "meet" the "Sorceress of the Atlantic"... perhaps he established her somewhere inland along the rivers. Certainly, one cannot found a settlement without women. Either the Sinclair expedition included women, or women were sent to the refuge once it was founded in the wilderness. It is possible, at least, that one of the refugees was a high-ranking women who governed the settlement for a while, as Esclarmonde de Foix governed a Cathar citadel a century before. The "de Bouillon complex" of which the Sinclairs were a part did not appear to be so "male chauvinist" as the usual feudal aristocracy of the times. A woman refugee-ruler might well be remembered as the "Sorceress of the Atlantic" if her community were protected by convenient taboos established by the mysterious strangers. She might even have been the "cruel queen" of Jeanne McKay's history.

But this is pure speculation.

Aside from Glooscap who "came and went" over a relatively brief period of time, is there any evidence that the Micmacs were exposed to any long term European influence before Columbus?

The answer to this is "yes", but the evidence leads in surprising directions. Henry Sinclair did voyage to Nova Scotia and he may well have been connected with the Templar mission to discover a refuge.

But perhaps he did not need to carve a refuge from virgin wilderness.

Perhaps a ready-made European site of great antiquity was already at The Cross. Perhaps Henry built on a foundation of earlier ruins. He did not necessarily plant the oak signposts. Maybe he followed them.

But before we follow the oak signposts ourselves, I should mention that there is evidence that Sinclair/Glooscap visited New England after leaving Minas Basin. Whether this New England visit was a short sojourn before returning to Orkney, or whether the New England interlude is of greater significance is a question that no one can answer at present. The following story of the intriguing effigy at Westford relies on Pohl's *Prince Henry Sinclair*.

The Micmac Indians of Nova Scotia were part of the Abenaki group of Algonkian-language speakers who inhabited Nova Scotia and New Brunswick in Canada, and from Maine to Massachusetts in what is now New England. Glooscap legends, though not nearly as detailed as the Nova Scotia traditions, extend as far south as Boston. Charles G. Leland in his Preface to *Kul skap the Master* stated: "A Penobscot woman once told me that it was Klus-kabe who divided the great mountain of which Boston originally consisted into three hills".[28]

There is intriguing evidence that Sinclair did visit Massachusetts after his Nova Scotia explorations. The evidence is an effigy of a medieval knight punched into gneiss along the old Tyngsboro trail near Westford, Massachusetts. Pohl speculates that Sinclair sailed away from Nova Scotia toward New England, sighted land in eastern Massachusetts, and made for the highest hill in sight. This was Prospect Hill at Westford, 465 feet in altitude. From the summit, Pohl speculates, Sinclair would have been able to see the general features of this new land he'd found. But the climb to the top of the hill seems to have proved too much for one of the knight's in Sinclair's entourage, for someone punched an effigy of a 14th-century knight into a ledge on the hill and this figure carries a broken sword, symbol of death.

For a long time, residents of Westford just assumed that the weathered figure on the ledge was the work of Indians and no one paid much attention to it. But in 1940 a man named William B. Goodwin saw the figure, looked at it carefully, and made out the much-weathered representation of the sword as well as some other details that argued a European origin for the figure. Later, Frank Glynn, president of the Connecticut Archeological Society, sent a drawing of the sword to Prof. T. C. Lethbridge, curator of the University Museum of Archeology and Ethnology,

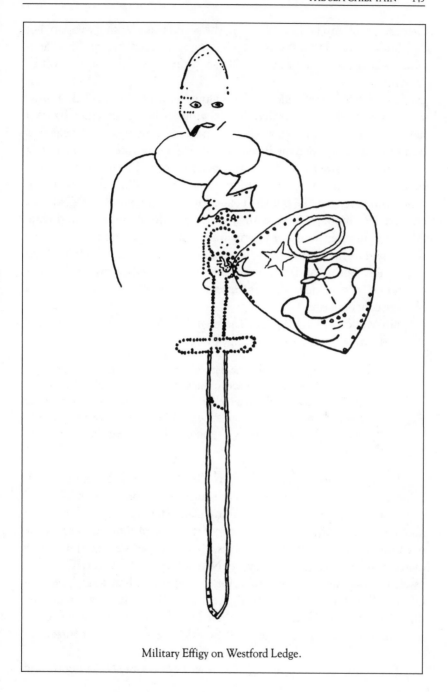

Military Effigy on Westford Ledge.

Cambridge. Glynn had assumed that the sword was a Viking weapon, but Lethbridge replied that it was not a Viking sword, but "a large hand-and-a-half wheel pommel sword" of 14th-century type.[29] It was a Scottish "claymore".

Glynn, and later Frederick Pohl along with Dr. Donnell B. Young, visited Westford and made detailed drawings of the entire effigy figure. I have reproduced Pohl's reconstruction here, and the figure is revealed to be a representation of a medieval knight. He wears a steel "helmet" of a type called a basinet which was in vogue for only 25 years, from 1375 to 1400. The sword is a type in fashion from 1350 to 1400. Glynn and Pohl were even able to make out the coat-of-arms on the knight's shield ... a crescent, a "mullett" (like a star) and a buckle above a masted ship. Although neither Pohl nor Glynn was aware of it at the time, because they were not heraldry experts, the coat-of-arms proved to be that of the Gunn clan (Sutherland) or Gunne clan (Caithness) bearing the "Galley of Orkney," according to Burke's *General Armory*, which lists a number of obscure coats-of-arms.

Iain Moncrieffe in his book, *The Highland Clans*, makes the following statement in acceptance of the effigy evidence:

> Startling enough, the earliest surviving example of the Gunn chief's coat-of-arms appears to have been punch-marked by a medieval armourer-smith on a rock in Massachusetts. The heater shaped shield there, borne by what appears to be the effigy of a fourteenth-century knight, appears to show a distinctively Norse-Scottish character.[30]

The cycle of Glooscap (Kulo-skap, Kul skap, Klus-kabe, etc.) legends insist that the hero ventured as far south as Boston, and at Westford there's an effigy of a knight of the Gunn clan, a family likely to have been allied with Sinclair, wearing the proper weapons of Sinclair's era. Aside from the Micmac legends themselves, then, Sinclair's expedition left its own document attesting the voyage. Needless to say, however, it is safe to assert that the majority of establishment experts either don't "see" the effigy at Westford at all (it *is* badly weathered) or prefer to attribute the crude figure to local Indians. How these local Indians could have been so well informed about obscure north Scottish heraldry is, or course, not explained.

The center of Glooscap legends, is without doubt, Nova Scotia and particularly the region around Minas Basin. However, the tradition *does* extend south to Massachusetts. We will remember that Sinclair *could have spent* two winters across the Atlantic, and did spend one of them at "Owokun", according to Nova Scotia Micmacs. It is therefore barely possible that Sinclair might have spent his second winter in Massachusetts, although no Abenaki (Penobscot or other) legends refer to this. But, if Sinclair did spend a winter in Massachusetts, it is possible that he established a "settlement" or outpost somewhere in New England. The Newport Tower discussed earlier also dates from about Sinclair's time, and then there are the alleged ruins along the Charles River in Massachusetts itself. Both the Newport Tower and the alleged Charles River ruins have been championed as "Norumbega" by American enthusiasts intent upon claiming significant pre-Columbian settlement for America in competition with Canada.

And, of course, the American enthusiasts may be right. There is no absolute proof of where Sinclair founded his settlement in Estotiland, and we have no idea of the geographical extent of Estotiland as Sinclair and Antonio Zeno may have conceived it. The "Zeno Map of the North" does show some land south of Estotiland. This is labelled "Drogio". Drogio may, indeed, represent Massachusetts. But there are no settlements indicated in Drogio.

Chapter Five

Doors

Nova Scotia is like a small country. Within the space of very few miles, you can traverse distinct regions. Not only does the character of the land change, but the orientation of the people changes as well. Nova Scotia is unlike Ontario in this respect, and equally unlike vast areas of the United States which now reflect a uniform North American "megaculture" for many hundreds of miles at a stretch.

Whereas around the Bay of Fundy, and Minas Basin in particular, is Glooscap country, just 25 miles away across the peninsular spine of the province "Glooscap the warrior" disappears entirely. He is replaced by no less dubious pirates. The Atlantic coast opposite Minas Basin is pirate country. The town of Chester is the centre of this buccaneer ethos. You can eat at "Blackbeard Take-Outs" and buy souvenirs at any number of "Pirate's Chest" curio shops. During the tourist season, both the Indian and the pirate orientations take on economic, if not historic, validity. The tourist season is short and Nova Scotians make the most of it. Canadian history has not predisposed them toward mercy for visitors from rich central Canada, to say no more.

Chester is just 17 miles from The Cross. It is the centre of pirate country because of Oak Island.

In 1795 three boys discovered a curious and roughly circular depression in the ground at one end of Oak Island. An oak tree grew beside this depression and one of its limbs extended out over it, and from this limb dangled (so some say) a ship's block, or pulley. Others deny the ship's block and say only that the limb was scarred, as if by the action of a rope against its bark. In any case, it was obvious to the boys that some pirate

Aerial view of Oak Island showing major landmarks on it. The mouth of the Gold River is in the upper left of this photograph. If you stand on the island, opposite the mainland and at the narrowest point of the chanel between the island and the mainland (where the causeway meets the island) the Gold River entrance is to your right. This photo is taken from a postcard printed by the Book Room in Halifax. The descriptive paragraph on the back of the card reads:

"It is believed that the notorious pirate Captain Kidd buried a vast treasure on this island, and since 1795 countless adventurers and many well financed companies have sought to wrestle this great treasure from the 'Money Pit,' as it came to be called . . . "

Captain Kidd was born in New York in the late 1600s and was hanged in the mid-1700s. He may have used the "Money Pit," though there is no evidence whatsoever to support this idea, but he did not dig it. Spruce planks recovered from deep in the pit have carbon dated to 860 A.D. and 1135 A.D., about 500 to 800 years before Captain Kidd's time.

Courtesy The Book Room, Halifax.

had used the limb to lower a treasure chest into a hole. The depression was caused by the re-filled earth settling. They dug.

Two feet down they came across a layer of purposefully laid stones. Ten feet further down, they came upon the first of many oak-log platforms laid across their path of descent. These oak-log platforms proved to be laid at a distance of 10 feet apart as one progressed downwards. These three boys, who seem to have been highly motivated, dug down more than 30 feet and encountered three oak-log platforms before calling for adult aid. This was not immediately forthcoming because the farmers in the area were too busy with more mundane tasks.

But adult interest was soon kindled.

Discovery of the laid-stone platform and of the multiple oak-log ones indicated beyond doubt that *something* of great value must have been buried in the hole. Or, so everyone assumed then and still assumes to the present day.

As early as 1802 some 30-odd financial backers got together to form the Onslow Company with the object of speedily recovering the undoubted treasure. They hired workers and began to dig the shaft that the boys had begun. The Onslow Company reached the 93-foot level, discovering the same oak-log platforms every 10 feet, before the pit began to flood. Soon, one bucket of water was being removed from the shaft for every two of earth. This flooding of the pit defeated the Onslow Company and has, in one way or another, thwarted every treasure-seeker since.

The Onslow Company gave up in 1804. It was not until 1849 that the Truro Company was formed to start a fresh assault on the mystery. When flooding made it clear that the shaft could not be excavated, the Truro Company turned to probing with a pod auger of the sort then used for prospecting for coal. Five probes were made. On its most promising exploration the augur went through a 5-inch oak platform at the 98-foot level and "dropped 12 inches and then went through four inches of oak; then it went through 22 inches of metal in pieces, but the augur failed to take any of it in except three links, resembling an ancient watch chain. It then went through eight inches of oak, which was thought to be the bottom of the first box and the top of the next: then 22 inches of loose metal, the same as before; then four inches of oak and six inches of spruce; then into clay seven feet without striking anything else.[1]"

For all the effort, the Truro Company recovered no treasure . . . only the three small chain-links. But there was general agreement that the augur had drilled through two oak chests, one on top of the other, that were filled with metal in pieces, hopefully coin.

The Truro Company, too, was defeated by the flooding. Although the augur probe results had been tantalizing, it was clear that no treasure could be recovered until the flooding was conquered, but this was beyond the technology of the times.

The Oak Island Association was formed on April 3, 1861 "for the purpose of making excavations on Oak Island in search of Hidden Treasures". They proposed to tackle the challenge of the flooded shaft itself and to bail continuously with newly-invented powerful steam pumps. This seemed to work for a time, but then, when workers reached the 105-foot level — almost within reach of whatever had been penetrated by the Truro Company's augur — the entire shaft seemed to collapse downwards. Its bottom seemed to drop out, or at least to drop many feet, and the presumed treasure dropped with it.

Other companies and other treasure-seekers continued in pursuit of the elusive pirate hoard. With the original pit in ruins, the technique became one of sinking other pits next to the original shaft, and trying to keep the water down by pumping from one or more of these secondary shafts, and then by digging horizontal tunnels from the secondary pits at a level where the treasure might be intercepted. In 1897 a probe drill apparently encountered the same two oak chests that the Truro Company's augur had penetrated almost 50 years before. These objects had fallen to the 150-160-foot level, and it was from this depth that a scrap of parchment was brought to the surface. It had writing on it, what looked like the letters "vi" or "ui" in a fancy hand script. Eleven feet lower, at the 171-foot level, the 1897 probe drill encountered an iron plate which seemed to be a true floor. In 1909, the most famous treasure-hunter, future U.S. President, Franklin D. Roosevelt, bought shares in the "Old Gold Salvage and Wrecking Company" which prepared to assault the mystery anew. Although this effort was no more successful than any of the others, FDR retained a lively and life-long interest in the continuing excavations of "The Money Pit". Even during World War II, Roosevelt wrote letters of enquiry concerning the latest attempt to recover the presumed treasure.

People are still at it.

The present searchers are represented by Triton Alliance Ltd., formed in April 1969.

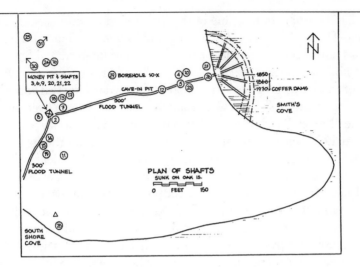

Plot of additional shafts dug by treasure-seekers on Oak Island.

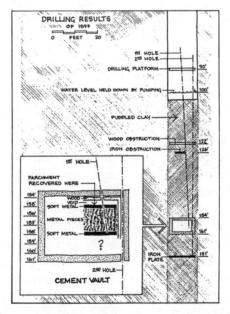

Cross-section of more important discoveries in the Oak Island "Money Pit."

Courtesy D'Arcy O'Connor.

This is the barest outline of the Oak Island treasure-seeking operations. The entire story is fascinating and extremely detailed. Plenty of books have been written about the Oak Island mystery, and one of the best and most recent is *The Money Pit* by D'Arcy O'Connor.[2] And. I understand, this 1972 book may soon be reissued in a revised edition.

The "treasure site" on Oak Island has become known over the years as the "Money Pit", but whether this is because of the money poured into it over 190 years (an estimated $2-million) or because of the treasure still hopefully thought recoverable from it, is hard to say. In order to offset the costs of excavation on the site, which is now a confusion of other shafts and a warren of horizontal tunnels, the present operators have established a tourist museum. Admission is charged and you can buy souvenirs. The museum is worth a visit because it displays items found throughout the island, not only things recovered from the pit. A pair of scissors of 16th Century Latin American workmanship is on display, odd bits and pieces of metal recovered from various levels of various shafts, an old shoe dating from the 18th Century. There are photographs of some of the inscribed stones found on the island, plus samples of the curious "putty-like" substance found in the Money Pit and the coconut-fibre found not only in the pit, but also on some of the island's beaches.

But the most interesting evidence must be the carbon dates obtained from wood found in the pit. The analysis done by Geochron Labs in Cambridge, Massachussetts raises some problems. All of the oak sample analyses have proved to date from between 1550 and 1600 A.D. which is, more or less, the proper "pirate era". But the spruce planks are another matter. Two have been recovered from the pit. Sample GX-1692 dated to about 860 A.D. Sample GX-1691 dated to about 1135 A.D. I have verified these dates with Geochron.[3]

Although these embarrassingly early and inexplicable dates are noted in the Triton museum, all of the attention and speculation is focused upon the artifacts dating from the proper and hopeful pirate era of the 1600s.

The treasure-seekers have now carried their investigations down past the 200-foot level in the pit. And, at this level, an important discovery was made: *the pit ended in a deep and natural cavern far underground.* Television cameras lowered into this cavern show it to be a natural formation. Some photos displayed at the museum also purport to show part of a chest, or at least a plank, and part of a human corpse. For what it is worth, I looked at these photos carefully but just didn't see these objects

KRUEGER ENTERPRISES, INC.
GEOCHRON LABORATORIES DIVISION

24 BLACKSTONE STREET • CAMBRIDGE, MASSACHUSETTS 02139 • (617) 876-3691

7-20-87

Dear Mr. Bradley:

I can confirm your information about two C-14 analyses done by Geochron Labs in December, 1969.

Sample Lab Number	Material	Age (C-14 Years Before Present) "Present" is AD 1950
GX-1691	Wood	815 ± 110 B.P. 1 sigma error
GX-1692	Wood	1090 ± 140 B.P. 1 sigma error

Please note that "C-14 Years" do not correspond exactly to calendar years. The dates as reported here are in "C-14 Years" before A.D. 1950.

Sincerely yours,

C. H. Sullivan
C-14 Lab Manager

SPECIALISTS IN GEOCHRONOLOGY & ISOTOPE GEOLOGY

Dear Mr. Bradley

I can confirm your information about two C-14 analyses done by Geochron Labs in December, 1969.

Sample Lab Number	Material	Age (C-14 Years Before Present) "Present" is AD 1950
GX-1691	Wood	815±110 B.P. 1 sigma error
GX-1692	Wood	1090±140 B.P. 1 sigma error

Please note that "C-14 Years" do not correspond exactly to calendar years. The dates as reported here are in "C-14 Years" before A.D. 1950.

Sincerely yours,

C.H. Sullivan
C-14 Lab Manager

in them, only a lot of murky shadows that could be interpreted as just about anything, or nothing.

In the absence of much "hard data" from the site, some attention has been paid to "psychic probes" of the pit. Psychics have been used successfully in "establishment archeology" to predict what may be found at a site and to map sites before excavation. Professor Norman Emerson at the University of Toronto used psychics to locate and "pre-map" a number of Ontario Iroquois sites.[4] "Psychic Archeology" is routinely used in the Soviet Union, Great Britain and is even recommended by the State Archeologist of Massachusetts. So, "psychic" probes are not necessarily bunk, but they may be in any given case. This forewarning having been duly delivered, it can be said that psychic Charles B. Thomas announced in 1954:

> It is my belief, which is based on an accurate knowledge of the divine plan of the ages, that the treasure will consist of a museum that will contain the sacred relics of the typical Kingdom of Israel, the gold and sacred things of the temple of Jerusalem, together with manuscripts and documentary evidence that will throw some light on human history.[5]

Another psychic investigator of Oak Island, a native of Huntsville, Texas, who chose to remain anonymous, said in 1976:

> And there will be things there that you cannot imagine. There is all kinds of religious material down there and all kinds of documents too. There'll be a blue book found down there with a cross on its cover. I'm sure of that. There'll be chalices and statues and possibly the Holy Grail. The dates of some of this stuff will go back three thousand years; things that were kept for centuries and then stolen from many parts of the world.[6]

The Holy Grail?

One may have grave reservations about the psychic opinions, but it seems at least rather odd that whereas the active diggers have been uniformly motivated by visions of pirate gold, the psychics have uniformly received visions of religious treasures.

If this all seems confusing, one fact is certain: the famed Money Pit is at least partly a natural feature. It is a deep limestone sinkhole leading up from a cavern below the island. The cavern and the sinkhole were probably formed by tidal action and by surface water draining down through a fissure which expanded through the ages. This is a common geographic feature.There are other similar sinkhole-and-cavern systems not far from Oak Island on the Nova Scotia mainland. A small hoard of pirate treasure was even allegedly found in one of them. No one dug the Money Pit. The pit was already there.

People merely adapted it for their own purposes. First, it seems that the bottom was sealed off with an iron plate. Then, successive layers of earth alternating with oak-log platforms had been added to make a more secure floor sometime in the late 1500s or early 1600s. Some pirate may have done this to hide his treasure. This treasure is not likely to be recovered easily if at all. Investigators have flooded and collapsed the pit with their frenzied digging. The floor fell out. Whatever was in the pit has now fallen down into the deep cavern.

But it seems that our hypothetical pirate was not the first person to use this natural pit.

Someone else apparently had the same idea, but earlier. They used spruce platforms instead of oak-log ones to reinforce their floor. These spruce planks date from 860 to 1135 A.D., long before Blackbeard and William Kidd.

Maybe there's a clue here. Did these "pre-pirate" people use spruce *because there were no oaks on the island when they were working?*

Did they, perhaps, plant the acorns to make the oak signposts so that when the pirates finally did come the island was over-grown with oaks and *that* timber became the obvious and natural one for the pirate platforms? So that oaks became ubiquitous and gave the island its present name?

Of course, it may be coincidence and no more that the two spruce planks happen to date 500 years older than all the oak logs.

The important point is that someone was busy making planks and working in the Money Pit five centuries before any pirates. Who were they? Why were they there?

Then, there might be other questions. What, precisely, was a pirate? How did the whole piracy bit start? And why is it that the traditional "Jolly Roger"pirate flag . . . you know, the skull and crossbones . . . *looks so damnably identical to the skull and crossbones on Freemason gravestones?*

*   *   *

Deanna and I strolled out of the Oak Island museum and began our

Masonic tombstone of the 17th Century, the "skull and cross-bones" familiar from the pirates' "Jolly Roger" flag. Were some pirates the Holy Blood's navy?

Photo by Michael Baigent.

tour of the island. The focal point of the trail, which is marked with signposts, is, of course, the Money Pit. But we were not much interested in seeing it. We were more interested in the fact that the island trail followed the route of something very familiar, a path of rubble-work stones like we'd seen often enough before at The Cross. This path or "lane" of laid stones disappeared and reappeared at intervals beneath the dirt trail like an undulating spine. The trail itself was much wider than this central stonework backbone because of the many tourists who wandered along it daily and who had widened the trail over the years. Still, the stonework seemed to have dictated the route of the trail, but was obviously older since the dirt of the trail often covered it for a distance of many feet or yards. Maybe the foundation of a ruined wall had once snaked through the underbrush and had formed a convenient footpath around the island.

Walls of stone branched off the trail to either side, too. They had not received any attention from treasure-obsessed investigators. It was impossible to tell their age. Some were marked on our souvenir pirate chart as "pirate walls". They looked like the stonework at The Cross. As far as we could discover from our research in the Nova Scotia Archives in Halifax, at least some of these walls already existed at the time of the first modern colonial survey. In fact, this survey seemed to sub-divide Oak Island in a very strange way because the divisions seemed to follow the course of the walls.

On the north shore of the island we looked past the swaying sailboat masts of the nearby mainland marina and saw the broad mouth of the Gold River beckoning at exactly 2 miles distance *to our right*. Enter the river and follow its course for 17 miles and you'd come to the same kind of stone walls on the hill top of The Cross.

We admired the oaks. The island was covered with mature oaks in the 1760s when it received its present English name. An oak takes about 200 to 250 years to mature. No one knows how many generations of oaks may have matured from acorns on Oak Island since they were first introduced from the mainland. Oaks were plentiful, obviously, around 1600 A.D. when the "pirates" laid all those oak-log platforms in the Money Pit. Oaks may not have been so plentiful 500 years earlier when someone used spruce instead. Assuming that the oaks cut by "pirates" in the 1600s were the first mature generation of trees, then they'd been planted 200 years or so earlier, or, at about the time of Sinclair's visit.

But there may have been many generations of oaks. There was no way to tell.

*   *   *

One of the most familiar landmarks in Halifax is the church at the corner of Spring Garden and Barrington. It has a bronze plaque on the front, easily visible to passers-by on Spring Garden, commemorating the work of Father Pierre Maillard. He was a Jesuit of the 1700s who preached among the Micmacs. He claimed to have invented an "alphabet" for them, to suit their language, and claimed to have translated the Bible and psalms into Micmac using this alphabet. This church is a familiar landmark, and the plaque commemorates comfortable history.

Haligonians accept the plaque without a second thought, as they pass by, but the history described is a lie.

Bishop Colin F. MacKinnon, Bishop of Arichat, and a leading authority on the Micmac Indians, wrote:

> When the French first arrived in Acadia, the Indians used to write on bark, trees and stones, engraving signs with arrows, sharp stones, or other instruments. They were accustomed to send pieces of bark, marked with these signs, to other Indians of other tribes, and to receive back answers written in the same manner, just as we do with letters and notes. Their chiefs used to send circulars, made in the same manner, to all their men in time of war to ask their advice, and to give directions.[7]

The French first arrived in Acadia in 1604. If the Micmacs had a writing system then, Maillard certainly did not teach it to them because he had not been born.

A rather closer look at the Micmac writing system shows that it isn't an alphabetic system. It is more like a hieroglyphic system. It has focused some scientific attention in recent years because it appears to be North African in origin. Professor Barry Fell of Harvard has compared Micmac hieroglyphs with an Egyptian hieroglyphic system which was in use over much of North Africa. The results are startling. I've included renderings of Psalm 116 in Micmac and in the North African hieroglyphs as compared by Professor Fell. There's also a list of common words compared in both scripts.

Maillard could not have invented this Micmac hieroglyphic system. It is obviously related to wide-usage Egyptian hieroglyphs. These were not

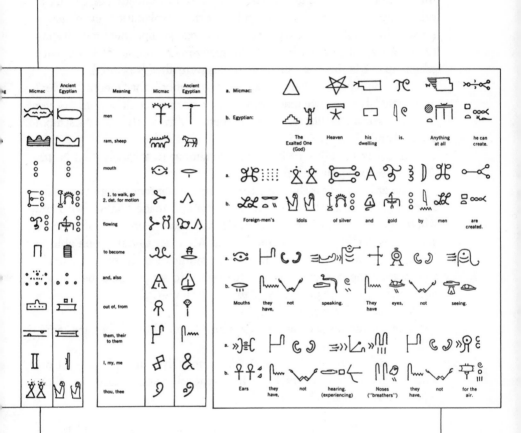

Left – Micmac and Egyptian symbols compared. After Barry Fell.

Right – Psalm 116 *Non nobis Domine* rendered in Micmac hieroglyphics by Maillard in 1738 and in Egyptian hieroglyphics. After Barry Fell.

deciphered until Champollion published his famous work in 1823. Maillard died in 1762. Maillard did not invent this writing system for the Indians . . . *He learned it from them.*[8] And he translated religious material into their language using the writing system they already possessed. No other explanation is possible, and no other explanation even makes sense. Why would a French priest invent a strange alphabet for his Indian flock? Why not just teach them the ready-made Roman alphabet with which all of Maillard's religious materials were already printed?

The comparative chart shows Micmac symbols for "metal", "silver" and "gold". But the Micmacs were a stone-age people. They did not use metal, or know the different kinds of metal. Why did they have a symbol for gold and silver?

And why is their writing system so similar to a widely-used North African hieroglyphic script?

The only answer is that North Africans, *or someone using an originally North African script,* came to Nova Scotia and made contact with the Micmac Indians. Further, this contact must have been maintained over some considerable period of time for the Micmacs to have been able to learn, and to adopt, a novel kind of communication. It isn't very likely that something so complex as a hieroglyphic script could have been adopted by an entire people from a short-term visit.

Who could have come? Why?

The answer has been around for a long time. The Celtiberians came. They came for metal.

Among Aristotle's "Minor Works", probably written by one of his students in the 4th Century B.C., there's the following passage in Section 84 of *On Marvellous Things Heard:*

> In the sea outside the Pillars of Hercules they say that an island was found by the Carthagenians, a wilderness having wood of all kinds and navigable rivers, remarkable for various kinds of fruits, and many days' sailing distance away. When the Carthagenians, who were masters of the western ocean, observed that many traders and other men, attracted by the fertility of the soil and the pleasant climate, frequented it because of its richness, and some resided there, they feared that knowledge of this land would reach other nations, and that a great concourse to it of men from various lands of the earth would follow. Therefore, lest the Carthagenian Empire itself should suffer injury, and the dominion of the sea be wrested from their

hands, the Senate of Carthage issued a decree that no one, under penalty of death, should thereafter sail thither, and they massacred all who resided there.[9]

About 300 years later, Diodorus of Sicily wrote in the last century B.C.:

> Over against Africa lies a very great island in the vast ocean, many days' sail from Libya westwards. The soil there is very fruitful, a great part whereof is mountainous, but much likewise a plain, which is the most sweet and pleasant part, for it is watered with several navigable rivers . . . The mountainous part of the country is clothed with very large woods, and all manner of fruit trees and springs of fresh water . . . There you may have game enough in hunting all sorts of wild beasts . . . This island seems rather to be the residence of some of the gods, than of men.
>
> Anciently, by reason of its remote location it was altogether unknown, but afterwards discovered on this occasion: The Phoenicians in ancient times undertook frequent voyages by sea, in way of traffic as merchants, so that they planted many colonies in Africa and in these western parts of Europe. These merchants succeeding in their undertaking and thereupon growing very rich, passed at length beyond the Pillars of Hercules, into the sea called the Ocean. At first they built a city called Gades. The Phoenicians, having found out the coasts beyond the Pillars, and sailing along by the shore of Africa, were on a sudden driven by a furious storm off into the main ocean, and after they had lain under this violent tempest for many days, they at length arrived at this island, and so they were the first that discovered it.[10]

Aristotle and Diodorus are writing about Carthagenians and Phoenicians. What do they have to do with the Celts? The answer is simple: *they were the original "Celts"*. Carthage was a colony of Phoenicia. "Phoenician" means "red haired". The Phoenicians and the Carthagenians expanded all across North Africa and western Europe. They pushed past the Straits of Gibraltar and founded the city of Gades (present day Cadiz) in Spain. While active in Spain, these Phoenician/Carthagenian descendants are called "Celtiberians" by archeologists. Later, some sailed away from Spain and colonized the British Isles, where they are simply called "Celts" by archeologists. In their migrations through the Mediterranean, these Celts picked up a number of different languages and alphabets.

These languages and writing systems were in use by different Celtic groups at different times. Memories of some of these scripts were retained up until the medieval period in Ireland. The *Book of Ballymote*, believed to have been composed about 1200 A.D., gives an alphabet, described as "African". Until recently, scholars considered that this "African" script was some sort of cryptic monkish secret alphabet, or maybe just gibberish, but since 1960 this alphabet has been shown to be an actual ancient North African one in use about 1000 B.C.[11]

The Celts of Ireland, Wales and England... the "Ancient Britons"... were at least partly of Phoenician/Carthagenian stock via Iberia. They used, or at least they preserved, a multitude of writing systems with which they had come into contact on their long migration from Palestine, through North Africa and Spain, and finally to the British Isles.

There would be nothing particularly strange about such Celts or Celtiberians bringing an Egyptian-like hieroglyphic system of writing from North Africa or Spain to Nova Scotia. They brought a North African alphabet to Ireland, preserved in the *Book of Ballymote*.

There is an undoubted Celtic or "Celtiberian" influence among the Algonquin Indian languages of the New England and Nova Scotia coasts. This has long been recognized by some scholars, and long disputed by others. Professor Barry Fell gives a list of Algonquin and Gaelic words having the same meanings and the same sounds. The list is lengthy and impressive. Even many phrases with the same meanings or descriptive force sound the same in both languages.[12] Further, Algonquin legends state specifically that some of their ancestors came from across the Atlantic, and that white men lived among them in times long past. Some traditions refer to the previous use of metals.

The Micmacs of Nova Scotia are a part of the northeastern complex of Algonquin-speakers, and they seem to have been exposed to rather more Celtic influence than some of the other related Algonquin-speaking groups.

Aside from linguistic peculiarities, it is a curious fact that many northeastern Indians did apparently once make use of metals, but subsequently abandoned the technology. No one knows why. Perhaps the number of Celtic immigrants with metallurgical knowledge was limited. When these died out then their mixed descendants could not maintain the skill of extracting and working metals.

This Celtic contact seems to have been a relatively massive and long-standing one. Phoenician/Carthagenian voyages beyond the Pillars of Hercules could have been made as early as 700 B.C. The "Celtiberians" and the "Celts" of the British Isles could have continued to voyage across the Atlantic for many hundreds of years. In fact, there are Celtic traditions of transatlantic voyages to a blessed western land even up to the Middle Ages. Saint Brendan was supposed to have visited this western country on a trip from Ireland not long after Arthur's time.

And, when the first Viking explorers reached North America, they reported people with auburn or light-brown hair among some Indian tribes in the northeast.[13] They were told of a "White Man's land" which was inland from the coast and whose inhabitants walked in processions carrying banners and chanting. This sounds like the religious practices of Irish monks. It is related in one of the Norse sagas that an Icelandic merchant named Ari Marson was shipwrecked in the new lands across the Atlantic *and was baptized there.*[14]

The Norse voyages recorded in the sagas date from about 1000 to about 1020 A.D., a matter of just a generation comprising half a dozen shiploads. For the most part, these visits touched only upon the coasts, so far as is known for certain, and no great knowledge of the interior comes out in the sagas. But, even so, there are indications of a Celtic presence of some significance among the Indians that the Vikings met.

There could have been sporadic Celtic voyages to North America over a period of 1700 years, from about 700 B.C. to at least 1000 A.D. Recent archeological finds in New England indicate, although there is great dispute and controversy over them, that there appear to have been fairly large Celtic settlements in the northeast.

Judging from the very great Celtic and Celtiberian linguistic influence upon the Nova Scotia Micmacs, it seems likely that there were a few Celtic settlements in Nova Scotia as well. They may not have been continuously inhabited by Europeans, but may only have been sporadically visited.

One thing is absolutely certain. The Celts of the British Isles never lost their knowledge of some "blessed" land to the west. They must have carried this knowledge to Britain from their Spanish and North African phases of migration when they sailed with Phoenicians and Carthagenians. The idea of some fruitful and almost magical land in the western ocean never left them. Their descriptions of it reflect the observation of Diodorus that the place seems "rather to be the residence of some of the gods, than of men." This almost magical place was sometimes called *Iargalon*, "the land beyond the sunset." *Iargalon* and *Avalon* seem to have been the same magical place in Celtic mind and myth.

A residence of demi-gods. A residence of heroes.

And this brings us to the matter of Avalon. Avalon is one of those annoying Celtic things which exist on several levels at once . . . just like *duir* means simply "oak" on one level, but means "door" and "right-handedness" and even "divinity" in other and cryptic senses.

Avalon means simply "apple trees" on one level. And, in that same sense it was a real place in the neighborhood of Glastonbury. But, on another level, it was another real place . . . a land across the Atlantic to the west. Probably the same place that Aristotle and Diodorus described. But then, on an even deeper level, Avalon was a sort of "fairy" land where the souls of dead heroes went. A paradise.

Therefore, when Geoffrey of Monmouth wrote of Arthur that he "was borne thence unto the island of Avalon for the healing of his wounds", he means two separate things: first, that Arthur was "healed" by death and was buried at Glastonbury; and, second, that his soul was "healed" by transport to that other Avalon in the far west.

The land to the west had not been forgotten by the Romano-Britons of Arthur's time, though specific knowledge about it may have become vague and it had acquired a magical tinge. This knowledge of land to the west passed with Arthurian refugees into France. It became incorporated into the "Grail Romances" of the southern French troubadours, and maybe helped to confirm the reality of western lands shown on maps brought back by Templars from the Middle East. When a refuge became needed, this "Avalon" sprang to mind, both as a spiritual concept and as a geographical one shown on Templar maps.

In the case of Henry Sinclair, the ancient Celtic Avalon and the new lands on Templar maps received powerful confirmation from another and independent quarter: the Norse sagas of Henry's noble colleagues. The Vikings had *been* there. And they knew that at least some Celts had been there before them, *and might be there yet.*

All this converging evidence must have been most impressive. Sinclair must have been relatively sure of what he would find before he set sail. Since he represented Arthur's mission himself, and may well have known it, the voyage to the American continent might not have seemed like an exploration into the unknown. It was more like a homecoming. Sinclair, like other heroes before him, was bound for Avalon.

All this is clear in a symbolic sense. Might it be real in a coldly factual and geographical sense? *Was Nova Scotia the Avalon across the Atlantic?*

Avalon means "apple trees". The area around the Bay of Fundy, and especially around Minas Basin near the mouth of the Gaspereau River, is justly famed for its apple orchards. Apples are *the* crop. Orchards cover hundreds, if not thousands, of acres. All of the towns around the Minas shore decline or prosper with the apple harvest. In fact, the local chamber of commerce has created the personage called "Dan D. Apple" who signs testimonials that various businesses have done their bit in supporting the annual Apple Blossom Festivals. In the spring, the land for miles around Minas is white with blossoming apple trees.

The Acadian French are supposed to have planted these orchards. They certainly tended them, and improved them. *But did they originate them?* I have been able to find only a few tantalizing hints that some of these orchards may have existed when the Acadians arrived. Nothing definite enough to publish. The botany of apples is more complicated than I could ever have thought as I tried to get a handle on this. Apparently, if I have got it all straight, there may be two species of apple native to Canadian North America, and neither are native to Nova Scotia.[15] If apples existed around Minas before the Acadians arrived, then they must have been purposefully brought across the Atlantic and planted by people. Perhaps by the same people who planted the oaks.

The origin of the Minas apple orchards might be a rewarding and surprising area of research for someone who knows something about botany. There may be good grounds for supposing that the Celtic Avalon had a precise geographical location.

Whether or not we can ever pinpoint Avalon because of its apple trees, the idea of Avalon had a powerful hold on colonial explorers. Several places in the New World were named Avalon, maybe the earliest to receive this name was the Avalon Peninsula of Newfoundland.

There does not seem to be much doubt that the Celts were busy in Nova Scotia from very early times. Aside from just being a good place to live, it provided wealth in the form of metal. Probably for export back to Europe. The first European explorer known to have made a detailed survey of the Fundy area, Samuel Champlain, was constantly coming across abandoned mines. There were so many in the neighborhood of the

Gaspereau River that he named the place "the bay of Mines". In the course of time, this became corrupted into the present "Minas Basin" which is a sub-bay of the Bay of Fundy.

The existence of the Oak Islands is definitely a Celtic touch, and there is Celtic linguistic influence apparent among the Micmacs. At The Cross, Jeanne McKay claimed to have found a Celtic-looking flint knife. And there was her Celtic-looking petromantic "Herm" with its alleged inscriptions. Similar petromantic sculptures of undoubted Celtic origin have been discovered in New England.

Except by thorough archeological excavation there is no way to determine whether the ruins at The Cross have an ancient Celtic origin. There's certainly enough circumstantial evidence to suggest that they might very well have such an origin.

If so, Henry Sinclair might have found his refuge partly ready-made. With signposts already leading to it. He may have only been confronting the job of raising new walls on an old foundation. And the place may already have been "special" to the local Micmacs. The depot on Oak Island may already have been in existence, ready to serve as a manned outpost on the crucial Atlantic approaches. The pit there may have stood waiting to serve as a temporary vault for treasures that would be hiked inland.

And, if some great holy relic was among the items later consigned to the transatlantic refuge, it may have spent some time in the pit.

Maybe it left powerful vibrations that endured to influence the psychic investigators of Oak Island.

Chapter Six

The French Connection

Our story opened with King Arthur. From a misty figure of myth and legend, recent archeological investigations at traditional Arthurian sites have revealed what British writers call "the Arthurian Fact". A powerful Romano-British war lord did apparently reside atop Cadbury Hill, the traditional site of Camelot. Cadbury Hill was the centre of an anti-Saxon defensive network in southwest England. There is reason to believe that the lord of Camelot was a leader of heavy cavalry who, possibly reviving an old Roman plan for the defence of Britain, sallied forth with *clibanarii* to assist beleaguered neighbouring chieftains and petty kings.

King Arthur is also associated in myth and legend with an early Christian community in southwest England, and with something called "The Holy Grail". There was found to be support for an early Christian community at Glastonbury, and even some evidence for a plausible "Holy Grail" as a religious treasure guarded originally by Joseph of Arimathaea.

Arthur perished at the Battle of Camlann and was buried in Avalon. He handed over his command to Constantine, but the Saxon darkness closed over him and the spark of civilization that was Camelot. Only stubborn memories remained, to be partly vindicated 1500 years afterwards by modern archeologists.

Then we jumped 500-odd years to the year 1099 A.D. when Godfroi de Bouillon emerged from relative obscurity in southern France to become King of Jerusalem. His place of origin, the Pyrenees and the regions of Languedoc and Provence, was unique in all of Christendom. The civilization there was relatively advanced. It was wealthy. It wasn't quite Christian. The knight-poets of the area, the troubadours, *created a literature based, of all things, on King Arthur and the Holy Grail.* Although my favourite troubadour is Wolfram von Eschenbach, who was Bavarian and might better be called by the proper German term *minnesinger,* the great majority of troubadours who wrote and sang Grail Romances were French, from the regions of Provence and Languedoc. The best known are Chrétien de Troyes, who wrote the first known Grail Romance, and Robert de Boron. There were many others, mostly all French.

De Bouillon's dynasty created the Knights Templar, and this order of chivalry was woven into the Grail Romances. They were portrayed as guardians of the Grail, as Arthur had been. The Templars immediately gained great prestige, and wealth to match. They began to assist trade and commerce in Europe. They may have helped to finance the building of Gothic "Notre Dame"cathedrals. They very probably came into possession of Middle Eastern maps that assisted maritime commerce in Europe and which showed new lands in the west across the Atlantic.

But de Bouillon's dynasty lost the Holy Land. Hostile forces which had been kept at bay by some mysterious power, felt bold enough to close in. The Albigensian Crusade was launched against the de Bouillon's not-quite-Christian constituency in southern France. The Cathars were crushed. The Templars were dispersed.

As we have seen, the surviving Templars fled to refuges on the fringe of Europe. To Scotland. To Portugal. And, plausibly, using the maps found in the Middle East, began a desperate search for transatlantic havens. The more southern probes, from Spain and Portugal, failed. But a northern probe from Scotland appeared to be successful. The haven scouted by Henry Sinclair was already known to the Celts, and to the Norse. It had been known since long before Arthur's time among the Celtic Roman-Britons. It was, in a way, Avalon.

There is a thread of connection. But what of the 500-odd year gap separating King Arthur from Godfroi de Bouillon?

Obviously, de Bouillon's troubadours conceived a connection between King Arthur and southern France. That mysterious object, the Holy Grail, links Arthur with the de Bouillons and the Templars the dynasty founded. Was there a connection between the "de Bouillon complex" and King Arthur? The troubadours insisted on one. Did they have access to information that we have lost?

We will recall that a broken Merovingian bowl was found on top of Cadbury Hill. That small ruin of glass will take us very far indeed.

The modern French village of Rennes-le-Chateau nestles in the eastern foothills of the Pyrenees near the confluence of the Aude, Blanque and Sale rivers. It is only about 2 kilometers, a bit more than a mile, from the larger town of Blanchefort. This larger town was in the past the family seat of Bertrand de Blanchefort, a Grand Master of the Knights Templar.

Naturally, because of all the traditional stories about Templar treasure, local legends have hinted that something of great worth had long been hidden near the village of Rennes-le-Chateau and the town of Blanchefort. This gossip seemed to be folklore no more. Several unsuccessful attempts were made, at various times over the centuries, to search for this reputed hoard, whatever it might be.

But, after all the centuries, it appears that something was found after all.

In 1891, the obscure and impoverished village priest of Rennes-le-Chateau, Bérenger Saunière, began the job of making repairs and renovations to his village church. He discovered that his church had been built on the foundations of an older medieval one. Most of this older structure had been destroyed, but the altar-stone remained. It was supported by two pillars. One of these columns proved to be hollow.

Inside the hollow pillar Curé Saunière found four pieces of parchment. Two pages were genealogies. Two others were a long and complicated message in code.[1]

The genealogies dated from 1244 and 1644. The first date is significant. It is the year that the last Cathar stronghold, Montségur, surrendered and when the remnants of the Cathars and de Bouillon's descendants and relatives went into hiding.

The two pages of code had been written in the late 1700s by a former village priest of Rennes-le-Chateau. This priest was also the personal confessor to the Blanchefort family. This coded message has exercised the imaginations of a number of French investigators. Some of it has apparently been deciphered, but even so the text does not always make much sense.

> Shepherdess, no temptation. That Poussin, Teniers, hold the key;
> Peace 681. By the Cross and this Horse of God, I complete — or
> destroy — this daemon of the Guardian at noon. Blue apples.[2]

Another passage reads:

> To Dagobert II, King, and to Sion belongs this treasure and he is there dead.[3]

This may sound like nonsense, but it is not altogether so. The mention of Dagobert II is important and ties in with the two pages of genealogies found along with the message. An article in the French press dated January 22, 1981 asserted that these genealogies preserved the lineage of Dagobert II through his son, Sigisbert IV, up to Godfroi de Bouillon and on into the 1700s.[4]

Whatever the significance of the coded message and the genealogies, Bérenger Saunière was able to make some sense of them. What he learned, and what he leaked out to the world, changed his life in a number of ways. Saunière immediately took the documents to his superior, the bishop of Carcassonne. Then the bishop just as quickly instructed him to take the documents to Abbé Bieil, Director-General of the Seminary of Saint-Sulpice in Paris.

After his visit to Paris, Saunière returned to Rennes-le-Chateau, but he returned as an amazingly changed man. This formerly impoverished village priest began to acquire . . . or at least to spend . . . vast sums of money. He spent it in peculiar ways.

He built a small medieval-replica castle in which to house his rapidly expanding library of books. He called it the " Tour Magdala", the Tower of the Magdalene.

Then he built himself a large country manor which he called Villa Bethania in honour of Mary of Bethany.

It has been estimated that Saunière spent several million dollars between 1891 and 1917. Not all of it was spent on private libraries and manors. He paid for the building of a modern road to Rennes-le-Chateau, and he supplied his village with a running water system.

His faith underwent a transformation along with his finances. It changed from orthodox Catholicism to some other belief which, though just as strong perhaps, he kept hidden for the rest of his life. He continued with the restoration of the village church which had been interrupted by his discoveries and his Parisian visit, but he restored the church strangely. Over the new door he placed this inscription in Latin:

TERRIBILIS EST LOCUS ISTE

It means: " This place is terrible".

The Tour Magdala, the "Tower of the Magdalene," built by Bérenger
Saunière to house his library in Rennes-le-Chateau.
Photo by Michael Baigent.

He decorated the inside of the church with painted panels depicting events from the life of Christ from birth to Crucifixion, but Saunière's illustrations departed from the Biblical accounts in incongruous ways. The Child is shown in swaddling clothes, but of Scots plaid! Now that we have learned something of Henry Sinclair's voyage to Nova Scotia and the possibility that he established a haven there, the Scots plaid swaddling clothes seem appropriate. There are equally incongruous details in all the other panels. Inside the church he placed a statue of the demon Asmodeus — "custodian of secrete, guardian of hidden treasures and according to ancient Judaic legend, the builder of Solomon's Temple."

Saunière's social life changed. Along with his inexplicable wealth, he acquired the friendship of Archduke Johann von Habsburg (cousin of the Austrian Emperor, Franz-Joseph), of the French Secretary of State for culture, of the famed opera singer of the times, Emma Calvé. He also apparently acquired a mistress, Marie Denarnaud, who inherited all of Saunière's wealth and properties. She also claimed to know his secret.[5]

Marie Denarnaud died on January 29, 1953. She announced that she would reveal Saunière's secret on her deathbed, but she suffered a sudden stroke, lay in a near-coma for 10 days before her death, incapable of speech, and the secret died with her.

The strange life of Bérenger Saunière and the odd church and Tour Magdala at Rennes-le-Chateau piqued the curiosity of a number of French investigators during the 1950s. And, as they dug for the facts in libraries, including the Bibliothèque Nationale in Paris, an even more mysterious state of affairs began to come to light. It soon became clear that someone had deposited a series of bewildering and tantalizing documents in these libraries, but most particularly in the Bibliothèque Nationale where they were certain to be stumbled upon by serious researchers. Most of these documents had to do with Godfroi de Bouillon, the Merovingians, Cathars, Templars or with the troubadours. Taken individually, these tracts often made no sense, or began and ended without really saying anything. These documents included genealogies, squibs of historical observation, clippings from obscure publications, and long dissertations about Cathar religion. Invariably, although they were deposited in the Bibliothèque Nationale, and sometimes recently during the 1950s, their origin was a mystery. The authors, when that information was given, turned out to have used pseudonyms. There were clippings from "publications", and neatly type-set, that never existed.

Serious researchers into the strange events at Rennes-le-Chateau increasingly came upon these no less mysterious depositions in the libraries. All were vaguely relevant to the "de Bouillon complex", none made much sense individually, *but taken together they told, and fleshed out, a remarkable story.* It slowly dawned upon the researchers that someone was way ahead of them. Someone knew the secret about Rennes-le-Chateau and had left a series of clues for researchers to discover, and it did not take too long before everyone began to realize that just a mere "someone" could not have deposited all of these documents. The mass of material was both too great and too varied to be attributed to any one individual. Then, how had so many documents been accepted by the Bibliothèque Nationale without proper author-publisher data? How had such documents been so speedily transferred onto *microfiche* minus the standard catalogue data?

The only possible answer seemed to be a well-organized and well-funded secret society with high-level contacts in the French ministry of culture. It was quite obvious that this secret society wanted the story of Rennes-le-Chateau to come out and was leading the researchers by a cat-and-mouse game of coy and carefully-timed revelations to get the story out. And this story gradually became larger and more momentous than most of the researchers would ever have guessed. In the beginning, soon after Marie Denarnaud's death, most of the curious journalists and writers had been content to assume that Saunière's wealth had somehow derived from some sort of very tangible treasure that he'd found, probably a hoard of Templar gold and silver.

But it gradually became clear that the treasure was some sort of secret information, not metallic wealth, and that this secret knowledge concerned nothing less than the essence of Western history. The *Dossiers secrets* gradually led investigators to a reconstruction of a fantastic underground history, and led them according to a time-table. Whatever the organization was behind it all, it wanted the story told, but wanted the information released over a number of years. It seemed that the researchers, and the general public, were being prepared for some momentous future revelation by increasing exposure to "mini-revelations" that were more digestible.

All manner of journalists and writers started to put the story together at about the same time, resulting in that spate of French-published books referred to earlier. These books naturally varied a lot in both content and interpretation, but to a remarkable degree these different authors' revelations were the same: *that the Cathars and Albigensians possessed some secret truth or doctrine that amounted to a human treasure.* And that, somehow, Godfroi de Bouillon's bloodline *was* this treasure, incarnate, and had been guarded by thie Templars. Various objects called collectively the "Holy Grail" provided proof absolute of this lineage's extraordinary origin and worth. This proof, likewise, had been guarded by the Templars. Contact with this secret truth was restricted to a chosen few. But once they did come into contact with it, and once the proofs of it were seen, they could never again accept orthodox religion whether Roman Christian, Judaism or Islam. The secret was something that transcended all of these "truths".

At least one small part of the great secret, *but by no means all of it,* has been disclosed by several French investigators and now by three British authors. It is simple, *Jesus had apparently been married to Mary Magdalene, they had children, and these children married into the bloodline that resulted in Godfroi de Bouillon.*[6]

The legacy of Jesus had not ended on the cross. The descendants of Jesus survived after his Crucifixion to form a "Holy" bloodline. This had merged into the lineage of the first kings of France, the so-called Merovingian Dynasty. Godfroi de Bouillon was a Merovingian.

This was the theme of many French-published books, aided and abetted by the information so coyly released by the *Dossiers secrets,* during the 1950s and 1960s. It suggested a solution to the mystery of Rennes-le-Chateau. Saunière had found proof of this divine lineage among the genealogies. It threatened Christian dogma and orthodoxy, and placed the Roman Church in the position of being the oppressor of Christ's descendants. Saunière had obtained his wealth by blackmailing the Vatican. Saunière had tapped into the real power of the de Bouillon bloodline, a power that no longer seemed so mysterious. Because of his discovery, Bérenger Saunière just accidentally became initiated into the secret that was ordinarily revealed only to a relative few. He also tapped into the underground of secret societies which replaced the Knights Templar. His faith was transformed, he acquired instant wealth, and he acquired friends and enemies in high places.

So much for the mystery of Rennes-le-Chateau. It was a mystery no more, if the Merovingian lineage was really related to Jesus, but there remained the tantalizing suggestion that the de Bouillon bloodline had not been exterminated by the Inquisition. The lineage had apparently survived the Albigensian Crusade, the fall of Montségur and the destruction of the Knights Templar. One of the genealogies that Saunière found traced the de Bouillon line up to 1644, or 400 years exactly after the surrender of Montségur. The "Holy" Merovingian lineage had survived. The *Dossiers secrets* leaked hints that it had survived until today and was busy molding Western history behind the scenes.

Who were these Merovingians? Maybe more important, *what* were they? Godfroi de Bouillon's "Holy" lineage did not depend only upon intermarriage with the descendants of Jesus. Jesus was only a part of the divine claim, one episode in a very long history.

What might be called "establishment history" can easily tell us what the Merovingians were, at least, on the surface. They were the Sicambrian Franks, a somewhat mixed Celtic-Teutonic tribe that during most of the Roman Empire had lived east of the Rhine in present-day Germany. They were far from being savages, although they were pagans. They had long been in contact with Rome, some of the leaders had adopted Roman dress. Some had become Roman citizens, and there were even Sicambrian consuls in the history of the Roman Empire. Many of the Franks served in the Imperial Army.[7]

When Roman power began to collapse during the late 300s and early 400s A.D., these Sicambrians moved westward across the Rhine and occupied Roman Gaul. This was not a "barbarian invasion" such as the Angles, Saxons and Jutes were launching from further north, for the Sicambrian Franks were not barbarians. They moved into the Roman power vacuum and filled it. This was just before the time of Arthur in Britain. When the Sicambrian Franks reached the Channel about 400 A.D., they probably established contact with the Romano-Britons in the generation of Ambrosius Aurelianus and Uther Pendragon. In fact, archeology proves this to be the case. Shards of Mediterranean wine amphorae have been recovered from most Arthurian sites, including Tintagel, the traditional place of Arthur's birth.[8] Excavation has demonstrated a lively trade across the Channel between Somerset-Cornwall and Brittany in the 5th Century. It was trade between the "Arthurians" and the Sicambrian Franks.

An alliance between the two peoples was almost inevitable. They played the same role. While the "Arthurians" preserved what was left of Roman civilization in Britain, the Sicambrian Franks did the same thing in Gaul.

One Sicambrian King was named Merovée. About 470 A.D. something noteworthy happened during Merovée's rule. The Sicambrian line was somehow enhanced in prestige from this time. The dynasty was called Merovingian afterwards in honour of this King Merovée who reigned about the time of King Arthur's birth.[9]

And that covers the Merovingian origins, on the surface.

But these Sicambrian Franks, or Merovingians, were peculiar in several respects. Not the least of their peculiarities was that they claimed to be Jewish! They claimed to represent the majority of the Tribe of Benjamin![10]

Benjamin was one of the Twelve Tribes of Israel and was in some way special. It was also powerful. God was somehow *in* the Tribe of Benjamin. In Deuteronomy 33, Moses says of the Tribe of Benjamin: "The beloved of the Lord shall dwell in safety by him; and the Lord shall cover him all the day long, and he shall dwell between his shoulders."

The Tribe of Benjamin held the land that included Jerusalem, as is spelled out in Joshua 18: "Zelah, Eleph and Jebusi, which is Jerusalem, Gibeath and Kirjath; fourteen cities with their villages. This is the inheritance of the children of Benjamin according to their families".

But it came to pass that most of the Benjamites left Palestine, and this was because of a civil war among the Israelites. The Tribe of Benjamin came into conflict with the other eleven Tribes because the Benjamites were apparently allied with the "Sons of Belial" and would not attempt to impose Israelite laws and customs upon them. This war is covered in Judges 21 in the Bible. The result was that most of the Benjamites left Palestine, or were expelled by the victorious eleven Tribes.

The "Sons of Belial" with whom the Benjamites were allied, or against whom they refused to go to war in order to enforce Israelite customs, were none other than the Phoenicians of Tyre and Sidon, the "red headed" ones who were "proto-Celts". It is possible that the Benjamites were related to these coastal people. They certainly had some affinity with them, and refused to go to war against them.

At the same time, the Benjamites had a very great holding in Palestine, a tract including the major Israelite cities and Jerusalem. Then, the mere fact that they were able to consider a war against all the other Tribes must mean that the Tribe called the Benjamites must have been the most powerful single tribe in the Israelite confederacy as well as being somehow "different".

The Old Testament has been doctored to reflect the cohesion and greatness of the Hebrews, just as the New Testament has been doctored to distort certain embarrassing relationships.

The Tribe of Benjamin, which had some special divine dispensation and significant geographical holdings, *may not have been within the "Semitic mainstream" at all.* They may have had closer genetic relationship to the "Sons of Belial" whom they refused to fight. If so, the later editors of the Old Testament could not allow this to come out. The most special Hebrew tribe, and the most powerful one, *was not descended from Abraham at all?* Was not a part of the Hebrew mainstream that would later become "Jewish"?

Whatever the truth of such speculations, the Benjamites seem to have been virtually exterminated in the war. The majority of the survivors took ship for Greece. Only a few stayed behind. This emigration is itself a powerful argument that the Benjamites and the coastal Phoenicians must have had close relations. The Israelites were inland herdsmen, not seamen. The refugee Benjamites must have sailed to Greece on Phoenician ships. But why wouldn't the Phoenician just have enslaved the remnants of a defeated inland tribe? Why should the Phoenicians have carried them to safety instead?

The answer can only be a close and sympathetic affinity between the Benjamites and the Phoenicians, and very probably a blood-relationship.

At any rate, the Benjamites arrived in Greece, in a region called Arcadia. It was their refuge for some generations. Then, they joined the general westward migrations of people in Europe. They followed the major rivers westward, like the Danube, and finally ended up along the Rhine at the close of the Roman Empire. They moved west across the Rhine when Roman power finally crumbled and reached Brittany and the English Channel.

And there, of course, they came into contact with people who had also, long before, been partly Phoenician/Carthagenian themselves. People who had undertaken an even longer migration westward by sea. People who were, in a way, long-lost relations, and they became allies. Aside from the matter of a distant Middle Eastern kinship, the Romano-British Celts and the Sicambrian Franks faced the same military foes.

But the Sicambrian Franks, or Merovingians, did not forget their past Jewish history as the Tribe of Benjamin. Merovingian geographical place-names and personal names were sometimes Jewish. In the 6th Century a brother of King Clothair II was named Samson, while Miron "Le Lévite" was a count. "Sion" and "Levi" were Merovingian towns in France. Scholars have even traced Merovingian "Salic Law" back to Judaic law. There was a very great "Jewish" component among the Sicambrian Franks/Merovingians and, because they practiced polygamy (another Merovingian peculiarity) they left a great number of offspring. These aristocratic Merovingian children married into almost all the noble families of Europe during the 5th, 6th and 7th Centuries. This has prompted more than one historian to suggest that the foundation of European nobility is Jewish![10]

In addition to being "Jewish", or partly so, the Merovingians claimed an ancient descent from God. This is even hinted in the Biblical allotments to Benjamin, as already quoted. In token of this descent, the Merovingians were believed to bear some physical mark, though different writers disagree on what this was. But most believe it was some sort of red cross-like birthmark, either on the chest or on the back. Some have assumed that the dwelling of God between the shoulders of Benjamin referred to this red cross birthmark. It is hard to say whether this curious birthmark really existed as a distinguishing characteristic of Merovingians. It is difficult to credit. Maybe only a few Merovingian monarchs ever had it, or maybe even only one, and something similar was tattooed onto other Merovingian children as a token of their descent. In any case, a red cross "pattee" became the Templar insignia[11].

Several symbols were associated with the Merovingians. They brought the fleur-de-lis into France where it became associated, off and on, with the French state and with French royalty. The present flag of the Canadian province of Quebec has four fleur-de-lis separated by a white cross. This symbol is a stylized lily and there is evidence that it was originally a Jewish symbol. Not only are lilies frequently mentioned in the songs of David, but Jewish coins depicted lilies that look very much like fleur-de-lis.[12]

The Merovingians are also associated with bees and, of all things, with toads.[13] Clovis was the most famous Merovingian king. His father was Childeric I. In Childeric's grave were found 300 small gold bee-figures. What these bees symbolized is not known, but it is known that Napoleon appropriated them for his imperial robe when he crowned himself Emperor of the Franks in 1804.[14]

Clovis himself merged the symbolism of fleur-de-lis and toads. In a tapestry that was once in Reims cathedral but which has now been removed to the Reims museum, Clovis is shown wearing a yellow surcoat decorated (if that's the right word) with three toads. At Orléans a bas-relief showing a battle between French and Germans has the French represented by two flags: one flag with three toads, the other with three fleur-de-lis.[15]

We cannot guess what these toads represented, but maybe they had something to do with the Merovingian claim of divine descent. Supposedly, the Merovingians had sprung from a union between humans and some sort of godlike sea-beast. Toads, or at all events frogs, are amphibious and exist on land as well as in water. Maybe the Merovingians chose this symbol to represent a union of land and water from which they had come. Although the French authors seem always to refer to toads (crapauds) when writing about these symbols, it would be hard to tell a toad from a frog on something like a tapestry or bas-relief. Maybe these Merovingian toads were really frogs and represented their divinely aquatic ancestor.[16]

This may not be wholly mythic gibberish, but may prove to be quite important. Or at least suggestive. We'll get to that later. But is it altogether accidental that the French are sometimes (and less than politely) called "frogs"? Could it be that this common epithet is a folk survival from Merovingian days?

A lot more could be written about curious things attaching to Merovingian lore, but enough has been given so that some sense can be made of a note found by researchers among the *Dossiers secrets*:

> ONE DAY THE DESCENDANTS OF BENJAMIN LEFT THEIR COUNTRY; CERTAIN REMAINED; TWO THOUSAND YEARS LATER GODFROI VI (DE BOUILLON) BECAME KING OF JERUSALEM AND FOUNDED THE ORDER OF SION.

This is typical of a lot of the material in the *Dossiers secrets* and it would at first seem to connect two totally unrelated matters, the Tribe of Benjamin and a rather obscure 11th Century French nobleman, and to connect them in a nonsensical way. It is the kind of thing that both frustrated and tantalized the French researchers. Only with a lot of study into pretty obscure history and legend did a note like this suddenly make sense. And, at the same time, it showed that some organization was more knowledgeable than the researchers.

The links between the Merovingians and Godfroi de Bouillon are now clear, thanks to the tireless detective work of a number of French and English investigators over the past three decades. We will cover the story as quickly as possible.

At the end of the 400s A.D. the Roman Empire was crumbling in the west. The Christian Church represented what was left of civilized knowledge, administrative know-how and literacy. But the Church was a spiritual power, not a military one. To a greater or lesser extent at many different times, the Church was threatened with utter extinction by influxes of pagan barbarians. To survive, the Church sought out some cohesive military and social structure with which it could ally itself. The Merovingian kingships in Gaul were that power, the heirs of Rome. Although they were pagans, they were at least semi-civilized ones. To some degree they appreciated civilization and the Church's role in preserving what was left of it. That being so, they could be converted. And the Church set out to do just that.

Clovis was *the* Merovingian king who became converted to Christianity. The kingdom of the Franks became converted with him. Clovis ruled between 481 and 511 A.D. and was thus probably a contemporary of King Arthur. He was baptised in 496 A.D. by St. Rémy. This baptism was considered to mark the birth of a new and reconstituted kind of Roman Empire, a sort of "Christian Roman Empire" in which the Church would have spiritual control and much administrative influence, and in which Clovis and the Merovingians would have military and secular responsibilities. In theory, this was to be a perpetual pact between the Church and the Merovingians.

It lasted, in name, for about 300 years. The problem was that, after Clovis, the Merovingian monarchs seemed to decline in vitality and in competence. With rare exceptions, they didn't prove to be the bold warriors that the Church so urgently needed. The last Merovingians were called "enfeebled kings", and they were. Real power passed from the kings to the Mayors of the Palace, the ancestors of Charlemagne.

The enfeebled Merovingian kings were a definite liability for the Church and for European civilization. Very vital Islamic armies invaded Spain and threatened to pour over the Pyrenees into France itself. In this desperate situation, the Church turned more and more to the Mayors of the Palace and ignored the Merovingian kings. It was Charles Martel, not the Merovingian monarch, who won the Battle of Poitiers in 732 A.D.

and stopped the Moorish invasion of France. In 754 A.D. his son, Pepin III, was anointed King of the Franks, and established the Carolingian dynasty which replaced the enfeebled Merovingian one in the eyes of Rome. In the year 800 A.D., Charles the Great, Charlemagne, was crowned as Holy Roman Emperor, and the Church had broken its "perpetual pact" with Clovis and the Merovingian lineage.

In the meantime, steps had been taken to dispose of the Merovingian kings and potential heirs. The last real Merovingian ruler, Dagobert II, was assassinated by a Carolingian Mayor of the Palace. It was thought that Dagobert's son and heir, Sigisbert IV, had died as well.

But it seems that the young boy was taken to safety in the south of France to live among his mother's noble family, and Counts of Razès.

Briefly, and leaving out unsuccessful attempts to re-establish the Merovingian kingship, various exiles and banishments and some close calls evading the Moors, this lineage survived and prospered in the foothills of the Pyrenees. It multiplied and inter-married with other noble houses in France, England and Scotland.[17] But the secret of Merovingian descent was not revealed to everyone.

Eventually, this bloodline culminated in Godfroi de Bouillon and the Kingship of Jerusalem.

The "power centre" of the bloodline was southern France, even though it established branches in many places. The family seat of the Counts of Razès was called Rhédae in the early middle ages. It later became known as Rennes-le-Chateau. Where Bérenger Saunière found the hidden genealogies that changed his life.

The Merovingians had always claimed a divine origin, or, at least, had always claimed a supernatural one because of this "sea-beast" who was an ancient ancestor.

But in the early "Dark Ages", this claim to "divinity" became much more immediately relevant to the people of the times, and especially to the Church.

We will recall that something noteworthy happened during the reign of Merovée which justified some sort of "new reckoning" and a new dynastic name for the line of Sicambrian kings.

Several French researchers and three recent English authors, led by clues in the *Dossiers secrets*, have concluded that an infusion of "Holy Blood" occurred during the rule of Merovée, an infusion of blood from the lineage of Jesus himself. It was this that justified a new dynastic name and it was this that gave the Merovingian kingship such enormous prestige among those who knew of it. It was secret knowledge reserved for those who reached very high positions in Church and State, and it was the reason for the Church's perpetual pact with Clovis, which was betrayed by Rome.

The Church's subsequent energetic attempts to destroy this bloodline, *and to deny that it ever existed,* were motivated by guilt over the broken pact and motivated by fear of popular reaction if people ever learned the truth. Then, too, the Church itself was gradually transforming its character, like any other bureaucratic organization. The bishop of Rome, who had once been no more powerful than any other bishop, was attempting to assert spiritual authority over all of Christendom. The bishop of Rome was, in fact, slowly becoming the Pope and a complicated spiritual dogma was being created to justify this process. The existence of any flesh and blood descendants of Christ would undermine Papal authority. Like any other large and powerful bureaucracy, the Papacy fought for its survival.

But . . . *were there any descendants of Christ?*

This is such a shocking question for most modern Christians that it will have to be dealt with at some length, and in easy stages. It is first easier to ask if Jesus was married.

The Bible never explicitly commits itself as to the marital status of Jesus, but there is a lot of circumstantial evidence that Jesus must have been married. First of all, marriage was very much an expected role for any Jewish male of Jesus' time. It was an absolutely necessary condition for being a rabbi ("teacher"). "The Jewish Mishnaic Law is quite explicit on the subject: 'An unmarried man may not be a teacher' ". Charles Davis, "a respected contemporary theological scholar", says:

> Granted the cultural background as witnessed . . . it is highly improbable that Jesus was not married well before the beginning of his public ministry. If he had insisted upon celibacy, it would have caused a stir, a reaction which would have left some trace. So, the lack of mention of Jesus's marriage in the Gospels is a strong statement not against, but for the hypothesis of marriage, because any practice of advocacy of voluntary celibacy would in the Jewish context of the time have been so unusual as to have attracted much comment and attention.[18]

The Gospel of John does, in fact, describe a marriage early in Jesus' ministry and it is apparently Jesus' own. It is the wedding at Cana. Inexplicably, somehow the mother of Jesus is also present at this wedding and she tells him to replenish the wine. This would be the function of a hostess. This is the well-known miracle when Jesus changed the water into wine. Neither Jesus nor Mary seem to be mere guests. "There is further evidence that the wedding at Cana is in fact Jesus's own. Immediately after the miracle has been performed, the 'governor of the feast' — a kind of major-domo or master of ceremonies — tastes the newly-produced wine ... 'called the bridegroom, and saith unto him, Every man at the beginning doth set forth good wine; and when men have well drunk, then that which is worse: but thou has kept the good wine until now.' "[19] The italics in this passage quoted from *The Holy Blood and The Holy Grail* belong to the authors of this recent bestseller. They point out that the "governor of the feast" refers to Jesus ("thou") and to the bridegroom in the same sentence and as the same person. For those who want to check the Gospels, the relevant passage is John 2:9-10.

There are rather too many Marys in the life of Jesus. In addition to the Virgin Mary, his mother, there are also Mary from Magdala, Mary "Magdalene", and Mary of Bethany, the sister of Martha and Lazarus.

Both Mary Magdalene and Mary of Bethany seem to be related to Jesus closely, but in strange ways. In two Gospels (Mark and Matthew) the Magdalene isn't mentioned until late in the accounts, while in Luke she features early when Jesus is still preaching in Galilee ... *and she apparently accompanies him to Judea.* As the authors of *The Holy Blood and The Holy Grail* point out ... "This in itself strongly suggests that she was married to someone. In the Palestine of Jesus's time it would have been unthinkable for an unmarried woman to have travelled unaccompanied — and, even more so, to travel unaccompanied with a religious leader and in his entourage ... her special relationship with Jesus and her proximity to him would have rendered both of them subject to suspicions, if not charges, of adultery".[20]

What was this special relationship? It is never quite spelled out in the Gospels. But, first of all, it was to Mary Magdalene that Jesus first reveals his Resurrection, and she is present at all of the significant events of Jesus'adult ministry. The unnamed woman who anoints Jesus has always been associated with Mary Magdalene. If this is so, then Mary Magdalene is revealed as a woman of means because the cost of the anointing ointment is stressed. "Throughout the Gospels Jesus treats the Magdalene in a unique and preferential manner . . . (which) may well have induced jealousy in the other disciples".[21]

Mary of Bethany was also a woman of means. Apparently Jesus and his entire entourage stayed at the home of Martha, Lazarus and Mary toward the final days. In Luke (10:38-42) there's a reference that would seem to indicate that Jesus is the husband of Mary. Mary's sister, Martha, complains:

> Now it came to pass, as they went, that he entered into a certain village: and a certain woman named Martha received him into her house.
>
> And she had a sister called Mary, which also sat at Jesus' feet and heard the word.
>
> But Martha was cumbered much about serving, and came to him, and said, Lord, dost thou not care that my sister hath left me to serve alone? Bid her therefore that she help me.
>
> And Jesus answered and said unto her, Martha, Martha, thou art careful and troubled about many things:
>
> But one thing is needful: and Mary hath chosen that good part, which shall not be taken away from her.

Apparently, then, Jesus could bid Mary to help Martha, *as a husband*, but does not.

There is a similar suggestion in the Gospel of John that Jesus is married to this Mary of Bethany. When Jesus arrives in Bethany, Lazarus is thought to be dead (before Jesus raises him) and Martha rushes out of the house to tell him . . . but Mary does not come out with her. Why not? Because, in the Jewish custom, she would have been sitting Shiveh (mourning) for Lazarus and by Judaic law of the time a woman sitting Shiveh could not leave the house *except at the bidding of her husband.*

Jesus could not have been married to two women at once. He could not have been married to Mary Magdalene and Mary of Bethany at the same time.

But there is a possibility that these two women with the same name, and with apparent wealth, *were the same person.* There is a direct inference of this in John 12:1-3:

> Then Jesus six days before the passover came to Bethany where Lazarus was which had been dead, whom he raised from the dead.

> There they made him supper; and Martha served: but Lazarus was one of them that sat at the table with him.
>
> Then took Mary a pound of ointment of spikenard, very costly, and anointed the feet of Jesus, and wiped his feet with her hair: and the house was filled with the odour of the ointment.

This Mary who anoints Jesus is clearly intended to be Martha's sister, Mary of Bethany, yet Mary Magdalene is also associated with the anointing of Jesus.

Both of these Marys are devoted disciples. Yet, in three Gospels Mary Magdalene is listed among those present at the Crucifixion while in the same three Gospels Mary of Bethany is not mentioned as being there. But surely such a devoted disciple would have been there. The perplexity is resolved if Mary Magdalene and Mary of Bethany are the same person. "Both" were there, in the same person.

"Could these women who, in the Gospels, appear in three different contexts in fact be a single person? The medieval Church certainly regarded them as such, and so did popular tradition. Many Biblical scholars today concur".[22]

There is, then, evidence that Jesus was married. And that he was married to Mary (Magdalene) and Mary (of Bethany) who were the same person.

Biblical geography gives support to this. Cana, where the wedding took place, is only a few miles from Magdala which was Mary Magdalene's home town. Both Cana and Magdala are in Galilee, and are neighboring places. After this wedding, Mary Magdalene joins Jesus' entourage and travels with him to Judea. Was Mary's family so wealthy that it boasted two residences, one in Magdala and a town house in a wealthy suburb of Jerusalem? Apparently. And this supposition will lead to interesting speculations.

It appears that the role and importance of Mary have been distorted by later editors of the New Testament. And confused. The profusion of Marys appears to have been a way of disguising the fact that Jesus had a very special relationship with "Mary" which aroused the jealousy of the male disciples and which threatened the "patriarchal" orientation of the later Church. The male disciples' discomfort with Mary comes out often enough in the Gospels and doesn't need to be stressed here. It is well known and was even used as a major theme in the musical *Jesus Christ Superstar*.

The authors of *The Holy Blood and The Holy Grail* speculate that Mary Magdalene/Bethany may have been a Benjamite and say:

> In the New Testament there is no indication of the Magdalene's tribal affiliation. In subsequent legends, however, she is said to be of royal lineage. And there are other traditions which state specifically that she was of the Tribe of Benjamin.[23]

Unfortunately, these "other traditions" are not cited by the authors with any reference one can check. But they go on to speculate that a marriage between Jesus and Mary Magdalene/Bethany would, *if Mary had been a Royal Benjamite*, have been of very great dynastic importance.

Israel's first king, Saul, was a Benjamite. David, of the Tribe of Judah, not only deposed Saul but also appropriated his capital of Jerusalem. David therefore deprived the Benjamites of the kingship and of their major city. A dynastic marriage between a descendant of David's royal line and a descendant of Saul's would not only reconcile the Jewish kingship but establish a double claim to it. It becomes understandable, in this context, that Mary, if she was a royal Benjamite descendant, could undertake the anointing of Jesus ... it was a ritual reconciliation, a passing of the usurped kingship to her husband.

None of this proves that Jesus was married to Mary Magdalene/Bethany, but it is suggestive.

If they were married, it is likely that they had children. If the marriage were, in fact, a dynastic alliance, children would have become a responsibility. Rabbis were expected to have children.

There are strong traditions that Mary Magdalene fled to southern France immediately after the Crucifixion. "As early as the fourth century legends describe the Magdalene fleeing the Holy Land and being set ashore near Marseilles — where, for the matter, her purported relics are still venerated. According to medieval legends, she carried with her to Marseilles the Holy Grail."

Not far from Marseilles is the shrine of "Les Saintes Maries" where these relics supposedly reside. Gypsy rumours and pilgrimages support the other popular traditions. Katherine Esty writes in *The Gypsies, Wanderers in Time:*

> Pilgrimages are nothing new to the Gypsies, of course. ... For the last seventy-five years, though, *the* Gypsy pilgrimage has been to Les Saintes Maries. There is a widely known Gypsy legend which

explains both the name of the village and why it is a pilgrimage spot. According to legend, after the death of Jesus, the Jews gathered together all those closest to Jesus, forced them into a small boat — without oars, sails, food or water — and pushed them out to sea. Death seemed certain for this pious crew . . . but gentle winds pushed them westwards until they approached the shores of the Rhone delta. Black Sara, queen of the local tribe of Gypsies, swam out to guide them in. The Marys converted her to Christianity at once and she spent the rest of her life helping the saints. Traditionally the pilgrimage centered around the showing of the relics, the bones of the two Marys.[24]

By "the two Marys", Katherine Esty means Mary the Virgin and Mary Magdalene. But some of these legends count *three* Marys among "Les Saintes Maries", including Mary of Bethany in the entourage, and therefore reflecting the confusion apparently purposefully engendered by editors of the New Testament. Joseph of Arimathaea is supposed to have been in this "pious crew" as well, and independent non-Gypsy legends also say he accompanied "Mary" to southern France.

The authors of *The Holy Blood and The Holy Grail* and most of the French writers are satisfied merely to trace "Mary" to southern France. Once there, she can conveniently connect up with Merovingians and with the "de Bouillon complex" that seemed to originate in southern France. It is just assumed that, sooner or later, the children of Jesus and "Mary" married into the Merovingian lineage. This infusion of "Holy Blood" happened during Merovée's rule and justified the "new reckoning" and the dynastic name. This Merovingian line eventually led to Godfroi de Bouillon and the Kingship of Jerusalem.

But what about Glastonbury's claims to Joseph of Arimathaea and the Holy Grail? And what about the connection between King Arthur and the Holy Grail?

It is understandable that the French researchers might be inclined to ignore the Glastonbury claims, and understandable that they might simply skirt the issue of King Arthur's presence in all of the southern French troubadour Grail Romances.

It is much less understandable that the British authors of *The Holy Blood and The Holy Grail* would do the same thing. But they do. And these British authors, like the French ones, seem content to ignore several problems besides King Arthur.

"Mary" arrived in southern France sometime around 35 A.D. if she fled, or was expelled, immediately after the Crucifixion. But the Merovingians didn't cross the Rhine until about 300 years later, and when the Sicambrian Franks did eventually cross over the river into modern France they occupied the north across to Brittany, not the south. Where was the "Holy blood" during this period of more than 300 years? How did this "Holy Bloodline" in the south eventually make contact with the Sicambrians/Merovingians in the north?

Neither the French authors, nor the British ones of *The Holy Blood and The Holy Grail*, give this much thought. And, as for King Arthur, the British authors commit an unpardonable sin (for Englishmen) and contradict archeology in Britain. Not finding any way of connecting a British King Arthur with "Mary's" refuge in southern France, they solve the problem by transplanting King Arthur and Camelot there!

These authors suggest that the "Wales" of the Grail Romances might be, instead, the region of "Valois" including southern France and some of western Switzerland!

This is a novel approach to the problem. But it is not supported by the popular traditions about King Arthur and the excavation of Arthurian sites in Britain. Archeological research in Cornwall and Somerset place some great warlord just where the traditions insisted that Arthur was, in Camelot atop Cadbury Hill.

The puzzle can be fitted together, and King Arthur can be restored to his proper place in both geography and the Grail literature. It can be done easily.

Mary Magdalene/Bethany and Joseph of Arimathaea may have arrived first near Marseilles in southern France, *but there is no reason to assume that they stayed there.* They may have lived there for some time before moving on to Glastonbury. Marseilles was even then a major port and in close contact with Rome. It would not have been a good permanent refuge. But Marseilles was a major city along the route leading further north along the Rhône, and then west, toward Britain. If Joseph of Arimathaea and Mary Magdalene/Bethany stopped at Marseilles on their way to Glastonbury, both bodies of popular legend, the French and the English, would be satisfied. And, if any Mary died near Marseilles leaving relics to be venerated until today, it is likely to have been Mary the Virgin, the mother of Jesus, if only because she was an older woman. Given the confusion around all these Marys, any Mary-relic is likely to be confused in identity, especially if tradition says that two (or three) of the Marys travelled together.

The speculation that Mary Magdalene/Bethany travelled on to Glastonbury with Joseph of Arimathaea solves several problems. First, it strengthens Joseph of Arimathaea's stubborn connection with the Holy Grail. The medieval Grail Romances of the troubadours agree that, somehow, he was a guardian of it.

Mary Magdalene/Bethany, if she had been the wife of Jesus, would make a plausible "Holy Grail" herself. She would have been, in a very literal sense, "a vessel of the Holy Blood". Her womb would have been such a "vessel", her children would have been the Holy Blood itself. And, by extension, *this Holy Bloodline was itself The Holy Grail.*

If Joseph of Arimathaea arrived in Glastonbury with Mary Magdalene/Bethany and was her companion and guardian, then he would be a guardian of the Holy Grail. The Grail Romances of the troubadours mysteriously connect Joseph of Arimathaea with the Grail lineage . . .

> Medieval tradition portrays Joseph of Arimathaea as a custodian of the Holy Grail; and Perceval is said to be of his lineage. According to other later traditions, he is in some way related by blood to Jesus and Jesus's family.[25]

Who was Joseph of Arimathaea?

Do we not, now, have enough information to make a plausible guess?

In the Gospels he is described as a rich man who was a secret disciple of Jesus. He supplied the shroud in which the body of Jesus was wrapped. *It was Joseph of Arimathaea who obtained the body of Jesus from Pontius Pilate. And he owned the land with the tomb in which Jesus was buried.*

The ownership of a private tomb indicates great wealth, the fact that he could obtain the body of Jesus from Pilate indicates not only great influence, but something else. Joseph of Arimathaea must have been a relative of Jesus in order to have claimed the body from the Roman authorities.

Then, there is the matter of the tomb. Was Jesus put into the same tomb, and resurrected from the same tomb, as the one in which Lazurus was buried and raised? It *seems* so from the Gospels because this is the only tomb mentioned during the final days before the Crucifixion and after it. This tomb was a cave whose entrance could be closed by a stone rolled in front of it. Lazarus was laid in it (John 11:38). Jesus was laid in it. At least, the descriptions of this cave-tomb are the same for both Jesus and Lazarus.

If this deduction is correct, then the cave-tomb was the property of Joseph of Arimathaea, and this cave-tomb was on the property at Bethany, at the house of Martha, Lazarus and Mary. The same house where Jesus and his entourage had been offered extended hospitality. Joseph of Arimathaea must have been the owner of this house in Bethany with its cave-tomb. He must have been the father of Martha, Lazarus and Mary. He must also have been the father-in-law of Jesus.

He was wealthy enough to have had at least two residences: a country place in the cool mountains around Magdala, where one daughter, Mary, had been born; and a "town house" in the capital, in the wealthy Jerusalem suburb of Bethany, more convenient for business. Maybe the country place was not in Magdala itself, but in the nearby town of Cana. Jesus seems to have been accommodated at both places, and possibly married in the Cana residence.

Is there any evidence to support such speculations? Yes, there is. Joseph was "of Arimathaea". Where was that? According to the Biblical authorities who composed the "Helps to the Study of the Bible" found as an appendix to the standard Oxford Press edition of King James version, the derivation of "Arimathaea" is not known, but it was the same place as "Ramah". *Ramah* means a "high place" and it is listed as one of the "fourteen cities with their villages" that was allotted to the Tribe of Benjamin. Part of this passage has already been quoted (Joshua 18:21-28). Joseph of Arimathaea was, therefore, a Benjamite. And, if Mary Magdalene/Bethany was his daughter, she was of Benjamite descent too. This gives some substance and support to those "other traditions", not specified in *The Holy Blood and The Holy Grail*, which insist that she was of Benjamite descent.

But the name "Arimathaea" rang some bells. Given the fact that "r" and "l" often become transposed as sounds in many human languages, might "Arimathaea" once have been "Almathea" or "Alimathaea"?

There was a sub-tribe of that name in ancient Palestine, or at least there was a group who called themselves the "sons" of a goddess variously named Alimathae, Almathae, Amalthea or Amathea. This generally means that a group counted their descent from some matriarch of the name. It is known that some tribes of ancient Palestine did have a matrilinear succession.

At any rate, Robert Graves informs us that these people of Alimathea or Amalthea lived in the neighborhood of Mount Tabor in Galilee.[26] The town of Ramah is on the shoulders of Mount Tabor which, indeed, is a "high place". The towns of Magdala, Cana and Nazareth are also clustered around Mount Tabor. In short, Joseph of "Arimathaea" came from this area and may have reckoned his descent from these Amaltheans (Alimathaeans", "Almathaeans", etc.). It also may be significant that Jesus, traditionally of Nazareth, and Mary Magdalene, from Magdala, came from the same area on the shoulders of Mount Tabor. The towns of Nazareth, Cana and Magdala are within 10 miles of each other.

Interestingly enough, these Amaltheans seem to have been of Phoenician and "proto-Celtic" stock. At least some of them joined the long westward migration of the Celtiberians and "Celts" and ended up in Wales, Cornwall and Somerset.

Which is to say that they ended up around Glastonbury. But they did this long before Joseph "of Arimathaea" arrived. One could say, in fact, that some powerful Celtic families of Ancient Britain were Joseph of Arimathaea's long-lost relations.

There has long been a popular tradition that Joseph of Arimathaea was a wealthy tin-merchant with business connections in southwest England. There is no evidence for this, no proof, but it is known that the Phoenicians and their Carthagenian colonial offspring were involved in this trade. The Amaltheans of Mount Tabor were doubtless engaged in it, too, because of their Phoenician associates. It is at least possible that Joseph "of Arimathaea", who came from Mount Tabor, knew of these British mining activities and might even have been involved in metal import-export.

There is a persistent legend in the little Dorset town of Priddy that Jesus came with Joseph of Arimathaea on a boyhood visit. Jesus was supposed to have been 12 years old at the time. Priddy is about 10 miles from Glastonbury, slightly to the northeast, and its location is easily visible from the Tor.

Nothing is known of Jesus' boyhood. It is at least possible that he was "adopted" by Joseph of Arimathaea at an early age, and it is possible that he was bethrothed to Mary of Magdala at an early age in a dynastic arrangement. Jesus, Mary and Joseph of Arimathaea all lived in close proximity during the early years of Jesus' life. It would have been perfectly possible for Joseph of Arimathaea to have made a business trip to Britain in Jesus' youth and to have taken the boy with him.

In any case, these connections, if they existed, explain why Joseph of Arimathaea would likely have chosen Glastonbury as a refuge. Not only was it on the fringe of the Roman Empire and as far away from Palestine as one could get in the civilized world, he may have had friends and associates there in the tin-trade, people who happened also to be distantly related to him. Further, if Mary Magdalene/Bethany was his daughter, it explains his traditional and legendary associations with her, and with the "Holy Grail" as one of its custodians and guardians.

This line of "Holy Blood" would surely have married into the royalty of Roman Britain. There's a hint that this did happen. One of the kings of Gwynedd (North Wales) was known as Math ap Mathonwy. "Math" means "treasure". Robert Graves has shown that the "Mathonwy" probably derives from Amalthean . . . it is a Celticization of "Almathea", "Amalthea", etc. Or, could it be a Celticization of *Arimathaea*? If so, then this king was called "Treasure of Arimathaea" in transliteration.

Math ap Mathonwy is one of the many, many Welsh kings, petty kings, princes and nobles who claim some distant kinship with Arthur. Math ap Mathonwy was a rather more major king than most. He was reputed to know a secret of great importance. A later Welsh bard boasted: "Old Math ap Mathonwy knew no more than I."

If the "Holy Blood" came to Glastonbury, then it had more than 400 years in which to multiply and marry into the Romano-Celtic royalty. It doubtless figured in most of the Celtic genealogies, in one way or another, after four centuries of inter-mixture. But it apparently culminated around King Arthur.

The Glastonbury sojourn of three or four centuries adequately explains what happened to the "Holy Bloodline" up to the advent of the Merovingians. It puts King Arthur in his proper perspective. He, too, was a guardian of the lineage until the Battle of Camlann.

When Arthur failed, the French connection took over. By Arthur's time, or a couple of generations before him, the Sicambrian Franks had crossed northern France and had reached the Channel. Sicambrians and the Arthurians came into contact, as we know from archeological evidence of trade, and they became natural allies not only because they faced the same military foes, *but because they were distantly related.* They both possessed an ancient and royal Benjamite legacy that could be rejoined after many centuries and many migrations.

We may recall that a broken Merovingian bowl was recovered from Cadbury Hill.

Is it too implausible to imagine the bitter-sweet conferences that must have been held between the Arthurian heirs of the Grail Dynasty and Sicambrians? Is it so difficult to guess the tragic-victorious arrangements that must have been made?

Britain was being engulfed by the northern barbarians. Its end was certain and even Arthur's valour could do no more than postpone it. Civilization, and security, would flicker out. Britain would be over-run, and cut off.

The Sicambrian Franks, on the other hand, not only represented a much greater military force than Arthur's Britain, they were a continental force which could not be cut off and isolated as an island kingdom could be. At worst, under pressure from the northern barbarians from Denmark and Scandinavia, the Sicambrians had only to retreat toward the south, with their strength consolidating onto a smaller "front" as they did so and with the barbarian strength being stretched to cover an ever-increasing front with an ever-longer route of supply. Not only that, but the Sicambrians would be, in this last extremity, retreating into areas long held by Rome and before, by Greece. They would be retreating into what was, ever-increasingly a civilized world. At some point, the northern barbarians would be stopped in France, whereas it was plain that they would conquer Britain.

The military situation would be as clear to modern strategists as to those of the time.

Safety for the Holy Blood now lay in Sicambrian hands. The Arthurians, for all their courage, were doomed. They fought on, not with any hope of victory, but only with the duty of postponing the inevitable darkness. And it is within that context that we must see Arthur, and that is how he probably saw himself. It is reason enough for the stature accorded him by the knight-poets of the Grail Romances. Arthur's struggle was the most glorious of all, great valour in the face of inevitable defeat for the most noble of causes. It was, and became, the ideal of chivalry. And it lived on deservedly, in the Grail Romances of the knight-poets of France even when Arthur's memory had perished among all in Britain except among the stubborn peasantry.

Camelot was a blaze in the growing darkness when these matters

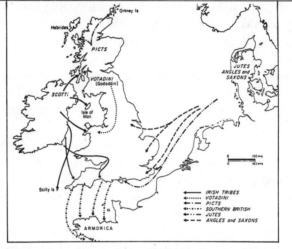

Map showing the groups which invaded Britain between 300 A.D. and 500 A.D. and the escape route of Arthurians to Amorica.

There was a British refugee movement to France at about the same time that Merovée claimed a special infusion of specialness from over the sea. Was this an intermarriage of Arthurian "Holy Refugees" into the lineage of the Sicambrian kings?

would have been discussed. It was about 500-525 A.D. that the details of the transfer would have been thrashed out. When the final, inevitable, defeat happened, then the human and documentary treasure would be taken down to the sea and shipped across the Channel to Brittany. The Holy Grail. The bloodline and the proofs of it.

The bloodline itself could only be preserved by marriage, and by dynastic inter-marriages between the Arthurians and the Sicambrians.

The ports of embarkation were in Somerset and Cornwall. The ports of arrival were in the westernmost part of Brittany. Not only was the Channel crossing shorter at that point, but it was further west. It was therefore further from the Saxon longboats. Because of the nature of the treasures that landed in this part of Brittany, and because of the dynastic partners who must have been landed safely there, this westernmost part of Brittany was known in those times as Amorica, in Latin, the land of the lovers. Or, the land of love. The treasure, human and otherwise, was transferred from the Arthurians to the Merovingians. The lineage lived on. The proofs of it were preserved.

And Arthur and his *clibanarii* charged into the darkness, and Camelot fell quickly into obscurity.

As Arthur fell, in his last battle, against Medraut, his son, on the water-meadow of Camlann on the River Cam, it is not so improbable that he remembered his life's work. Not so improbable that he would have recalled the feasts of happier days, when Camelot blazed, and when pacts of loyalty and common purpose were sealed with draughts of imported Mediterranean wine, as the shards of Mediterranean wine amphorae excavated by archeologists show. This wine of many covenants was drunk from bowls. With visiting Sicambrian lords. And, maybe, it was during one of these pledges that the Merovingian bowl got broken. The one whose shards were found on Cadbury Hill in 1955. The ruin of glass.

It was, in its own small way, a Holy Grail also.

Chapter Seven

Map Memorials

During 1982-1983 we made weekend excursions to Nova Scotia places that had become relevant to our research and our study of old maps.

Naturally, a fair number of these trips were to The Cross. We kept our promises to the Ministry. We measured the site and had a plan of it drawn up to scale by a Halifax civil engineer who had sometimes worked with us on boat blueprints. We obtained samples of the well water for analysis by Nova Scotia government labs.

Jason went along on these trips whenever possible, not only because he became interested in the story and wanted to help with our investigation, but also because he was able to see a good deal of the province in the process. The field trips were combined with fishing, picnics and mineral-collecting.

We also hoped that Jason's presence might come in handy at The Cross. One of our objectives was to trespass on neighbouring properties to see what else might be discovered on the hill top and Jason served as camouflage for any apprehensive villagers. The three of us looked like an innocent family out on a country ramble. Two adults methodically searching the ground with a metal detector would have caused talk, whereas Jason could only be searching for dropped pennies or old nails. He was very methodical with the metal detector, too, because we'd told him about the natural gold deposits around The Cross and about the apparent connection with Oak Island. Like every Nova Scotian 10-year-old, Jason knew about the Money Pit, and he was sure there was pirate gold in it. If some of this gold had come to The Cross, he was determined to find it. He surveryed the McKay ruins and a lot of the hill top with dogged persistence and an intent look.

The instrument indicated a lot of buried metal.[1] Jason had slim interest in archeology and wanted to dig it all up immediately.

Naturally, we had warned him about Jeanne.

From ground level, while walking over Jeanne's back yard, it wasn't possible to see the correct proportions and perspective of the ruins. If Jeanne accompanied us on a tour, or stood around while we were measuring, it was impossible to concentrate on seeing the ruins in *any* sort of perspective. She kept up a non-stop description of the site with more gushing enthusiasm than any Hollywood tour guide to Beverly Hills . . . over there were the remains of the stables, in another place was the foundation of the Stuart mansion (the one that Inigo Jones had built), while in a third spot was the location of the gold smithy. Jason looked puzzled but, perhaps noticing the large number of toads in Jeanne's garden, refrained from making comments except under his breath.

It was all impossible, of course. Jeanne's back garden was generous by centre-city standards, but it simply wouldn't hold all the things that she was trying to put in it. This was as obvious to Jason as to Deanna and me. Crowding stables, a mansion and a gold forge into her rectangle of grass would result in horses the size of terriers and a house and workshop suitable only for elves. A place for *eohippi* and Smurfs, as Jason succinctly put it, showing the combined influence of his latest library book on prehistoric animals and Saturday morning TV.

When the site plan was finally ready we drove it up to The Cross. Everything was reduced to scale on one piece of paper, and the scale itself was clearly marked. Jeanne looked at the plan carefully for several minutes and then congratulated us on our work, saying that it confirmed everything she'd been saying. She then insisted on showing us the paintings she had done of her castle, and she brought out a number of painted canvases and pencil sketches.

These were really quite good considering that Jeanne had had no formal training and simply dabbled with brush or pencil when the spirit moved her, as it apparently did quite often with respect to the castle. Her work showed the same 5-towered and 5-sided castle from a number of perspectives. It was a Late Medieval affair with round towers and pointed roofs. The kind of thing you see in travel posters of France and Switzerland. Her castle brooded among the dark spruces on the hill top overlooking the Gold River. From its location on the hill, and the hill was

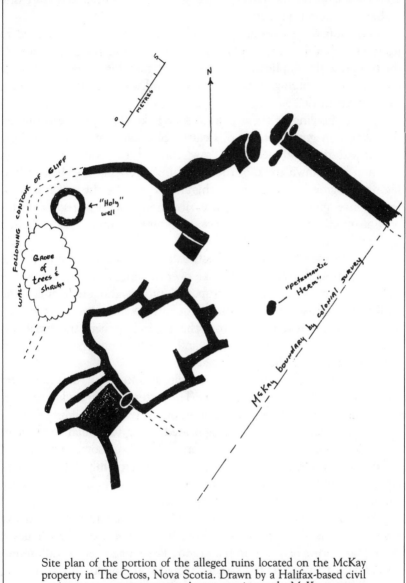

Site plan of the portion of the alleged ruins located on the McKay property in The Cross, Nova Scotia. Drawn by a Halifax-based civil engineer to our measurements. Apparent ruins on the McKay property include part of an exterior wall, a well and the foundation of a small interior building. Ruins extend onto neighbouring properties of The Cross.

accurately rendered in all her artwork, Jeanne had painted all of the castle on her own modest property.

Jason rolled his eyes and we smiled politely. It never occurred to Jeanne that her property would not accommodate such a castle. Nor did she recognize the implications of the site plan and its scale. Yet, Jeanne McKay was an intelligent woman. Her mind was just blocked when it came to the castle.

While showing us these paintings and sketches, Jeanne confessed that she often got visions of this castle. She sometimes induced these visions with rites and spells. She "saw" some of the people of the castle, too, and had drawn some of them. Again, witchcraft had helped her. Jason's eyes grew large listening to this and he regarded the lemonade that Jeanne had given him with grave suspicions, perhaps regretting his previous snide remark about *eohippi* and Smurfs . . . maybe remembering the garden toads . . .

All of this seemed to be hopelessly balmy, yet it wasn't wholly so. The explorations we'd been able to make over the entire hill top traced the walls that ran off the McKay property onto neighbouring ones. The outline did suggest a 5-sided structure of fairly large extent. At intervals, at the corners, were tumbles of stone that might have been the remains of 5 towers. There were other walls and patterns that may have been outbuildings around the central one.

The castle that Jeanne "saw" was an idealized one, and her mind insisted that it was all on her property. The patterns in her back yard were, in reality, only one small wall segment, one very small building foundation, and a well. The building appeared to be too small for human habitation, only about 15 feet square. There was some evidence of collapsed chimney-like ruins and, given the proximity of this small building to the well, it might have been a structure for some activity requiring water, anything from a forge to a bakery.

Aside from the fact that most of the castle could not be on her property, it was obvious that it had not been the sort of Late Medieval thing that Jeanne had seen in her vision. There had been no tall, round towers with pointed roofs. No crenellated battlements. It had looked nothing like a story-book illustration of Camelot.

But it might have looked similar to the real Camelot, and similar to the fortress that Henry Sinclair built in the Orkney Islands in Kirkwall when he began the conquest of his earldom.[2]

Rather than walls, the perimeter of this construction could better be described as "barriers" or "palisades". The walls had been formed of piles of stone, incorporating large boulders which had been rolled into position. The outline of the whole thing seemed to have been laid out with the idea of including boulders too large to move. This resulted in an irregular 5-sided shape. I was inclined to think that the towers had been merely larger and taller piles of stone, and not at all "hollow" constructions of any sort. They were vantage-points where cannon could be sited, and archers placed, so as to fire down upon anyone trying to scale the walls themselves. Judging from the amount of stone lying around, I guessed that the stonework had been perhaps 6 feet high or less. The towers might have been 4-6 feet higher than the walls.

It would have been easy to build a wooden palisade on top of the stone one. Vertical logs could have been jammed down into the interstices between stones and boulders, and horizontal logs stacked up between these vertical ones. Any wood in the walls had long since rotted away.

There was a quantity of fine sand mixed among the stones, and this didn't seem to exist anywhere else on the hill top except within the stone patterns and piles. Jeanne believed that this sand was all that remained of mortar. Mortar is a mixture of cement, lime or gypsum plaster, and sand and water. Cement is a mixture of burnt clay and limestone. Lime mortar generally is superior to gypsum mortar. All of these materials are ready to hand in Nova Scotia. The lime would have been the only difficulty. It could have been extracted by burning clam shells, and any Micmac kitchen midden would have provided a good supply of these, but the nearest source would have been the coast. The sea was 17 miles distant to the east (the Atlantic) and about 20 miles distant to the west (Bay of Fundy).

The builders may have decided to use gypsum instead of lime since there are easily visible gypsum deposits only a mile away. If so, it was very possible, as Jeanne had concluded, that this inferior mortar had gradually deteriorated leaving only the sand behind. But, if this stronghold had been constructed in great haste, the builders might not have used real mortar at all, but simply a filler of sand and clay. This would have cut the wind, but would have leached away fairly quickly to leave only sand.

One thing seemed clear to us. There seemed to have been a large construction of some sort on this hill top. It had nothing to do with colonial settlement because the walls sometimes cut across the boundaries that had been established by colonial surveys and which were marked on maps, and which still constituted some present property lines.

Jeanne's ideas were both strangely wrong and disconcertingly accurate. Her visions had contained the right sort of shape, but the wrong architectural style. They had shown her the correct relative sizes of the parts of the ruins, but had inexplicably compelled her to shrink the whole complex of ruins down to fit on *her* property. Nonetheless, the visions she had were generally correct, and it was hard to explain this. Her visions lent substance to her assertion that she and John had known about the place before immigrating to Canada and had come at least partly to search for it. They'd bought the only available property on the hill, and it did have a small fraction of the ruins on it. Jeanne had adopted the whole, which all the other villagers ignored and denied, and, in her imagination, placed all of the castle on her land.

Perhaps she'd had visions in England. I asked her this, but she continued to maintain that she knew about the site from stories in her family (who were Stuart pretenders). The visions had started to come only after she'd moved to Nova Scotia.

Jeanne's visions seemed to be a part of that mysterious *something* that has always moved beneath the blanket of history. The not-quite-tangible hints, clues and connections that, nevertheless, resulted in very real things: like the stones of The Cross, the Money Pit, the two Oak Islands, Sinclair's voyage, Godfroi de Bouillon and the Templars, Joseph of Arimathaea and Glastonbury, the Marys and the Holy Grail.

But, as for the ruins themselves, it seemed virtually certain that some large structure and community had once existed on the hill top of The Cross. I say "virtually" because it seemed just as clear that the structures had been purposefully and efficiently destroyed at some later date. The suggestions remained, the patterns, but there was not one undeniable piece of wall still standing. Someone had clearly tried to erase all obvious evidence that there had ever been a castle and a community, but they had not quite succeeded.

It was not quite tangible, like so much else we had been pursuing. You *could* attribute the stone patterns to chance, or to glacial action. I couldn't swear in court that there was a genuine ruin, but I thought so.

If it was the sort of structure I have described, then it could have been made by a force of about 20 men over a period of 3 or 4 months, or less if there was some of it already existing. Some of the boulders looked

damnably like collapsed dolmens, some groups of standing stones looked
for all the world like British megaliths. There were suggestions of ancient
occupation.

The well water turned out to be exceptionally good water, and in an
area with a contamination problem. Nova Scotia is mineral rich. A lot of
Nova Scotian wells penetrate heavy metal deposits and the resulting
water can be unfit for consumption. The town of Waverly outside of
Halifax has a problem with arsenic-contaminated water. Harrietsfield,
also a suburb of Halifax, has a uranium problem. These cases of pollution
from natural deposits make the headlines in Nova Scotia regularly. As the
detection methods have improved, and as the health hazards of heavy
metal contamination have become appreciated, this issue has become a
topic of general public concern in Nova Scotia. The Cross, too, has a
uranium problem. There are deposits not far below the surface. Wells and
some surface water are contaminated. The health authorities have not yet
announced this officially pending further study and a better assessment of
the danger. We learned this from our talks with the people who analysed
the water for radioactivity and non-radioactive metals.

The water from the McKay property was completely free of any heavy
metal content. It was also "soft" in an area of rather "hard" water.
Perhaps, over time, the Indians observed the harmful effects of the water
around The Cross, except for the pure water in this well, and regarded it
as holy or special for that reason. We were never able to confirm Jeanne's
assertion that the well pre-dated the known colonists in the area, nor
were we able to speak with any Micmac Indians who could confirm or
deny Jeanne's insistence that the Indians had considered it holy. The two
Micmacs who, she said, had told her this story had both died 10 years
before.

Nor was I able to confirm Jeanne's statement that the Indians knew of
Europeans at The Cross before the known colonists. One Micmac, the
oldest man on a reservation near Berwick about 25 miles away, but who
had once lived near The Cross, told me that he "could tell me some
things", but that I was "asking too much." He was very reluctant to talk.

This brings us to an observation that must be made in order to clear
up a misapprehension. Our university libraries are crammed with eth-
nological studies that purport to describe and relate the beliefs of "primitive peoples." Generally, some anthropologist or ethnologist visits some
tribe for a few weeks or months, asks some questions and records a lot of

chants and stories that the people are willing to let him hear. Then, the "expert" returns to write his book. The shelves are filled with many "studies" and they are 99 percent bunk.

Aside from the problem of interpreting what these people are saying through their myths, allegories and legends, there's the much bigger problem that they tell the white man what he wants to hear. Or, what they *think* he wants to hear. Or, maybe, they tell him nonsense just to get rid of him as soon as possible. They do not tell white men the truth for the very good reason that they don't trust any Europeans out of long and tragic experience. European arrogance has led to ridicule of everything they really do believe, and to exploitation.

Few anthropologists and ethnologists are likely to admit that "studies" by such doyens as Boaz, Margaret Mead and Malinowsky are so much wasted pulpwood, but a couple of examples (the first one will become relevant to a sequel to this book) suggest that this is so.

French anthropologists Marcel Griaule and Germaine Dieterlen lived among the Dogon people of West Africa *for 20 years* and had already written volumes about their supposed beliefs and social structure. It was only when the Dogon learned that Griaule was terminally ill that they held a meeting of elders and decided to reveal the real tribal secrets which they'd disguised and hidden for 20 years and which neither Griaule nor Dieterlen had ever suspected. Apparently, this decision was made only because of the immense respect that Griaule and Dieterlen had earned over the period of a generation among these people. The revelations of the Dogons were shocking, and even had repercussions at NASA. These are of great relevance to *this* story, but in a sequel book. The present point is just that these real secrets of the Dogon actually dictated and molded their social structure. For 20 years they'd been telling Griaule and Dieterlen much less than the truth. The Dogon revelations required another book, *Le Renard Pâle*, to correct all of what had been written previously. Maybe another, similar example emphasizes the point.

Halfway around the world, the Polynesians had said all along that they came from the east into the Pacific. European "experts", however, decided that this couldn't be true and agreed instead that the Polynesians must have come from the west, from Malaya. The latest *National Geographic* migration map of the Pacific still reflects this nonsense. Finally, the Polynesians just gave up talking to anthropologists and ethnologists and began to feed them what they wanted to hear. Everybody was happy that the Polynesians had seen the error of their ways. Then, Thor Heyerdahl proved beyond doubt that the Polynesians had, in fact, migrated into the Pacific from the east, from America. This is gradually becoming accepted now, as those "experts" die off who are responsible for so many textbooks which are mere rubbish.

Now, if Griaule and Dieterlen can live among the Dogon, and be respected over a period of 20 years and yet still not learn the real beliefs of these people, then how can some hot-shot academic spend a few weeks or months with a tribe and expect to come away with any idea of what they know and believe?

I knew very well that the Micmac Indians don't differ from other exploited peoples in their views toward white men. I didn't expect to get anything out of them. Their beliefs and knowledge have been ridiculed and distorted by white "experts" for so long that they just clam up. I have often wondered, for instance, whether there was always a perfectly straightforward account of who Glooscap really was, and what he really did, and that the "myths" and songs were composed to entertain patronizing Victorian folklorists who expected "mythological" accounts. The Micmacs have, after all, suffered the indignity of having their writing system attributed to a man who was manifestly a liar and a fake, but who has a plaque commemorating his good work among the benighted savages. Why should they talk to anyone?

Since the Micmac sources were closed to us, except for the scraps that Pohl managed to salvage from the Glooscap legends as told to Victorians, that left us with only European records to rely on.

These records do refer to a refuge in Nova Scotia. The records are the earliest maps of Nova Scotia.

Jeanne had told us about these early on, and we had confirmed their existence and strange references in Ganong's *Crucial Maps*. Many of our excursions involved trips to see, with our own eyes, the coastal areas shown on these maps and described by early explorers.

It is always helpful, when checking old maps and early accounts, to see the country described with your own eyes if at all possible. This policy enabled us, as we'll see a bit later, to discover that Champlain's accounts are purposefully distorted when it comes to the Bay of Fundy, for instance. An incident he relates is utterly impossible, but significant. Our trips helped us to appreciate what some of the early cartographers were trying to tell some mariners. Some of the map-makers apparently knew a secret.

Henry Sinclair decided to found a settlement, as *The Zeno Narrative* tells us. He stayed behind to do it, wintering in Estotiland which was Nova Scotia. "The Zeno Map of the North" shows two settlements in Estotiland and these are, in the usual medieval convention, represented by little castles. One of these settlements is shown on the map at just below 63 degrees at the far right, the other is shown further down on the right just below 62 degrees. This more southerly settlement is *to the east of a large river or estuary.* Since Estotiland can only be Nova Scotia because of the open pitch deposits encountered there and all the other geographic features which fit the narrative and apply only to Nova Scotia, then this large river must be an attempt to show the Bay of Fundy. The castle is mid-peninsular, just like the ruins at The Cross.

I take these two castles to represent Pictou, the "town of a hundred wigwams", in the north, and The Cross in the south. This "Zeno Map of the North" is, in many ways, in much the same class as the portolans. Although "The Zeno Map of the North" as it comes down to us was created by Antonio (most probably) about 1400 A.D., it betrays proof that he based it on another and much more accurate map. This was the one that probably came from the Middle East with refugee Templars to Rosslyn. But, from Antonio's point of view, the problem with this Middle Eastern map was that he didn't understand it completely. Although it did show lands across the ocean, which was the main thing, it was drawn on a conic projection.

This is not supposition or speculation on my part, but a fact that has been demonstrated by Professor Hapgood and the Strategic Air Command's mapping department. Hapgood transferred "The Zeno Map of the North" onto a modern and highly accurate polar projection and, when that was done, the relative longitudes and latitudes of the places showed amazing accuracy.[3]

Because Antonio didn't understand the conic, polar projection, he changed it on his copy to something he did understand, more or less, and this distorted everything. As for the lands themselves, Antonio relied on the accurate original when he copied Greenland because he'd never been there and he had no choice. *No known European had been to northern Greenland,* yet, Greenland is the most accurate land on "The Zeno Map of the North." As for places that he had visited, or had heard of, Antonio "im-

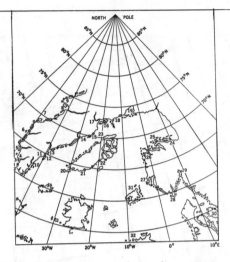

The entire Zeno map drawn on modern polar projection. Professor Charles Hapgood found that the geographic positions of 32 places were represented with remarkable accuracy of latitude and longitude. Antonio Zeno must have based his map on a source map with a projection like this, which he did not understand, and imposed his own meaningless and inaccurate grid system.

proved" the original from his own knowledge. This is why the coastlines look so primitive and inaccurate whenever Antonio "improved" things.

A detailed analysis of this map can be found in Hapgood's book (*Maps of the Ancient Sea Kings*) for anyone who's interested, and I have covered only enough here to make a point: Antonio's map almost proves that Glooscap was Henry Sinclair.

Antonio left Sinclair in Nova Scotia and there's no evidence that Antonio sailed further than the harbour of Trin with its headland extending eastwards out into the sea, Cape Trin. This harbour and headland are drawn with great emphasis on Antonio's map, but the map also shows, quite clearly and much more accurately than many later maps, the inlet that is the Bay of Fundy. Yet, *Antonio had never been there*. His narrative says that he sailed back almost immediately. He could only have learned about the Bay of Fundy from Henry Sinclair when the "Prince" finally returned home. Only then could Antonio draw more than Cape Trin and the harbour of Trin. Only from Henry's account could Antonio draw the rest of Estotiland and place the settlements in it.

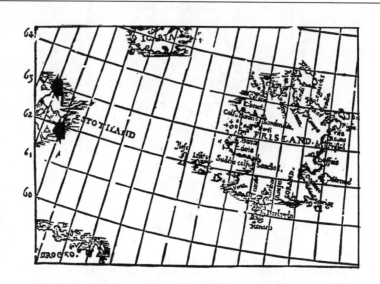

Part of the "Zeno Map of the North" showing two settlements, represented by castles, at the edge of the map at 63 and 62 degrees. Estotiland is Nova Scotia.

If Sinclair told Antonio about the Bay of Fundy, then Sinclair must have been there, *just as Glooscap had explored the Bay of Fundy*. The Micmac itinerary for Glooscap is reflected in Antonio's map based on Sinclair's voyage.

The map has another "almost-proof" that Glooscap must have been Sinclair. Up to the time Antonio sailed back he referred to Estotiland as an island. He had no reason for suspecting it might not be an island. Nova Scotia is almost an island. It is attached to the continent by a narrow isthmus only 17 miles wide. It is a peninsula, not an island. Glooscap would have discovered this fact while exploring the Bay of Fundy. From Cape D'Or it appears that the Bay of Fundy comes to an end, and that salt water might not completely surround Nova Scotia. Sinclair would have explained this when he returned to Orkney and discussed his explorations with Antonio. Only then could Antonio have drawn the new land as a peninsula, and not as the island he originally thought it was and which he called it in his letter home to Carlo in Venice.

Estotiland is right on the edge of the map, unfortunately, and we cannot tell whether it is an island or a peninsula of a larger continent. We do not know what Antonio intended to convey. Cartographers had a convention of labelling islands that were not immediately obvious as islands, such as islands that were cut off on the edge of maps. This was a safety precaution for mariners. An island labelled as such on the edge of a map could be sailed around, with due caution, in relative safety. Any land on the edge of a map not labelled as an island indicated an extensive coastline immediately beyond toward which a sailor could not sail with any safety. Antonio does not label Estotiland as an island, and, as it appears, it is a much better representation of peninsular Nova Scotia than any other map up until about 1570. If he did learn that Nova Scotia was a peninsula from Sinclair, and if he intended to present it that way by omitting the "island" label, then it proves that Sinclair explored Fundy to its headwaters to make absolutely certain that it had a termination.

According to Glooscap's itinerary as reconstructed from the legends, he did exactly this. The Bay of Fundy ends in two sub-bays which both penetrate far inland. Glooscap supposedly explored both of these sub-bays to the very end. Pohl deals with this important point in great detail, but, of course, he has no idea of why Glooscap/Sinclair should have gone to so much trouble to find out that the new land wasn't an island.

Why was it so important to determine whether Estotiland was an island or a peninsula? The answer is simple: if a refuge was being planned, *Sinclair would have wanted to know how many water approaches he had to deal with*. Glooscap, by completing a rather hectic schedule of explorations in Fundy headwaters, established that only two water approaches had to be guarded, not three or four. The fact that Estotiland proved to be a peninsula was of great strategic importance for any planned secret haven.

"The Zeno Map of the North" doesn't prove anything beyond doubt, but it is suggestive of a great deal.

Many other maps are just as suggestive, if not more so. The Caspar Vopell map of 1545 illustrates the coast of Nova Scotia with a Templar knight! Aside from the matter of the knight, this map is worth reproducing because it shows how "good" Antonio's map was compared to one made 150 years later. Vopell doesn't know nearly as much as Zeno did. "C. Raso" on Vopell's map must be Cape Race on the east coast of Newfoundland, but he's sort of combined Newfoundland and Cape Breton Island into one amorphous mass of imaginary island groups.

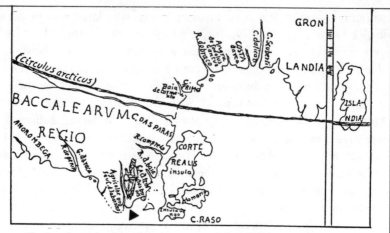

Tracing from the Bjornbo photocopy of the 1570 engraved copy of Caspar Vopel's map of 1545, after Ganong. Note the decorative illustration of the Templar knight on the coast of Nova Scotia. Also, just across the river from the knight is the legend: "Agricolae pro Seu. C. d. laborador."

Reproduced from Crucial Maps in the Early Cartography and Place Nomenclature of the Atlantic Coast of Canada, by W. F. Ganong, by permission of the University of Toronto Press.

Nonetheless, this "Corte Realis insula" serving double-duty as both Newfoundland and Cape Breton does provide a focus of a sort. The Templar is southwest on what passes for the coast of Nova Scotia.

Although "experts" claim to be able to distinguish a lot of individual features on maps like this which, they say, represent known bays, capes, islands, etc., I don't think that a map as crude as this allows much specific comment. The knight seems to be on the Atlantic coast of Nova Scotia, and where he is on that coast simply can't be guessed. If the "R. de penin" (River of the Peninsula?) is supposed to represent the entrance of the Bay of Fundy (even though it extends northwest instead of northeast), then the knight would be about half-way along the Atlantic coast of Nova Scotia, somewhere near Mahone Bay and the famous Oak Island.

Then, there's "Agricolae pro Seu C. d. laborador." "Labrador" has been a highly mobile geographical place-name. It was originally applied to the coast of Nova Scotia, but, as Nova Scotia became better known and many features recieved names, there came a time when room for "Labrador" got scarce. "Labrador" then began a migration on maps until it finally ended up where it is today, north of the St. Lawrence River on the eastern edge of Canada opposite Newfoundland.

No one really knows what "Labrador" means, either. The obvious idea is the Iberian word for "labourer". But it could also mean something like "Le bras d'or", "the golden arm" of water, perhaps, at sunrise or sunset. This is not so far-fetched. The interior of Cape Breton Island is a sort of inland mini-sea with two outlets to the Atlantic via very narrow channels. This is called "The Bras d'Or Lake" even though this "lake" is salt water. Was this lake first called "Labrador" when the name passed through Cape Breton on its long migration northward? Or was it originally named for something to do with "golden arms"?

Either is possible, and probably the name stuck because of a combination of both. The salt water lake is divided into a number of long and narrow channels, and these are oriented northeast-southwest, which is to say, toward sunrise *in the summer* when foreign mariners were likely to have visited the place. And, the lake is an ideal harbour. I have seen summer dawns on Bras d'Or when it would have been easy to swear that the water was a cast arm of molten gold stretching away into the distance.

But, on the Vopell map, this "laborador" occurs in a longer place-name and it makes some sense, after a fashion. The "Agricolae pro Seu C. d. laborador" means "Farms (or farmers) for the Lord of the cape of labourers" ... or rather, that's the gist of the notation in a deliberate mixture of several languages, along with the abbreviations that map-makers of this period were apt to use. Cartographers of the 1500s used a combination of Latin, Italian, Spanish, French and English in a kind of "pidgin" that, hopefully, could be understood by their multi-national seafaring clients. That is what the notation seems to mean in this patois. We are stuck with the idea of some Lord who controlled a cape of labour or labourers, and who had some farms (or farmers).

Which Lord? What labourers? And what farms ... in 1545? This "Agricolae pro Seu C. d. laborador" is next to the Templar knight, right across the river to the west.

This knight *is* a Templar, too. He has a cross on his shield and no other insignia. Only the Templars were allowed to have just the cross on their shields, or maybe it is more accurate to say that they were required to have the cross on their shields and were forbidden to display any other device. Templar recruits had to give up all their lands and titles, swearing loyalty only to Christ. Vopell clearly intends to convey the idea of a

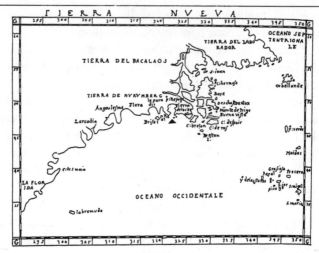

Tracing, much reduced, of a photo of the original Gastaldi map in the Venice Ptolemy of 1548, after Ganong. The map may have been drawn as early as 1539. Note the "p:Refuge" a little to the right of centre.

Reproduced from Crucial Maps in the Early Cartography and Place Nomenclature of the Atlantic Coast of Canada, by W. F. Ganong, by permission of the University of Toronto Press.

medieval Templar and has correctly drawn the "Crusader" type of shield, not the shape in vogue in 1545.

Maybe some Templars were mining with labourers and needed farms to feed them.

The Gastaldi map first appeared in the Venice Ptolemy of 1548, three years after the Vopell map, but may have been drawn as early as 1539.

At first glance, it doesn't look much like the coast of Canada either, but a careful look will reveal some place names to give a focus. Just to the right of centre is "c: de ras", which is Cape Race in Newfoundland again. Just west of this is "c:breton", Cape Breton, correctly shown as an island.

Then things start to get a bit interesting. Just west of Cape Breton we have "tierra de los brator" which actually means nothing at all in any known language, but you get the idea by now. This is applied to the Nova Scotia mainland. Right beside this name, and almost exactly in the centre of the map is a roughly circular bay. Above it is written "p:Refuge", Port Refuge.

The authoritative volume on Nova Scotia place-names assures everyone that Port Refuge received its name in 1620 because a foundering ship needed a haven in a storm. The authoritative opus doesn't explain how the name pops up on a map made about 80 years earlier. There are other interesting place-names on this map: "Larcadia", "Angoulesme", "Flora", "le paradis".

As our historical research progressed, the place-names on the Gastaldi maps began to fascinate us because they can be made to form a message which has relevance to our story: " The *flower* of *Angoulême* has found a *refuge* in *the paradise* of *Arcadia* in the *land of Norumbega*."

Tradition says that the treasure of the Cathars was taken out of doomed Montségur before the citadel surrendered. It was supposedly hidden in moutain caves for a while. But true safety demanded that the treasure be taken out of the Pyrenees, and even out of France, eventually. This could most easily be done using the Garonne River which flows out of the Pyrenees to the Atlantic. Now, it may be recalled that the Templar port was La Rochelle on the Bay of Biscay north of the Garonne estuary. The largest nearby town and fortress was Angoulême in the 14th Century. We considered the possibility, therefore, that the "Holy Grail" (or other Cathar treasure) might well have spent some time in Angoulême before arrangements were made to ship it out of La Rochelle. Montségur fell in 1244. The Templar fleet disappeared from La Rochelle in 1307, never to be heard from again. The Holy Grail could have resided in Angoulême for sixty years or so before being evacuated from France. If we are indeed talking about a special lineage of people, then a couple of generations of Holy Blood could have sheltered in secret in Angoulême, in close proximity to La Rochelle, waiting for a propitious time to leave Europe. During this long stay, we thought it possible that the bloodline might have become known as "the flower of Angoulême". The justification for our suspicion was, admittedly, quite slim ... but in addition to Angoulême's strategic position from the Cathar-Templar point of view, we discovered that Angoulême's town seal is a *dragon writhing in flames*. Since the dragon was a Cathar symbol for knowledge or "gnosis", one could translate the meaning of this town seal as "knowledge tormented", a true description of the fall of Montségur and the fate of its defenders. They were all tortured and then burned at the stake.

But perhaps the creation of a "message" in these place-names is just the result of imagination on our part. However, while on the subject of place-names, we considered the possibility that "Cape Race" in New-

Tracing, somewhat reduced, from the Stokes photo of the Gastaldi map of 1556 in Ramusio's Vol. III, after Ganong. Note "Port du Refuge" at the head of Mahone Bay illustrated (correctly) with many islands.

Reproduced from Crucial Maps in the Early Cartography and Place Nomenclature of the Atlantic Coast of Canada, by W. F. Ganong, by permission of the University of Toronto Press.

foundland, variously called "C. raso", "C. de Raz", etc., on old maps might be a memorial to the House of Razès which sheltered the young heir of Dagobert II, Sigisbert IV. Then, given the somewhat disreputable status of Mary Magdalene in the 16th-Century Roman Church, we found it odd that Jacques Cartier would have named the Magdalen Islands after her. And is it merely coincidence that "Montreal" was not only a Templar stronghold in the Holy Land but also a Cathar fortress near Carcassonne?

Gastaldi made another map in 1556. A segment from this later effort shows things more clearly. The circular bay below "Port du Refuge" has now acquired a number of islands. This is meant to represent Mahone Bay which does, in fact, have 350 islands in it and which was sometimes called, on other maps, "the bay of many islands". Port Refuge, then, *is at the mouth of the Gold River.*

Further to the left (west) just next to the word "Terra" there's a large indentation in the coast and, to the west of it, another bay with many islands and a river leading from it. This all reflects the confusion referred to earlier about latitude. The large indentation is the entrance to the Bay of Fundy, while the bay with islands beside it is Passamaquoddy Bay (which also has many islands) in Maine. The river is the Penobscot. Gastaldi is confused about the distribution of land and water because three major bays have roughly the same latitude because of Nova Scotia's east-west orientation.

Gastaldi calls the whole country "La Nvova Francia" ("New France") and calls the region of Nova Scotia "Terra De Nvrvmbega" ("Land of Norumbega"). He gave the region of Nova Scotia the same name in his earlier map, too, "Tierra de Nvrvmberg".

This is not the only map on which "Norumbega" appears, and you'll see it on others reproduced in this section. The important point is that it was first applied to Nova Scotia. Later; like Labrador, it got pushed into the hinterland as Nova Scotia filled up with more specific place-names. Norumbega eventually ended up in southern New Brunswick or Maine, and then disappeared from maps altogether in the 1600s because there was no room for it and regions had by then acquired more familiar names.

Norumbega (or "Anorumbega", "Nuremberg", etc.) is a minor mystery. It is supposed to have been a city about "15 miles" up a river. Several well-known explorers claimed to have visited it in the early 1500s. Verrazano said he travelled to a "Norman villa" in 1524 and found that its inhabitants were rich in furs and gold. In 1525 Estevan Gomez claimed to have captured some people of Norumbega and to have taken them back to Spain.

The word "Norumbega" (or "Nurumberg", etc.) could mean "new city", "northern city". Verrazano, being an Italian, would quite naturally call it something like "Norman villa" (ie. Norman ville) which would mean "Northman town".

There's always been a general agreement that Norumbega, if it really existed, had some connection with Norse. Eben Norton Horsford pointed out as early as 1896 that "Norumbega" was simply the name of Norway during the medieval period and occurs on a number of maps of Scandinavia.

When the word "Norse" is used, everyone immediately thinks of Vikings, but, during the medieval period, a lot of people were "Norse". Normans like William the Conqueror were "Norse", descendants of Northmen raiders of Brittany. Although we think of something like the Bayeux Tapestry as being a "French" creation, it told the story of William the Conqueror's invasion of England. In the words of art expert Eric Maclagen, the Bayeux Tapestry "is a purely Norse thing." Henry Sinclair was "Norse", too, and doubly so. First of all, he was a Norman descendant. His ancestors fought for William and, in fact, no less than nine Saint-Clairs were at the Battle of Hastings. Then, Sinclair became "Norse" when he became the Earl of Orkney because he held the islands as a vassal of the King of Norway.

An Eric the Red or a Lief Ericsson is not required to account for Norumbega. Henry Sinclair could be the explanation. Whereas he might have called the immediate locale around his settlement "Arcadia" after his Orchadie earldom, he might have named the larger region of the peninsula "Norumbega" in honour of Norway and the king, his liege-lord. In fact, that would almost be expected of him. The name would also honour his Norse colleagues who had discovered land to the west in Viking times 400 years before.

We now have a Templar knight illustrated on a coast that Henry Sinclair is known to have explored, with a place-name of Port Refuge at Mahone Bay where the Gold River and Oak Island are located. We have evidence of some ongoing "labouring" activities and of farms.

The "Pseudo-Agnese" map of 1556-1560 shows a very curious feature. It shows a track going across the ocean to end up at Mahone Bay and "p: del refuge". In the middle of this track is a rectangle called "y: de Sabion" ("Island of Sabion"). What is this?

The most obvious notion is that it is a representation of Sable Island, that sandy island with off-lying shoals that has been called "The Grave-yard of the Atlantic" because of all the ships that have run aground on it. The experts almost unanimously agree on this identification.

But a perfectly square island?

Map-makers of this period prudently drew islands with irregular shapes. Not only did this make them look more realistic and natural (when they were often works of imagination), but mariners were warned to beware of any land in the vicinity. No mariner of the time would credit a square island. Further, the track goes across the ocean. Are we to assume a shoal all the way across the Atlantic? There wasn't one, as sailors knew well because, by 1556, there had been plenty of crossings. Pseudo-Agnese's transoceanic shoal was inviting ridicule, or, more aptly, even more ridicule than was usually dumped on map-makers.

Just like "l" and "r" change places (and back again) in the develop-

Tracing, reduced, from a photo of the original "Pseudo-Agnese" map of 1556-1560. Note curious dotted track across the ocean to Port Refuge. After Ganong.

Reproduced from Crucial Maps in the Early Cartography and Place Nomenclature of the Atlantic Coast of Canada, by W. F. Ganong, by permission of the University of Toronto Press.

mental course of languages, so do "v" and "b". Did Pseudo-Agnese know this from a study of old books? It *was* the Renaissance, and cartographers were eagerly reading Greek and Roman texts to get hints of any ancient knowledge of land to the west.

If we substitute "v" for the "b" in Sabion, we get Island of the Saviour, more or less. This would be a ship, maybe, a sort of moveable island with Holy Refugees aboard crossing the ocean to Port Refuge.

Was Pseudo-Agnese indulging in a coy code?

Many of the maps of the 1500s show some or all of these features on the Canadian Atlantic coast, and I think it is fairly obvious by now that a secret refuge was being hinted at. There's really no other explanation.

The "Holy Refugees" would have enjoyed relative peace in Sinclair's haven only for about a century, from 1400 to 1500 A.D. By the early 1500s, traffic was starting to get a bit heavy on the Atlantic. Fishermen from Brittany, Basque whalers and people engaged in the fur trade were all voyaging across the Atlantic from the first decade of the 16th Century. In fact, one gets the impression that the official explorers commissioned by various European monarchs were definitely Johnny-come-latelies in the discovery business.

Given the geographic knowledge of the time, and the fact that our hypothetical refuge was inland and concealed by confusing geography, the refugees could probably have remained beyond the knowledge of casual entrepreneurs if they wanted to. But the handwriting was on the wall. With the advent of official explorers from Europe, purposeful colonization wouldn't lag far behind. Sooner or later, the haven would be discovered.

But, in a way, the refuge had already served most of its purpose. The 1400s had been the really crucial century. Although the religious wars raged during the 1500s and 1600s too, the world started to change. Modern commercialism was beginning to motivate people as much as religion. The "Age of Faith" was giving way to the "Age of Money", and partly because of the mercantile sabotage of feudalism begun by the Templars long before.

Europe's social structure was evolving at an ever-quickening pace. Every year that the refuge could be concealed brought the Holy Bloodline rapidly closer to the dawn of a more modern, and more tolerant, age. Still, the 1500s were very nervous years for descendants of Godfroi de Bouillon, while the 1600s were only a little better.

By the late 1500s, discovery of any hypothetical refuge in Nova Scotia was inevitable in the not-too-distant future. Something would have to be done to establish a more secure haven until the world could evolve just a little more toward tolerance, and something would have to be done to keep official explorers and colonizers in the dark about the Nova Scotia refuge until the relocation could be planned and accomplished. The new site seemed to have been reconnoitred in 1534,[5] but it would take years to prepare. It could not be some nearly-unknown new land whose existence was the secret of a few, as Nova Scotia had been in Sinclair's time, because by 1534 there weren't many places like that left. The new haven would have to be concealed in another way, by disguise and by influence in high places, and, above all, by the promotion of conflict and confusion.

Meanwhile, until the covert operators could complete their infiltration of high places in Europe, the nosy official explorers and colonizers would have to be infiltrated first and led away from The Cross.

There were a lot of people engaged in this task, it appears, and they did it both by accident or design, knowingly or unwittingly. One of them was particularly prominent in early Canadian history. Was Samuel Champlain an agent for the Holy Blood? If so, did he do his work purposefully or was he used without suspecting anything? The evidence suggests that Champlain knew what he was doing.

Before venturing into the journals of Champlain which indicate that he was trying to hide part of New France while trying to map the rest of it, something has to be said about the religious background of the times and the position of the "Holy Blood".

It has been suggested that the Cathars were a sort of "proto-Protestant", and this is true in a general way from one point of view. But this is not to suggest that Protestantism by about 1550 was in any way a "Holy Blood" movement, or a slightly more successful kind of "secret society" that had survived the Templar and Cathar defeats. The Holy Blood is something "other". It is a secret doctrine that compels obligations that few can accept. Organized major religions have been built around *part* of the truth of the Holy Blood, but have not been able to embrace or incorporate *all* of the truth.

Religions attracting a great number of people have inevitably jettisioned more and more of the whole truth until only a digestible portion is left that can be swallowed by average intelligence, average commitment and average imagination.

Therefore, although the Cathars may have been "proto-Protestants" of a sort, Protestantism, as it evolved and grew, became an organized and mass religion that could no longer appreciate, or tolerate, the secret that had once been part of its own origin and philosophy. Just as the Church broke its pact with Clovis' descendants for practical and populist reasons, Protestantism increasingly repudiated its origins as it gained adherents.

So, although the Holy Bloodline came into conflict with the Roman Church, and although Protestantism may have received some impetus from the Cathars, Templars and "Holy Bloodline secret", Protestantism as a whole grew away from the philosophy and truth represented by de Bouillon's lineage. It came to pass that Protestants could be, and were, just as intolerant as Roman Catholics, as the Salem witch trials show.

The Holy Bloodline is neither "Protestant" nor "Catholic", but was forced to infiltrate both sects of Christianity in order to protect itself in European affairs. Some individuals, whether "Catholic" or "Protestant" knew the secret and were actively engaged in protecting the de Bouillon lineage irrespective of their nominal and professed faith. Often, indeed, they were able to work best when disguised as religious zealots of one sort or the other. It is hard to distinguish such infiltrators from *real* religious zealots. Therefore, in relating some curious facts about the exploration of Acadia and New France, it is not so simple as opposing teams at a football game, or "Good Guys vs. Bad Guys". The agents of the Holy Blood were a *third* team which infiltrated both of the others and which had its own scoring system. All Protestants were not "pro" Holy Blood and in on the secret, just as all the Roman Catholics were not "anti" Holy Blood and determined to eradicate the lineage.

The great majority of Catholic and Protestant worshippers could not have suspected the Holy Blood's existence during the 16th and 17th Centuries any more than 20th Century churchgoers do. During the 1500s and 1600s the Holy Blood was a reality (and a problem) only for those who knew the seed within the shell of organized religion and established royalty, and they were few: the descendants of de Bouillon themselves; and the kings, princes, popes, cardinals and Protestant reverends they manipulated or blackmailed. Or recruited. This realization of the Holy Blood's existence, which was characterized by inconsistency and intrigue in the highest stratum of European society, was operative among a few although it molded nations.

Before leaving this general religious background, it must also be said that the other two major religions of the Western world, Judaeism and Islam, exhibited exactly the same evolution as did Christianity. They, too, gradually came to reject the entire original foundation in favour of only a small part.

The secret doctrine of the Holy Blood cuts brutally through the most cherished beliefs and dogmas of all three major Western religions. It mocks the small part that each has chosen to promote as the "whole" truth, and threatens the all-too-human hierarchies that have been established to promote these rival "mini-parcels" of the truth as the entire story. All three major organized religions of the West are hostile toward the secret and the threat represented by the Holy Bloodline, but I've been forced to tell this story through its impact upon European and "Christian" society, not only because that context is more familiar to readers, but because it is more familiar to me. The same story could be told differently.

The rabbis of the Exilic period, who "edited" the Old Testament, were no different from the Catholic churchmen who "edited" the New Testament. The schism in Islam between the Shi'ites and Sunnis reflect the same sort of development toward a more palatable and chauvinistic truth.

And, just as there are some Catholic priests and Protestant ministers in Europe who know the truth and who either fear it or try to promote it discreetly to those who can accept it, some Jewish rabbis and Islamic mullahs possess the same knowledge and must make the same choice.

In what follows, therefore, one must be careful not to adopt a "Good Guys vs. Bad Guys" or football fan approach, but simply appreciate the fact that inexplicable events happened and that personalities (whether Catholic or Protestant) behaved in very inconsistent ways. One can chalk this up to human foible if that's easier to digest, or, one can realize that the inexplicable happenings and inconsistent relationships do form a pattern.

And, to get back to where we were before the general religious background, that pattern suggests the concealment of the Nova Scotian refuge and the establishment of a new haven in Montreal.

Samuel Champlain appears to have been prominent in the conceal-ment operation, and relating a bit of what he did and didn't do will pave the way for an appreciation of the underground nature of the colony at Montreal.

Samuel Champlain was supposedly born in Brouage around the year 1567. The exact date and year are uncertain. Brouage was once a fairly major seaport, but since 1586 its harbour has been silted up with sand. Brouage is about 17 miles from the old Templar port of La Rochelle. Some authorities suspect that Champlain may have been born a Protestant, but he later became a Catholic.[6]

He is known, of course, because of his explorations of New France and Acadia which, at that time comprised any and all of the new western lands north of 40° latitude (roughly, modern New York City). "Acadia" extended from this lower limit of 40° to 46° (even more roughly, the middle of modern Cape Breton Island). Nobody knew exactly where any of this was, or how far inland it might extend.

> Well has Champlain earned the title of 'father of New France'. From 1603, when he first visited the St. Lawrence, until his death he devoted all his energies and all his thoughts to the discovery, occupation and colonisation of that country. His works dispel the

darkness in which hitherto New France had been enshrouded ...
from the Bay of Fundy on the east to Lake Huron on the west, and
from Lake Champlain in the south to Lake Nipissing in the north.[7]

In researching all that follows, I've consulted many sources on
Champlain but have chosen to rely upon, and quote from, the most
authoritative English-language work on the subject of Champlain's explorations. This is entitled *The Works of Samuel De Champlain*, in 6
volumes, and was the effort of six Canadian scholars under the general
editorship of H.P. Biggar. This massive work was originally published by
The Champlian Society of Toronto between 1922 and 1936, and was
reprinted by the University of Toronto in 1971. It includes all of Champlain's journals in both original French and English translation, many
notes by the six contributing scholars, and reproductions of Champlain's
maps and sketches (the most important in a portfolio, Vol 7.).

Although this is *the* authoritative work, in English, on the subject of
Champlain's explorations, and although the six notable Canadian
scholars are almost irritating with the profusion of their comments,
observations and their identifications of various places that Champlain
mentions, not one of them expresses curiosity about what Champlain
fails to do and fails to mention. Not one picked up on the curious manner
in which Champlain avoids describing certain important features, and
not one realized that Champlain's statements about latitude can sometimes refer to two places at once.

The most puzzling omissions in Champlain's explorations happen to
concern two places that are significant in this story of a possible refuge in
Nova Scotia. These two places are Mahone Bay and Minas Basin, the
locations of the two Oak Islands which, we have suggested, may have
been "doors" to an inland haven as well as lookout posts to give warning
about the approach of unwanted visitors.

Champlain first came to Acadia, old Nova Scotia, in 1604 as a
member of de Monts' colonization expedition. De Monts, a French
nobleman and a Protestant (or "Huguenot"), had obtained a monopoly
in the New France fur trade from the French king. The first man in the
17th Century to have been granted the fur monopoly was Pierre Chauvin,
another Protestant, who died in 1603. De Monts proposed to the king
that the fur trade could pay for the cost of colonization without, in
Champlain's words, "drawing anything from the royal exchequer".

Champlain then proceeds to describe the voyage in detail, and the quoted passages are from the English-language translation referred to. The italics in the following passages are mine.

> The Sieur de Monts, having by virtue of his commission made known throughout all the ports and harbours of this Kingdom the injunction against fur-trading granted to him by his Majesty, collected about 120 workmen whom he embarked in two vessels: one of the burden of 120 tons wherein commanded the Sieur de Pont-Gravé, and the other, of 150 tons, wherein he himself took passage along with several noblemen.
>
> We set out from Havre de Grace on the seventh of April, one thousand six hundred and four, and Pont-Gravé on the tenth, with a rendezvous at Canso, twenty leagues from Cape Breton. *But when we were on the high sea, Sieur de Monts changed his mind, and set course towards Port Mouton, because it is farther to the south and also a more convenient place for making land than Canso.*
>
> *On the first of May we sighted Sable Island . . . distant about thirty leagues from Cape Breton . . .*
>
> On the eighth of the same month, we sighted cape La Have, *to the eastward of which lies a bay* containing a good many islands, covered with firs, *and on the mainland are oaks, elms and birches.*[8]

We will have to take this slowly because Champlain crams many red herrings into the descriptions of his Acadian voyage of 1604.

First of all, what responsible commander would change his mind about the agreed-upon landfall with no way of communicating this to his other ship? Then, the reasons that Champlain gives for this not only make no sense, but are false. The fact that Port Mouton is father south is neither here nor there. The more southerly latitude of Port Mouton would make no difference, weather-wise when they could expect to arrive, which would be sometime in May. Then, there's the consideration that no captain could set a course for Port Mouton from any distance out at sea. Latitude sailing was not exact enough to quibble about a landfall at Canso or Port Mouton. The navigator would just end up on the other side, hopefully not too far from his intended destination, and quest north and south until he found it.

And this was why, undoubtedly, Canso had been agreed as the rendezvous in the first place. *It is the most conspicuous cape on the Atlantic coast of Nova Scotia*, with high ground immediately inland, and can be seen for miles from the north or south. It is not just coincidence that

Henry Sinclair also made a landfall in the lee of Cape Canso, as we will remember. It is hard to miss.

So, when Champlain writes that Port Mouton was "a more convenient place for making land" . . . he's lying. Port Mouton is not only at the opposite end of Nova Scotia from Canso, it is the exact opposite kind of place. Port Mouton is a bay whose entrance is partly screened by islands, not a cape. Port Mouton is as hard to find as Canso is easy to find.

But this is all more or less irrelevant since, whatever the course steered, de Monts' ship ended up near Canso *anyway*. On the first of May they "sighted Sable Island". It isn't "about thirty leagues from Cape Breton", but more like 100 (Champlain's leagues are about 2 1/2 miles). This is probably just an honest mistake since Champlain had never been there before and was speaking from hearsay. The curious thing is that Sable Island is closer to Canso than to Cape Breton, and it is *much* closer to Canso than to Port Mouton. About twice as close. Sable Island is low and cannot be sighted from any great distance, which is why so many ships have run aground there and the reason it is called the Graveyard of the Atlantic.

That being the case, de Monts' ship was close to Sable Island and therefore, whether he wanted to be or not, was twice as close to Cape Canso as to Port Mouton. Since he was almost there *anyway*, why not keep the Canso rendezvous with Pont-Gravé?

They could not have known exactly where they were until they sighted Sable Island. This uncertainty in navigation is confirmed by the fact that de Monts' ship was itself almost wrecked on the island. In a part of the account I skipped, Champlain mentions:

> . . . we ran the risk of being lost through the error of our pilots, who were wrong in their calculations, making us forty leagues further on than we really were.[9]

In short, de Monts fixed his position at Sable Island, and *then* turned south for Port Mouton instead of north for Canso in spite of the fact he was much closer to the agreed rendezvous than to his changed destination, and then proceeded to hide his ship in bays instead of heading for conspicuous headlands where Pont-Gravé might sight them. One rather gets the impression that de Monts tried to avoid Pont-Gravé for a little while. Pont-Gravé was a few days behind them, heading for Canso, but his navigation could be no better than that of de Monts' own pilots. He could turn up anywhere along the coast. The only way that de Monts could be certain of avoiding a chance discovery was to embay his ship whenever possible while working down the coast toward Port Mouton. And that's what he did.

On the eighth of May they reached Cape La Have, "to the eastward of which lies a bay containing a good many islands", as Champlain rather coyly tells us.

In a footnote to this passage, one of the six scholars tells us that this bay is the mouth of the La Have River, but this is wrong. The mouth of the La Have River is to the *west* of the cape.[10] To the east of Cape La Have is none other than Mahone Bay, and Champlain's grudging observation of "a good many islands" is something of an understatement because there are no less than 350 islands in Mahone Bay. It is obvious, too, that de Monts ran his ship deep into this bay because the trees "on the mainland" are described. De Monts was screened from the sea by a confusion of 350 islands. Champlain mentions that the islands had "firs", while stating that "oaks" grew on the mainland. We know that at least one island had oaks on it too. Did Champlain specify only firs on the islands in order to disguise the fact that one of them had oaks predominantly?

By the twelfth of May they had reached a place that was just five leagues from Cape La Have, that's only about 12 to 15 miles, which means that de Monts' ship must have spent some two or three days in Mahone Bay. Time enough to do *something* at Oak Island. Champlain doesn't say much about this bay and, for once, the scholars point this out . . .

> Although Champlain made so elaborate a map of this port, and apparently remained there for two or three days, he makes no mention whatsoever of this place in his narrative. It is probable therefore that something has been dropped here in the abbreviation of his journals for publication.[10]

More than that has happened. Champlain did draw a map of the Port and Cape of La Have, and it is a red herring. Champlain's maps are pretty accurate when he had an opportunity to study a place for any length of time. In this case, he was *somewhere* for two or three days. The map he offers as the Port and Cape of La Have, which still bear the names that Champlain gave them, does not have the standard of accuracy usually associated with him. In fact, he rather obviously drew it *while sailing past*

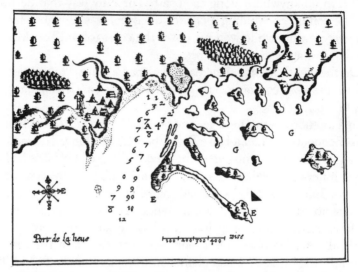

Champlain's map of La Have. Note incorrect shape of the major island
when compared with a 19th Century map below.
Courtesy The Champlain Society.

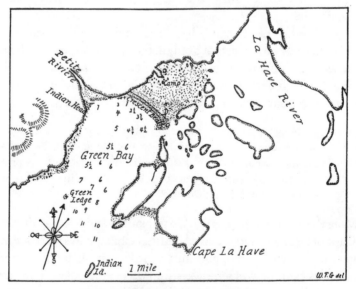

Modern (19th Century) chart of La Have.
Courtesy The Champlain Society.

offshore because he shows the largest and most prominent island, now called "Cape La Have Island" in honour of Champlain's deception, as a long and thin piece of land. But it is not. Not only is it the largest island in this bay, it is not long and thin. It is a piece of land almost as wide as long. Further, a low-lying area in the middle almost splits it in two parts and is shown as a shoal on 19th Century charts. Seen from the sea, however, these two parts seem to overlap, one behind the other, so that the low-lying spit would not be suspected.

If Champlain had really spent 2-3 days in *this* harbour, the one called La Have today because of him, and if he'd gone close enough inshore to distinguish the kinds of trees, then he could not have failed to notice that the largest island in the bay was anything but long and thin. And he could not have failed to notice the shoal-like spit between the island's two halves.

The whole map is an exercise in disinformation. Champlain was not in the place called Cape la Have today in honour of his map. He saw it sailing past to seaward, drew it inaccurately, but *in accordance with the view from seaward* and called the place the Cape and Port of La Have.

In fact, the name of "Cape" La Have is not justifiable at all, not when compared with the real "cape" that projects very prominently out into the Atlantic immediately north and east of the La Have area. In fact, there are two more prominent capes, that would be seen first from de Monts' ship coming from the direction of Sable Island and coasting a safe distance offshore. The most prominent of these is the Lunenburg Peninsula and just west of it is Rose Point. Of the two, Champlain's functional "Cape La Have" which would be a conspicuous landfall from Sable Island must be the Lunenburg Peninsula. It extends a half mile or so seaward of Rose Point. Also, eastwards of Lunenburg Peninsula *is* a bay with "a good many islands", Mahone Bay with its 350 islands, whereas eastwards of Rose Point there's only Rose Bay, a small bay less than a mile across with only two islands in it (Conrad Island and The Long Rock).

The real headland in this vicinity, as is suggested by its name is the Lunenburg Peninsula. The bay with the many islands to the eastwards is Mahone Bay.

Champlain has confused the issue, apparently purposefully, by referring to this prominent headland and the bay with the many islands as La Have in the narrative, and drawing a map of *another* location and giving it "La Have" place-names. The commentators note that there is no description of La Have Cape and Port, *just a map which is inaccurate*. The answer seems to be that Champlain did not spend 2-3 days at the place he calls "La Have" on his map, but viewed it from seaward, as they sailed on toward Port Mouton. He therefore dared not describe it in detail because he really didn't know anything about it.

And he did not want to describe the *real* prominent headland that they saw first coming from Sable Island, nor did he want to describe the bay eastward of it with many islands where he spent 2-3 days.

This is the first time that Champlain ignores the existence of Mahone Bay. But it is not the last.

> On the twelfth of May we entered another port five leagues from La Have, where we seized a vessel that was carrying on the fur trade in violation of the king's injunction. The master's name was Rossignol, and his name clung to this port, which lies in latitude 44°15′.
>
> On the thirteenth of May we arrived at a very fine port, seven leagues from Port Rossignol, called Port Mouton . . .
>
> As soon as we landed, everybody began to construct camps, each after his fancy, upon a point at the entrance of the port close to two ponds of fresh water. *At the same time* the Sieur de Monts despatched a shallop, wherein, with some Indians for guides, he sent one of our men *carrying letters*, to search along the coast of Acadia for Pont-Gravé . . . This man found him *at the Bay of All Isles* . . . and to him the man delivered our letters. As soon as Pont-Gravé had read them, he returned towards his ship at Canso, where he seized some Basque vessels which were trading furs notwithstanding his Majesty's injunction, and sent their captains to the Sieur de Monts, who meanwhile had commissioned me to go and make a survey of the coast and of the ports suitable for the safe reception of our vessels.[11]

The first thing that jumps out is the amount of traffic on this supposedly unexplored coast. De Monts seized one ship at Port Rossignol, while Pont-Gravé seized "some" Basque vessels at Canso. A quarter of a century previously, Sir Humphrey Gilbert found no less than 36 ships in the harbour of St. John's in Newfoundland! The traffic was, indeed, brisk for "unofficial" vessels. The official explorers were Johnny-come-latelies. Perhaps the Holy Refugees, if they existed, survived quite well by trade with renegades and freebooters from Europe . . .

Champlain writes that "as soon as we landed" they started to make camps and "at the same time" de Monts sent someone to look for Pont-

Gravé. This is not true, according to Lescarbot's account of the same voyage. No one was sent to look for Pont-Gravé *for three weeks*. One of the scholars admits that Champlain's statement is "misleading".

The messenger sent by de Monts found Pont-Gravé at the "Bay of All Isles." Where was that? Champlain does not tell us at this point in his narrative, when he logically should, but refers to it only much later, and then curiously. In a passage relating to later explorations in Acadia he says:

> On leaving cape La Have, we went to Sesambre (Sambro), which is an island so named by some men of St. Malo, and distant from La Have fifteen leagues. On the way are a large number of islands which we had named the Martyrs, because some Frenchmen had once been killed there by the Indians. These islands lie in several coves and bays in one of which is a river called Ste. Marguerite . . .[12]

Once again, this can only be Mahone Bay. It is between La Have and Sambro and the "large number of islands" fits. But, again, Champlain refrains from mentioning any name for this bay or telling us much about the geography, except for the Martyrs, named because "some French-man" had "once" been killed there. Who were these Frenchmen? And when were they killed? Champlain's "had been" and "once" implies an event in the distant past. And, a "martyr" is a religious term. Champlain published this account in 1613. Up to that time, no known French priest or "religious person" had been killed on the Atlantic coast of Acadia. Who were these Martyrs in Mahone Bay? Could they have been some of the inhabitants of Norumbega that the Spanish captain, Estevan Gomez, claimed to have captured in 1525? We will return to this possibility in the next chapter.

Champlain seems more than a bit vague in this passage. There is a large number of islands in Mahone Bay, and a large number of coves and smaller bays within it. It is not very helpful for Champlain to say that "in one of" these coves and bays there is a river called Ste. Marguerite. There are many rivers that empty into Mahone Bay. He is trying to call oblique attention to something. But what? Champlain gives a bit more information when he says that "the river called Ste. Marguerite" is:

> . . . seven leagues from Sesambre, which is in latitude 44° 25'. The islands and coasts are covered with quantities of pines, firs, birches . . .[13]

I think it is at least possible that Champlain is saying something in code here, either out of some wistful need to honour a place, or to call attention to it in a way that could only be appreciated by people already in on a secret and who might need up-to-date (for the times) navigational directions. Champlain was by now aware of the northeast-southwest trend of the Nova Scotia coast and aware that several places could have the same latitude as a result. Whereas this fact could lead to confusion, it could also be used to pinpoint a secret location in code while disguising it from all except those needing to know.

Briefly put, *the latitude of Sambro is the same as the latitude of Oak Island and the mouth of the Gold River* . . . at least, *well* within Champlain's usual margin of error. From the general description of his trip to Sambro, a navigator would know that the mouth of the "river called Ste. Marguerite" was southwest of Sambro, a prominent headland where the famous "Sambro Light" now marks the promontory of Chebucto Head, and at latitude 44° 25'. Was the Gold River once called the "Ste. Margaret River" by some martyrs?

Champlain, in the same passage of this later account, makes another curious reference, again followed by a latitude. Passing Sambro, and continuing the passage quoted above, he says:

> We went to a harbour, distant from Sesambre some eight leagues . . .
> We named this place St. Helen's harbour. It lies in latitude 44° 40',
> a little more or less.
>
> From this place we went to a bay called bay of All Islands, which
> is some fourteen or fifteen leagues in circumference . . . the land
> being covered with the same trees I have mentioned above.[14]

Champlain's league was about 2½ miles. This "Bay of All Isles" was, therefore, *about 35-50 miles in circumference*. The scholarly commentators tentatively identify this bay with the present Musquodoboit Harbour or Jeddore Harbour.

But this cannot be. Neither is anywhere near 30-50 miles *in circumference*, and "circumference" is a word implying a circular shape. These harbours are both narrow arms of the sea with a much smaller length of coastline, perhaps 10-15 miles, or a third of what Champlain says.

The latitude he gives in this passage. 44° 40', *happens to be the latitude of the ruins of The Cross with an error of less than 5 miles*, again well within his usual error for latitude. Then, he relates this latitude to the Bay of All

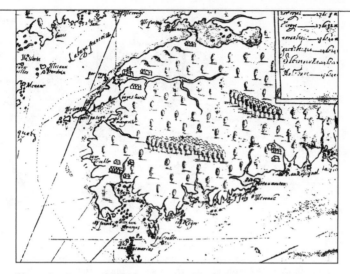

Champlain's map of 1607 begins at La Have and omits Mahone Bay to the east.

Courtesy The Champlain Society.

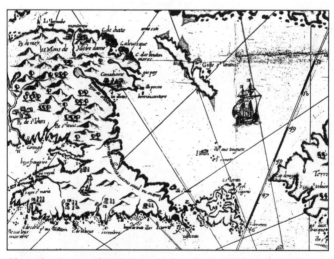

Champlain's map of 1612 does not show Mahone Bay but the "baye de toute illes" would be a good rendition of Mahone Bay if folded over at Sesambre onto the southwest shore.

Note reasonable representation of Minas Basin showing that Champlain must have explored it, yet his description is wrong.

Courtesy The Champlain Society.

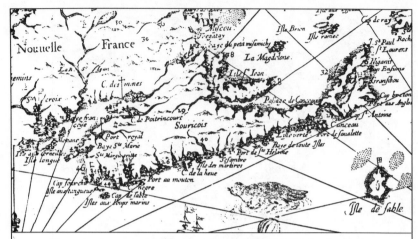

Champlain's map of 1632. Again, the Bay of All Islands can be
transposed onto the southwest shore to yield a reasonable representation of Mahone Bay in *about* the right place . . . but there is no large bay
with islands on the northeast coast of Nova Scotia short of Canso.
Also, note how the map of 1607 is more accurate in general than the
later maps of 1612 and 1632.
                    Courtesy The Champlain Society.

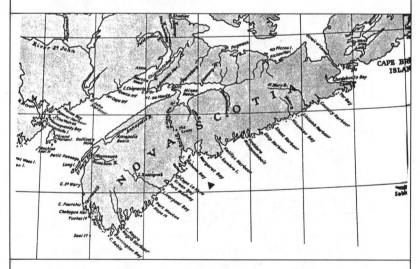

Modern map of Nova Scotia. Compare with Champlain's maps. Note
that Mahone Bay is the largest bay on the entire Atlantic coast, yet
Champlain does not show it although he states he passed by it.
                    Courtesy The Champlain Society.

Isles in the very next sentence. And, in describing this Bay of All Islands, he refers to the trees "mentioned above" where the latitude 44° 25′ is stated in a sentence about the Martyrs and the Ste. Marguerite River, which are doubtless in Mahone Bay.

This "Bay of All Isles" is, then, linked in a cunning series of statements with Mahone Bay. As I have said so many times before, Mahone Bay is a "bay of all isles". Further, the circumference of Mahone Bay *is* about 35-50 miles which Champlain gives for this Bay of All Isles and, moreover, Mahone Bay is circular in shape. It is a regular curved semi-circle, not a long and narrow fiord.

This all might seem a bit forced, and maybe it is, except for one overwhelming fact: Mahone Bay *is the largest bay on the entire Atlantic coast of Nova Scotia, and yet Champlain never once overtly refers to it.* Not only is Mahone Bay the largest bay on Nova Scotia's Atlantic coast, it is very prominent. It is a huge island-filled indentation deep into the peninsula. Its entrance is in no way obscured or hidden behind bars, spits or large offshore islands. In short, it simply cannot be missed, and Champlain admits that he must have passed Mahone Bay when going from La Have to Sesambre because the bay fills this space, but he mentions only the Islands of Martyrs.

Champlain's maps are more informative. Neither the map of 1607 or 1612 shows Mahone Bay. The map of 1607 starts with La Have and Mahone Bay would therefore be off the edge of the map to the northeast. If there was any attempt to disguise matters, Champlain did it easily enough by simply making his map begin immediately west of Mahone Bay.

But the map of 1612 shows all of Nova Scotia. Mahone Bay does not appear on it, just some offshore islands called Islands of Martyrs. Interestingly enough, however, Champlain's "Bay of All Islands" *does* appear on this 1612 map about as far northeast of Sambro as Mahone Bay is southwest of Sambro. Champlain's drawing of the Bay of All Islands is a very good rendition of Mahone Bay, but in the wrong place. It is the shape of Mahone Bay, the size of Mahone Bay and the many islands are shown.

The problem is that there is no such bay northeast of Sambro along the entire coast of Nova Scotia up to Canso. Champlain passed this coast. He must have known all this because it is impossible to miss.

How could he omit the largest bay on the Atlantic coast, and then draw it accurately but in the wrong place? Or did he?

Sambro or "Sesambre" is the key. The imaginary coast for a distance of about 50 miles northeast happens to be a mirror image of real geographical features along the coast for about 50 miles southwest of Sambro. If Champlain's map were mentally folded at Sambro, then the Bay of All Islands would accurately represent the size and shape of Mahone Bay in the correct place. Champlain correctly gives the latitude of the folding point at Sambro, 44° 25', and in his narrative he gives the length of coast to be transposed, about 15 leagues, or about 35-50 miles.

Is there any justification for suspecting some sort of transportation code on Champlain's map. Yes, there most definitely is. Sambro is the modern name of a prominent headland. "Sesambre" is what Champlain called the place and the word from which the modern name has been corrupted. Champlain named this headland after Cézambre, an island lying off St. Malo in France, or so one earlier commentator on Champlain, Abbé C.H. Laverdière, suggested in 1870.

And so it may have been, although, if Laverdière's speculation is correct, it shows that French spelling of the 1600s was as flexible as English spelling. Given this inconsistency of spelling, Champlain may have been punning in the interest of a coded instruction. The year that he returned home to write his account of the Acadian explorations, 1607, saw the introduction of a new family of words based on the verb root *cesser*. *Cessible* was first used in 1607, while the form *cessable* occurs in 1609. These are adjectives meaning "transferable". They were trendy words when Champlain sat down to write about his explorations.

This new group of words derived from an older coinage of words that first appeared in the French language in 1570 and were current during the time Champlain was growing up. This older family of words was based on the Latin *sesamum*, the root of our word for the sesame seed. The introduction of this group of words based on *sesamum* was due to the phrase "Open Sesame!" which had caught the fancy of the French reading public because of the newly-published stories about Ali Baba and his treasure cave. Everyone will recall that Ali Baba's cave (large enough to accomodate his 40 thieves and their loot) could be opened by the secret words: "Open ... Sesame!" All sorts of verbs, nouns, adjectives, and adverbs grew from this complex of *sesamum* and *cesser* roots between 1570 and 1650.

Cesambre, *sesambre* or even *sesembre* would have been a likely form derived from this complex with the general meaning of "open unto you", "transfer unto you", etc., with the connotation of a *transferred revelation*, like learning the secret of how Ali Baba's cave opened. These mostly extinct word forms survive in some legal contexts with the meaning of "cede", or to transfer some commodity or valuable property. Champlain grew up familiar with the "s" words of this family based on *sesamum* and may have refused the use of the "c" words of this evolved group based on *cesser*, but meaning roughly the same and identical in pronunciation. In any case, the spelling of this period was highly variable.

Of all the many place-names appearing on Champlain's map of 1612, only "Sesambre" has no obvious (to moderns) meaning. Other Champlain place-names have immediate geographical relevance (Cape of Two Bays), or refer to some member of the de Monts expedition (Cape Poutrincourt) or were bestowed in honour of saints (St. Mary's Bay) or religious connections of some sort (Saint Croix Island), or referred to Indians and animals of the region (i.e. Isle of Cormorants). La Have, for example, was named after the roadstead of Havre du Grace where the expedition set sail for the transatlantic voyage. Only "Sesambre" is obscure, or *was* obscure, although now it is clear that the word has connotations of "transferring" a relevation or a secret.[15]

If this is not sheer imagination on my part, it was a very apt choice of name on Champlain's. By folding his map at Sesambre according to the general trend of the Nova Scotia coast, the Bay of All Isles reveals the true size, shape and position of Mahone Bay. Sesambre's latitude gives the latitude of Oak Island and the mouth of "a river called Ste. Marguerite". The latitude given for the area of the Bay of All Islands gives the location of The Cross. Open, Sesame! Indeed.

By the way, Ali Baba's invocation is not at all magical, but simply very practical. Sesame seeds contain oil used as a lubricant in the Middle East. If something is stuck, or won't open, sesame oil might help. Ali Baba's "Open, Sesame!" is, in fact, an Arabic joke.

So much for the Atlantic "door" that Champlain managed to obscure. What about the Fundy "door"?

De Monts arrived at Port Mouton on May 13. He sent Champlain to explore the coast southwest and all the way around into the Bay of Fundy. Champlain left on this mission in a pinnace of 8 tons. He left on May 19 and returned to Port Mouton about a month later having gone as far as St. Mary's Bay. De Monts decided to transfer the entire expedition to St. Mary's Bay and his ships arrived there before the 15th of June.

A curious incident then occurred. One of the expedition members, a cleric named Nicolas Aubry ("a Parisian ecclesiastic of good family") got lost.

> ... one of our priests named Master Aubry, of the city of Paris, on going to fetch his sword which he had forgotten, lost his way in the woods so completely that he could not find the vessel again; and was seventeen days in this state without anything to live upon except some sour and bitter herbs resembling sorel, and little fruits of small substance, which creep upon the ground. Being at his wits' end, and without hope of ever seeing us again ... when one of our shallops, going out to fish, caught sight of him ... and brought him away.[16]

Lescarbot, in relating the same incident, says that Aubry was lost for twelve or thirteen days and that some of the Catholics in the expedition suspected that Aubry had been murdered by a Protestant with whom he'd argued about religion. Aubry was supposedly lost on Long Island.

It is impossible to be lost on Long Island for 17 days (Champlain) or 12-13 days (Lescarbot), for, as Champlain says of Long Island:

> This island is six leagues in length (about 15 miles) and in some places nearly a league (nearly 2½-3 miles) in width, though elsewhere only a quarter of a league (900 yards).[17]

The island is a long and narrow spit. It is also fairly high in elevation with hills up to 200 feet. From Long Island all of St. Mary's Bay is spread out below like a gigantic map and from any hill top you can see exactly where you are, where the Bay of Fundy is and where St. Mary's Bay is. It is barely possible that Aubry could have been lost for a few hours. De Mont's ship lay at anchor in St. Mary's Bay and must have been clearly visible. Then, there were other and smaller expedition vessels scurrying about all over the bay on other business, like the fishing shallop that finally picked him up.

Everyone knew that Aubry was missing because,

> The Sieur de Monts had a search made for him both by his own men and by the Indians, who had scoured the woods everywhere but had brought back no news of him.[18]

In short, even after a massive search, expedition members would have kept their eyes open for him.

Almost every commentator of Champlain's account has been troubled by this incident because some of them had visited St. Mary's Bay, as we did also, and realized that the story made no sense. Laverdière decided that both Champlain and Lescarbot must have made a mistake and that Aubry was lost for only 2-3 days, which is barely possible, I suppose. The scholarly commentators to the 6-volume edition of *The Works of Samuel De Champlain*, also knowing that this story is absurd, heave a collective sigh of relief at Laverdière's verdict, and write definitively in a footnote:

> When Lescarbot says that Aubry was lost twelve or thirteen days after the arrival of the expedition at St. Mary's Bay, he means two or three, as Laverdière has shown.[19]

Laverdière didn't "show" anything in the academic sense of demonstrating a fact beyond doubt. He merely said that there must have been a mistake.

Lescarbot and Champlain often differ on details in relating the same events. There is more than a hint of jealousy between the two. Lescarbot was a man of letters, Champlain was an explorer. Lescarbot stayed aboard the main expedition ships, or stayed at the settlement at Port Royal, and did not participate in the many dangerous coastal explorations that Champlain undertook. Yet, Lescarbot published his description of Acadia before Champlain was able to, largely because he was writing his account while Champlain was working at exploration. Lescarbot wove Champlain's descriptions into his own publication before Champlain himself had time to assemble his field notes, draw his maps, and write a publishable book. Lescarbot beat him to the punch using Champlain's own material. Champlain was bitter. Their disagreements in their accounts sometimes, therefore, include put-downs about the other's accuracy.

In this case, however, Lescarbot and Champlain agree with each other, at least, more than either agrees with modern scholars. Champlain says 17 days, Lescarbot says 12-13 days. A period of 2-2½ weeks is the time that Aubry was lost, and this is simply not plausible.

The most obvious explanation is that Aubry went somewhere on a delicate and secret errand.

De Monts and Champlain may not have known the exact location of the Fundy "door". The Gaspereau River flows west, but then turns north to empty into Minas Basin. The Fundy Oak Island "door" is therefore about 60 miles north of the Atlantic Oak Island even though both the

Gold River and the Gaspereau lead to the same place. Even if the Bay of Fundy (or "French Bay", as de Monts called it) had been described to them, Champlain and de Monts would have had some trouble finding the Gaspereau River immediately.

Champlain, because he was a navigator and a map-maker, might have suggested an easier way to make contact with the inland refugees. If, as I have suggested, the expedition really explored Mahone Bay for 2-3 days and not the modern "La Have", then Champlain could have taken the latitude of Oak Island and the mouth of the Gold River. This is about 44° 25', the same as the latitude of Sesambre, as we've seen. Therefore, once reaching the Fundy side, a messenger could be sent from latitude 44° 25' with instructions to travel due east. Sooner or later, the messenger should come across the inland settlement, or at least meet up with a similar probe that Pont-Gravé may have been making from the Atlantic *at the same time*.

We will recall that de Monts didn't send a messenger to find Pont-Gravé until the first week in June. We do not know how long this messenger took to reach the "Bay of All Isles" or how long Pont-Gravé remained there.

It just so happens that latitude 44° 25' is the position of Boar's Head on the northeastern tip of Long Island. The very place where Aubry became impossibly lost for 2-2½ weeks. De Monts may have sent the French searchers in all the wrong directions, and some of the Indians may have been helping Aubry to travel inland rather than searching for him.

How would Aubry travel due east? He was not a navigator. Champlain might have taught him how to use a compass, even though at that time, compass lore was rather esoteric. But, in any case, it would not have been so easy to use a compass because Champlain could not have been certain of the local magnetic variation from north. In Nova Scotia this variation from magnetic north can be considerable, from 15 to 20 degrees west, and would result in a large error at Aubry's hypothetical destination.

Champlain would have immediately seen an easier and more certain way of assuring a due east course. The summer solstice occurs about June 20-22 when the axis of the earth inclines the Northern Hemisphere toward the sun and when the sun's declination is on the Tropic of Cancer 23½ degrees north of the Equator. Now, although the sun is actually well south of the latitude of Nova Scotia, the earth's spherical shape causes what navigators call "the obliquity" of the horizon. What this means in practice is what anyone can observe in June: the sun appears to rise in the northeast and to set in the northwest. At the latitude of Nova Scotia, the sun happens to appear to rise almost precisely northeast. That being so, Champlain could have provided Aubry with a very simple "instrument" . . . a 45-degree angle. This could be anything. A piece of iron or wire bent into a 45-degree angle, a triangular piece of paper with a 45-degree angle, or a triangular piece of a plank with a 45-degree angle. Aubry would use it this way: he would hold the "instrument" with the 45-degree apex close to his eye, and, as the sun rose in the morning he would direct one side of the angle where the sun was peeking over the horizon. The other side of the angle he would keep *to his right* and he would pick out a distant landmark along the line of the angle. That landmark would be almost exactly due east of his position. He would march toward it and his day's travel would be due east. To return due west Aubry could either mark and retrace his route, or he could reverse the procedure described above. He could direct one side of his angle toward the setting sun, keeping the other side of the angle *to his left* this time, and pick out a distant landmark that would then be almost exactly due west.

Assuming that Aubry could be dropped off at the proper latitude of 44° 25′ sometime around June 15, then even a "Parisian ecclesiastic of good family" should have been able to manage a due east probe and due west return over the course of a couple of weeks. The summer solstice would occur exactly in the middle of this period, and the sun's deviation from a northeast sunrise and northwest sunset would be very small. This timetable dictated by the summer solstice may be the explanation for why de Monts so hastily transferred his part of the expedition from Port Mouton to St. Mary's Bay, even though they had already made camps at Port Mouton and even though Champlain had not yet found a good place for a settlement on the Fundy shore.[20] Coincidence or not, Aubry was "lost" at the correct latitude, and at the right time in June, and was missing the right number of days to have made a probe inward toward The Cross.

Champlain and de Monts seem to have been in a hurry to make a probe of their own, and they seem to have known just where to head. On the 16th of June (while Aubry was still "lost"), they set off in some sort of auxiliary boat, leaving the larger vessels in St. Mary's Bay, and sailed toward Cape D'Or. They must have made excellent time, knowing where to go, because they *left* Cape D'Or on the 20th of June, just four days later.

Yet, they must have remained at least a day or two in Advocate Harbour, *which is literally at the foot of Cape D'Or,* because Champlain drew an excellent and very accurate map of the harbour ... a map much more accurate than his La Have effort where he supposedly spent a few days. I have reproduced Champlain's chart of Advocate Harbour, and a modern one, to show exactly how good it is. These should be compared with the La Have maps and, when that is done, I don't think that anyone can argue too much about my suggestion that Champlain was never in La Have for any period of time and drew his chart from the deck while sailing past.

Cape D'Or is almost exactly 180 miles from the exit of St. Mary's Bay. That distance is two full day's sail. Even modern yachts do not *average* more than about 100 miles per day. To have reached Advocate Harbour in two days, *they must have sailed directly for it,* nonstop, and they must have known where it was by some sort of chart or description because Cape D'Or is not visible from the area of St Mary's Bay. Not only is it much too distant to be seen, but the coast curves to hide it.

Champlain offers another piece of disinformation in his narrative when he says that they discovered Port Royal, the future site of de Monts' settlement, on their way to Advocate Harbour.

> ... Having found in St. Mary's Bay no place where we might fortify ourselves, except after a long delay, we determined to ascertain whether there might not be some more suitable place in the other bay. Standing to the northeast six leagues, we came to a cove ... Continuing two leagues on the same course, we entered one of the finest harbours I had seen on all these coasts, where a couple of thousand vessels could lie in safety ... which I named Port Royal.[21]

It is Champlain who is lying in safety, for no expert has questioned his account. He proceeds to give a long description of this extensive port, including an enumeration of various rivers flowing into it, the kinds of fish to be found there, the kinds of trees, and so on, all with the clear suggestion that they did all this on the way to Advocate Harbour and Cape D'Or.

Yet, this simply cannot be. If they *left* Advocate Harbour on June 20th, they had obviously arrived earlier. Champlain needed at least a day or so to draw his very accurate map of the place. But it is two full day's from St. Mary's Bay.

There was no time to explore Port Royal on the way. Champlain is being misleading. They must have surveyed Port Royal on the way back from Advocate Harbour.

In short, Champlain and de Monts sailed *directly* and at full speed for Owokun, Glooscap's winter quarters, while Aubry was still "lost".

The stated reason for this rapid trip was a search for a copper mine that was supposed to be around Cape D'Or. Champlain calls Advocate Harbour the "Port des Mines". They'd heard about this supposed mine from a certain Sieur de Prévert of St. Malo who had sent some men to look for it earlier, probably in 1603.[22]

It is here, in Champlain's "Port des Mines" that he makes another curious omission. Cape D'Or is called "the golden cape" because of copper ore that gives it a golden hue. It is an impressive sight, this golden cape, and not only because of its metallic colour. It is the highest land for miles about, as the photograph of the lighthouse reproduced on an earlier page shows clearly enough. Cape D'Or looms over Champlain's "Port des Mines", towering over Advocate Harbour. In fact, from the top of the cape you get an excellent bird's eye view of Advocate Harbour, and can see the channels in the water, and I'm inclined to think that Champlain drew his chart from these heights to make it so accurate. It would have been a stiff climb, and a time-consuming one, requiring a full day to get to the summit, draw a chart, and come down again. It is certain that Champlain did climb the cape since, on his chart, he *incorrectly* shows Spencer Island, which is invisible from Advocate Harbour because of intervening higher ground. He can only have seen this island in its true insular nature from above, for from seaward it appears to be a peninsula unless viewed from close inshore. But it is too near Cape D'Or on the map, evidence of altitude foreshortening.

We are faced with another coincidence. How is it that Champlain and de Monts end up at Glooscap's winter quarters so soon after arriving in a supposedly unknown country?

Champlain and de Monts must have stood on the very same ground atop the cape where Glooscap, alias Henry Sinclair, had stood 205 years previously. *The very same spot.* Isn't it just a bit too coincidental that they reached Owokun, of all places, just over a month after making landfall in a previously unexplored country?

Then, Champlain is as coy about Cape D'Or as he is about Mahone Bay. He never mentions it! Although this cape is one of the most

Champlain's map of Advocate Harbour, which he calls the "Port of Mines." This harbour is the location of Sinclair's "Owokun." Note the accuracy of this chart when compared to a modern chart.

Champlain must have climbed Cape D'Or to get a bird's eye view of the harbour to have drawn it so accurately. He shows Spencer's Island too close, which indicates that he must have climbed Cape D'Or because from the high elevation the island appears to be closer to the promontory than it really is.

Courtesy The Champlain Society.

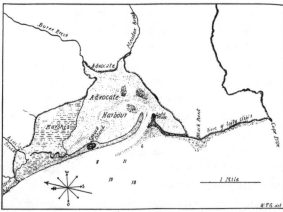

Modern chart of Advocate Harbour. Note that Spencer's Island is not shown because it is actually too far east to appear on this scale.

Cape D'Or is one of the most spectacular capes in Nova Scotia, and literally looms over Advocate Harbour, and yet Champlain never mentions it. But he must have climbed Cape D'Or in order to draw his chart.

Courtesy The Champlain Society.

spectacular ones in the Bay of Fundy, Champlain gives it no name. He ignores its existence in his narrative. He does not, apparently, want to call any attention to it.

Champlain's account of his exploration of Minas Basin is not only confusing, it is deliberately misleading. He never specifies when he makes his various trips into Minas Basin, but he made several between 1604 and 1607. He gives a general description of Minas Basin only at the end of his narrative, a distillation of all the previous explorations. He says:

> We went to the head of this bay, but saw nothing except certain white stones for making lime, which were few in number, and many sea-gulls, which are birds that were upon some islands. We captured as many of these as we wished. We made a circuit of the bay in order to visit the Port of Mines, where I had been already. I conducted thither the Sieur de Poutrincourt, who gathered some small pieces of copper which were obtained with great difficulty. This whole bay is about twenty leagues in circumference, and at its head is a small stream which is very shoal and has little water. There are a number of other small streams and certain places where there are good harbours, but only at high tide, which here rises five fathoms. In one of these harbours, three to four leagues north of Poutrincourt Cape, we found a very old cross, all covered with moss, an unmistakable sign that formerly Christians had been there. This whole country is covered with very dense forests, and the land is not very pleasant except in certain places.[23]

There is no doubt that Champlain did explore Minas Basin very carefully. His maps show it extremely accurately in terms of general shape and even coastal detail. Cape Blomidon ("Cape Poutrincourt"), Cape Split and Cape D'Or are well drawn. He saw it and he doesn't give an attractive description of it. The place would attract few colonists.

Except that Champlain's description is a lie. A deliberate one. *The largest rivers in Nova Scotia flow into Minas Basin*, the Shubenacadie River and the Avon River. Far from being a "small stream which is very shoal", *both* of these rivers are navigable for long distances. The *smaller* of the two, the Avon, still has ocean freighter traffic as far as Hantsport. Then, in addition to these two very large rivers (the Avon is more than a mile wide in places), there are several smaller rivers which are navigable for some distance: the Cornwallis River and the Gaspereau River, although the Gaspereau isn't navigable very far for large craft.

As for the land, to say that it is "not very pleasant except in certain places" amounts to a purposeful falsehood. The land around the eastern shore of Minas Basin, especially around Cape Poutrincourt, is the best farmland in Nova Scotia. It is *the* garden of Nova Scotia, the famous Annapolis Valley, a country of rolling hills, deep and rich earth (a relative rarity in Nova Scotia), lovely and stately elms, oaks and other shade trees, and those innumerable apple orchards referred to earlier. This land is the best agricultural land in the province.

The Acadians belatedly discovered this. Possibly discouraged for a number of years by Champlain's description of the place, the Acadian French eventually did inhibit this bountiful part of the province and the majority of Acadians came to live there. This was the land of the Acadian heroine, Evangeline, not de Monts settlement at Port Royal 200 miles to the southwest. Evangeline Beach, from which the Acadians were deported, is near Wolfville not far from the mouth of the Gaspereau River, about three miles from Oak Island. Today, Acadia University is in Wolfville, within sight of Cape Poutrincourt.

Champlain could not have been mistaken about the rivers because he saw them and he drew them. He could not have been "mistaken" about the quality of the land, either. Whereas a lot of Nova Scotia is covered with birch, fir and spruce forests struggling on relatively thin soil, the land of old Acadia is famous for its tall and stately elms and oaks. These are deciduous trees with deep root systems. They can only thrive in deep and rich soil. Champlain must have known this, and he must have seen these magnificent trees. Some of the tall elms that shade the streets of Wolfville, Kentville and New Minas were alive in Champlain's time.

Champlain was not "mistaken". He was trying to discourage people from going to the Minas Basin area. Even the "mines" which they'd come to assess, turned out to be worthless according to the opinion of Master Simon, the miner they'd brought with them. Champlain's published account nipped in the bud any French rumours of valuable mines. The little copper there was at the "Port of Mines" could only be obtained with great difficulty, while the "certain white stones for making lime" at the head of Minas Basin "were few in number". The copper of Cape D'Or has been mined commercially as recently as 1960. As for the scarce white stones for making lime, they are the gypsum deposits on the Avon River, whole shining white cliffs of gypsum, and a remarkable feature for tourists. These cliffs of gypsum support several commercial operations today. The gypsum is shipped out on freighters from Hantsport on that "small stream" with "little water".

Before leaving Champlain and this chapter, one more thing deserves attention. Norumbega. Champlain relates, with great derision, how he attempted to find this city by ascending the "River of Norumbega" (the Penobscot), but with no success. He ridicules those who claimed to have visited the place and, for readers of his narrative, explodes a myth.

The Penobscot River is, of course, in Maine. The country of Norumbega was in Maine and part of New Brunswick, according to Champlain.

But . . . who ever said it was there? Norumbega was first and originally in Nova Scotia. It only later migrated across the Bay of Fundy to appear as a place-name in New Brunswick and Maine. Champlain must have known this very well. By searching for it in the place where the name had only recently been transferred, Champlain was again being deliberately misleading.

Champlain seems to have been playing a double game, and, possibly, a potentially dangerous one. He had to map and explore Nova Scotia for the king and for plans of future colonization, but apparently his job was also, at the same time, to obscure parts of the province and to discourage anyone from bothering to go there. Champlain seems to have been infiltrated into the official colonization policy in order to deflect it from certain sensitive areas. Champlain seems to have been a secret agent for the Holy Bloodline. According to Champlain's maps and narrative, Mahone Bay didn't exist, Minas Basin was a place of no worth, former Christian occupants had abandoned the area, and Norumbega was a fable.

Except for these places, Champlain's maps and descriptions are generally accurate, given the time he had and the great dangers he braved during his explorations.

But can it be mere coincidence that all of these places have relevance to the construct offered in this book? The prominent Canadian historian, W. F. Ganong, has written:

> . . . It has been the greatest satisfaction to me, with Champlain's narratives and maps in hand, to follow in his footsteps over most of the ground he has described and over all that he mapped in detail. The results of these combined labours has been, I believe, to make Champlain's work more completely known, and I doubt if much is left to be learned . . . unless his original journals are discovered.[24]

So much for academic arrogance. Champlain's maps and narratives raise some very curious questions for anyone truly familiar with the areas he explored. Perhaps, by asking some questions which no one has bothered to ask before, we have learned something else about Champlain.

It appears that in addition to being a great explorer and accomplished cartographer, he may also have been an agent of the Holy Bloodline of Godfroi de Bouillon. Was his major labour not to explore and map New France and Arcadia, but to buy a little more time for Henry Sinclair's refugees?

It may be worth noting that *both* de Monts' and Champlain's fur monopolies were revoked because neither undertook any steps toward serious colonization, which was originally the whole idea of de Monts' proposal. Between them, they hindered effective colonization for 19 years, from 1603 to 1622, the major reason why colonization of New France was painfully slow. A royal edict in 1626 noted "with some bitterness that the holders of the monopoly had taken out to New France during the past eleven years only eighteen colonists" and "in 1628 Quebec could boast of not more that forty or fifty persons who might be described as ordinarily resident there".[25]

To some degree, this difficulty in finding colonists resulted from the reluctance of Frenchmen to leave France: " ... even as late as the days of Richelieu, emigration to Canada was so much of a joke that a man pursued by creditors might say jeeringly that all that was left for him to do was to go 'to Canada to marry the Queen of the Hurons' ".[26]

Champlain's descriptions might have fuelled this reluctance. The only people that did go to Canada were Protestant Huguenots, and they came to trade, not to settle. Champlain, that "ardent Catholic", headed those who petitioned the king to exclude even Huguenots, while, of course, Champlain had been a friend and faithful companion of de Monts, a Huguenot. Further, Champlain himself had formed a trading company in 1614 with a majority of Huguenot associates! How can one explain this inconsistency? It is simple. It appears to have been adept manipulation of all the factions which might pose any threat to the Holy Refugees. The possibility of truly massive colonization by France's Catholic majority of agriculturalists was countered with descriptions of worthless places like Minas Basin and the terrible cold and scurvy suffered during the winters.

Huguenot fur traders, who were necessary to provide a screen for transatlantic contact, were kept to a minimum by raising ardent Catholic objections about heretic influence. The kind of objections that Champlain raised in 1621. Greed was manipulated, in that the Protestant fur trade contributed to the Catholic king's coffer. He continued to grant licenses and trading monopolies, and *this* was manipulated as well to include the right to seize unauthorized shipping. Again, the conspiracy could limit the number of visitors, as de Monts and Pont-Gravé did in seizing Rossingnol's ship and those of the Basques at Canso.

Finally, the conspirators sided with the zealots of the Catholic Church who wanted to make conversion of the Indians the major activity in New France. Ironically, the zealots realized that massive Catholic colonization by Frenchmen would hinder this missionary work more than occasional and casual contact by Protestant traders. The zealots were manipulated to support royal approval for a minimum number of these Huguenot businessmen while, at the same time, the Church discouraged colonization from French pulpits.

In short, all factions posing any danger to the Holy Refugees were adroitly manipulated by their own strengths, weaknesses and special interests. As a result, a handful of people effectively controlled and regulated transoceanic contact with New France. They insulated the haven at The Cross as much as possible while keeping open the necessary trade to assure supplies and communications. Champlain seems to have been a key figure in this process, the conspiracy's major field operative.

It was not an entirely rewarding role for Champlain in a personal sense. Overtly, his primary claim to personal fame was as an explorer and map-maker in the king's navy. Yet, as we have seen, Lescarbot beat Champlain into publication, announcing the cream of Champlain's discoveries before the explorer himself could do so. Perhaps worse, Lescarbot was a better writer. He knew what the public wanted and he gave it to them. His book, largely based on Champlain's efforts, was more successful than Champlain's own.

Covertly, as an agent of the Holy Bloodline, Champlain's accomplishments were even more important, but they could never be revealed for reasons now very obvious. Had Champlain given way to any temptation to proclaim his important role, he would have been branded a traitor several ways at once: to king and country, to the Catholic Church, to the Grail Dynasty.

Is it possible that Champlain left us the smallest hint of his role? Some little reference that, someday, might indicate his real impact on history? Perhaps he did.

In one of his journals, Champlain says:

> On June 17 (1613) we arrived at the rapids of St. Louis, where I found L'Ange, who had come out to meet me in a canoe, to inform me that Sieur de Maisonneuve of St. Malo had brought a passport from Monseigneur the Prince (de Condé) for three ships . . . On landing, Maisonneuve came to see me with the passport from Monseigneur the Prince, and as soon as I examined it, I allowed him to take advantage of it with the rest of us.[27]

The rapids of St. Louis are the Lachine rapids. The site of this meeting between "Sieur de Maisonneuve" and Champlain was, therefore, the future site of Montreal, the refuge that would be founded 29 years later.

Champlain does not mention this Sieur de Maisonneuve "of St. Malo" further. Who is he?

The first leader of the Montreal colony was a "Sieur de Maisonneuve". It cannot be the same one, unless he was born at least 15 years earlier than all the biographers claim. But it could be the father. If so, this man had just had a son, born the previous year (1612) who would become Paul de Chomedy, Sieur de Maisonneuve, the first governor of Montreal. In the above passage, Champlain "allows" him to set foot on Montreal.

Is Champlain telling us that he was high up in the great conspiracy? That he was the steward of the future haven of Montreal? That he knew the newly-born de Maisonneuve heir was to be groomed to be the first governor of the new refuge (or that he knew de Maisonneuve's real age which would be concealed from history)?

And if he's trying to hint at all of this, or at any of it, then he is also sending a message down to future historians: Samuel Champlain was a paladin of the Holy Blood, and worthy to stand beside King Arthur, Jacques de Molay, Henry Sinclair and all the other heroes.

At this point we may as well confront a question, and some readers may well feel that it is long overdue. Has this entire reconstruction been a mare's nest of unrelated facts and unfounded speculations, or, does it have some claim to truth? Is it history, or is it imagination?

Since I'm responsible for much of this reconstruction, but by no means for all of it, I may as well answer honestly that I just don't know. On the other hand, I've studied history for some years and have lectured on it. I don't know what history is, either. Napoleon is supposed to have said that "history is the lie commonly agreed upon". Ben Johnson had equally caustic things to say about it. Scholars choose facts and ignore others when they create history to be read in books. Or, sometimes, they're just remarkably uncurious.

It seems a bit far-fetched to suppose that de Monts and Champlain were heirs of some Templar mission begun long before, but . . .

It is very difficult sometimes to come to grips with the facts behind ordinary history, the kind offered in authorized texts. How much more difficult must it be, then, to come to grips with a history that has been purposefully suppressed by friend and foe alike? One is forced to become a suspicious detective, and to glean clues that others might miss, or dismiss. One cannot expect proof when seeking hidden history, one can only hope to find stray hints of a pattern that goes beyond the acceptable "warp and woof".

Champlain mentions a de Maisonneuve at the close of his accounts. At the very beginning, he mentions another mysterious figure. Champlain's first known voyage was to the West Indies between 1599 and 1601 and it was this experience that gave him the credibility to join the later French explorations which won him fame. Without going into all the details, Champlain owed his participation in the Spanish West Indies voyage to "a nobleman named Don Francisco Coloma, a knight of Malta", as Champlain describes him, who was leader of the expedition. Champlain needed permission to join this voyage and

> . . . we sought out General Coloma, to know if it would suit him that I should make the voyage. This he freely granted me, with evidence of being well pleased thereat, promising me his favour and assistance, which he has not since denied me upon occasion.[28]

We do not really know when the "since" was in this passage because we do not know when Champlain composed his notes on this voyage for publication in France. It may have been 1601, 1604 or even as late as 1613. Champlain may have been a long-time protegé of this Don Francisco Coloma, a knight of Malta, who held so high a position in the Spanish navy, and whose name means "Dove".

I have spared the reader any history of the Knights of Malta until now because of fear of complication of an already too-involved story. But, briefly, the Knights of Malta were a sort of Templar back-up Order. They, too, were established in the Holy Land under the de Bouillons at about the same time as the Templars. Whereas the Templars were headquartered in Jerusalem at the Temple of Solomon, the Knights of Malta were originally headquartered in Acre. They "relocated" to Rhodes, and then Malta, when the Moslems regained the Holy Land. They retreated to a succession of island fortresses.[29]

Where the Templars were high-profile, the Knights of Malta were low-profile, but still attracted the flower of nobility. Like the Templars, they were sworn to chastity and poverty as individuals, but the Order itself became immensely wealthy. They, too, were answerable only to the Pope. And where the Templars specialized in finance and banking, the Knights of Malta took to hospital work. In fact, before the move to Malta, the Order was known as St. John's Hospitalliers, of which today's St. John's Ambulance is a descendant. They also engaged in sea-commerce.

The Grail Dynasty throughout history has shown itself always to be one step ahead of everyone else through careful contingency planning. While the Templars seemed to be the overt "sword-arm" of the Holy lineage, the Knights of Malta seem to be a sort of low-profile back-up contingency group. The Templars got into trouble fighting de Bouillon's enemies, the Knights of Malta remained neutral toward the Albigensians, and carefully orthodox.

So it came to pass that when Phillippe le Bel staged his dawn raids upon Templar priories and warehouses in 1307, such treasure as did get confiscated was awarded, by order of the Pope, *to the Knights of Malta*. It is difficult to figure out if the Knights of Malta were "anti-Templar" and were therefore rewarded for orthodoxy, or were just a carefully planned contingency for the de Bouillons. At any rate, it is simply a fact that Templar assets and money ended up with the Knights of Malta, in a secure island fortress, and it is another fact that for all their supposed orthodoxy and martial zeal, the Knights of Malta were strangely reluctant to fight *anyone* on behalf of the Vatican. They stayed in their Malta fortress and amassed huge fortunes by various means.

Don Francisco Coloma, who started Champlain on his career, and who had assisted him "since", was a Knight of Malta.

It appears that Champlain's long-term friend and business associate, the Sieur de Monts, also had Templar and Knights of Malta connections. A notation in Anthiaume's *Cartes Navales* reads: "La succession du commandeur de Chastes fut recueille par Pierre du Guast, sieur de Monts, *gentilhomme d'origine italienne*". In other words, it is said that de Monts was of Italian origin. This has been disputed, but if it is a fact, he may have been named after a relative, Pietro del Monte, Grand Master of the Knights of Malta from 1568 to 1572.

However that may be, it is an undisputed fact that de Monts purchased the castle of Ardennes *on the ancient estate of Godfroi de Bouillon* as a retirement home. This had been a Templar stronghold. The oldest surviving document about this castle is the will made by Guillaume de Blanzac in 1232 A.D. upon the occasion when he left on a pilgrimage to Santiago de Campostelle. It says:

> One donation with special allotments provides for the peace of his soul, one or two monasteries, priories, churches and ten gold sols to the Templars of Ardennes.[30]

Philippe le Bel seized the Chateau of Ardennes along with other Templar property in France, but it passed on with much else to the Knights of Malta. The altar in the chapel is decorated with Maltese crosses. This is the castle that Sieur de Monts was able to buy, even though he was frequently bankrupt, and the place where he died, most probably in the year 1628.

Around the year 1635 during the last days of Champlain's term as governor:

> ... in Paris the Hundred Associates, under the guidance of Cardinal de Richelieu, were meeting to choose a new governor. The reason is not clear — whether Champlain was regarded merely as too old, whether his policy had crossed that of the Cardinal, or whether some intrigue was at work. There was indeed a plan afoot to turn Canada over to the Knights of Malta; but for all we know, Champlain may have approved the project in advance.[31]

Turn Canada over to the Knights of Malta?

Yes, this proposal is a historical fact, as are the Maltese crosses on the altar of the old Templar castle that de Monts acquired, as is the existence of Don Francisco Coloma, Knight of Malta, who aided Champlain from the beginning of his exploration career.

Even though the history as a whole has been supressed and obscured, there are enough curious and orphaned facts to support the construct suggested in this book.

In spite of the incongruous facts and inconsistencies that collectively hinted that Champlain and some of his closest associates were double-agents in some secret cause, I confess that when I finished the text of this chapter I felt great apprehension. I was not even a native-born Canadian. Who was I to dare to suggest that Samuel Champlain was anything other than four-square and straightforward, the "Father of Canada" as the scholars have unanimously agreed? Who was I to contradict the "common knowl-edge" of Canadian history which insisted that Champlain devoted all his energy to the accurate mapping and efficient colonization of Canada?

I was both considerably surprised and heartened, therefore, to dis-cover that an obscure but respectable French scholar had harboured similar suspicions about Champlain and published them in his obscure but respectable book. I had, as I thought, completed the text of this chapter and was checking bibliographic references to Champlain for the Notes and Bibliography sections of this book in the Toronto Reference Library when I noticed in the Canadian History card catalogue a book entitled L'incroyable Secret de Champlain ("The Incredible Secret of Cham-plain").[32] It had been published in Paris in 1959 and never translated into English so far as I could discover. The author was Florian de la Horbe who wrote it in collaboration with M. Meurgey de Tupigny, Conservator-in-Chief of France's National Archives. There was only one copy in the Reference Library and it couldn't be taken out, so Deanna and I were forced to wade through it, French-English dictionary in hand, on the spot, and to make photocopies of some of the more interesting pages.

It did not appear from the stiffness of the book that anyone had ever cracked it open before us. What we discovered inside was intriguing enough to justify a brief extension of this chapter so that you can read about it here rather than in a note in the back of the book.

De la Horbe's suspicions were kindled initially by some apparently newly-discovered material in the Bibliothèque Nationale . . . where have we heard that before! But de la Horbe seems unaware of any "Holy Blood" research. He does not mention the Dossiers secrets nor does his book refer to the de Bouillon conspiracy as outlined in this book. What caught de la Horbe's interest were the apparent lies that Champlain told in the account of his first voyage to the West Indies in 1599.

Champlain says that his uncle, called "le Provençal", was captain of a

French ship named the *St. Julien*, but the documents in the Bibliothèque Nationale stated that one Guillaume Hélaine was captain of it all during the time that Champlain's account covers. This information agreed with the archives in Madrid which listed one "Guillermo Eleno" as captain of the *St. Julien*. On checking out the Madrid archives further, it transpired that Champlain nowhere appears in the list of personnel that sailed with Don Francisco Coloma although the inventories of the armada are extremely detailed in terms of people and equipment.[33]

To cut a long story short, de la Horbe subsequently spent several years of research and came to the conclusion that "Samuel de Champlain" was an alias created by Guy Eder de la Fontenelle, one of history's most colourful rogues. De la Fontenelle was a pirate and a brigand who was involved on all sides, at one time or another, in the European wars of religion of his time. According to his own words, de la Fontenelle "believed in neither God nor the Devil", and was as unprincipled as he was brilliant. He spent most of his early career either in prison or acting as a special operative for European monarchs, including Champlain's nominal patrons King Henry IV of France and Catherine de Medici.

De la Fontenelle drops suddenly from the stage of history in 1602, and Samuel de Champlain appears just as suddenly in 1603 with the publication of his account of the West Indian voyage and his first trip to New France. De la Fontenelle and Champlain knew the same people, were the same age, filled the same role as literary adverturers, mapmakers and navigators, and shared the same predilection for young girls (a taste of Champlain's that has been almost completely expunged from Canadian history books). Both Champlain and de la Fontenelle apparently enjoyed high-level contacts that cut across French-Spanish-English rivalries, and both somehow enjoyed the favour of the King of France and the Stuarts of England. De la Horbe gives a great deal of circumstantial evidence apparently supporting the fact that "Samuel de Champlain" was a personality invented by de la Fontenelle because of some crisis which impelled him to undertake a mission under another identity. De la Fontenelle somewhat "changed his life" when taking on some great and secret task as Champlain, but certain proclivities remained to be exhibited by Champlain.

De la Horbe's research led him only to conclude that Fontenelle/ Champlain was a secret agent working for high-level English-French interests against those of Spain (but with many high-level covert contacts within Spain and the Spanish Navy). De la Horbe does not know what the conspiracy, or mission, was, but it obviously took Fontenelle/Champlain to Acadia and New France.

De la Horbe's conclusion is not at odds with the one suggested in this book, although, as stated before, de la Horbe seems innocent of any knowledge of the "Holy Blood-related" revelations of other French researchers. The same inconsistencies we have noted about Champlain did not escape the attention of de la Horbe. After acknowledging that Champlain, that "ardent Catholic", married a girl from a Protestant family, de la Horbe makes a caustic observation about Champlain's commitment to colonization of Acadia and New France:

> . . . Champlain a toujours pretendu qu'il voulait implanter au Canada une population francaise et doubler le commerce par agriculture. Mais il y a une contradition absolue entre les efforts qu'il aurait faits dans ce dessein et l'inanité des resultats.[34]
>
> (. . . Champlain always pretended that he wanted to establish a French population in Canada and to double trade by agriculture. But there is an absolute contradiction between the efforts that he made in this design and the inanity of the results.)

De la Horbe attributes the inane failures of colonization to the incompetence of someone who was essentially a rogue, pirate and brigand, not an administrator. De la Horbe had no reason to suspect that Fontenelle/Champlain was anything other than a rogue, pirate and brigand. But we have reason to suspect that Champlain may have been a very special rogue with a momentous responsibility. His failures may not have been the result of incompetence, but due to a secret purpose. Inanity has disguised genius before.

There is no proof that Champlain was really Guy Eder de la Fontenelle, as de la Horbe claims, or that he was an agent of the Grail Dynasty as I have suggested in these pages. But if there is no proof of a secret mission, surely the accumulation of Champlain's deceptions, inconsistencies and disinformation is sufficient to warrant a re-evaluation of his role in history.

We do not have to abandon the vision of Champlain as brave, courageous and devoted, nor can we question his competence as an explorer, map-maker and navigator. He was, obviously, a most unique individual and a great man.

No authenticated portrait of Champlain is known to exist, but we do know that he was thin and wiry, and of a height below average.

But what we may well have to abandon is the idea of Samuel de Champlain as being representative of comfortable Canadian history. Being the "Father of Canada" may not be his real claim to fame, while being a paladin of the Holy Blood may have been his true life's work.

There had been, indeed, a 17th Century proposal to transfer Canada to the Knights of Malta and "Champlain may . . . have approved it" but the Holy Blood had learned by long and desperate experience that the only guarantee of security lay in infiltrating *both* (or *all*) sides of any confrontation. While it is easy to suspect Grail Dynasty interest in the Knights of Malta, the bloodline had also taken steps to promote a rival plan for the future of Canada. The group that finally accomplished real colonization in Canada was not the Knights of Malta, but the founders of Montreal. This group, too, seems to have been a Holy Blood operation.

By infiltrating and controlling two rival plans for the future of Canadian colonization, the Grail Dynasty seemed to have developed a "no lose" scenario for the safe establishment of a new haven to replace the Arcadian refuge.

The founding of Montreal represented a triumph of organization and clandestine operations, one in which just pride could be taken by the brilliant agents involved.

Yet, the new haven nearly proved to be a disaster through unforeseen circumstances.

Chapter Eight

The Shepherds of Arcadia

If our hypothetical Holy Refugees did, indeed, find themselves established in a Nova Scotia haven founded by Henry Sinclair, surely they explored their new environment. And, if they explored their Atlantic seaboard they would shortly have discovered milder and more fertile places for settlement in New England and perhaps even further south. If the initial refuge was established in 1398, it is reasonable to assume that exploratory probes, or even relocation to a new haven, would have been accomplished within a century.

We will probably never know what happened in North America during that intriguing century before Columbus, but there is some evidence that a fair sprinkling of Europeans were active in the northeast during the 1400s. Some of these Europeans may have been southward-probing Holy Refugees. Others may have been lingering Norsemen from the doomed Greenland colonies. Still others may have been Irish priests and their half-caste descendants. These priests were sworn to celibacy, it is true, but perhaps more than one succumbed to temptation. Algonquin women must have been curious about these white men among them, and Algonquin tribal morality emphasized premarital experimentation, to say no more. We are told that Sinclair established a settlement. We know that the Norse called North America "Greater Ireland".

Someone constructed the Newport Tower during the 1400s. There are supposedly some rubblework ruins along the Charles River in Massachusetts which, from the descriptions I have read, are similar to the ruins at The Cross. There is curious stonework at a place called "Mystery Hill" in New Hampshire and, although these ruins seem to be very ancient, there may well have been a 14th or 15th Century period of European occupation when later visitors adapted the ruins for their own use.

Then, there are some very obscure European records which indicate that furs from North America, including buffalo skins, may have been known in parts of Europe before Columbus. This is possible because the woodland bison once ranged as far as the Atlantic before being rapidly exterminated by early colonists. Buffalo, New York, was named after one of the last of these eastern bison. Also, it seems that American bird's eye maple objects, and American turkeys, were known in Europe before Columbus, and neither bird's eye maple nor American turkeys are native to Europe.[1] If they were known, it could only have been through trans-atlantic contact. In short, there is some evidence that a fair number of Europeans were active along the Atlantic seaboard in the century before Columbus.

What is certain, however, is that any Holy Blood refugees among them would have immediately retreated northward again as soon as the grim news of June 7, 1494 reached them.

That was the date when the Treaty of Tordesillas was signed by Spain and Portugal. It was a treaty dictated by Pope Alexander VI in an effort to keep Spain and Portugal from going to war over their new geographic discoveries. But it was also an attempt on the part of the Vatican to ensure that the entire world, through the efforts of Spain and Portugal, would become Roman Catholic. The mind of Alexander VI conceived the Inquisition established throughout the world and his method for doing it was simple, if a bit grandiose: he divided the whole world between the two most loyal Catholic powers, Spain and Portugal.

Alexander administratively split the world from top to bottom along a line running 100 leagues (originally) west of the Cape Verde Islands. This line was subsequently modified to be 370 leagues west of the Cape Verde Islands by mutual agreement between Spain and Portugal.[2] This imaginary line ran through both poles and on into the other side of the world . . . no one knew quite where, because Magellan had not yet circumnavigated it. With the earth's sphere thus neatly divided from top to bottom into two equal halves, like a great apple, Portugal was awarded the eastern half of the apple while Spain got everything westward.

Portugal got Africa, the Indian Ocean and (hopefully) China as being included on their half while Spain got the Americas and anything else that might be found in the Pacific as far as the line that began Portugal's territory somewhere in the Asian and Pacific unknown.[3]

As far as the Vatican was concerned, all other European nations were excluded from world discovery and colonization. None were loyally Catholic enough to undertake the business of missionary work throughout the pagan world, and this was the justification for discovery and conquest. The economic exploitation was merely a happy coincidence.

The Treaty of Tordesillas caused an interesting situation on the North Atlantic. The coast of North America trends northeast. It was believed that, at some point in northern latitudes, the "Line of Demarcation" (as the Pope's division was called) would intersect with this coast. Naturally, no one knew just where this would happen because no one could tell longitude with any accuracy at all. As this coast became better known, the best guesses were that the Line of Demarcation probably met the Atlantic North American seaboard somewhere between the present-day Carolinas and Maine. Everything west belonged to Spain. Everything east belonged to Portugal.

This was the legal state of affairs in the minds of the Vatican, the Spanish and the Portuguese. It is why the entire southeast part of the modern United States was called "Florida" until after Champlain's time. "Florida" was the name given by the Spanish to easternmost of their new discoveries, and nobody was sure how far north and east "Florida" might extend. DeSoto explored "Florida" for Spain: the modern states of Florida, Georgia, Alabama, Mississippi, Louisiana and part of Texas, but he was careful not to go too far east and north. In 1500, Portugal sent Gaspar and Miguel Corte-Real to explore what might lie east of the Line in the far north. They sailed to the modern Cape Breton Island area, and around Labrador and Newfoundland, and were careful not to sail too far south and west. Their discoveries are the "Corte Real insula" of the Gastaldi Map (and others).

Both Portuguese and Spaniard stayed away from that very large questionable area on the Atlantic coast between the Carolinas and Maine where the Line might intersect the North American seaboard. No one wanted to plant a colony that might turn out to be on the rival's territory. Neither Spain nor Portugal wanted to provoke a war against the other.

The Portuguese were not much interested in the north. They were interested in Africa and their proven route to the Indies and China that existed via the Cape of Good Hope. The northern lands in their half of the apple seemed poor in comparison with the wealth represented by African slaves and East Indian spices. They made only the occasional probe into their northern possessions. But maybe there was another factor at work behind the scenes in high places. We will recall that Prince Henry "The Navigator" of Portugal had himself been a Grand Master of the Knights of Christ, the new and more politic name for the Templars in Portugal. It seems likely that the Portuguese royal house had some special knowledge of, and sympathy for, the Holy Bloodline.

Someone had given the Portuguese accurate charts showing the possessions that founded Portugal's medieval wealth; the chart of Martin de Boheme which showed the Straits of Magellan before they were discovered, the chart of Fra Mauro showing the Cape of Good Hope before it was discovered. Refugee Templars very possibly supplied these charts. In repayment, it is not too unlikely to suppose that Portugal agreed to turn a blind eye toward Holy Refugees in its northern possessions, especially since these lands didn't seem too attractive anyway.

The Treaty of Tordesillas prevented the Holy Refugees from settling anywhere southwest of Maine. It was a danger zone subject to Spanish probes and attacks in a no-man's-land created by the Line of Demarcation.[4] Given the restrictions imposed by the Treaty of Tordesillas, the original Nova Scotian refuge area began to look pretty attractive. At least, it was the best of a bad bargain.

Although there is good agricultural land in the interior of Maine and New Brunswick, the winters inland are much more severe. Because Nova Scotia is almost completely surrounded by water, and because it extends out into the Atlantic a little closer to the Gulf Stream, its climate is less severe than the climate of inland Maine and New Brunswick. Then, because the Holy Refugees had to remain near the coasts in order to maintain contact with Europe, Nova Scotia alone seemed to offer the best compromise of all that they required. It boasted a relatively mild climate for the latitude, excellent agricultural land in the Annapolis Valley and numerous hidden coves and harbours where careful ships could arrive and depart in secrecy. Whether they wanted to be or not, the Treaty of Tordesillas forced the Holy Refugees to become Arcadians.

These observations effectively answer the immediate and natural objection that Canadians would raise against the reconstruction of their early history offered in these pages. If the Holy Refugees did tend to migrate southward to New England during the 1400s, they had to scurry back to Nova Scotia after the Treaty of Tordesillas in 1494.

Perhaps it is justifiable to indulge in a small digression here because, while the Treaty of Tordesillas supports the reconstruction of the romantic history argued in this book, it simultaneously contradicts the drab authorized history in Canadian textbooks. This is the matter of "John Cabot". He was dredged up when the British required a claim to New France.

No first-hand account or map of "Cabot's" discoveries exist. All accounts are second-hand. Cabot supposedly sighted land on June 24, 1497 and described the country as "excellent and the climate temperate, suggesting that brazil and silk grow there."[5] This "brazil" is a tropical dye-wood and, of course, silkworms require a *very* moderate climate. As every Canadian school child knows by heart, Cabot wrote of the incredible numbers of fish that were spawning in the rivers of the new land when he came to anchor in the estuaries.

Testimony given before the Commission of Fisheries pertaining to the Treaty of Washington (1877) states that the river-spawning fish at the latitudes of Newfoundland, Cape Breton and Labrador do not set upon the coast until July 12th at the earliest. If Cabot saw runs of salmon on June 24, then he was far to the south of the present-day Cabot Strait. He was somewhere in southern New England. Could he have seen these fish later? Not likely. He could not have lingered on the coasts of Newfoundland or Cape Breton until July 12, when the fish start to spawn at these latitudes, because he was back in London by August 10.

He must have left the coast of North America almost immediately after he sighted it and have begun his return voyage to England. This supposition agrees with Cabot's own "record" (such as it is) because he said he had to turn back through want of provisions.

The return voyage would have taken at least a month. Cabot returned to Bristol before continuing on to London. The over-land journey from Bristol to London would have taken at least 2-3 days. Yet he was in London on August 10. This means that he must have left North America no later than July 7 or so, but probably earlier, sometime around the end of June. He saw no spawning fish in the rivers of Cape Breton or Newfoundland.

Contemporary experts thought that Cabot had sighted the mid-Atlantic coast. Gomara, in his *General History of the Indies*, says that

Cabot reached land at about 38° north latitude, or about the position of present-day Delaware.

There is a theoretical reason why this is probable. It is a magnetic phenomenon called "Westward Variation". Magnetic compasses point west of north increasingly as one nears North America. Early mariners had no way of suspecting this phenomenon. The practical result of it was that anyone who thought he was on a due west compass course was, in fact, sailing to the southwest unwittingly. All early transatlantic explorers "dropped their latitude" without knowing it, which simply means that they ended up in America far to the south of where they thought they were. Columbus, sailing west from the Canary Islands in 1492, fell 240 miles to the south without suspecting it by the time he reached the other side. On his third voyage, when his point of departure was the Cape Verde Islands, he dropped 293 miles to the south by the time he reached Trinidad.[6,7]

Cabot, sailing only 5 years after Columbus, had the same compasses and the same problem, only more so. It happens that "Westward Variation" increases the further north you happen to be. Cabot sailed out of Bristol, far to the north of Columbus' routes, and took his transatlantic departure from Land's End at about 50° north latitude. If he sailed what he thought was a due west course, he would have fallen to the south by 10° or 12° by the time he reached North America, a matter of roughly 400-450 miles. This would place his landfall at between 38° and 40°, just like Gomara says, somewhere between Massachusetts and Delaware.

This, of course, was smack in the middle of the danger area created by the Treaty of Tordesillas in 1494, just 3 years before Cabot's voyage. Cabot's discovery was, therefore, of little value to the English king, Henry VII, because the king was in no position to go to war against Spain. The king awarded Cabot the sum of £10 for his discovery! Not a very handsome reward, because the discovery was of very little use. And then the king, and everybody else, promptly forgot about John Cabot.

He was resurrected in the mid-1700s when the British needed a claim to New France. The fact that he could not have reached the latitude of New France was ignored. The problem was solved by printing "Cabot Strait" between Cape Breton and Newfoundland, a place "John Cabot" could never have seen. And the British claim was emphasized by rather shamefully Anglicizing the explorer's name. He was, of course, the Venetian, Giovanni Caboto.

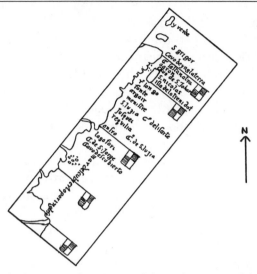

Juan de la Cosa map of 1500, one of the earliest maps of the North American Atlantic seaboard. According to Ganong, it shows the results of the first Cabot voyage. But does it?

"Cavo de Ynglaterra" (i.e. "Cape of the English, or Britains" = Cape Breton) indicates that "Isla de la Trenidat" is intended to represent Cape Canso, Henry Sinclair's "Cape Trin". Cabot's own landfall, if he made the voyage at all, was "Cavo Descubierto" ("Discovery Cape") far to the south and east.

Did Cabot hear rumours of a "Trin" island which had been confused in waterfront gossip with the island of Estotiland with its Cape Trin? He was from Venice like the Zenos were and doubtless heard rumours of the Zeno voyage 100 years earlier.

Courtesy The Trustees of the British Museum.

If he crossed the Atlantic at all.

On July 25, 1498 a Spanish diplomat in London, Pedro de Ayala, wrote to the king of Spain saying that he had obtained a chart from "John Cabot" and would forward it forthwith to Madrid. He did. The ranking Canadian expert on early maps, Ganong, concluded that information from Cabot's voyage found its way onto the Juan de la Cosa Map of 1500, and this is generally accepted.[8] This map is reproduced here.[9] It is damning to authorized Canadian history. It has "Isla de la Trenidat" in the north and "Discovery Cape" far to the south. "Discovery Cape" is obviously Cabot's own landfall, but what is this "Isla de la Trenidat" ("Trinity Island")?

We have run across this name before. I think it is Sinclair's Cape Trin . . . Cape Canso . . . but shown as an island.

This map suggests two things at once. First, we know that Cape Canso ("Trin") is itself well south of Cape Breton and Newfoundland. It is a full 240 miles south of the "Cabot Strait". But Cabot's "Discovery Cape" is well south of "Trin". If this map reflects Cabot's voyage, as the ranking Canadian expert has concluded, then it proves that Cabot was nowhere near the lands so conveniently claimed because of his discoveries.

Second, I think that this map hints that Cabot never crossed the Atlantic at all. The name "Trenidat" in the north can only have come from knowledge of Sinclair's Cape Trin. Yet, *The Zeno Narrative* wasn't published until 1558, 58 years after this map was made. It is only after 1558 that some of the Zeno place-names occur on other maps drawn by European cartographers. Mercator's map (1577) shows "Estotiland", indicating that he'd consulted this published Zeno account. How did Cabot know about Trin 60 years earlier?

I think that the answer is simple. Giovanni Caboto was a Venetian, from the same city as Nicolo, Antonio and Carlo "The Lion". Caboto was a navigator and sailor. He'd *heard* about the previous Zeno adventures through waterfront gossip in Venice. He *heard* about places like "Trin", but he didn't know where or what it was exactly, because the documents themselves had not yet been published.

Armed with this waterfront knowledge, the Cabotos went to England where, along with a lot of other Venetian navigators of the times, Caboto tried to get the king to sponsor him as an explorer.

A lot of Italian navigators were doing this. It was in vogue. It was almost obligatory. Cristoforo Colombo had set the pattern, a Genoese who had flogged his proposal to both Portugal and Spain and who had made good. Many European monarchs were being plagued by Italian navigators urging various courts to get in on the ground floor of the discovery business. Henry VII was being propositioned by just another Italian navigator, Giovanni Caboto.

I'm inclined to the suspicion that Cabot's "first voyage" of discovery, the 1497 one, was concocted to tempt the king into hiring him. It was concocted from waterfront information picked up in Venice and based on the Zeno adventure. Cabot's first voyage was remarkably swift, a quick trip to North America and back, barely possible but not very probable.

At the time, Henry VII wasn't impressed and "rewarded" Caboto with £10. About 250 years later, when the British needed a claim to New France, Caboto's effort was remembered. His name was Anglicized, his subsequent career was embellished: a second and more definitive voyage was concocted and his son, Sebastian, was presented as an expert navigational and exploration consultant to the crown.

The irony for "establishment" history is that the British *did* have a valid claim to New France, but no one knew it. This claim was Henry Sinclair's voyage, well documented in *The Zeno Narrative*. But the British didn't know about Sinclair's voyage when they needed the claim in the 1750s. *The Zeno Narrative* was an Italian document and was dismissed as a "boastful claim of Venetian discovery" before Columbus. Moreover, because of the handwriting and spelling of the document, it took scholars until about 1800 to figure out that *The Zeno Narrative* was referring to Henry Sinclair. The Canadian expert, Ganong, does not refer to *The Zeno Narrative* or to Sinclair when writing in the period 1900-1930 because there was still, at that time, lingering doubt about the authenticity of the document and the certain identification with Sinclair.

The authenticity and the identification are now accepted.

But, it must be admitted, even if Henry Sinclair's exploit *had been known and accepted* during the mid-1700s, there was a small fly in the ointment from the British point of view. This was the problem of the Scottish Stuarts. Rulers of Scotland since the accession of Robert II (1371) and "stewards" of Scotland since about 1160, this family became also the rulers of England through intermarriage when the son of Mary Queen of Scots, James IV of Scotland, also became James I of England in 1603. Thereafter, for 150 years, the English struggled with the curious situation that while Catholic monarchs ruled, the population became increasingly Protestant. This eventually culminated in a bloody civil war and Cromwell. Finally, the Stuart and Scottish claim to the English throne was adroitly "solved" to English satisfaction, but in Scotland the Stuarts still ruled and, in theory, claimed the crown of England as well. They had support enough to be a serious threat until the Battle of Culloden Moor in 1746 where Prince Charles Edward Stuart ("Bonnie Prince Charlie") was decisively beaten by the English. But "Bonnie Prince Charlie" did not die until 1788, and his brother, Henry Benedict Stuart, the last Stuart claimant to the throne of England (as Henry IX) did not die until 1807.

Therefore, even if the British had known of Sinclair's voyage in the mid-1700s, there was the embarrassing fact that Sinclair had been *Scottish*, not English, and the still-powerful Stuarts would have been presented with a claim to New France, as well as England! From the English point of view, it was better for everyone to forget about Henry Sinclair until after the "final solution" of the Stuart Problem. This may be one reason why Henry Sinclair has only recently become an accepted and acknowledged explorer who truly equalled, or surpassed, Columbus.

It is easy to see why the British preferred the dubious claims of a "John Cabot" for propaganda purposes, rather that the actual achievements of Henry Sinclair.

This digression has been longer than I intended, but justifiable, I think. Real, solid "authorized" Canadian history pertaining to John Cabot is revealed as a very shaky ediface constructed for Caboto's personal machinations to gain employment and Britain's colonial machinations to gain New France, both based on hazy waterfront rumours of the very same romantic historical outline presented in this book.

Before leaving this, as an aside, it should be mentioned that "Westward Variation" supports the conclusion that Henry Sinclair reached Nova Scotia. His departure was far to the north of Cabot's. From the Orkney Islands north of Scotland, Sinclair would have dropped 400-450 miles in latitude by the time the Atlantic was crossed. This would make his first landfall dead-center on the coast of Newfoundland, the island of "Icaria" as it is called in *The Zeno Narrative*. Then, as it says, they sailed some days to the southwest to reach Estotiland, Nova Scotia. Sinclair's voyage conforms to "Westward Variation", Cabot's alleged discoveries do not. Sinclair's descriptions are accurate, Cabot's are not.

It seems that John Cabot's contribution to early Canadian history is a "lie commonly agreed upon". The accounts of Cabot's alleged voyages are acceptably dull and undramatic.

The Treaty of Tordesillas forcefully transformed the Holy Refugees into Arcadians and effectively confined them to Nova Scotia. "Larcadia" first appears on the Gastaldi map of 1548, applied to part of Nova Scotia and the name has lingered since in various forms, including the more familiar "Acadia", which are still applied to Nova Scotia regions, highways and a university. The origin of the name is not known for certain, although I've suggested some ways it might be related back to Sinclair's island earldom of "Orchadia". But, we may also remember that Arcadia in Greece was the refuge of expelled Benjamites long before. These Benjamites migrated into Europe to become known as the Sicambrian Franks, ancestors of the Merovingians and of Godfroi de Bouillon. It may be that the Holy Refugees named their Nova Scotia refuge after the old Greek one.

In time, the Benjamites had migrated away from their ancient Arcadian refuge in Greece, probably because of pressure exerted by new migrants from the east. Exactly the same thing seems to have befallen them again in the Nova Scotia Arcadia. The increasing tempo of transatlantic shipping and the imminent threat of official colonization demonstrated that their haven could not remain undiscovered for long. Steps were taken to survey a new refuge, and meanwhile the exploratory and colonization expeditions were infiltrated by Holy Blood operatives whose job it was to disguise the location of the Arcadian haven and lead potential colonists away from sensitive areas. It seems that de Monts, Champlain and perhaps Pont-Gravé were involved in this delicate mission. At least two of these men, the Sieur de Monts and Samuel de Champlain, had proven connections with the Templars or with the Knights of Malta, or with both. There was a scheme about this time (1620 to 1633) to cede Canada to the Knights of Malta. The Knights of Malta, like the Templars, were founded in the Holy Land during the rule of the de Bouillon dynasty.

Although it is impossible, from the present evidence, to figure out exactly what was going on and who was doing it, the undeniable result was that colonization was delayed for a generation by the combined efforts of de Monts and Champlain and their various companies which lobbied for fur-trading monopolies. Although the original proposals were that this fur-trade would pay for the cost of colonization, and although successive monopoly-holders were supposed to undertake serious colonization, this was not done. Both de Monts and Champlain had their fur-trading monopolies revoked by the king because of failure to undertake colonization. Their various companies included each other as shareholders, along with others, Catholic and Protestant alike.

Champlain's religious behaviour and geographic descriptions are both inconsistent. Although supposedly an ardent Catholic and leader of the colony at one point, and a man who petitioned the king to limit Huguenot influence, he was simultaneously a life-long associate of Sieur de Monts, a Protestant. At the time of sending the petition, Champlain was also chief executive officer of a fur-trading company of which de Monts was the major shareholder, while the majority of the other shareholders were also Protestant.

Champlain omits any mention of the largest bay on Nova Scotia's Atlantic coast, and fails to show it on his maps, but there is reason to suspect that he may have shown it through the use of a transfer code centred on Sesambre using the "Bay of All Islands". His description of the Minas Basin area was inaccurate and discouraging. Rumours of mineral wealth there, already current in France, were discredited by Champlain. The land was described as not particularly suited to settlement, the rivers and harbours were described as inadequate. This description is contrary to the facts, and it cannot be the result of accident.

This is how matters stood as of about 1620 to 1625. Exploration had been deflected, colonization had been delayed. About 20 years of security had been obtained for the Holy Refugees through the combined efforts of Samuel de Champlain and the Sieur de Monts.

Meanwhile . . .

In France itself, supporters of the Holy Blood were working frantically to prepare the new haven. The site had to be purchased, administration had to be organized, funds had to be raised and, most important, personnel had to be recruited to staff the refuge and to arrange for the transfer and reception of the Holy Refugees. Exceptional people were needed to shepherd this flock from Arcadia. Exceptional people were found. They became the Shepherds of Arcadia.

Canada's respectable scholars have not failed to blanch a bit when confronted with the story of Montreal as it has come down to us. E.R. Adair of McGill University, writing in *The Canadian Historical Review*, says:

> . ... In regard to colonization the French had done badly: from 1608, when Quebec was founded, down to 1640, less than three hundred immigrants had come to New France; yet in 1641 at one blow a small and almost unknown company had sent out fifty settlers to establish Montreal, and it had succeeded in gathering enough recruits during the next twenty years to enable the settlement to survive its very real dangers on the frontier and to show signs of steadily growing importance . . . This is a naive story, filled with more accidental coincidences than history would willingly accept; but it is not impossible to produce from it a rational and intelligible account of what really happened.[10]

Adair correctly identifies a secret society, the Compagnie du Saint-Sacrement, as the real power behind the founding of Montreal. But the true nature of this secret society eludes Adair as he wonders about it while trying to produce a "rational and intelligible" account along the lines of mechanistic history:

> Why was all this secrecy necessary? Sometimes some of the provincial members (of the Compagnie du Saint-Sacrement) away from the dominance of Paris officials wondered; they even inquired and were told that it arose from a desire "d'imiter la vie cachée du Sauveur dans cette Euchariste". But there were far more practical reasons than that. An open association of so many powerful and wealthy men would have aroused suspicion on the part of church and state alike. Constant pressure for certain objects by one single society would have created bitter and concerted opposition, while the apparently spontaneous action of separate individiuals appeared to be merely the result of a natural growth of public opinion. Moreover, it was soon realized that secrecy gave a romantic and semi-confessional glamour to the whole business, a glamour that proved very attractive to wealthy but well-born members of the middle class, to pious and prosaic lawyers and especially to rich women with nothing better to do.[11]

Adair is waffling. He has already identified the Compagnie du Saint-Sacrement as an ardently Catholic and orthodox organization determined, at last, to effect real colonization. As such, its secrecy was truly unncessary. There was no reason for an overtly ardent and orthodox Catholic organization to "arouse suspicion of church and state" alike in trying to promote colonization of New France. The king had been trying to do it for years and only a small fringe group of religious zealots would really oppose it on missionary grounds. The best that Adair can come up with is that this secrecy was "glamourous" and assisted in fund-raising.

And it probably did.

But what Adair does not suspect, and what justified the secrecy, was that the Compagnie du Saint-Sacrement was apparently a Holy Blood operation. It posed as an ardently orthodox Catholic society, but it was not. It recruited ardently orthodox Catholics, and took their money, but it was run from the top by people who were not so orthodox. Adair does not appreciate the significance of the explanation for secrecy that was fed to provincial members by Parisian officials of the Compagnie: *"d'imiter la vie cachée du Sauveur dans cette Euchariste"*.

"To imitate the hidden life of the Saviour in this community."

And we can appreciate that this was literally true, although somewhat misleading under the circumstances. The Compagnie du Saint-Sacrement had to be as secret as the Holy Refugees themselves had to be in the existing "community" of the day. It was a truth with bite, and a grim joke on the part of Parisian officials "explaining" things to provincial members.

The headquarters of the Compagnie du Saint-Sacrement was the Seminary of Saint-Sulpice in Paris. We have heard of this place before. It was the place where the Bishop of Carcassonne instructed Abbé Bérenger Saunière to deliver the cryptic genealogies and the coded messages that he'd found in the hollow altar-column in the church of Rennes-le-Chateau. This Parisian trip to the Seminary of Saint-Sulpice profoundly changed Saunière in many ways. He returned to Rennes-le-Chateau a wealthy man, he had suddenly acquired friends high in society and politics, he experienced some deep change of faith. Something learned at the Seminary of Saint-Sulpice apparently induced him to put that inappropriate inscription above the door of his church: THIS PLACE IS TERRIBLE. He built a small medieval-looking castle, the Tower of the Magdalene, to house his library and called his own estate Villa Bethania. We are now in a position to realize the significance of these names, to guess the secret he learned from the parchments in the hollow altar column.

Clearly, somehow the Seminary of Saint-Sulpice was connected with these rapid changes in Bérenger Saunière's life. We may now be able to guess what this mysterious power seems to have been. Bérenger Saunière apparently found evidence of Godfroi de Bouillon's lineage, including some sort of proof that the bloodline had survived until the 1700s. Bérenger Saunière may not have blackmailed the Vatican at all, as some French writers have supposed. He may have delivered the documents to high agents of the Grail Dynasty at the Seminary of Saint-Sulpice and thereafter have been paid very well to keep silent.

The Seminary of Saint-Sulpice was founded by Jean-Jacques Olier. Jean-Jacques Olier was one of the pivotal personalities in the establishment of Montreal. The Société de Montréal grew directly from the Compagnie du Saint-Sacrement. McGill University historian, E.R. Adair, noted in *The Canadian Historical Review*:

... on March 21, 1650, a legal act set forth the names of the members of the Society as joint holders of the island of Montreal: two in New France — d'Ailleboust and Maisonneuve — and nine at home — Dauversière, Faucamp, Olier, Bretonvilliers, said to be the richest priest in France, Nicholas Barreau, Roger du Plessis, Duc de Liancourt, Henry-Louis Habert, seigneur de Montmort, King's councillor and master of requests, Bertrand Drouart, and Louis Séguier, Sieur de Saint-Firmin. Six of these nine were members of the Compagnie du Saint-Sacrement: Dauversière, Olier, Barreau, Liancourt, Drouart, and Séguier, and Bretonvilliers was to succeed Olier as Superior of the Order of Saint-Sulpice.[12]

In short, we have Montreal being founded by members of a secret society that had connections with the Seminary of Saint-Sulpice where Bérenger Saunière deposited his documents about the de Bouillon bloodline, and subsequently acquired instant wealth.

It took a great deal of money to found Montreal, too, some 200,000 livres during the first 30 years of the colony's existence. That is about $2 *million* dollars in 1980 currency. Some of this was collected from the orthodox and ardent rank-and-file members of the Compagnie du Saint-Sacrement under what can only be called false pretenses. But a lot was contributed by the wealthy and powerful members of the Parisian "Directorate" of the Compagnie.

Some of it was contributed by wealthy women, but Adair's cynicism backfires on him when he describes one of them as being among the "rich women with nothing to do" in the passage quoted above. One of the most generous contributors to Montreal was Madame de Boullion. She had, very literally, *nothing* better to do with her money. She may have been a direct descendant of Godfroi de Bouillon and if so, was contributing to the continued survival of her own bloodline.

Perhaps, after all of this, the establishment of Montreal doesn't seem to be dull Canadian history any longer.

The traditional story of Montreal is full of simultaneous visions and miraculous mutual recognitions among people who had the same spiritual convictions. This is the "naive story" that Adair referred to and which, somehow, Canadian school children are supposed to accept as fact. As we shall see, some Canadian authors felt compelled to disguise the implausibility of it all with extra-orchidacious prose. The first simultaneous vision, according to Canadian historian, Gustave Lanctot, happened on

February 2, 1636, the Day of the Purification of the Virgin. On that day, Jerome Le Royer de la Dauversière had a vision which impelled him to select Montreal as the site of a future hospital he wanted to establish in the wilderness. And, as Lanctot tells us:

> ... But it happened that on the very same day a former 'man of the world who had reformed his life', Abbé Jean-Jacques Olier, a young priest twenty-eight years of age, felt equally called to give himself to the conversion of the sauvages of New France.[13]

Dauversière had already established a hospital training school at La Flèche, France, sometime between 1630 and 1634, but on that day he determined to locate it eventually in Montreal, while Jean-Jacques Olier, similarly "called" at the same time determined to form the Seminary of Saint-Sulpice to undertake missionary work among the Indians of New France. One might doubt the visionary origin of these decisions when one considers that Abbé Alexandre Le Regois de Bretonvilliers, "said to be the richest priest in France", was Dauversière's assistant at the La Flèche training school. He also succeeded Olier as head of the Saint-Sulpice seminary.

Quite obviously, these people were "destined" to meet, and they did, and made the acquaintance of others. This meeting took place in 1639 at the Chateau de Meudon, then owned by the Grand Master of a neo-Templar secret society according to The Holy Blood and The Holy Grail. On August 7, 1640 the island of Montréal was bought from its current owner, de Lauzon, by Dauversière and Baron de Faucamp with funds provided by anonymous backers. As we know, the island was later transferred to the joint ownership of the 9 members of the Société de Montréal, of whom 6 were members of the Compagnie du Saint-Sacrement.

While all this administrative and financial infrastructure was being developed, a remarkable young woman was being inspired by visions too. As J.K. Foran tells it, in April, 1640:

> As when a sudden flash of lightening leaps across the darkness, revealing for an instant the entire landscape and plunging it back into a deeper obscurity, so came to Jeanne Mance the vivid inspiration. She saw at a glance the field of her future labours, the region that called her to its shores, the Indian and the colonist, the missionary and the pioneer, the struggles with the savage and against

the obstacles that nature raised in the pathway of civilization; she saw the tortured and the wounded, the sick and the dying; she saw, as if by inspiration, the grandeur of the part she might play in that sublime drama of a country's dawning history.[14]

Yes, Jeanne Mance had decided to go to Montreal too. The visions of Jeanne Mance have been burned into the memories of Canadian school children by flights of unforgettable prose like this and no one need fear that Canadian history will be lessened by learning that Jeanne Mance was also a member of the Compagnie du Saint-Sacrement. This interesting fact was discovered by historian Marie-Claire Daveluy, but no one has to be concerned because her book, *Jeanne Mance 1606-1673*, has not been translated into English.[15]

It seems likely that Jeanne Mance was recruited. She was intelligent, industrious . . . and, she seemed to have another asset as far as the Holy Bloodline was concerned. Her background was just as obscure as that of Champlain, de Monts or Maisonneuve.

How was a single young woman in the France of 1640 supposed to live out a vision of serving Montreal when she had no funds, no apparent society connections and no overt religious connections? It was, of course, impossible, yet, it happened. Her local advisor, the Canon of the cathedral in Langres (near her home town of Nogent-le-Roi), suggested that she travel to Paris and meet Father Charles Lallemant who was in charge of the Jesuit missions to Canada. Jeanne Mance took this advice and journeyed to Paris in the spring of 1640, staying with her cousins near the Seminary of Saint-Sulpice for several months. She met with Father Lallemant and was subsequently screened by several other clerics. Eventually, she made contact with Madame de Bouillon whom she met four times during the summer of 1640.

> On the occasion of her fourth visit to her new patroness she was asked to unfold all her plans. Jeanne had to admit that she had no fixed program, that her desire was to go out to Canada, look over the ground and discover in which way God wished her to be of use to the colony.[16]

This is, quite obviously, "creative history" forced upon the author because he doesn't know what transpired at the fourth meeting, or any earlier one. Neither does anyone else. What is known is that Jeanne Mance received 1,200 livres from Madame de Bouillon (about $12,000) and eventually set off for the old Templar port of La Rochelle where she hoped to find a ship bound for Canada.

In point of fact, Jeanne Mance did not arrive in La Rochelle until June, 1641. A year is missing from the slim record that exists of her life in France, but she was probably being intensively briefed by operatives of the Compagnie. Consider that when she finally did arrive in La Rochelle she sought out a Father Laplace, a Jesuit missionary who was also bound for Canada and, as she entered his home a strange coincidence occurred:

> As she was introduced into the parlour a gentleman, who had been talking to Father Laplace, arose and made way for the lady visitor. This was M. de Faucamp, who had been sent from Paris by the Company of Montreal to oversee the embarkation of the recruits that were to be sent out from Canada. After the priest had said a few words to Jeanne concerning her splendid undertaking, he remarked: "That gentleman who has just gone out gave this year twenty thousand livres for an undertaking connected with the country to which you are going. He is called Baron de Faucamp and he is associated with a number of prominent persons who are expending large sums for the establishment of a colony on an island called Montreal, in Canada. "That", said Jeanne, "must be the very place indicated to me in a wonderful manner." And she then and there concluded that this island of Montreal must be the theatre of her future activities.[17]

On the following day, another coincidence happened. As Jeanne Mance was walking to a nearby church in La Rochelle:

> . . . she met a gentleman coming out of that ediface. At once, as if by inspiration, she recognized him as M. de la Dauversière, and at the same moment he recognized her. They met, saluted each other, called each other by name and immediately, without any formality, entered upon a conversation regarding the island of Montreal. They entered the church together and prayed for a long time. What was said during that interview has not been recorded, but until the very day of her death Jeanne spoke of it with a fervour that amounted almost to ecstasy.[18]

Jeanne Mance and Dauversière had supposedly never met before and their mutual recognition was regarded as miraculous, but it may have been the fruit of a year of careful training in Holy Security Procedures. But the revelation in the church was a different matter. We can now appreciate the emotional impact of it a bit better . . . if she was informed, for the first time (after careful screening and a year of training) of the Holy Bloodline and her service to it. Jeanne Mance's response was no different than the response of many paladins down through history. She became utterly committed to the secret and to what it meant to humanity.

I've dealt with Jeanne Mance's story at some length, as far as is possible considering the small number of real facts that survive about her, in order to make a few points.

First, just as modern scholars are starting to suspect, the establishment of Montreal was not dependent upon visions and inspirations, except, maybe, on a very general level. The specific activities of people were not regulated by miraculous "calls" but by careful planning of a secret organization with significant financial resources.

Then, although I have quoted some rather naive passages intended for junior readers in Canadian schools, I did not do so in order to be at all cynical. I did it to show how very little is really known about Jeanne Mance, just as very little is known about others apparently recruited for service with the Grail Dynasty. We know *nothing* about Samuel Champlain's birth and early life, *nothing* about Sieur de Monts, *nothing* about Maisonneuve and virtually nothing about the birth and early life of Jeanne Mance. One careful historian, William Inglis Morse, who wrote a book about the life of the Sieur de Monts, continually expresses a mixture of disappointment, frustration and perplexity that so little documentation exists. He notes that the archives of de Monts' ex-Templar castle were destroyed by fire, which is unfortunate. But it is *puzzling* that some documents in other places, which were known to exist, suddenly disappeared when he tried to look at them.[19]

Isn't it rather strange that the major figures in the very early history of Canada are so utterly without backgrounds?

The third point that I wanted to make by quoting from the "creative history" of Foran is that he's essentially accurate in trying to communicate the sense of commitment and wonder that Jeanne Mance felt, lived and was a part of. If Foran's style of writing seems unbearably over-blown and corny, the problem may lie with us and the self-indulgent cynicism we choose to adopt when viewing what we call "reality". Jeanne Mance saw another reality. As did a *dux bellorum* named Arthur, and a "prince" called Sinclair, and Jacques de Molay, Esclarmonde de Foix, Champlain, de Monts. And many more who have not been mentioned. All devoted lives of sacrifice and hardship for *something*. They were not fools.

Also, by lingering just a little while on the inspiration of Jeanne Mance, I'm trying to show that paladins of the Holy Blood have always come in both sexes. In thinking carefully how best to structure a very complicated story which most people are not inclined to want to believe anyway, it happened that I chose episodes featuring male paladins. I did this only because of the mechanical links that some episodes offered more obviously than others. But other episodes could have been used which are a part of the same story. Joan of Arc could have been featured because she, too, was a paladin of the Holy Blood and bought time when it was desperately needed. I was tempted to tell the story of Esclarmonde de Foix and the fall of Montségur, but I did not because the historical connections would have been too unfamiliar.

Something both dramatic and profound has motivated exceptional men and women over thousands of years and, in trying to draw an outline of what it is, I have not been able to give proper due to the many courageous women in this story. It is quite obvious that this failure reflects my own limitations of "expertise". I've had to stick to episodes and evidence that betray the existence of a secret history through its impact on discovery, exploration navigation, and old maps.

With the recruitment of Jeanne Mance all but one of the major roles in the drama of Montreal had been filled. Still required was someone to act as a military leader and governor, a soldier. The man chosen was Paul de Chomedy, Sieur de Maisonneuve. Maisonneuve, too, was interviewed by Father Lallemant, screened by several other assessors, and in due course ended up in La Rochelle in time to embark with Jeanne Mance for Montreal.

Again, nothing whatever of Maisonneuve's birth and early life is known beyond the bare facts that he was *supposedly* born in February, 1612, in the town of Neuville-sur-Vanne. He had been a soldier, but retired from his regiment at the age of 29. He, too, wanted to serve in Montreal.

> He opened his heart to Father Charles Lallemant who put him in touch with M. de la Dauversière. After an interview with the latter, the Associates were quick to add to their group this rare fellow who wanted to use "his life and purse in an undertaking in which there was no ambition beyond serving God and the King his master". "A

man of prayer", he possessed a great deal of feeling for his fellow man, a profound sense of justice and a firm judgement. Moreover, he had no desire for honours and sought neither advantages nor riches. On the contrary, he gave generously from the income from his own personal fortune. Of cool bravery and unshakeable firmness, he was to reveal himself as the leader who refused to yield to the Iroquois, the malevolent governors and the theocratic authorities.[20]

For once, this sort of eulogy seems fully deserved. Maisonneuve was a remarkable individual. Canadian historian, Francis Parkman, summed up Maisonneuve's character with brief eloquence: "Maisonneuve was a great man, knightly in bearing, brave as a lion, and devout as a monk."[21]

Jeanne Mance had many of these qualities herself, plus seemingly boundless compassion and infinite patience. Maisonneuve and Mance made a formidable team and, between them, established a remarkable community and ensured its survival against rather unbelievable odds.

> They resembled to a remarkable degree the early Christians in the Catacombs. They lived in hiding and in constant fear of attack; not, as of old, from the spies and soldiers of Nero, but from the scouts and warriors of the Iroquois. There was no money in circulation to any great extent; rather did they live by barter and the exchange of commodities, of work and of services. There was an absolute absence of crime, because there was no selfishness, no sordid ambitions, no amenities . . . and we find Père Leclercq, a Recollet priest of the time, calling the community at Montreal "The Holy Colony".[22]

Jeanne Mance, Maisonneuve and the other colonists bound for Montreal left La Rochelle in June, 1641. They spent their first Canadian winter at the previously-established settlement at Quebec. Meanwhile, back in France, when it was known that the colonists were safe in Quebec, the principals of the project formally announced their commitment. They chose a symbolic date, the anniversary of the simultaneous visions experienced by Dauversière and Olier which, so the "naive story" goes, had started the whole thing.

> On the 2nd of February, 1642, the Associates of the Company of Montreal met in the church of Notre Dame, Paris, and there, in the presence of M. Olier and de la Dauversière, dedicated the Island of Montreal to the Holy Family. About the same time, M. Olier founded the Order of Saint-Sulpice, a community of gentlemen destined to take charge of the spiritual requirements of the new colony.[23]

The following spring, the colonists arrived at the island of Montreal at the confluence of the Ottawa and St. Lawrence Rivers. The date was May 17, 1642. They numbered 72 souls.

This is no place to look at a detailed history of Montreal, although any researcher who does so from the perspective of the Holy Blood's existence is likely to glean some interesting, and perhaps important, facts and insights. The colonists did not call their settlement "Montreal", *that* was the elevation rising above the town on the shore of the St. Lawrence, a sort of high hill that does not quite merit being called a mountain. Montreal means "Mount Royal" and it was possibly named after a Cathar fortress near Carcassonne, or after a Templar stronghold in de Bouillon's Kingdom of Jerusalem. The town itself was called "Ville Marie", the Town of Mary, and it was dedicated to the Holy Family.

The town grew fairly quickly, in spite of Iroquois warfare, and the first census in 1666 listed a total of 627 persons by name, age, sex and occupation ... except that, inexplicably, the known heart of Ville Marie's population was not listed in this census. This core was Jeanne Mance and her hospitalliers, together with some Sulpician priests. They do not appear on the rolls even though they should logically head the list of inhabitants after Maisonneuve. Jeanne Mance's hospital was Ville Marie's *raison d'être*. Modern researchers have figured out that at least 17 people are known to have been in Ville Marie at the time, but are not mentioned in any way. These 17 include Jeanne Mance herself and her closest colleagues but might, of course, involve many more than 17 whose existence could not be guessed by modern scholars. Why were these people, the most important ones, left out?

The only explanation must be that the French officials did not want to know exactly how many people might be attached to Jeanne Mance's group. A purposefully blind eye seems to have been turned toward the people who were the soul of Ville Marie.

There is some evidence to show that the new haven of Montreal, if that is what Ville Marie was, had been conceived as early as 1625 to 1627 because that is when the Compagnie du Saint-Sacrement appears to have been formed. Because of the secrecy, however, everything about the Compagnie must be highly conjectural. It may have existed much earlier. Champlain's curious mention of a Sieur de Maisonneuve at the site of the Lachine Rapids in 1613 is surely thought-provoking. Maisonneuve is supposed to have been born in 1612 and to have died on September 9, 1675. He was therefore 63.

I have searched through a fair number of biographies and historial encyclopaedias for some additional information on his birth and background, including some authority for this birth date. I have not been able to find anything beyond the date itself. If there's not some document I have overlooked, I'm inclined to believe that his dates 1612-1675 must come off his gravestone, and dates on gravestones can be faked. People grew up younger then. Maisonneuve, in the authorized story, told Lallement that he joined his regiment at 15. This was an average age for being considered a functional adult in those times. If Maisonneuve were only 15 years older, then, he could have met Champlain as the Sieur de Maisonneuve in 1613 and still have been the Maisonneuve who governed Ville Marie in co-operation with Jeanne Mance. That would make him 44 years old when he arrived at Montreal, 68 when he left Ville Marie in 1666, and 78 when he died in 1675. This is not impossibly old by any means. Champlain was 68 when he died.

This is an intriguing speculation, but one whose only importance is likely to be an indication of when Montreal began to be actively planned. Even this is not a crucial point since, if Arcadia was a refuge, some relocation would have been recognized as eventually necessary by the mid-1500s at the latest because of reasons given earlier. But there is a reason why the tempo of planning might have speeded up in 1603, the year that Champlain first voyaged to Canada. James I, son of Mary Queen of Scots, came to the throne of England and inaugurated the Stuart dynasty of England. Everybody could predict that this would cause trouble sooner or later. The Catholic Stuarts were bound to come into conflict with their increasingly Protestant subject, as they did.

This threat was immediately compounded in 1625. That was the year that Charles I, the son of James, became king. Charles I married Henrietta Maria, daughter of the king of France. In some mysterious fashion, as soon as this marriage occurred, Arcadia passed into partial Stuart control and possession for a while and started to be called "Nouvelle Écosse" — Nova Scotia — on some maps. This partial transfer, or sharing, of the place seems to have been more of a verbal deal "in the family" than any formal treaty. The Stuarts began creating "Baronets of Nova Scotia".

It takes little imagination to reconstruct some hypothetical discussions between the royal in-laws on the subject of Acadia/Nova Scotia. The Stuarts had something of a claim on it because of Sinclair's voyage, and they may very well have known it. The Stuarts and Sinclairs intermarried too. Knowledge of the 1398 voyage may well have been preserved as secret family history. One can almost hear the cordial barbs and innuendoes flying back and forth between the kings of England and France regarding the ownership of Acadia/New France, and hints about the repercussion of any overt claims to it. If Acadia/Nova Scotia really was a Holy Blood refuge at this time, the complications become virtually limitless. A little careful thought will disclose a few of the delicate considerations.

Both Catholic monarchs become guilty of harbouring *the* enemy of the Vatican and to have knowingly done so for a couple of centuries. Both monarchs should, by reason of national policy and national obligation as leaders, claim the place and dispute its ownership, yet neither could because of what such a revelation would mean. Then, both monarchs may have had more allegiance to the Holy Blood than to the Catholic church as represented by the Vatican and the pope. Henry IV of France had previously been Protestant. He became Catholic when he became king. It seemed more politic. As for the Stuarts, they had married into the lineage of de Bouillon in the 11th Century. They had also crossed blood with the Sinclairs, who had themselves mixed with the de Bouillons.

The Stuart claim to "divine right" of rulership had nothing to do with "Vatican Catholicism", it resulted from their partial Merovingian descent. They were "Catholics" only nominally, although the average British Protestant-on-the-street could not be expected to know the ironic truth, just as the average orthodox Catholic supporter of Stuart royalty could not be expected to know the truth either, nor could either be told the truth. The fact of the matter was, for all their outward and orthodox Catholicisim, the Stuarts knew, and were an offshoot of, a secret that threatened Rome far more than overt Protestant opposition and religious warfare.

The formerly Protestant French king seems to have been in a similar position. Family loyalties, and much higher ones, dictated continued protection of the Holy Bloodline, obligatory Catholicism dictated concessions to orthodox-appearing behaviour and policy, while newly emerging national and economic realities compelled still other decisions for the welfare of the state and population as a whole. We've seen how the obligation of protecting a refuge conflicted with the national obligation to promote colonization, and how both (in different ways) opposed factions of orthodox Catholicism. We've seen the curious compromise of all these conflicting forces in early New France: colonization was effectively postponed by giving fur-trade monopolies to Protestant entrepreneurs who were responsible for promoting Catholic colonization and Catholic missionary work!

The separate forces of familial loyalty to the Holy Bloodline, the political necessity of appearing to be orthodox Catholic, the dictates of newly emerging national economics and politics, all these forces were like gravitational pulls of major planets swirling around the European heads of state, spiced with ever-present personal ambitions of kings and ministers. The resulting "resolution" of these forces often appeared to be inconsistent and inexplicable policies.

Astronomers can sometimes pinpoint the position of an unseen planet by analysing the motions of planets in other orbits and the motion of the central sun. If strange and unexplained perturbations are observed, then it indicates the presence of some unsuspected body exerting a significant gravitational pull. By measuring the magnitude of these deviations from smooth curves, astronomers can calculate the probable mass of the unseen planet and its orbit and can approximate its importance in the entire system.

European history has *always* indicated the presence of such an unseen force whether during the "Arthurian Age", the crusades and the Kingdom of Jerusalem or the "Age of Discovery". But, nowhere are the perturbations more clearly seen than in the period between 1500 and 1815 when colonialism was establishing the conflicts of our own 20th Century world. *Something* was compelling inconsistent and inexplicable policies, which often resulted in unnecessary national conflicts later on. One could say that there really "shouldn't" have been any development of Protestantism at all, but just a modification of Catholicism, except for the idea of the Holy Blood. One could say that there "shouldn't" have been any conflict between Catholic orthodoxy and colonialism, except for the idea of a Holy Blood haven. The Holy Bloodline is the unidentified gravitational force in the system. It has not *quite* been seen by historical observers, but the perturbations it has caused have been a source of puzzlement in trying to make sense of European history.

As for the Stuarts and Henry of France, they *knew* what the hidden gravitational pull was, could not overtly acknowledge its existence, and yet had to reconcile its pull with the other forces acting upon the French and English thrones and nation-states. The resolution-of-forces arrived at was surely unique in the annals of European colonialism. *For a while, the French and English royal houses simply shared Acadia/Nova Scotia without any quibbles over ownership or boundaries.*

This family compromise bought a little extra time for the Holy Bloodline, but only at the cost of increased threat a few years down the road, because two forces were not totally satisfied with the royal compromise. National identity and colonial competition could not be reconciled with such a compromise for long. English religious conflict would not ignore this compromise for long. It could only be a matter of time before the English people repudiated the Stuarts and got back into the mainstream of colonial attitudes and expansion.

The Holy Blood and its supporters had always boasted a number of very astute and agile political minds, such acumen had proved to be *the* prerequisite for survival over a number of turbulent centuries. By about 1620 at the latest, the eventual vulnerability of Acadia/Nova Scotia would have become evident to these sharp political analysts. A new refuge would have to be found a bit more quickly than previously planned because it was only a matter of time, and not too much time, before Acadia/Nova Scotia would be drawn into the conflict between the Stuarts and the English Parliament. Stuart heads were vulnerable to the axe and Acadia/Nova Scotia was vulnerable to attack from the Puritan colonies in Massachusetts. The danger of this was evident to Holy Blood political analysts by the mid-1620s, which explains why the Compagnie du Saint-Sacrement appears to have been formed around this time and why the preparations for the Montreal colony progressed so quickly in comparison with other French colonial schemes.

These political considerations also explain the choice of Montreal. The new haven could not be a coastal one because it would be vulnerable to sea-borne attack by the British once they got back on the rails of colonialism after the Stuart side-track. The new haven would be safest in the heart of New France, protected by downstream fortresses on the St. Lawrence, like Quebec. Such a haven could no longer be a secret geographically, as Acadia had been, but would have to be disguised. The best disguise was religious, a missionary community. Politically, in France, such a community *had to be* nominally and overtly Catholic, and it was, but, somehow the newly-created Order of Saint-Sulpice managed to control its "spiritual requirements" and the older established Catholic orders, such as Jesuits, Recollets, Dominicans and others were excluded from any influence for many years.

This explains why the tempo of planning and organization speeded up from about 1625-1627. The new refuge had to be established before Stuart problems came to a crisis and Acadia/Nova Scotia was attacked by Puritan Roundheads. An organization had to be welded together more quickly than anticipated in order to establish the new haven and to found a financial and religious structure that would insulate the refugees from the machinations of truly orthodox and ardently Catholic orders which represented Vatican interests.

While the core of the conspiracy was labouring to do all this between 1620 and 1642, other relatives and supporters of the Holy Blood had to be reassured about what was happening. Anyone could appreciate the converging dangers to the refugees represented by increased Atlantic traffic and colonization, and suddenly compounded by Stuarts on the throne of England.

Those who had a stake in the bloodline, but who did not rank high enough to be in the core group of planners, had to be assured that appropriate steps were being taken to shepherd the refugees from Arcadia.

This could not be done overtly, of course, because of the Vatican. And, before the days of mass communications like newspapers, radio and TV, it could only be done through coded messages in literature and art. And, on cue, Arcadia suddenly became a popular theme for writers and painters. Sir Philip Sydney wrote the epic *Arcadia* about a half-mystical haven. Charles I read it in the last few hours of his life while awaiting the axe at Whitehall. It presumably meant something to him, and afforded some comfort, although that would not be its effect on modern readers since it is long, dull, complicated and implausible.

Painters used the Arcadia theme too. The years 1618 to 1642 saw the creation of a curious series of paintings called "The Shepherds of Arcadia" or "I am in Arcadia", both clearly showing shepherds gathered around a tomb. Although in some paintings they look serious, these shepherds are not tragic. In some paintings they even look animated and excited. The first of these paintings was created by the Italian, Guercino, in 1618. The last was painted by Nicholas Poussin in 1642. The same theme was picked up by many more minor artists.

Three of these paintings are reproduced. In the 1618 work by Guer-

"Et in Arcadia Ego" by the Italian painter Guercino, created circa 1618. The first of a series of curious paintings to use this phrase. Note the bumble bee resting on the skull.

Courtesy The Museum of Antique Art, Rome.

Two gold bee figurines recovered from the tomb of the Merovingian king, Childeric I, father of Clovis.

Courtesy French Ministry of Culture.

"Et in Arcadia Ego" by Nicholas Poussin in 1630. Shepherds crowd around a tomb with this phrase carved in it. The first painting of this theme by Poussin.

Courtesy The Louvre, Paris.

Poussin's more famous "Les Bergers d'Arcadie" now in the Louvre. Who are these shepherds? Compare tomb and background with photograph on following page.

Courtesy The Louvre, Paris.

Photograph of an actual tomb near Rennes-le-Chateau discovered by the authors of *The Holy Blood and The Holy Grail*. Note the crag in the background and compare with tomb and landscape in Poussin paintings.

Photo by Michael Baigent.

cino, a bee is depicted on the skull. Bees were a Merovingian symbol. The inscription on the tomb reads: ET IN ARCADIA EGO. This means "I am in Arcadia".

Two paintings by Poussin are reproduced, both showing this same theme. One is also called "Et in Arcadia Ego", while one is entitled "Les Bergers d'Arcadie" ("The Shepherds of Arcadia").

The British authors of *The Holy Blood and The Holy Grail* called attention to the possible significance of these paintings for English readers. They even managed to locate a real tomb that seems to be the one shown in Poussin's "Les Bergers d'Arcadie" which was completed in 1642. Not only does the tomb look the same, but even the actual landscape near the real tomb seems to be reproduced in Poussin's painting. I have reproduced the photograph of this real tomb located by the authors of *The Holy Blood and The Holy Grail*. The cliff in the background is similar to the crag in the background of the Poussin painting, the tombs are identical. The real tomb in the photograph *is near Rennes-le-Chateau,* where Bérenger Saunnière found the genealogies.

Poussin's "Les Bergers d'Arcadie" is now in the Louvre, but it was once owned by Louis XIV of France who went to a great deal of trouble to obtain it between 1656 and 1660. When he did finally get it, he hid it away in his private apartments so that only a trusted few could view it in his lifetime.

These paintings, so similar in theme but painted by many different artists over a period of a quarter of a century, obviously mean something. But what?

The authors of *The Holy Blood and The Holy Grail* in company with earlier French investigators, can only suggest that, somehow, these paintings must refer to the ancient Arcadian refuge in Greece that was once important to the exiled Benjamites who were claimed as ancestors by the Merovingians. One of the coded messages that Bérenger Saunière found at Rennes-le-Chateau was:

> SHEPHERDESS, NO TEMPTATION, THAT POUSSIN,
> TENIERS, HOLD THE KEY . . .

The French and English researchers realized that the reference to a shepherdess must hint at the curious series of shepherd paintings. Teniers (father and son) were also painters, but their creations of this sort, if they ever made any, have been lost. That leaves Poussin and the others. The idea that these paintings must have something to do with the Greek Arcadia would seem to be clear because the draping of the figures is "classical", but no more obvious connection came to the minds of the investigators.

In the mid-1600s, the old Arcadia in Greece was firmly in control of the Turks and was no refuge for the Holy Blood. And, why should a French king in 1660 want to hide something from ancient history? It did not seem to make much sense, and French and British researchers alike could only speculate that these paintings must have had some mystical relevance to the history of the Holy Blood. The British authors of *The Holy Blood and The Holy Grail* suggest that an "underground stream" of knowledge is being reflected in these paintings because of the underground rivers of Greek mythology.[24]

Readers who have gotten this far will immediately understand the significance of these paintings, and maybe even suspect why a king of France would want to hide "The Shepherds of Arcadia" away from too-public viewing.

The only Arcadia important to the Holy Bloodline in the mid-1600s was that very real and geographical Arcadia across the Atlantic, the one endangered by colonization and Stuart political problems. The "Shepherds of Arcadia" could only have been those whose job it was to establish a new haven and transfer the Arcadian refugees there. These shepherds established their new haven in Montreal, and began their active field work, in 1642, the same year that Poussin completed "Les Bergers d'Arcadie" which the king tried so hard to obtain and hide.

Poussin's painting "The Shepherds of Arcadia" shows four shepherds, three men and a woman. Maybe the king hid the painting because these people were identifiable, not because they were mythic figures from ancient Greece. Identifiable shepherds of the geographical Arcadia might have caused the Catholic king some embarrassment, more especially as these shepherds had been established in the field during his reign and since his census-takers were about to turn a blind eye to the exact size of this particular flock.

As we have seen, service with the Holy Blood could have its down side. Sacrifice and death (sometimes, by particularly hideous means) were accounted an occupational hazard. Jesus, Arthur, Joan of Arc, Jacques de Molay, Geoffrey de Charnay, Esclarmonde de Foix and many others could attest to this.

But, as a "perk" or fringe benefit, Holy Blood operatives seem to have had the guarantee that their contributions would be recognized, consistent with the policy of secrecy and according to the problems of inserting such recognition into the accepted history and culture of Western humanity. Sometimes, in order to guarantee the recognition spelled out in the fringe benefit clause, the Holy Blood had to resort to "reverse-snobbishness" for secrecy's sake in order to secure recognition for its truly noble-born operatives.

Jesus, who was very much a king and the scion of a long lineage with powerful dynastic claims to Jerusalem, failed in his bid to re-establish the Jewish kingship, and could best be remembered as a humble carpenter from Nazareth. As another example, Joan of Arc, who has been remembered in history as a mystical (or, perhaps insane) peasant girl, la pucelle, who "heard voices" and who somehow came to command armies, has now been revealed by modern scholarship to have been connected with the powerful dukes of Anjou, but only now.

Their fringe benefit clause has molded our understanding of history and is the foundation for our major religions.

The Holy Blood seems to have been an equal opportunity employer, recruiting people on merit without regard to sex and with the same guarantee of recognition (as and when possible, depending upon circumstances, with no obligation for immediate acknowledgement and full discretion over the media to be employed, etc., etc.). The lower-born operatives posed an even bigger problem of recognition in status-conscious Europe. They could hardly be passed off as nobility in order to find their way into history. Even the Holy Blood could not fudge so many genealogies. Besides, lineage was the keystone of European society, and any strangers injected into family trees would be quickly discovered and repudiated. The easiest thing to do would be to insert the lowly-born operatives within the comfortably amorphous mythic ambience of the Ancient World, such as among the classical-looking "Shepherds of Arcadia", for instance.

Poussin created this painting between 1640 and 1642, just when the Montreal personnel were being selected through the screening by Father Lallement and others. The bodies of these shepherds were "stock shots" for any Renaissance Master, as Poussin was. All that he needed to know was that the shepherds consisted of three men and one woman. His problem would be the facial portraits.

It is tempting to suppose that these shepherds were: Olier and Dauversière (the real founders of the colony), Jeanne Mance and Maisonneuve. Three men and a woman who were all in Paris in the years 1640-1641 and could have posed for Poussin's portraits. The shepherds suddenly became identifiable, and embarrassing to the French throne.

Canadian historians often complain about the lack of authentic pictorial representations of people prominent in early Canadian exploration and colonization. There are no reliable portraits of Cartier, Champlain, Maisonneuve, de Monts, Pont-Gravé or Jeanne Mance, or of a number of others.[30] Maybe Canadian historians should take the hint from the coded message found by Bérenger Saunière in Rennes-le-Chateau: "Poussin, Teniers, hold the key".

Maybe these people are immortalized within the allegorical-seeming series of paintings dealing with the "Arcadia" theme, maybe their faces can be found among the shepherds in the paintings created by Guercino, Poussin and Teniers between 1618 and 1642. Although any specific "Shepherds of Arcadia" painting by the Teniers seem to have been lost, other examples of their work survive. Perhaps significant faces appear on fishermen, peasants and other figures in these paintings. Certainly, the shepherds in Guercino and Poussin are worth checking out. Poussin's "The Shepherds of Arcadia" was created while the Montreal leaders were concentrated in Paris, the three men and a woman would seem too much of a coincidence and almost *must* be Olier, Dauversière, Maisonneuve and Jeanne Mance, and the fact that the king hid this painting indicates that these people must have been identifiable *at that time*.

Art history is not my strong suit. Careful study of these "Shepherds of Arcadia" and allied paintings should be undertaken by someone with the appropriate fine arts background. Having traced the Holy Blood's activities through many centuries, and having come to appreciate its little ways, I'm willing to bet pretty heavily that clues have been provided to permit specific identification of these faces. It has not been possible for us to follow up this line of research for lack of time and proper training.

The crisis between the Stuarts and Parliament came to a head in 1649 when Charles lost his. Just 5 years later, in 1654, the peninsula of Acadia/Nova Scotia *was* attacked by Robert Sedgewick of Massachusetts. The Holy Blood had only 12 years, from 1642 until 1654 to establish a refuge at Montreal capable of accommodating, and hiding, any hypothetical Holy

Blood personnel and treasures that had to be transferred from Acadia/ Nova Scotia. It is known that Montreal did have an influx of settlers in 1650 and in 1653, just before Sedgewick's attack in 1654.

I do not pretend to know how, or when, the necessary transfer took place, but it is obvious that there would have to have been some justifiable and plausible possibility of contact between Acadia and Montreal to act as a cover for this transfer. De Monts' old settlement at Port Royal had been abandoned in 1607 when his fur-trading monopoly had been revoked. Although it is impossible to be absolutely certain, it does not appear that anyone stayed in Port Royal after de Monts' withdrawal under royal displeasure.

Obviously, Acadia would have had to have been re-occupied in order to justify any voyages between it and Montreal. This was done by Isaac Razilly in 1635 who came with 300 settlers to Port Royal. The census of 1686 lists 592 people then at Port Royal, 15 at Cape Sable at the southwest extremity of Nova Scotia (not to be confused with Sable Island out in the Atlantic), 19 at La Have, 127 at Beau-bassin at the head of the Bay of Fundy near Cape Chignecto and 57 settlers at Minas near the mouth of the Gaspereau River.[31] These locations were not necessarily the best for farming, but are strategic lookout points. We will probably never know how Razilly's colonists of 1635 were distributed originally. What is certain, however, is that the mere presence of these Acadians would "explain" any casual contact between Acadia and Montreal. These settlers quickly built their own shallops for coastal voyaging and they were visited by ships from France. It would not cause much comment if a ship from France happened to call at Acadia before proceeding on to Quebec and Montreal. The necessary transfer of people and objects could have been effected by these ships and coastal shallops using the 1635 settlements as a screen.

Further, as any hypothetical Grail Dynasty refugees abandoned Acadia, these Acadian settlers could have occupied their previous sites and would have muddled the matter nicely for anyone who might have suspected prior Holy Blood habitation in the area. Frederick Pohl found rather suggestive house sites atop Cape D'Or, but also found *very early* Acadian artifacts in them. Acadians later occupied the fertile farm land around the mouth of the Gaspereau River, as well as the more obvious look-out points around the peninsula. In this way any previous Holy Blood occupancy could have been disguised.

Who tried to "erase" the inland settlement at The Cross? It is known that Sedgewick sacked and burned Port Royal during his attack in 1654, but no evidence that he probed inland to do the same with The Cross, at least, none that we have been able to find.

However . . .

There are the traditions of the Nauss family of Lunenburg. The famous fishing and ship-building port of Lunenburg was supposedly settled in 1753 by immigrant German families. But at least one member of the now large and widely-scattered Nauss family has stated that the family originally arrived near the present Lunenburg in 1623 as immigrant German carpenters engaged to build an inland mansion! Sketches of this mansion have passed down from generation to generation within the Nauss family. I have reproduced some of them here.

This story was originally told to Jeanne McKay, the sketches were copied for her by a member of this family who shall remain nameless here (but who is known to the Nova Scotia Ministry of Culture, Recreation and Fitness). I have attempted direct correspondence with him, but my letters have gone unanswered. According to the tale told to Jeanne McKay, the mansion was built within the already-ruined walls at The Cross. Because of the problem of obtaining good-quality mortar, it was built entirely of wood in the end. It was surmounted, however, by a golden-looking dome and it boasted 12 pillars. Inset into the foyer was a mosaic of the lion of Scotland, which happens also to appear on Nova Scotia's present provincial flag.

It is not completely implausible that the Holy Blood handed over their inland haven to the Stuarts after they ceased to have any use for it, or during the period when the new haven of Montreal was in the planning stage. It may be that Stuart carpenters began their mansion while the Holy Blood refugees still inhabited The Cross. James I died on March 27, 1625, or 2 years after the start of this mansion's construction (if we are to believe this tale), but in any case he could never have used it because his whereabouts are well accounted for by history. Charles I, his son, was beheaded on January 30, 1649 and he could never have used such a refuge either, and for the same reason, he's too well known in history. But . . . the sons of Charles I *could* very definitely have been hidden in such a haven for a while, although, I believe, they are generally thought to have found refuge in France during the time of Cromwell's Protectorate, which was established in 1653. Whether they did or not, or

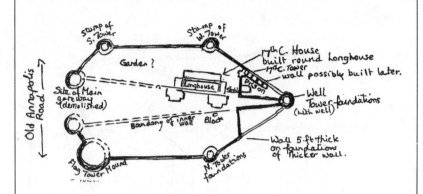

Jeanne McKay's sketch of the "castle's" alleged shape, copied from sketches in the possession of the Nauss family of Lunenburg, Nova Scotia.

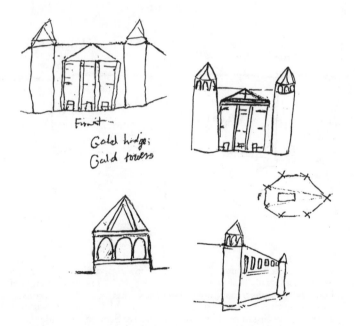

Jeanne's sketches, supposedly based on Nauss family drawings, of the "castle's" guard towers, main gate with pillars, and golden-coloured "dome" (or cone).

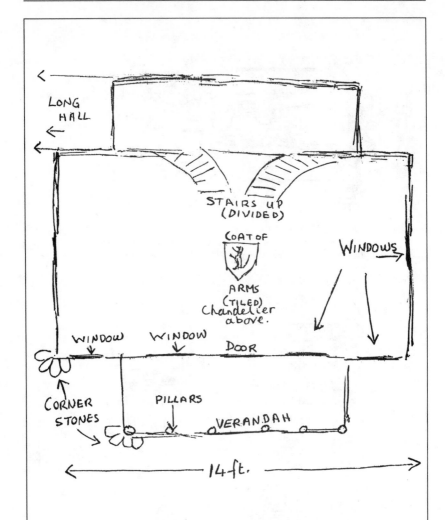

Jeanne's sketch, based on Nauss family drawings, of the 17th Century mansion allegedly built within the "castle" walls. The Nauss family of Lunenburg claims to have arrived in Canada in the 1620s as carpenters to work on the mansion, according to Jeanne McKay, which was used as a refuge for Stuart princes. The royal lion of Scotland was inlaid into the main hall of this mansion which Jeanne claims was probably designed by Inigo Jones.

But note the scale that Jeanne has given this "mansion" . . . just 14 feet wide!

whether there was really such a mansion, I'm in no position to say. But this is the tale told to Jeanne McKay by a young man of the Nauss family.

There is a little more to this story. It is claimed that Sedgewick did probe inland to this mansion in The Cross, destroyed it thoroughly, and carried the dome and the 12 columns back to Massachusetts with him, where they were incorporated into the present Boston State House! Personally, I can't see how any such dome could have been easily wrestled down to the sea along with 12 pillars. However, some architectural student in Boston might find it interesting to try to trace the origin of the dome and pillars on the Boston State House. We have not been able to do this.

According to Jeanne McKay, she was able to find two Micmac Indians who knew of this "mansion in the woods" and inland occupation by white men before the 19th Century colonists arrived. As I said previously, I spoke with several Micmacs but was unable to verify this story. The Indians who confided to Jeanne McKay are now dead.I have spoken to their relatives, and to other Micmacs, and I have gotten the definite impression that they know *something*, but are unwilling to talk about it. The names of the Indians I contacted are known to the Ministry of Culture, Recreation and Fitness of Nova Scotia.

If any of this is true, then it is possible that The Cross sheltered its last refugees in 1653. Refugee Stuart princes. If Sedgewick did not destroy it out of anti-Stuart malice, then maybe Acadian settlers themselves did what they could to erase obvious signs of the inland haven which had sheltered the Grail Dynasty since 1398.

At the end of the last chapter it was noted that the Montreal operation was almost compromised by unforeseen circumstances. The Holy Blood planners made a miscalculation in under-estimating the very real danger posed by the Iroquois to the colony. Schooled in the bitter rivalries of Europe where 20,000 victims could be commonplace in the sack of a city, the dimensions of the Indian "wars" described by Champlain must have appeared comical to Holy Blood military experts. They doubtless figured that a few musketeers could deal with any Indian attack.

What no one anticipated, and what everyone continued to fail to appreciate in Europe (whether Holy Blood military men or official French ones), was the power of the Iroquois confederacy. Although it was nothing by military standards in Europe, it was capable of utterly destroying the sparsely-populated colonies along the St. Lawrence. People back in

Europe could simply not credit the danger. This nearly caused the extinction of any Holy Blood personnel along with everybody else in Montreal.

The Iroquois were not a "tribe". They were a confederation of 5 formerly mutually-hostile tribes that inhabited the finger lakes region of New York State: Onandagas, Cayugas, Mohawks, Oneidas and Senecas. "Iroquois" means "five nations". Sometime around 1450 A.D. these five tribes were welded into a confederacy by a remarkable man named Hiawatha who, apparently, used the occasion of an eclipse to impress these people. They immediately began to fight everybody else instead of fighting among themselves as had formerly been their practice. The result was dramatic in the extreme. The Iroquois immediately began to expand by a program of conquest previously unknown among North American tribes. They eventually carved out an empire which stretched from the Mississippi to the Atlantic and from the Ohio River to Lake Superior, an area about half the size of the Roman Empire at its height. This process was going on when the French arrived between Cartier's voyage in 1534 and Champlain's explorations in 1603.

Most unfortunately for the French, they happened to first meet Indians, and become allies of Indians, who were enemies of these Iroquois. The French became enemies of the Iroquois in consequence, and it is not an exaggeration to say that this eventually cost the loss of New France. Although it has been estimated that the Iroquois never put more than 1,500 warriors in the field,[25] they absolutely controlled the hinterland in northeastern North America between approximately 1600 and 1720. Their ferocity and cruel tortures terrorized their enemies and left them powerless to fight the Iroquois even when greatly outnumbering them. As late as 1689 the Montreal suburb of Lachine was destroyed, and the inhabitants massacred, by the Iroquois. The Montreal colony had been in constant danger of massacre during the previous 47 years of its existence.

It is not inaccurate to say that the Iroquois, not the English, really defeated the French in Canada. These Indians confined the French to major river valleys, and the hinterland was never settled.

The English immediately perceived this, allied themselves with the Iroquois, and at one stroke gained the use of an entire inland empire that had always been denied to the French. In later military campaigns, this greater area of operations gave the English a great strategic advantage over the French.

But, in spite of the Iroquois, Montreal *did* survive. Although it cannot have proved the secure haven that might have been desired by the Holy Blood, it was a refuge from the much worse religious warfare in Europe. For many years it remained under the control of the Sulpicians of Jean-Jacques Olier.

It isn't possible to say how long the Holy Blood remained in Montreal. What is possible to say definitely is that any Holy Blood refugees in Montreal would have survived to see the dawn of the modern age. By the time the British won New France, in the mid-1700s, religious polarization had ceased to be *the* social force, and religious violence had given way to national conflict based on domestic and foreign-market economics we moderns understand today. In short, the Acadian refuge and the later one in Montreal had together served their purpose by preserving the Holy Bloodline from 1400 A.D. to the 1700s.

By 1750 it was safe to return to Europe.

The Knights of North America, the paladins of the Holy Blood, seemed to have performed their age-old duties very well in the new land. The flower of chivalry appears to have been active in North America, as it was in Europe, fighting in defence of the same Holy mission.

Although it seems that the Holy Blood was able to re-establish itself directly in European affairs by the mid-1700s, it also seems that it had become truly "American" to some extent during its 350-year sojourn across the Atlantic. Its representatives became interested and involved in the social experiments that were about to take place in North America. It is more than possible that the formation of the American republic was molded from Canada as well as from Europe. The Seminary of Saint-Sulpice established branch operations from Montreal in future major cities of the fledgling United States: Baltimore, New York and Boston. And Washington.

As we shall see, the character of the new republic seems to have been influenced in mysterious ways by secret operatives and curious people who contacted revolutionary leaders and early Presidents. Unknowingly, Americans carry with them daily tokens of this influence.

At the same time, in France itself, a possible dynastic heir worked hand-in-glove with North American agents to give the new American nation room enough to pursue a great social experiment on continental scale. It begins to appear that Holy Blood intrigues have molded much modern history, right up to today's crises and headlines.

Chapter Nine

The Bees of Childeric

A number of contemporary historians are of the opinion that the truly modern age began with the era of Napoleon. The major social, political and economic facts which shape our own time had their origin then and, except for amazing technological progress, little has basically changed. Even our technology has been applied to expressions of national philosophical and economic and military expansion that can be easily traced back to the epoch of the Corsican's dominance in Europe. Will and Ariel Durant, for instance, completed their multi-volume outline of the world history with their final work, *The Age of Napoleon*.

There's no doubt that Napoleon rudely jolted Europe out of a lingering semi-feudal orientation and catapulted the continent brutally into a completely modern kind of national rivalry requiring mass participation in warfare, industry, economics, education and politics. The modern world of the 20th Century is a direct descendant of the social changes dictated by the massive scale of Napoleonic warfare. Mass participation was absolutely necessary to wage the kind of wars that Napoleon fought and, in the fullness of time, but really over the astonishingly short period of only about 170 years up to the present, this mass participation in society evolved into the society we live in today.

Napoleon lived during the time of the French Revolution and reached the apogee of his power a short generation later. Without him, the democratic tenets of the Revolution would not have become disseminated nearly so widely in so short a space of time among friends and foes alike. The ideals of the Revolution thankfully outlived the extremes of it among the many people introduced to the new orientation by exposure to

Napoleonic armies. Without this obscure Corsican, it is very probable that the ideals of the French Revolution . . . "liberty, fraternity, equality" . . . would have been contained within France itself by an alliance of powers representing semi-feudal vested interests. In 1796 allied armies were invading the French republic from practically all directions at once, imminent defeat seemed a certainty and the pre-Revolutionary *status quo* of semi-feudalism seemed certain to be re-established to the relief of everyone on European thrones.

Then Napoleon arrived on the scene and transformed seemingly inevitable defeat into a series of crushing French victories. There's no doubt that his primary impact was purely military. Very simply, Napoleon magnified the scope of warfare beyond anything imagined previously, and simultaneously brought a scientific approach to it. Napoleon *calculated* power, time and distance, and on a massive scale, for the first time in history. Although he paid lip-service to glory, and although his wars certainly gave ample scope for it (which many French officers appreciated), his perspective was coldly administrative and analytical. And immediately successful.

As an example, it was accounted a great feat that the Duke of Marlborough was able to march 30,000 men a distance of 250 miles, and concentrate them at the right place without incredible confusion back in 1702. Just 110 years later, Napoleon, working within the same technological limitations as Marlborough, mobilized 1,000,000 men for the invasion of Russia in 1812, and marched 500,000 of them in several different co-ordinated lines of attack a distance of 750 miles from Paris to Moscow.[1]

Napoleon's defeat in Russia, and his subsequent one at Waterloo, are used now as derisive examples of overweening ambition that was thwarted, but we forget that European society was completely transformed in order to ensure Napoleon's defeat. The "Revolution" he represented *really* won, and all across Europe, even though the "Corsican Ogre" was finally overthrown and caged in exile.

The sheer scale of Napoleonic warfare required the participation of entire populations. War changed from the pastime of the nobility into the domain of mass, regimented, common and modern man. Industry on an unheard-of scale was required to feed the needs of the new size of war machines in all nations. The heyday of the Industrial Regolution coincided with Napoleonic war and its aftermath. The average man and woman, more or less superfluous within the feudal scheme of things, suddenly became intimately involved in society. Initially, for the worse. Untold thousands of men died as cannon-fodder in Napoleonic battles, while untold other thousands of men, women and children were exploited in the sweat shops of the new industrialism that supplied war materiel. But, for the first time in history, these people had been introduced into society and eventually they made themselves felt because their allegiance as soldiers and workers made them *necessary*, for the first time, and therefore creatures to be accommodated.

Warfare and industry increasingly required educated participants so that soldiers and workers could cope with evolving strategical and technological innovations. And, along with their education, came increasingly strident demands for greater representation in society's economic and political decision-making systems. Because the mass of people had suddenly become necessary in the kind of world that Napoleon molded, they gradually obtained more and more economic and political power. After about 170 years, we have arrived at the present democratic social profile of the Western World.

Although it has been the European tendency outside of France (and, sometimes, even within it) to regard Napoleon as a monster who uprooted decent society, and even though the mass of school children are generally encouraged to view him this way, it is hard to see what else besides Napoleonic warfare could have accelerated the painfully slow pace of European social progress. Even Marxists and neo-Marxists, who have a "class struggle" and mechanistic view of history and who repudiate the "great man" notion of historical change, owe the very existence of their industrial proletariat to Napoleon.

Is it too far-fetched to suppose that Napoleon may have been bred, or genetically engineered, to kick European progress into a higher gear?

Napoleon was born on August 15, 1769 at Ajaccio in Corsica, into a family eventually consisting of five boys and three girls. The father, Carlo di Buonaparte, a lawyer and supposedly a member of a very minor nobility, could trace his lineage back to Florence. Carlo di Buonaparte maintained close relations with a Corsican patriot and rebel, Paoli, but somehow also maintained close relations with the French military governor on the island, General de Marboeuf.

Some have suggested that the relations between the Buonaparte family and General Marboeuf may have been a bit too close. David G. Chandler of the Royal Military College, Sandhurst, and author of the definitive modern study of Napoleon, *The Campaigns of Napoleon*, has noted with respect to Marboeuf's frequent visits to the Buonaparte house that "scurrilous gossip has suggested that he was Napoleon's father".[2] Whatever the truth of such rumours, Marboeuf *was* related to Tallyrand who, as Foreign Minister to Napoleon and to the later restored Bourbons, succeeded in negotiating the national survival of France and the Revolution's better ideals after Napoleon's final defeat.[3] Tallyrand also paved the way for the restoration of Napoleon's heirs when the "legitimate" Bourbon line petered out with Charles X. If this "scurrilous gossip" has some foundation in fact, Tallyrand and Napoleon were blood relatives (probably cousins). This would explain a great deal for historians. Tallyrand's loyalty, and machinations, become a bit more explicable.[4]

Whether or not Marboeuf was Napoleon's real father, he treated the boy with fatherly concern, ensuring that Napoleon received the best possible education. With Marboeuf pulling some strings, Napoleon entered the College of Autun at age nine for a 4-month crash course in the French language. On April 23, 1779, and still only 9 years old, Napoleon was accepted into the Royal School of Brienne where he stayed for 5 years studying French, Latin, mathematics, history and geography.

> ... de Marboeuf undoubtedly played an important part in Napoleon's early life by being instrumental in gaining him a place at the school at Brienne in France. It took time to prove that the Buonapartes possessed the necessary four generations of nobility to qualify for entry, but eventually the young Napoleon was notified that a place awaited him.[5]

We may be reasonably assured that Napoleon's pedigree must have been doctored to some degree to prove this 4 generations of nobility, because modern scholars have not been able to trace the family back to any noble Florentine lineage.

From Brienne, Napoleon went on to the École Militaire in Paris and continued his studies of mathematics, history and geography, adding a fair knowledge of German to his attainments. In due course, he emerged an officer in the French artillery. It is unnecessary to trace his origins and early career in further detail. Eventually, his military abilities proved indispensable to the revolutionary governments and, because of this, he came to power himself; first as a partner with others, later as an absolute

The Empress Josephine, ex-wife of Alexandre de Beauharnais and supposedly a Merovingian descendant. She came originally from Martinique in the West Indies. Napoleon was advised to marry Josephine by Abbé Sieyès who was aware of the genealogical research of Abbé Pichon using material captured from the royal archives by revolutionaries. Napoleon's dynastic successor, Napoleon III, was the grandson of Josephine.

ruler. He transformed the Republic into an Empire with himself as Emperor.[6]

But one important turning point in his career cannot be overlooked. In 1796 Napoleon was one of three revolutionary "Directors" heading the government. Another "Director" was Abbé Sieyès, who knew of certain genealogical researches that had been undertaken by one Abbé Pichon. Pichon had access to the royal archives captured by the revolutionary government, where some important genealogies had been hidden away, and he discovered that a direct descent from Dagobert II had been maintained up to then.[7]

It is one of the stranger facts of history that these genealogies seem to have been a major objective for at least some of the people involved in the storming of the Bastille. It might not be too much of an exaggeration to suggest, especially in the light of later events, that these genealogies were *the* objectives of those who planned and provoked the riot and assault. Certainly, at least a few minds, or master-minds, viewed the revolution as a blow struck for the de Bouillon lineage. Several historians have called attention to a curious revolutionary vignette: as a group of priests was being herded toward the guillotine, a man jumped out of the mob and into the street and began to beat the victims, crying out: "There's one for the Templars!" and "There's one for the Cathars!" with each blow he rained upon them.

In any event, Abbé Sièyes urged Napoleon to marry Josephine Beauharnais *because she was a Merovingian descendant,* and to adopt her two children by a previous marriage who were of this anciently royal stock. Napoleon took this advice and married the beautiful Creole on March 9, 1796. As First Consul, and later as Emperor, Napoleon commissioned Abbé Pichon to continue his genealogical studies, in an official capacity, between 1805 and 1814. The reason for this was that "Napoleon was interested, among other things, in indications that the Bourbon dynasty was in fact illegitimate.[8]

Two years after his marriage to Josephine and the Merovingian line, Napoleon planned to leave the European theatre of warfare altogether and initiate an adventure in the Middle East. His armies sailed from various French ports between May 19 and May 23, 1798, bound hopefully for Egypt if the ships could elude the British naval patrols of Nelson and Sir William Sidney Smith.

On the way to Egypt, Bonaparte detoured to capture Malta and the treasure held by the Knights of Malta.

> . . . It was fortunate for the French that there was little fight left in the Knights of St. John . . . the last Grand Master, the apathetic von Hompesch, made only a show of resistance before accepting Bonaparte's terms . . . For the cost of three men killed, the French secured an invaluable naval base and a great deal of treasure . . .
>
> Over the five days following the island's capture, Bonaparte tore apart and refashioned every aspect of Maltese life. The Order of St. John was abolished and its members deported, apart from a handful who were persuaded to join the Army of Egypt . . . The treasures of the Order, amassed over 500 years, were promptly sequestered . . . and seven million francs' worth was diverted to the military chest.[9]

This seems to have been a straightforward sack of a wealthy fortress defended by knights "long since decayed into soft living", and maybe it was. But, on the other hand, perhaps von Hompesch's even token resistence was a show put on for the outside world and that the Knights of Malta would have bowed to Bonaparte *anyway.* Bonaparte hints at this sort of sham, and more, when he served warning of battle on the Knights of Malta. He said: "General Bonaparte will take by force what should have been accorded to him freely." And, as it happened, the "battle" was not so very fierce after all. The sham of defence may have been necessary to disguise the hand-over because . . . "both Austria and Russia had long coveted possession of this strategic island, and its high-handed seizure by the French was bound to lead to international repercussions."[10]

Did Bonaparte over-awe spiritless knights? Or, was Malta purposefully handed over to him under the disguise of token opposition? Was Bonaparte, as he seems to say, somehow in a position to claim the Maltese treasure legitimately?

There's no necessity to follow Napoleon's disastrous Egyptian campaign in detail. The military aspects of it are not relevant to our story, but the cultural aspects of it are. Bonaparte added a unique noncombat corps to his armies, a legion of 150 scientists of all sorts, supported by writers and artists. This group of *savants* was organized in typical Bonapart fashion into the "Institute of Egypt" whose job it was to study Egypt as Bonaparte conquered it. This was unique departure in the history of military affairs, and the victories of the *savants* endured long after the defeat of Napoleon's armies was forgotten.[11]

Napoleon, the military man, had at one stroke founded the modern science of archeology and began the *scientific* study of our human past. The French scientists were ordered to record everything they could about Ancient Egypt. Measurements of the pyramids and other monuments were obtained. The Rosetta stone was discovered, which gave the key for the decipherment of the Egyptian hieroglyphs. Ancient Egyptian art was recorded and preserved in the superb sketches of Dominique Denon, formerly renowned for a series of superb pornographic etchings, whom Napoleon later made a Baron in recognition for his Egyptian work. The results of the savants' discoveries were published over the next 25 years in 9 massive folio volumes of text and 12 volumes of plates, requiring 400 engravers working full-time.[12]

Napoleon established the science of Egyptology. What was discovered in Egypt stimulated other researches into other ancient civilizations: Sumerian, Mycenaen, Cretan and so on, leading to our modern understanding.

The Egyptian Campaign had a profound effect on Napoleon as well. On the 25th of Thermidor according to the revolutionary calendar (ie.

Painting of Napoleon in the King's Chamber of the Great Pyramid on August 12, 1799.

the 12th of August, 1799) Napoleon visited the Great Pyramid with Imam Muhammed as his guide. Bonaparte asked to be left alone in the King's Chamber. This was likely a gesture dictated by the dramatic part of Napoleon's character because Alexander the Great, whom Napoleon greatly admired, had done the same thing 2000 years before. Nonetheless, Las Cases relates that Napoleon emerged pale and shaken from the chamber. He commanded that no one ever question him about what happened in the pyramid. In *Memoirs of the Emperor Napoleon*, Las Cases claims that near the end of Napoleon's life, while in exile on the island of St. Helena, he seemed about to confide what had happened in the pyramid to Las Cases, but instead he shook his head and said: "No. What's the use. You'd never believe me."[13]

The Egyptian Campaign has always been a curious and bewildering episode in Napoleon's career. He had just finished a brilliant campaign in Italy and was about to return to Europe to achieve another Italian strategic and tactical coup. Then, it was on to the massive victories of Ulm, Austerlitz, Jena and 30 other battles which demonstrated his military virtuosity.

Why did he fight the Egyptian Campaign at all? He must have known that it was hopeless. Moreover, the French troops committed in Egypt were urgently needed for the direct defence of France in Europe. Britain absolutely controlled the Mediterranean, and the French forces in Egypt could not be supplied regularly or even withdrawn. The survivors of the war of attrition trickled back to France as best they could. Although they won every battle, only half the soldiers who set out in 1798 ever saw France again.

Napoleon was the master strategist of his age. He, better than anyone else, knew that the Egyptian Campaign must end in disaster. And yet he undertook it, while also adding an army of *savants* to his other military problems. But maybe the unique scientific contingent in the Army of Egypt was the heart of this military fiasco, perhaps the objective was always only to control Egypt long enough to give the *savants* time to make their studies and establish the science of archeology, so that we might begin to learn scientifically and systematically about our past.

We may possibly never know the real motivations in Napoleon's mind, but what is certain is that he returned to France in 1799 very much the same military master he'd been before his "oriental interlude", revealing, in war and peace, his towering intellect. By 1800 he was Consul, by 1804 he was Emperor. Aside from the military leadership that made France the dominant European power for a generation, Napoleon gave France the legal codes that characterize it today and which have been partly adopted by other countries:

> Urged on by Napoleon, the laws of France were progressively cod-
> ified and clarified; the Civil Code was promulgated between 1802
> and 1804, and was followed by the Commercial (1807), Criminal
> (1808) and Penal Codes (1810). In all, this represented an amazing
> legal achievement, the effects of which are still felt in France,
> Belgium, Holland, Italy and parts of Germany. As one prefect wryly
> put it: "God created Bonaparte and then he rested."[14]

Upon becoming Emperor, Napoleon was obliged to create a new nobility. Unlike the old one, however, Napoleon's was based upon rewards to exceptional individuals who served him and the state in some valuable capacity.

> By 1814 there were 31 dukes, 450 counts, 1500 barons and many
> more knights.[15]

This new nobility was not the success that could be claimed for the new legal codes, which is hardly surprising since Napoleon elevated merit where he found it, and sometimes it came from the gutter. One of his dukes had been a butcher, another had been an Italian smuggler. Both were rewarded with dukedoms because they were among the best field commanders of the age, responsible for many French victories. These gruff children of the revolution were not comfortable in their new grandeur.

In addition to his nobility, Napoleon created the Legion of Honour for those who made significant contributions in the arts and sciences.

Napoleon's new nobility was something of a parody of the "real" thing, and maybe it was intended to be just that. Europe had to live with his dukes, counts, barons and knights for many years after his personal exile. Returning Bourbon nobles had to accommodate these Napoleonic creations with what good grace they could muster. The whole exercise undermined the mystique of nobility and royalty during what remained of the 19th Century.

There can be no doubt that Napoleon considered himself to be a restorer of the legitimate Merovingian lineage, if not through some secret of his own birth which has been lost to historians, then by virtue of his marriage to Josephine and the adoption of her two children as his heirs. As was mentioned previously, at his coronation as Emperor in 1804 he adorned his imperial robe with the gold bee figurines which had been discovered in the tomb of Childeric I, father of Clovis. Napoleon styled himself *Emperor of the Franks*, not "Emperor of the French", and one can only suppose that this was the slim justification for carrying his wars of conquest beyond French borders onto lands once held by the Sicambrians across the Rhine in Germany (and, by adroit extension, almost everywhere else in Europe). Napoleon, however, was careful not to make the same mistake as Clovis. Clovis had allowed himself to be crowned by Rome. Napoleon snatched the crown from the Pope and placed it on his own head with his own hands.

As it turned out, Napoleon left no surviving heirs of his own. His dynasty, restored in 1848 in the person of Emperor Napoleon III after the Bourbon interlude, were descendants of Josephine Beauharnais.

Merovingians ruled in France up to the dawn of the 20th Century. Bonaparte had, indeed, restored the legitimate first dynasty of the French. As we shall see, scions of this dynasty apparently hold positions of power today in the French Republic and in other countries.

Napoleon did more than create the science of archeology, the law of much of modern Europe, the unparalleled war machine that was the Grande Armée, modern industrialism and much modern social structure. It can also be said that he created the United States.

True, the American Republic did, technically, exist before Napoleon's empire. But the republic was a small country, hemmed in on the Eastern Seaboard, and prevented from growing much larger by French Possessions west of the Mississippi River. By agreeing to the Louisiana Purchase, Napoleon allowed the American social and political experiment to proceed on a vast, continental scale. And, when the fledgling republic was in danger of losing this vast tract of territory to British invaders during the War of 1812, French pirates inexplicably turned up to help Andrew Jackson win the Battle of New Orleans. A curious sight it must have been, the Jolly Roger and the Stars and Stripes flying side by side, and unexplained.

Napoleon affected the United States in another and apparently more mundane way. It is said that a mysterious cloaked stranger approached Thomas Jefferson and gave to him the design for the Great Seal of the United States. It appears on every American dollar bill. It is, of course, the pyramid and the eye. The symbol was created in response to the *savants'* study of Egyptian antiquities and, just possibly, as a result of whatever Napoleon had learned while alone in the Great Pyramid.

What does it mean, this cryptic symbolism? It is easy enough to say that it really means nothing, that it was adopted because of the interest in Ancient Egypt generated by Napoleon's recent combined scientific and military enterprise.

But there *is* another explanation. It seems that some people had attached a meaning to the pyramid and the eye long before Napoleon. In fact, it may be that Napoleon was inspired or instructed to undertake his Egyptian Campaign, and to include the *savants*, merely to begin the overt and scientific study of our past. Perhaps Napoleon's disastrous campaign had no other purpose than to begin the revelation of humanity's ancient history. Perhaps the curious symbolism of the Greal Seal is supposed to be a daily reminder of the very ancient origins of the secret which has always directed our progress. If it was supposed to be such a reminder, we cannot plead that it is a rare clue. It is as ubiquitous as American money. It is displayed on the currency that has molded the Western world in the 20th Century.

Great Seal of the United States, appearing on every dollar bill, was purportedly given to Jefferson by a mysterious cloaked figure. The motif obviously has some connection with Napoleon's Egyptian researches, but what?

Conventional historians have been loath to admit even the possibility that both the French and American revolutions, and the republics these upheavals spawned, were partly orchestrated by a secret society. In this case, the facts themselves are not in dispute because they are well known. The interpretation of them is the bone of contention. For if the influence of a coherent and organized secret society is admitted by conventional historians, then dramatic chapters of recent history cannot be explained in purely material, political and social terms but take on a very disquieting aura of a higher long-term "spiritual" or "occult" *purpose* known to an elite of conspirators. Are the facts significant? Or, are the facts merely "coincidental"? Without taking a stand on this debate, I will simply state the facts.

All but two of the signatories to the Declaration of Independence were Masons. George Washington, the first U.S. President, was a Mason, and the next three American presidents were also Masons. All of the generals in the American revolutionary armies were Masons. Below the rank of general, 1500 other officers were Masons. The city of Washington was designed by a Mason, and the Washington Monument itself is a Masonic ediface, it was officially opened with Masonic ceremonies and, of course, its general form, like the motif of the U.S. Great Seal, was inspired by the obelisks and pyramids that Napoleon's *savants* found in Egypt and brought to popular attention.[17]

Within the context of the evidence so far presented in this book, it seems inane to regard these facts as mere "coincidence" because they lead too clearly back to Prince Henry Sinclair and refugee Templars of the 14th Century.

We will recall that the Sinclair family castle at Rosslyn was a refuge for outlawed Templars, and that a Templar cemetery is still a tourist attraction on the old Sinclair domains. Then, we may remember that the "oldest specifically Masonic document in existence" names the Sinclairs as hereditary heads of Scottish Freemasonry.[18] It begins to look as though the Freemasons were a kind of neo-Templar organization formed in response to the brutal crushing and dispersal of the real Knights Templar by Philip IV of France in 1307. And, in fact, this has been claimed by more than one writer on the subject of Freemasonry. This may explain why modern Shriners (who are all higher-ranking Masons) call their lodges "Temples" and sport symbols redolent of the Crusades and the Holy Land like scimitars, fez hats and crescent moon insignia.

Whether modern Masons and Shriners are knowledgeable about this connection is, perhaps, questionable. Whether modern Masons are as serious as their 18th Century colleagues in revolutionary France and America is also, perhaps, questionable.

But the link is certainly there, going all the way back to Henry Sinclair, his supposed establishment of a settlement in the New World, the subsequent founding of Montreal by an order of Sulpicians, and the establishment of Seminaries of Saint-Sulpice in major cities of the American colonies. Although, to my knowledge, there are no known documents to assert it, it seems logical enough to suppose that American Masonic revolutionaries sometimes found it convenient to meet in Seminaries of Saint-Sulpice in Boston, New York and Philadelphia. Certainly, the last place that British authorities might look for Masonic revolutionaries would be within the walls of a nominally Catholic religious order.

And here is as good a place as any to say something about this "Saint Sulpice". According to Norma Lorre Goodrich, this person, "Sulpice", was a 6th Century *British* religious notable who gave Galahad good advice on how to attain the Grail. Is it not a strange coincidence, then, that Jean-Jacques Olier named his religious order after a British priest who had a connection with King Arthur? Is it mere coincidence, then, that we can trace a pattern of circumstantial evidence and connections leading from King Arthur, through Henry Sinclair, and on to the French and American revolutions? Is it actually possible that a secret bloodline and its supporters molded much of Western history including the formation of democracy in Europe and North America? Personally, I hesitate to answer this question with an unqualified "yes", but I must admit that the Great Seal of the United States is disquieting in its associations and too plentiful, being printed on each and every American dollar, to be ignored.

The Great Seal speaks eloquently of a very ancient power of some sort literally "looking after us" . . . or, perhaps, "supervising" us. Did Napoleon, Sinclair, the Templars, the de Bouillons, the French and American Freemasons know the origins of this power?

Perhaps.

Napoleon's decision to decorate his coronation robe with Childeric's gold bees was an apt one. Bees are pollinators, and cross-pollinators. They disperse fertility widely and allow things to flower, grow and come to fruitation. Napoleon, for all the necessary brutality of his methods, performed the same function in Europe and America. New sorts of societies were seeded, flowered and have come to a degree of maturity.

Bees are the ancient insignia of those engaged in this human pollination, and cross-pollination, leading to the development of new and more evolved varieties of social structure. John G. Bennett, Personal Intelligence Officer for the Commander-in-Chief, General Milne of the British Army in the Middle East (during the Greek-Turkish War), wrote:

> One such clue . . . is the mention . . . of the Sarmoun or Sarmàn Society. The pronunciation is the same for either spelling and the word can be assigned to old Persian. It does, in fact, appear in some of the Pahlawi texts . . . The word can be interpreted in three ways. It is the word for bee, which has always been a symbol of those who collect the precious "honey" of traditional wisdom and preserve it for further generations. A collection of legends, well known in Armenian and Syrian circles with the title of *The Bees*, was revised by Mar Salamon, a Nestorian Archimandrite in the thirteenth

century. *The Bees* refers to a mysterious power transmitted from the time of Zoroaster and made manifest in the time of Christ.

A more obvious rendering is to take the *màn* in its Persian meaning as the quality transmitted by heredity and hence a distinguished family or race. It can be the repository of an heirloom or tradition. The word *sar* means head, both literally and in the sense of principal or chief. The combination *sarman* would thus mean the chief repository of the tradition . . .

And still another possible meaning of the word sarman is . . . literally, those whose heads have been purified.

. . . ancient Armenian texts, including the book *Merkhavat* . . . referred to the "Sarmoung Society" as a famous esoteric school that according to tradition had been founded in Babylon as far back as 2500 B.C. and which was known to have existed in Mesopotamia up to the sixth or seventh century of the Christian era. The school was said to have possessed great knowledge containing the key to many secret mysteries. The date of 2500 B.C. would put the founding of this school several centuries before the time Hammurabi, the greatest lawgiver of antiquity, but it is not an impossible one.[19]

This date is interesting because it is about the time that some people, later to be called "Hebrews", began a migration out of Mesopotamia to the present area of Palestine. Whether the Benjamites were with them at this point is hard to say. But it was a time of mixed migrations of many peoples, including Indo-Europeans, toward the west.

Did the Benjamites take this *sarmàn* knowledge with them, and did it pass on into Europe with the Sicambrians to end up as symbolic bees of Childeric that eventually adorned Napoleon's coronation robe?

The Bees of Childeric are those people born into a relationship with what we've been calling the "Holy Blood", or those deemed suited to be initiated into the nature of a great human secret and judged capable of accepting it and guarding it. They have been allowed measured glimpses of the secret, but only as the truth has been draped in various fashions appropriate to various epochs. Probably, there are only a handful of people who know the undraped, naked truth. Only a handful could accept it, or believe it.

But even those who have had just a glimpse of it, suitably presented in a frame of reference understandable to them, have generally committed their lives to it. They have been profoundly changed, inspired to great loyalty and greater sacrifice. Since the Crucifixion, the secret has mostly been draped in the Christian cloth for Europeans: perhaps it was enough for Henry Sinclair, Jacques de Molay and Jeanne Mance to know that they laboured to preserve and protect the bloodline of Jesus. Perhaps it was enough for the French revolutionaries, Napoleon and his marshals to know that they were labouring to restore a legitimate royal dynasty whose blood was augmented by Christ's own.

During its long existence, and in pursuit of its apparently long-term purposes, the Grail Dynasty has operated within all the different social and religious orientations in the Western world. Its heirs, agents, supporters, devotees and paladins have either naturally or purposefully adopted the religious and social presentation expected by humanity around them. People with some degree of initiation have been able to work within Judaeism without being "Jews", within Christianity without adopting the dogma of Catholic or Protestant, within Islam without becoming fanatical Moslems. Whatever the outward "shell" demanded of them by their time and place, they have usually been able to recognize each other. This explains the rapidity with which European operatives of the Holy Blood were able to forge links with similar agents operating within Judaic or Islamic orientations in Spain and Palestine during the Crusades, links that finally came to the attention of polarized humanity. The larger truth has always been intolerable to those too small to accept more than their tiny crumb of it. The Bees of Childeric, when discovered, have been branded as heretics and traitors which had to be destroyed, affronts to the mass of humanity.

Initiates or representatives of the Grail Family have been repudiated by Judaeism, by Christianity, by Islam. The Moslem *Sufis* have suffered the same persecution as the Cathars did at the hands of Rome and as Jesus at the mercy of the Pharisees.

By operating in the world in which they found themselves, but not *of* it, the Holy Blood operatives have laboured in the Ancient Holy Land, in Roman Catholic Europe, in Atheist Revolutionary France, in Materialist North America and, you may be sure, in Communist Russia. They labour still. Often, they have been the leaders of social and religious communities, and also economic ones, that did not suspect their orientation, and still do not.

They have, in fact, been just like bees, outwardly similar to all the others working in the Western world's hives, but having larger purposes than most of the drones and knowing an allegiance beyond the local queen.

These are special bees, secret outcasts among us. We ordinary bees, whenever we have identified them within our hives, have forgotten that they always worked hardest for us, and we have stung them to death or to loneliness.

Chapter Ten

The Dynasty in the 20th Century

We have traced the activities of one family, or bloodline, from the Benjamites of the ancient Middle East up to the early 1800s and Napoleon Bonaparte. In the process we have covered about 4,000 years of Western history, and have been forced to pick various episodes in this long history and simply sketch in connections.

Sometimes, actual members of this lineage seem to have been directly involved in dramatic events. Jesus apparently tried to establish a dynastic kingdom in Palestine, but was thwarted in his attempt. Joseph of Arimathaea, whom we have conjectured may have been an in-law of Jesus, took the survivors of the bloodline to safety in distant Britain. The Sicambrian Franks, who claimed to be of this lineage because of descent from the Benjamites, moved into Europe and inter-married with the bloodline of Jesus, thereby reinforcing their ancient connections with this family. The enhanced familial connection was honoured with a new dynastic name: Merovingian. Godfroi de Bouillon, who was a Merovingian heir, tried to re-establish a kingdom in Palestine a thousand years after Jesus. He failed as well.

Thereafter, it seems, the actual members of the family went into hiding for many centuries. They were hunted by the Inquisition. Overt activity was left to their supporters. Templar knights apparently dispersed with the mission of finding a haven for the survivors of the bloodline. We have suggested that Henry Saint-Clair was successful in finding a transatlantic refuge in what is now Nova Scotia.

Later, as the Americas began to be better known, and as fisherman, fur-traders and whalers visited the western continent more frequently, European sovereigns began to think of colonization. We have suggested that colonization of Nova Scotia, then called Arcadia, was postponed and purposefully delayed in an attempt to disguise the existence of the bloodline's refuge. Evidence has been presented that Samuel Champlain and the Sieur de Monts were involved in this delaying operation.

Meanwhile, another haven for the lineage was being planned, to be disguised as a religious community at Montreal. A group of supporters and agents known as the Compagnie du Saint-Sacrement organized the establishment of this new refuge.

We have assumed that the more tolerant religious atmosphere of the period after about 1750 would have allowed the members of the bloodline to come out of hiding to some extent and to take a hand in European affairs.

It is difficult to tell whether Napoleon was actually of the Merovingian lineage or not, but he married into it. His legal heirs were the children of a Merovingian descendant, Josephine Beauharnais.

There is some evidence that this lineage has not been concerned only with its own survival, but that its primary objective seems to be the encouragement of human progress. The bloodline and its supporters have contributed to human progress even at the cost of great personal sacrifice and in the midst of great danger. Jesus is an obvious example, sacrificed while trying to introduce a new philosophy of humane attitudes and behaviour. Arthur's struggle contributed to the eventual civilization of the northern barbarians. Templar maps may well have assisted commerce and the development of European discovery. Napoleon, for all his brutal methods, swept away the feudal world and instituted the modern industrial and democratic age. He promulgated laws that are still in use in much of Europe, and founded the science of archeology to begin the modern study of our own past. In addition, Napoleon's agreement to the Louisiana Purchase made the young American republic a continental power where a great social experiment could take place.

It has been impossible to give this lineage an adequate label. It seems to have been connected with Jesus, so we have called it the "Holy Blood" or the "Holy Bloodline" for convenience. This group of people seems also to be associated with an object known as the Holy Grail ... or with an idea called the Holy Grail ... and so we have sometimes called it the "Grail Family", or "Grail Dynasty".

But these labels are not very accurate or helpful. The lineage seems to be older than Jesus, he was just one heir of the bloodline, and it claimed some sort of "holiness" because of the Benjamite heritage in the ancient past. This family is not the "Holy Blood" only because of Jesus. In fact, Jesus may have been holy because he represented this bloodline. It is not very helpful to call the lineage the "Grail Family" because we do not know what this Grail was, and, in any case there is reason to suspect that this bloodline may *be* the Grail.

If these people have been active throughout 4,000 years of Western history, then it is reasonable to assume that they are active yet. We have hinted at this. What have they been doing since the early 1800s and Napoleon?

And here we encounter a difficulty, not because there is too little evidence but because there is too much. The "secret" of the Grail Dynasty has been gradually revealed, as we have seen. Starting in Revolutionary France, certain people became interested in records showing that the bloodline of the Merovingians had survived. Since Bérenger Saunière discovered hidden genealogies in 1891 and built his curious Tower of the Magdalene and Villa Bethania in Rennes-le-Chateau, not to mention his very unorthodox church, the interest of many more people has been stimulated. By the time of World War I, a large number of researchers were investigating the genealogy of the bloodline itself, the identification of the Holy Grail and trying to trace the survivors and current activities of this lineage.

Then, there were *known* relations of this bloodline who were prominent in European affairs. Napoleon III, who was Emperor of France up to the 1870s, was the descendant of Josephine Beauharnais who was supposedly a Merovingian.

Instead of being a *real* secret, the Holy Bloodline started to become an "open secret". There were some people who *may* have been related to the Holy Blood in a fairly distant way, but whose antics do not seem consistent with what the direct and purest descendants of it have apparently always tried to do. The Holy Bloodline is like any other family. It has branched out over the four millenia or more of its existence. In the late 19th Century thousands of people were distantly related to it, and thousands are related to it today. Distant relationship to the Holy Blood does not guarantee the qualities of competence, commitment, courage and responsibility that the core descendants have exhibited.

The attitudes and behaviour of people like Charles I and Napoleon

III seem to be an affront to the thrust of what the heart of the Grail Dynasty has always apparently represented. They were distantly related to the lineage, but allowed this to fuel all-too-human vanity instead of all-too-rare responsibility.

Aside from people who may have been distantly related to the Holy Blood but who failed to exhibit its historic qualities, there are those who learned of the "secret" and pretended that they themselves, and the organizations they formed, were a part of it. They did this in order to delude themselves and to delude others, to give themselves and their followers a bogus sense of importance and identity.

The Nazis fall into this group.

The Nazis began to appropriate the Holy Grail long before World War II. It became a central motivator of their self-image and a significant justification for their aggression. It may surprise most North Americans to learn that the Nazis claimed a connection with the Holy Grail, but it is nonetheless a fact. It would not be any exaggeration to say that, from the Nazi point of view, World War II was a religious conflict. They saw themselves as latter-day Templars, guardians of the Grail, or at least seekers after it.

The Nazi Party sent a man named Otto Rahn, later a colonel in the SS, to look for the Grail in 1931 and again in 1937.[1] Rahn was a medieval scholar and he also researched everything he could in order to learn what the Grail might be, and where it might be. He came to the conclusion that the Grail was an inscribed cup which had been given to the Aryans in the distant past. Somehow the Jews had obtained it, falsely claimed it as their own in order to substantiate their equally false claim to divine favour, and had kept it in the Temple of Solomon. This temple was subsequently sacked by a number of people and its treasures made various perambulations, but the bulk of the treasure, including the Grail, ended up in Rome. In its turn, however, Rome was sacked by Alaric in 410 A.D. who took the Grail to his Visigothic kingdom in Spain. The Grail passed to the Moors when they defeated the Visigoths at the Battle of Jerez de la Frontera in 711 A.D. Later it was acquired by the Cathars who kept it at Montségur until the crusade against the Albigensians. Just a few days before the citadel was surrendered on March 16, 1244, the Grail was carried to safety by four knights.

Otto Rahn believed that the Grail was hidden in one of the many caverns in the Pyrenees near Montségur and that's where he looked for it.

This Nazi Grail has no connection with Jesus, Joseph of Arimathaea, Arthur or Godfroi de Bouillon. It is a definite object which originally belonged to the Aryan race and which was stolen from the Aryan race. Rahn equated the Grail with an object known as "Solomon's Jewel Case", which did seem to have existed and which is mentioned in Spanish-Moorish sources.[2] Rahn wrote two books about the Grail. One of them was entitled *Kreuzzug gegen den Gral* (*"Crusade Against the Grail"*) which was required reading for SS recruits.

The Nazis appropriated the citadel of Montségur, too. During their occupation of France Montségur was considered German territory and French nationals were not allowed on it except by special permission.[3] In June 1943 a group of German scientists visited Montségur, apparently with the idea of searching for the Grail again with the latest equipment. Some writers have concluded that they actually found it, and that in the closing days of the war spirited it away in the obligatory Nazi submarine. Where it is now, according to this theory, is anybody's guess. Probably Argentina.

What does seem to be a fact, since the report comes from fairly reputable French Underground sources, is that on the 700th anniversary of the fall of Montségur, March 16, 1944, a Fieseler "Stork" aircraft with skywriting equipment aboard created a huge Celtic cross in the sky above Montségur.[4]

Apparently, Hitler and some of the other high Nazis believed they had a connection with the Grail, or *wanted* to believe it, because of a line in one of the troubadour poems:

> Al cap des set cens ans,
> verdegeo el laurel.[5]
>
> (At the end of seven hundred years,
> the laurel will be green again.)

Hitler took this to mean 700 years from the fall of Montségur. He admitted something of this sort of belief to Rauschning when he said:

> Creation is not finished. Man is clearly approaching a phase of metamorphosis. The earlier human species has already reached the stage of dying out . . . Humanity climbs up one more notch every 700 years, and the stake of battle, in the longer run of things, is the coming of the sons of God. All of the force of creation will be concentrated in a new species . . . This new species will infinitely

surpass modern man . . . Do you understand now the profound meaning of our National Socialist movement?[6]

There's no doubt that Hitler conceived of the SS as an Order of knighthood along thoroughly modern lines. Several medieval castles were set aside for SS training purposes in order to provide recruits with the appropriate atmosphere: Krössinsee, Vogelsang and Sonthofen. A visitor to Vogelsang, Alphonse de Chateaubriant, wrote about his impressions:

> All this whiteness was due to an array of a thousand immaculate place settings, each enveloped in its impeccable napkin, folded in the shape of a flower, while near each glass, in its crystal vase, reposed in its vast flowering bloom a large, satiny, shiny royal marguerite, reflecting its white light . . .
> As for myself, before this perfect whiteness in whose midst are gathered these thousand young knights of Vogelsang, I cannot help from thinking about the souls of Lohengrin and of Parsifal . . .[7]

It is difficult to figure out what, if anything, the Nazis really believed. Otto Rahn was a medieval scholar, but the Grail described by him and the history he constructed for it bear no resemblance to the Grail of the troubadours, and the troubadours introduced it into Western culture.

Up to now I have avoided quoting from the Grail Romances because, although they were exciting literature in their time, they make dull reading for moderns. However, the Holy Grail and the Grail Family must be described to a minimal degree from the original troubadour sources in order to show that the Nazi-concocted Grail of the 1930s was art deco.

The four original Grail Romances were all created within 20 years after de Bouillon's dynasty lost Jerusalem in 1187 A.D. The first known one, *Le Roman de Perceval, ou Le Conte del Graal* ("*The Romance of Perceval, or the Tale of the Grail*"), was written by Chrétien de Troyes just a year after the fall of Jerusalem, in 1188 A.D., and stands as the first mention of the Grail anywhere in Western literature.

Chrétien's poem is about Perceval, "Son of the Widow Lady", who leaves home to win his knighthood:

> . . . During his travels he comes upon an enigmatic fisherman — the famous Fisher King — in whose castle he is offered refuge for the night. That evening the Grail appears. Neither at this point nor at any other in the poem is it linked in any way whatever with Jesus. In

fact, the reader learns very little about it. He is not even told what it is. But whatever it is, it is carried by a damsel, is golden and studded with gems. Perceval does not know that he is expected to ask a question of this mysterious object — he is expected to ask 'whom one serves with it' . . . Perceval neglects to ask it; and the next morning, when he wakes, the castle is empty. His omission, he learns subsequently, causes a disastrous blight on the land. Later still he learns that he himself is of the 'Grail Family', and that the mysterious 'Fisher King', who was 'sustained' by the Grail, was in fact his own uncle . . .[8]

Chrétien's poem is rendered all the more perplexing by the fact that it is unfinished . . .

In any case Chrétien's version of the Grail story is less important in itself than in its role as precursor. During the next half century the motif he had introduced at the court of Troyes was to spread through Western Europe like a brush-fire. At the same time, however, modern experts on the subject agree that the later Grail romances do not seem to have derived wholly from Chrétien, but seem to have drawn on at least one other source as well — a source which, in all probability, pre-dated Chrétien. And during its proliferation the Grail story became much more closely linked with King Arthur — who was only a peripheral figure in Chrétien's version. And it also became linked with Jesus.[9]

It seems as if Chrétien de Troyes heard a story, or, rather, garbled rumours of a story, and rushed into print with it without understanding his material. He thereby won the distinction of first mentioning the Grail, but at the same time it is clear that people writing a few years later had access to more complete and coherent information.

Robert de Boron's *Roman de l'Estoire dou Saint Graal* ("*Romance of the History of the Holy Grail*") is believed to have been written between 1190 and 1199 A.D. and it draws from a different and earlier source than Chrétien. It differs from Chrétien's version in important respects. Robert says that he based his story on the contents of a great book whose secrets were revealed to him. He furnishes a history of the Grail: it was the cup of the Last Supper which came into possession of Joseph of Arimathaea whose family became keepers of the Grail. Robert's poem concerns the adventures of this family of Joseph of Arimathaea — Galahad is his son, while his brother-in-law, Brons, carried the Grail to England. Brons became the Fisher King and in Robert's story, Perceval is his grandson.

Robert's poem, like Chrétien's, is very vague on chronology. Both poems set the story in England, but Chrétien makes his action happen during the Arthurian Age while Robert's action takes place at least 4 centuries earlier.

Another version of the tale, *Perlesvaus*, was contemporary with Robert's creation and was written by an anonymous author sometime between 1190 and 1212. Barber, in his *Knight and Chivalry* has argued that the *Perlesvaus* was written by a Templar. In any event, whether created by a Templar or not, it seems to have been composed by a fighting man because of its

> . . . extraordinarily detailed knowledge of the realities of fighting — of armour and equipment, strategy and tactics, and weaponry and its effects on human flesh.The graphic description of wounds, for example, would seem to attest to a first-hand experience of the battlefield — a realistic, unromanticised experience uncharacteristic of any other Grail romance.[10]

The *Perlesvaus* has it that Joseph of Arimathaea was Perceval's great uncle, not uncle or grandfather, yet it is also set in Arthur's time about 4 centuries after Joseph of Arimathaea was alive. The Grail described in *Perlesvaus* is obviously not just a cup. When Sir Gawain sees it . . .

> . . . seemeth to him that in the midst of the Graal he seeth the figure of a child . . . he looketh up and it seemeth him to be the Graal all in flesh, and he seeth above, as he thinketh, a King crowned, nailed upon a rood. [11]

At a later point in the story, the Grail . . .

> . . . appeared at the sacring of the mass, in five several manners that none ought not to tell, for the secret things of the sacrement ought none tell openly, but he unto whom God hath given it. King Arthur beheld all the changes, the last whereof was a change into a chalice.[12]

In the *Perlesvaus*, what might be called the "shape-changing" Grail makes its appearance. One more small bit from *Perlesvaus* should be noted because it holds a clue to unravelling at least some of the confusion evident in the three versions so far referred to.

> . . . At a red cross erected in the forest, a beautiful white beast of indeterminate nature is torn apart by hounds. While Perceval

watches, a knight and a damsel appear with golden vessels, collect the fragments of mutilated flesh and, having kissed the cross, disappear into the trees. Perceval himself then kneels before the cross and kisses it:[13]

And, quoting directly from the *Perlesvaus* . . .

and there came to him a smell so sweet of the cross and of the place, such as no sweetness can be compared therewith. He looketh and seeth coming from the forest two priests all afoot; and the first shouteth to him: 'Sir Knight, withdraw yourself from away from the cross, for no right have you to come nigh it': Perceval draweth him back, and the priest kneeleth before the cross and adoreth it and boweth down and kisseth it more than a score of times, and manifesteth the most joy in the world. And the other priest cometh after, and bringeth a great rod, and setteth the first priest aside by force, and beateth the cross with the rod in every part, and weepeth right passing sore.

Perceval beholdeth him with right great wonderment and saith unto him, 'Sir, herein seem you to be no priest! wherefore do you so great shame?' 'Sir,' saith the priest, 'It nought concerneth you of whatsoever we may do, nor nought shall you know thereof for us!' Had he not been a priest, Perceval would have been right wroth with him, but he had no will to do him any hurt.[14]

The first thing that is obvious is that these French troubadours are drawing upon some *French source* that must have been readily available to them. Yet, this French source has foreign elements in it and the troubadours do not know what these elements mean. But the passage about the knight and the damsel picking up pieces of the mutilated flesh and putting them into golden vessels is very suggestive. It is an echo of a Welsh cycle of tales about the "caldron of Carridwen", a magical vessel that can regenerate people from pieces placed in it.

This indicates that the French source-tale, whatever it was, had been imported from Celtic Britain. Evidently, too, this source-tale had been imported from Britain in the distant past as far as the troubadours were concerned because they are all confused about when the story takes place, whether in the time of Arthur or in the time immediately after Joseph of Arimathaea 4 centuries earlier.

Something else is indicated also. However long ago the story had come into France from Britain, it had existed for many years in Celtic

Britain before ever reaching France. The "caldron of Carridwen" which is a pre-Christian Celtic motif has been mixed up with the Christian cup of the Last Supper. This would be a natural confusion during the time when the British Celts were first being exposed to Christianity.

The Last Supper was, in a way, the first Communion, or, at least, it was when Jesus gave instructions to his disciples that formed the basis for the rite of Communion. Jesus, knowing he was doomed through betrayal, told the disciples to think of his blood whenever they took wine and to think of his flesh whenever they ate bread. Although Christian transubstantiation is not exactly the same as Carridwen's regeneration, it would seem similar to recent Celtic converts. Any cup of the Last Supper would naturally be associated with Carridwen's caldron, *but only during an early phase of Celtic conversion to Christianity.* Once Christianity was well and truly established, its motifs would almost entirely supplant pagan ones. Most modern Irish and Welsh people have never heard of Carridwen's caldron and they certainly do not associate it with the Communion.

The tale, then, must date from the earliest centuries of Celtic exposure to Christianity and reflects the transitional period when Christian and pagan motifs jostled together. A long time later, but still many years before the troubadours, the tale came into France as the history of an important family. The troubadours we have looked at so far could not make much sense of this story but simply used it as best they could.

Things get much better with the creation of *Parzival* by Wolfram von Eschenbach. He was a Bavarian knight and wrote his Grail Romance between 1195 and 1216 A.D. It is an acknowledged literary masterpiece and "may stand as the noblest literary achievement of the Middle Ages, with the sole exception of Dante's *Divine Comedy.*"[15] Although Wolfram was a Bavarian, he seems to have gotten closer to the French source-tale of the story than any other troubadour and to have understood it better. It might be more correct to say that Wolfram seems to have had it explained to him so that he was able to grasp it. He says that he got the story from Guiot of Provence, "a troubadour, monk and spokesman for the Templars."[16] Wolfram calls him "Kyot", which probably better approximates how the name was pronounced at that time. It is known that Guiot visited Mayence, Germany, in 1184 when knights from all over Christendom gathered to witness the Holy Roman Emperor elevate his sons to knighthood. Wolfram and Guiot met at this time, most likely, and Guiot told him the story, obviously in very great detail. Wolfram says that Chrétien got it all wrong.

> If Master Chrétien de Troyes did not do justice to this story, that may well irk Kyot, who furnished us the right story . . . From Provence to Germany the true facts were sent to us . . . "I, Wolfram von Eschenbach, shall tell no more of it now than the master told there."[17]

As a sort of introduction, Wolfram describes how Guiot of Provence learned of the story originally.

> Kyot (Guiot), the well-known master, found in Toledo, discarded, set down in heathen writing, the first source of this adventure. He first had to learn the abc's . . .[18]

Guiot received some help from a heathen scholar . . .

> A heathen, Flegetanis, had achieved high renown for his learning . . . was descended from Solomon and born of a family which had long been Israelite . . . wrote the adventure of the Grail . . . A host of angels left it on earth. Since then, baptised men have had the task of guarding it . . .
>
> Kyot, the wise master, set out to trace this tale in Latin books, to see where there had ever been a people dedicated to purity and worthy of caring for the Grail. He read the chronicles of the lands, in Britain and elsewhere, in France and in Ireland, and in Anjou he found the tale.[19]

In short, as scholars have long concluded, the tale certainly originated in Celtic Britain and came into France later, into Anjou in northwestern France near Brittany. This record in Anjou was probably the French source-tale of which other troubadours had heard rumours.

We have quoted from the early Grail Romances sufficiently to show that the Nazi Grail created by Otto Rahn did not reflect what the troubadours themselves said about it. All of the Grail Romances insist that King Arthur had some sort of association with the Grail, yet Otto Rahn's reconstruction ignores King Arthur. Aside from King Arthur, the *Perlesvaus* reflects the Celtic "caldron of Carridwen" myth and many of the names in Wolfram's *Parzival* are obviously Celtic, yet Otto Rahn's Grail has none of these connections. In two of the four early romances, the Grail is a Christian symbol and Perceval is said to be related to Joseph of Arimathaea, yet Rahn avoids mention of this.

The Nazis did what all other Western religions have done, they took a very small part of a very large story and pretended that their crumb was the whole banquet.

Although we do not need to quote further from the Grail Romances in order to discredit Otto Rahn's Grail, Wolfram's poem is very suggestive in the light of the reconstruction offered in this book. Before returning to evidence of the Holy Blood's activities in the 20th Century, we will let Wolfram describe his Grail and we will also look into the curious mathematical structure of *Parzival*. Wolfram has left clues that he knew a great deal, and what he knew supports the speculations of many recent French writers.

Wolfram's description of the Grail occurs in the core of his poem, Book IX. Its first appearance . . .

> She was clothed in a dress of Arabian silk. Upon a deep green achmardi she bore the Perfection of Paradise, both root and branch. That was a thing called the Grail, which surpasses all earthly perfection. Repanse de Schoye was the name of her whom the Grail permitted to be its bearer.[20]

This is not very enlightening, but in a later passage Wolfram tells us that the Grail is a kind of "horn of plenty":

> A hundred squires, so ordered, reverently took bread in white napkins from before the Grail, stepped back in a group and, separating, passed the bread to all the tables. I was told, and I tell you too, but on your oath, not mine — hence if I deceive you we are liars all of us — that whatsoever one reached out his hand for, he found it ready, in front of the Grail, food warm or food cold, dishes new or old, meat game or tame. "There was never anything like that", many will say. But they will be wrong in their angry protests, for the Grail was the fruit of blessedness, such abundance of the sweetness of the world that its delights were very like what we are told of the kingdom of heaven.[21]

He adds that the Grail has the power to renew life:

> It is called *lapsit excillis*. By the power of that stone the phoenix burns to ashes, but the ashes give him life again. Thus does the phoenix molt and change his plumage . . . Such power does the stone give a man that flesh and bones are at once made young again. The stone is also called the Grail.[22]

In addition to all of these attributes, the Grail has a purpose: to provide leadership, in secret, to peoples of the earth.

> . . . the maids are sent out openly from the Grail, and the men in secret, that they may have children who will one day enter into the service of the Grail and, serving, enhance its company. God can teach them how to do this.
>
> . . . Upon the Grail it was found written that any templar whom God's hand appointed master over foreign people should forbid the asking of his name or race, and that he should help them to their rights. If the question is asked of him they shall have his help no longer.[23]

This may sound like medieval magical gibberish, and maybe it is just that, but Wolfram seems to have structured his work in a quite complicated way which scholars are just starting to appreciate. Perhaps we shouldn't consign his description to a harsh judgement until we know more about him.

Parzival is composed of 24,810 lines of rhymed couplets. In the middle of all this, in Book IX, the Grail Family, the Grail itself and the origin of the story are all described. *Literally in the middle.*

> . . . Each book is of course a unit, and even the small sections of thirty lines for long stretches form individual paragraph-like units. Professor Springer has shown in a recent article with what mathematical precision these units are arranged in relation to the core of the work, Book IX . . . there are 324 sections before and 324 sections after Book IX, which itself numbers exactly 70 sections . . . Tantalizing mystery besets every side of this poem.
>
> . . . Consistent, symbolically meaningful and artistically admirable also is the time analysis which Wolfram creates for his poem out of disparate elements of tradition. In an article of 1938, Professor Hermann Weigand contrasted the vague, implausible time sequence of Chrétien's version with the minute exactitude which Wolfram bestows upon his narrative. Six years' time accounts for the total work, and the line of development arches from a first Pentecost when Perceval is made a knight in name to a seventh Pentecost when he became truly a knight in spirit. Within this six year period no specific date is ever mentioned, yet twice the author introduces such elaborate time calculations that one is led to believe he intended the reader to compute his schedule of events. Professor Weigand discovered a close-reasoned calendar . . .[24]

Why structure a long poem so carefully just to frame magical gibberish precisely between 324 units before and 324 units after? Why conceal a calendar within a tale that makes no sense anyway?

Before going back to Wolfram's Grail descriptions, we will make one speculation about a date that can be computed from his poem's structure. The entire work is called "Parzival" and relates the story of a family in the past. How far in the past? This is a natural question and we have seen that the other troubadours seemed to have had no idea what period of history this French source-tale referred to. Does Wolfram know?

Perhaps. If you add up all of the units of which *Parzival* is composed, you get a total of 718: 324 before Book IX, 324 after and the 70 of Book IX itself. Wolfram may have been saying that the entire story of "Parzival" began 718 units before he finished it, and if we assume that these units are years, that the story of "Parzival" began 718 years before he wrote it. Wolfram von Eschenbach is believed to have composed the work between 1195 and 1216 A.D., a 21-year spread, this gives us dates between 477 and 498 A.D. when the story as told in *Parzival* began. Since *Parzival* is about a very special knight of Anjou, but one somehow related to Arthur's Britain, we can conjecture that these years between 477 and 498 A.D. are the time when the specialness of Parzival's lineage came to Anjou. This computation may be unjustified, and Wolfram may never have meant to hint when the story occurred, but the dates arrived at are astonishing and suggestive. They take us squarely back to the time of Arthur and the time that the Merovingians claimed some special holiness. Was Wolfram pinpointing the time when the Holy Blood was transferred from Arthurian Britain to the Merovingian French?

The transfer of such a treasure would have called for a large escort and a major military operation. Not only were religious relics proving the ancestry of the Holy Blood possibly involved, but also living descendants of a bloodline inclusive of Jesus and anciently holy because of an earlier divine dispensation. Every care would have been taken to guard this treasure.

Is there any historical record that the Arthurians were able to mount such a military expedition with their slim resources?

Yes. Just once. Geoffrey Ashe published a study of certain newly-discovered and very obscure continental records in *Speculum*, the journal of the Medieval Academy of America, in April 1981. These records refer to a "king of the Britons" who undertook a military expedition in France in the year 469-470 A.D.[25]

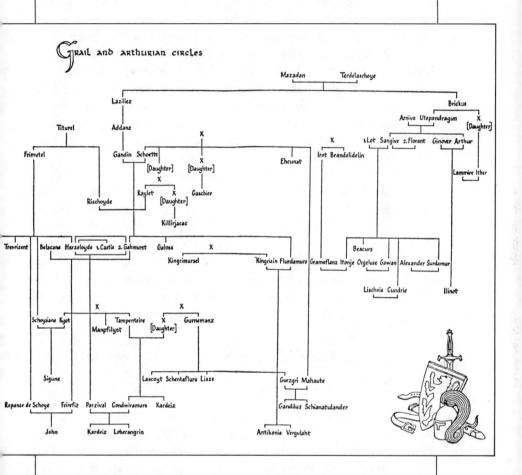

Grail and Arthurian circles

Genealogy described in *Parzival* by Wolfram von Eschenbach. Repanse de Schoye in the lower left is the bearer of the Grail in Wolfram's romance. King Arthur, although distantly related to the Grail Family is not in the direct line of descent.
Genealogy prepared from the Parzival text by Helen M. Mustard and Charles E. Passage for the Vintage edition.

Until about 30 years ago Arthur was considered totally mythical by most scholars. Even when his existence began to be conceded, his life was placed in a vague "sometime" between 400 and 600 A.D. It is only within the last 20 years that this range has been halved. Arthur is rather confidently thought to have lived between 450 and 550 A.D., but no date in this "Dark Age" is at all certain. No one knows for sure exactly when Arthur was born, when he died, or exactly when Merovée claimed the infusion of specialness from over the sea. Is it not suggestive that the date arrived at by adding up the units of *Parzival* bring us right back to the most likely time for this transfer activity? Either this is a meaningless coincidence resulting from chance and incorrect methodology, or Wolfram knew what he was talking about.

Parzival includes a complicated background and inter-relation between the characters. The translators and introducers of the Random House edition ("Vintage Books") of 1961, Helen M. Mustard and Charles E. Passage, prepared a genealogy according to Wolfram's story. It spans several generations. Arthur, "Ginover" ("Guenevere"), and "Utepandragun" ("Uther Pendragon") occur a few generations before Perceval and Repanse de Schoye. And the Arthurians are on another branch of the family tree, far removed from Repanse de Schoye who bore the Grail in Perceval's time. Arthur is in the background . . .

> . . . *Parzival* is, by definition, an "Arthurian Romance", a tale about King Arthur, yet the astonishing fact remains that neither this, nor any other such romance, for all the homage paid his name, really deals with the famous monarch as a primary figure.[26]

This failure to deal with Arthur is not astonishing, it is natural. For the French, the story really begins when the lineage came into France from Britain. Arthur preserved the lineage, and very possibly effected its transfer and therefore looms large in tale, but also foreign and remote. I'm inclined to suspect that Perceval was *the* first French-born heir of the direct Holy Blood lineage, and that his mother "Herzeloyd" (as Wolfram spells it) was Welsh. The name has a Welsh ring to it, as do many others in *Parzival*, if we can trust Wolfram's Germanic transliteration.

I think that Wolfram gives us hints about what the Grail is that are every bit as straightforward as his hints about when the story took place. One has only to pay attention and not second-guess him. Then, Wolfram has a sense of humour, as we've seen . . .

I was told, and I'll tell you too, but on your oath, not mine — hence if
I deceive you we are liars all of us.[27]

And, when talking about how Guiot found the story he says that
Guiot first had "to learn the abc's".[28] Wolfram is quite informal.

His first description of the Grail is not magical, but obstetrical. I will
re-quote the passage.

> She was clothed in a dress of Arabian silk. Upon a deep green
> achmardi she bore the Perfection of Paradise, root and branch. That
> was a thing called the Grail, which surpasses all earthly perfection.
> Repanse de Schoye was the name of her whom the Grail permitted
> to be its bearer.[29]

For readers unfamiliar with Wolfram I will guarantee that he knew his
audience and seldom neglected to describe the colours and textures of
clothing. His noble readers were titillated with such details. Why, then,
would he fail to describe the exotic (Arabian silk) dress of the bearer of the
Holy Grail at the climax of his story? The answer is that he does not fail to
describe it and, I think, he does in the very next sentence. He tells us that
Repanse de Schoye bore this Grail "upon a deep green achmardi". An
achmardi is a pillow, one usually covered in silk. Personally, I think that
Wolfram is only saying that Repanse de Schoys was pregnant, wore a
maternity gown of deep green Arabian silk, and that this pillow was a
distended tummy carrying a child of the Holy Blood in the direct lineage
("both root and branch").

I think that Wolfram is similarly straightforward with his other Grail
descriptions. When he says that the Grail is a sort of cornucopia supplying
all kinds of food, he means only that the Grail Dynasty originally introduced humanity to agriculture and animal domestication. We owe our
harvests to them. As we shall see, this seems to be no more than the truth.

When Wolfram says that the Grail enables the phoenix to arise to
new life in new plumage, he's saying only what we've observed several
times in this historical reconstruction: the Holy Bloodline periodically re-
surfaces in human history always clothed in the outward social, cultural
and religious "plumage" dictated by the times. When he insists that the
Grail can restore human vitality, he's saying only that this secret resource
can supply extra motivation to human lives and history, as we have seen it
do with Jesus in the Ancient World and with the maps of discovery in the
Medieval World.

In describing the Grail as a stone, Wolfram is indulging in a little joke based on a well-known religious pun. Peter, the disciple, is considered to be the founder of the Church, the "rock" upon which Christianity as an organized religion was built. "Peter" means "stone" in Latin, and Peter was the foundation of the Papacy. So Wolfram is just saying that the real foundation of Christianity is the Grail Family, of which Jesus was a part, and not Peter.

The Grail Romances are about a lineage. The anonymous author of *Perlesvaus* has Perceval seeing the image of a child in the midst of the Grail and, if our interpretation isn't completely wrong, this is what Wolfram wrote about also, a lineage more than any specific object. Within the entire troubadour context it was a lineage and not any specific object that was important. The Grail Romances were nothing more or less than eulogies, and epitaphs, for the de Bouillon Bloodline. It had just lost Jerusalem and had failed in a second attempt to establish a kingdom of the dynasty on earth. Not only was it unlikely that Jerusalem would be retaken, but the more astute minds might be able to envision the inevitable papal repercussions. In failure, the bloodline also faced extinction.

The Grail Romances, blossoming so quickly after the loss of Jerusalem, were not only a monument to what had almost been re-established, but were also intended to be monument to the very foundation of the Merovingian blood royal. In case it did not survive the rapidly converging forces of orthodox retribution.

Maybe this thought can lead to a brief digression. Was some genealogical information "leaked" to the troubadours so that this Arthurian-holy foundation of de Bouillon's clan could be preserved for posterity in literature? Chrétien de Troyes was one of the best-known troubadours of his day with many other successful compositions under his belt. Wolfram hints that Guiot gave the story to Chrétien first, but that he might have been "irked" at what Chrétien did with it:

> If Master Chrétien de Troyes did not do justice to the story, that may well irk Kyot . . .

Perhaps Chrétien, an establishment court bard, didn't grasp the real importance of the material he was handed and tossed off a stock epic dedicated to a potential eminent patron, Philippe, Count of Flanders. At the time, Philippe was a principal suitor for the hand of Marie of

Champagne, Chrétien's nominal liege.[30] Philippe had visited Troyes several times during the 1180s on urgent romantic (and dynastic) errands. Marie was newly widowed, Philippe was powerful, and maybe Chrétien decided to flatter a probable future patron by dedicating a vague epic about Perceval to him. And it may be that the Holy Blood was displeased with Chrétien's motivations and the accuracy and quality of the resultant work. What was of life and death importance to agents of the Holy Blood was sycophant flattery to Chrétien. In any case, it is merely a fact that there was a fire at Troyes in 1188. Chrétien is not heard from thereafter and no sure copy of his Grail Romance survives. It is on the slim evidence of uncertain copies of an unfinished work that he's credited with introducing the Grail into Western literature.

The Holy Blood may have turned to less-established, but also to less self-centred poets. We do not know when Guiot met Wolfram exactly, nor how long they stayed in contact, but we do know that storm clouds brooded on the Holy Blood's horizon by 1200 A.D. Guiot may have been desperate to find media outlets for the story and may have approached several lesser troubadours to see what they would do with it. In the obscure Bavarian knight he hit the jackpot. Wolfram apparently had the intelligence to grasp what the tale was all about, the skill to tell it in a way that would "sell" in his own time and therefore be preserved in numerous copies, and the wit and humour to disguise what he was saying so that *Parzival* would survive the Inquisition's scrutiny. Guiot found his man in the nick of time. Wolfram did not create *Parzival* overnight, and he must have been working on it during the crusade against the Cathars that Pope Innocent III launched in 1209 A.D.

The need to disguise the tale was plain. Whereas it seems that Chrétien unconsciously disguised things by paying little attention to the material he was given and tossing off a careless work, it appears that troubadours like Robert de Boron and the anonymous author of *Perlesvaus*, while conscientiously trying to do what they could with the story, were sincerely confused by it. Only Wolfram seems to have grasped what it was all about, structured a careful poem inviting various historical computations, and to have purposefully disguised the characters beneath nonsensical names (which nontheless furnish clues) and magical descriptions.

While all the Cathar writings were destroyed by the Inquisition, Wolfram's *Parzival* lived on. Is it only coincidence that Chrétien's was

destroyed by fire when many copies were immediately made of *Parzival?*...
or did agents of the Grail Family arrange this?

Otto Rahn, whatever else he may have been and chose to become,
was a meticulous medieval scholar specializing in the troubadour period.
His major and favourite source was Wolfram von Eschenbach, not only
because Wolfram was German, but also because he's by far the most
careful Grail author. Rahn knew that the entire body of Grail Romances
were, basically, an eulogy for the dynasty of Godfroi de Bouillon. He
knew also that the tales led back to Arthur and Celtic Britain and that
they had a legitimate Christian content. Nonetheless, Rahn chose to
ignore all this and to assist the Nazis in the theft of the Grail, in the
appropriation of someone else's history. Rahn later committed suicide.
Out of desperate regret?

Meanwhile, all through World War II, the real owners of the Grail
symbolism fought against the Nazis in Occupied France and in the Free
French forces. If we are to believe investigative journalists, the heirs of
the Merovingian dynasty survived into the post-war period and are
planning a political resurrection for the near future.

France has a weekly government publication called the *Journal Of-
ficiel* in which all groups, organizations and political or social clubs must
be declared. In the issue of July 20, 1956 the "Prieuré de Sion" declared
itself as being a knightly organization for Catholic traditionalists. It
claimed a membership of 9,841 divided into various ranks ranging from
"Knights" to "Constables" with a secret leader called a "Nautonnier"
("Navigator"). According to a tantalizing snippet in the *Dossiers secrets*
deposited in the Bibliothèque Nationale before 1956, the "Prieuré de
Sion" had existed continuously from the time of Godfroi de Bouillon and
its Grand Master had always been called a "Nautonnier".[31] And we may
recall that other nonsensical fragment from the *Dossiers secrets* deposited
sometime in the 1950s for researchers to find.

ONE DAY THE DESCENDANTS OF BENJAMINE LEFT THEIR
COUNTRY; CERTAIN REMAINED; TWO THOUSAND
YEARS LATER GODFROI VI (DE BOUILLON) BECAME
KING OF JERUSALEM AND FOUNDED THE ORDER OF
SION.

Certain researchers had, by 1956, concluded that this Order of Sion
had been *the* super-secret organization behind the more overt Templars,

Knights of St. John (Maltese Knights), Compagnie du Saint-Sacrement, etc. In short, this Order of Sion seemed to be *the* Grail Dynasty's core group. Was this new "Prieuré de Sion" registered in 1956 a legitimate descendant of the medieval Order of Sion?

The Prieuré de Sion did not reveal the name of its leader, or Nautonnier, but it did list some officers and its Secretary-General, one Pierre Plantard de Saint-Clair. A Saint-Clair again . . .

Researchers quickly discovered that the Plantards were an ancient lineage originating from the Pyrenees while, of course, it had long been appreciated that the Saint-Clairs were age-long paladins of the de Bouillon bloodline. The Prieuré de Sion claimed a house organ, or "newsletter", called *Circuit*, but the addresses given for both the Prieuré de Sion and for *Circuit's* offices did not exist.

A Swiss journalist named Mathieu Paoli spent several years researching the Prieuré de Sion and articles published in *Circuit* and, in 1973, published a book entitled *Les Dessous d'une ambition politique* ("*The Outline of a Political Ambition*")[32] in which he presented evidence of an international conspiracy, but one mostly centred in France, to return the de Bouillon dynasty to political power. A lengthy article in *Circuit* had outlined the necessary political changes on a step-by-step basis. Paoli could not figure out whether this was a serious movement with some very high-level support or the scheme of some pathetic and harmless Merovingian royalists.

Indications that all might not be so simple had been provided in the early 1960s with the rapid emergence of a new oil company in France which made its début with much publicity. This was (and is) Antar, which has a logo of a Merovingian king carrying a sword in one hand and a shield with a fleur-de-lis in the other.[33] Antar's slogan is "Discover France with Antar", the company is a subsidiary of ELF Petroleum.

Was the de Bouillon lineage emerging again, with their mysterious age-old power now augmented by the mundane clout of a major oil company? Or was it all coincidence? The researchers were undecided and puzzled. The Antar Merovingian king seemed a humourous cartoon figure, and the Prieuré de Sion described itself as a knightly organization for Catholic traditionalists — not the sort of thing that might promote de Bouillon interests.

Yet . . .

By this time the researchers were getting used to the Dynasty's little ways. Its penchant for appearing in the cultural, social and religious "plumage" that was most acceptable. Antar's cartoon king was modern plumage in a very modern industry. And, the Prieuré de Sion's "Catholic traditionalism" could be interpreted in two ways. How far did one choose to take the "Catholic traditionalism" back in history? To Clovis?

It seemed, the more researchers delved into things, that there *was* movement afoot to restore the Merovingian bloodline in France. A cover design from *Circuit* makes this objective obvious. A Star of David and a Merovingian sword are super-imposed over a map of France. And it *is* a Merovingian sword, because the hilt on the publication cover is a faithful rendition of the hilt of the sword of Childeric I (father of Clovis) found in his tomb in 1653. The symbolism was unmistakable.

Paoli, along with other journalists and investigators, felt forced to conclude that the Merovingian dynasty was probably the "legitimate" royalty of France, that heirs of it probably existed in the country and that there was obviously a conspiracy to restore the Dynasty to power, maybe with the financial backing of Antar if its Merovingian king-logo had any significance.

But, of course, it was all pathetic lunacy. What would be the point of restoring a bloodline that had been deposed for 1,300 years even if it were "legitimate"? What possible relevance could this lineage have today, even if it somehow proved that Jesus had had children? Christ's children granting that there had been any, were not Christ himself. Christian dogma might be rocked a little by such a revelation, but would find a way to weather the storm. The modern age was not particularly religious. A "Merovingian Revelation" would make the headlines for a few days, perhaps, and spawn an outpouring of books and magazine articles, but could it seriously affect government and international political economy? Paoli thought not, and most of the researchers agreed with him, but they remained puzzled.

We do not know whether Mathieu Paoli died still puzzled, either. Perhaps he discovered the significance of what he'd researched before he was executed. We will never know. It may be that his researches led him to go to Israel, where he worked in television journalism in Tel Aviv as late as 1977 or 1978. There all trace of him ends, and the rumour is that he was shot as a spy for trying to sell secrets to the Arabs.

Paoli's book of 1973 apparently caused some consternation in official diplomatic and espionage circles. Several secret agents were killed while

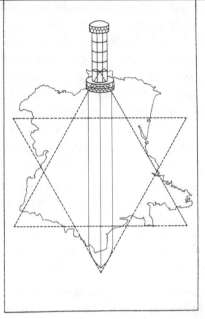

Cover of *Circuit* showing obvious Merovingian symbolism of re-emergence. The sword shown is that of Childeric I. Compare with hilt found in Childeric's tomb below.

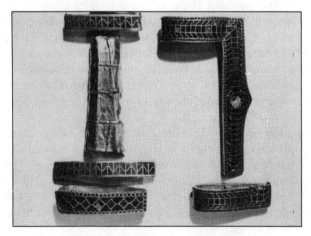

Gold hilt of the sword of Childeric I.
Courtesy French Ministry of Culture.

prying into Merovingian-related matters. In spite of the evident dangers of looking too closely at the mystery, it was too delicious for self-respecting reporters to shy away from. The Prieuré de Sion had named a "front man", the Secretary-General, Pierre Plantard de Saint-Clair. Who was he? And was it possible to discover the identity of the *real* leader, the "Nautonnier"? Would this real leader of the Prieuré de Sion turn out to be the current direct-blood heir of the Dynasty?

In 1973 a French magazine called *Le Charivari* published what claimed to be the transcript of a telephone conversation with Pierre Plantard de Saint-Clair. He didn't say much.

> . . . You must explore the origins of certain great French families, and then you will comprehend how a personage named Henri de Montpezat could one day become king.
>   . . . The society to which I am attached is extremely ancient. I merely succeed others, a point in a sequence. We are guardians of certain things. And without publicity.[34]

The magazine also published a character sketch written by Plantard's first wife, Anne Lea Hisler. According to this, Plantard was

> . . . the friend of personages as diverse as Comte Israël Monti, one of the brothers of the Holy Vehm, Gabriel Trarieux, one of the thirteen members of the Rose-Croix, Paul Lecour, the philosopher on Atlantis, the Abbé Hoffet of the Service of Documentation of the Vatican, Th. Moreaux, the director of the Conservatory at Bourges, etc. Let us remember that during the Occupation, he was arrested, and suffered torture, by the Gestapo and was interned as a political prisoner for long months. In his capacity of doctor of arcane sciences, he learned to appreciate the value of secret information, which no doubt led to his receiving the title of honorary member in several hermetic societies. All this has gone to form a singular personage, a mystic of peace, an apostle of liberty, an ascetic whose ideal is to serve the well-being of humanity. Is it astonishing therefore that he should become one . . . from whom the great of this world seek counsel? Invited in 1947 by the Federal Government of Switzerland, he resided for several years there, near Lake Léman, where numerous *chargés de missions* and delegates from the entire world are gathered.[35]

The British authors of *The Holy Blood and The Holy Grail* were able to substantiate some of the points of Hisler's sketch:

... our own research eventually yielded documentary evidence. As early as 1941 Pierre Plantard had begun editing the resistance journal *Vaincre*, published in a suburb of Paris. He was imprisoned by the Gestapo for more than a year, from October 1943 until the end of 1944.

... We wrote to the historical service of the French Army asking for details of the resistance activities of M. Plantard. We received a letter from the French Ministry of Defence informing us that this information was personal and confidential.[36]

Hisler's biographical sketch includes a lot of eccentric and direputable-seeming friends and associates of Pierre Plantard de Saint-Clair. What are we to make of "Paul Lecour, the philosopher on Atlantis" and "Comte Israël Monti, one of the brothers of the Holy Vehm" and "Gabriel Trarieux, one of the thirteen members of the Rose-Croix"? Then, what is a "doctor of the arcane sciences", and why should it be a credit to Pierre Plantard that he was an "honorary member in several hermetic societies"? Hisler's sketch asserts that Plantard was "invited" to reside in Switzerland and made his home there "near Lake Léman (ie. Lake Geneva), where numerous *charges de missions* and delegates from the entire world are gathered", yet Hisler never gives any evidence that any of these diplomats ever *consulted* Plantard about anything although she infers that he was one from whom "the great of this world seek counsel".

The picture we have of this Pierre Plantard is of a hopeless eccentric trying to "horn in" among the greats of the post-war world. And maybe that's all he is (because he's still very much alive and a ranking officer in the Prieuré de Sion).

On the other hand, maybe we of the democratic and mechanistic world-view should not snicker at all loudly. The Marshall Plan, the financial and political plan for the reconstruction of Europe, was thrashed out at Lake Léman in Switzerland. The American President, Franklin Delano Roosevelt, had approved this plan, and two of his closest friends and advisors had backgrounds and interests as disreputable as Pierre Plantard's. One such advisor, the financial wizard, Bernard Baruch, was a graduate of a French "hermetic" school and was the financial architect of the so-called Marshall Plan. He visited Lake Léman frequently in the immediate post-war years. FDR's other close friend and advisor was the architect, Frank Lloyd Wright, whose estate, "Taliesin", was named in honour of that boasting Welsh bard we have already

referred to in the section about evidence that Joseph of Arimathaea may
have come to the Glastonbury area . . .

> "Old Math ap Mathonwy knew no more than I."

And we may recall that FDR was the most notable shareholder in the
"Old Gold Salvage and Wrecking Company" which was engaged in
delving for "pirate" treasure on Oak Island. What did they wreck?

No, we dare not snicker. Because we do not have the faintest idea
what has been going on beneath the comfortable blanket of history, the
kind of history that Will and Ariel Durant have dealt with, and Barbara
W. Tuchman.

Pierre Plantard was listed only as a high official of the Prieuré de Sion.
Who was the leader? Could he be the actual heir of the Dynasty?
Reporters got onto that, too:

> . . . On February 13 (1973) the *Midi Libre* published a lengthy feature
> on Sion, Saunière and the mystery of Rennes-le-Chateau. This fea-
> ture specifically linked Sion with a possible survival of the Mer-
> ovingian bloodline into the twentieth century. It also suggested that
> the Merovingian descendants included 'a true pretender to the
> throne of France', whom it identified as M. Alain Poher.
>
> While not especially well known in Britain or the United States
> Poher was (and still is) a household name in France. During the
> Second World War he won the Resistance Medal and the Croix de
> Guerre. Following the resignation of de Gaulle, he was provisional
> President of France from April 28th to June 19th, 1969. He occupied
> the same position on the death of Geroges Pompidou, from April
> 2nd to May 27th, 1974. In 1973 . . . M. Poher was President of the
> French Senate.
>
> As far as we know, M. Poher never commented, one way or the
> other, on his alleged connections with the Prieuré de Sion and/or
> the Merovingian bloodline.[37]

As early as 1966 the French author, Saint-Loup, noted the birth
of a new mass-movement in Europe. It has not yet spread to North
America. Some people had begun to put together what they considered
to be the truth about human history. They became "Cathars" and began
to make pilgrimages to the monuments of the great struggle, Camelot
and Montségur. Saint-Loup's book was entitled *Nouveaux Cathares pour
Montségur ("New Cathars for Montségur")*.[46] By 1971 the new pilgrims

had swelled to a flood. French historians Michel Bertrand and Jean Angelini describe them.

> . . . men of all ages, but with a majority of young, these groups have a paramilitary appearance. Bearing banners and standards, and wearing parts of uniforms (berets and special neckerchiefs, insignia, etc.), they have a structure by ranks. Thus, there are among them knights and valets . . . There hardly passes a day when one of these groups does not come to one of the hotels of Montségur and fill up a page in the guestbook.[38]

The observant tourist can see this same kind of pilgrim any day in Glastonbury. They may have just have arrived from Cadbury Hill, or may just be planning a climb up the Tor, or be browsing among the Arthurian books in The Glastonbury Experience. Their numbers have increased since the 1960s. It may be the most astonishing kind of mass-movement in a century already too-familiar with populist frenzies. Who could have predicted a return to dynastic loyalty in our democratic age? And it is not a loyalty for the various monarchs who happen still to reign in our time, it is a commitment to the royalty which fought and died at Camelot and at Montségur, and, simultaneously, it is a denial of the late 20th Century view of human history.

The popular historians who have been published and honoured in our time have presented the human tale as a mindless and mechanical drone-like response to environmental and economic forces as the human juggernaut rumbles pilotless down the centuries. Historians like Will and Ariel Durant in their multi-volume outline of human history, and Barbara Tuchman in several Pulitzer Prize-winning studies of historical epochs, have seen the human story as a runaway "vehicle" sometimes breaking down, sometimes falling into potholes of disaster and sometimes progressing smoothly along the ages, but powered and guided only by human population expansion.

For these historians, there is no one at the steering wheel, and it was simply inevitable that the human historical wagon would some day bumble and lurch its way to our present 20th Century technological level, political developments and social perspectives. Barbara Tuchman has described some of the potholes we have encountered on the way which delayed our arrival at modern attitudes: the religious miasma of the 14th Century was covered in her *Bible and Sword*, wherein the British legends of Joseph of Arimathaea are adequately dealt with in 4 pages and dismissed as a psychological need; the *Guns of August* where she shows how we bumbled our way into World War I.

The tragedy is that the Durants and Tuchman are accurately describing human history as it has been lived and experienced by most people.

But not by all people.

Some people seem to have provided what guidance they could as the genetic cartload of humanity careened down the centuries. Danger ahead was perceived, potholes, and some provisions were made to soften the bumps. The mad chariot could not be made to avoid the holes altogether, but the wheels were nudged a bit. On steep grades, a little extra motivation was supplied in order to get us to the crest of a crisis and start the acceleration again.

It is the evidence of minimal guidance that has escaped the notice of our mechanistic and established historians. Guidance is denied altogether.

Yet . . . Jesus was predicted in Old Testament writing long before he made his appearance in Palestine. Who planned this? The portolans and maps showing the New World were around before the "Age of Discovery". Who created them? Who released them to the mariners at the right time? It seems to have been one family, one bloodline, that did all of this. Either you recognize their effect on history, or you do not. Either you accept the evidence for this dynasty's guidance of Western history, or, you reject it, explain it away or just ignore it.

But, if you accept this evidence then you must ask what makes this one family superior to the rest of us oblivious passengers on the careening cartload of historical experience? Could it be that the Prieuré de Sion is, after all, the legitimate descendant of a very ancient society. Did Plantard and the unknown Nautonnier guard a terrible secret?

During the Second World War, while Poher was doing something heoric in the Resistance to win the Resistance Medal and the Croix de Guerre, and while Plantard defied the Nazis and suffered torture for it, the Cross of Lorraine was adopted as the symbol of the Free French forces under Charles de Gaulle. This cross, having two cross-bars instead of one, originated with the ancient French house of Anjou, where Guiot found his tale about Perceval. It was later adopted by the Merovingian-descended rulers of Lorraine in the old Sicambrian heartland on the Rhine. It has never been explained why the Cross of Lorraine should have been chosen as the symbol of the Free French forces during World War II. Could it have been because of the secret underground leadership of the de Bouillon dynasty? The leadership offered by men like Poher and Plantard? Was such leadership still offered in the post-war world? In 1958, for example, when Algeria revolted, why did Charles de Gaulle, President of France, turn to Plantard for assistance?

It seems that the Cross of Lorraine, the old symbol of Anjou, had a secret significance right up to the end of World War II and today. And at least some fighting under the Cross of Lorraine seem to have known the dual nature of the secret it symbolized, Poet Charles Peguy wrote:

> Les armes de Jésus c'est la croix de Lorraine,
> Et le sang dans l'artère et le sang dans la veine,
> Et la source de grâce et la claire fontaine;

> Les armes de Satan c'est la croix de Lorraine,
> Et c'est la même artère et c'est la même veine
> Et c'est le même sang et la même fontaine.[52]

> (The arms of Jesus are the Cross of Lorraine,
> The blood in the artery and the blood in the vein,
> The source of grace and the clear fountain;

> The arms of Satan are the Cross of Lorraine,
> And the same artery and the same vein,
> And the same blood and the same fountain.)[39]

Was the Cross of Lorraine double-barred because one bar was Jesus and "holy", while the other bar represented Satan and the damned? Did just one family in the Western world have cause to know that what muddled humanity distinguished as good and evil, holy and damned, flowed from the same blood?

We will see (in a sequel book) that journalist Mathieu Paoli was apparently wrong in 1973 when he concluded with puzzlement in his book, Les Dessous d'une ambition politique, that the emergence of the Dynasty today could hardly make any difference.

The revelation of the Dynasty's secret, whether from France or any other country, would topple governments and transform society, both in the "free world" and in the Soviet bloc. Humanity would be rocked to its very foundations. None of the half-truths we have erected would survive. They would totter and fall.

What is the Grail Dynasty?

*   *   *

Summer gave way to autumn and the evenings came earlier. With the start of the school year, John and Jeanne McKay had left The Cross so that John could take up his new teaching duties out of the village. The villagers breathed easier.

We continued to visit the ruins when we could, after work, enjoying the drive through the fall landscape.

The truth is that Nova Scotia's seasonal glory is not the summer, which can often be cool, cloudy and wet, but the autumn. The Nova Scotians know this well enough and, as they watch the tail end of the tourist cavalcade retreating toward the provincial border after the Labour Day weekend, they settle down to enjoy the most magnificent autumn in North America. It may last until the middle of November, a succession of dazzlingly bright days, often with higher temperatures than the days of summer, but with an exhilarating night-time crispness.

Autumn is especially rich on the Fundy side of the province, in the Annapolis Valley, where the earth is deep and where the deciduous trees outnumber the evergreens. Gentle hills, clothed in maples, elms and oaks, magically adopt the lustre of precious metals, a cloth of gold over hill and dale with adornments of copper splashes. Small towns nestle in the golden folds, small towns settled by early colonists on the banks of small rivers and streams of old Acadia that pick their way between the hills to the sea. Always, these little towns proclaimed their presence by white church steeples soaring above the trees. These communities live by farming, drawing their wealth from the land, and it is wealth as golden as the autumn environment itself. Apples are the major crop of the Valley. Apples are rendered into applesauce, cider and juice. The people of the Valley harvest, liquify and export their autumn in the form of cider and juice as crisp as the days themselves.

We drove through this richness when visiting The Cross, were treated to perfumed breaths of mixed apples and woodsmoke when speeding through the evening haze that settled in the dells.

The sun was already low, on these autumn days, by the time we could reach The Cross from Kentville. A hint of royal purple lay over the Atlantic to the eastward by the time we could climb the hill toward the ruins, and the first shy stars twinkled in harvest constellations. Deanna and I would stroll among the ruins for a few minutes, generally in silence, thinking of other people drawn to other hill tops for the same reasons. Across the Atlantic, we knew, pilgrims watched the night descend from the earthworks of Camelot and from the ruined battlements of Montségur. We felt very close to these places and people, and the 3,000 miles of the Atlantic seemed inconsequential.

Sometimes we would break our silence with quiet talk as the shadows lengthened, recounting personal experiences to each other or re-examining some aspect of our joint research, wondering whether the Holy Grail existed as we had come to suspect. And wondering whether, in our own time as well as anciently, the Grail still performed its apparent function. Or, was everything that we had been pursuing just romantically imaginary?

Our thoughts were sometimes drawn down the cascade of darkening hills toward the Atlantic coast seventeen miles away where we could see the reflected, modest glow of Chester village nestled snugly beneath the indigo east and its first blazing stars. We thought of Oak Island with its money pit, wondered what (if any) treasure had ever been concealed there, and marvelled at the participation of American president, Franklin D. Roosevelt, in "The Old Gold Salvage and Wrecking Company". By now we knew enough to appreciate the significance of this company's name, but was the "significance" a real clue or an illusory coincidence? "De Bouillon" ("Bullion", etc.) meant only "golden" or "gold" and it was perfectly possible that Godfroi de Bouillon and Madame de Bullion had adopted the name to indicate their descent from or loyalty to the Holy Grail. Their names may not have been legitimate family ones . . . we had come to appreciate the Bloodline's little ways, just as French researchers before us had grappled with the coy, cryptic revelations of the *Dossiers Secrets*. That being the case, what aspect of the "Old Gold" was Franklin D. Roosevelt determined to salvage? What was to be wrecked?

We often spoke of this most popular President in American history and the apparently inconsistent role he played. Scion of a wealthy "Eastern Establishment" family, Roosevelt first won the Presidency in 1932, in the darkest days of the Depression. Immediately, he offered his "New Deal" to a despairing nation, but it was a domestic economic policy denounced as "socialist" by the class he himself represented. He introduced America's social security program, he got people off the breadlines with massive "make work" projects financed by the government. The Tennessee River was tamed with a series of dams, and a huge hydro-electric surplus was created. Roosevelt's government financed a massive, and unprecedented, construction of interstate highways. But, maybe even more important than these economic measures to employ the destitute, were Roosevelt's continuing radio-broadcast "Fireside Chats". He was the first U.S. president to use radio to keep in contact with the people on a continuing basis, and not just as a campaign media tool. Quietly, he told the American people what he planned in order to end the Depression and alleviate unnecessary suffering in the meantime, and quietly he told the American people that they need not despair but instead should be motivated by hope for they had "nothing to fear but fear itself". And the American people responded — even if the industrial establishment denounced him as a near-communist — and elected him to four terms in the White House.

What Roosevelt had done during the 1930s uncannily fitted the desperate requirements of the 1940s. Without the network of highways he created, called useless and worse by political opponents at the time, America could never have mobilized its industry and military to cope with World War II. And, without the huge electrical surplus generated by the TVA, the Allies could never have been able to win the desperate race to get the atomic bomb before Hitler got it. Scientists from the United States, Britain and Axis-held countries (German-Jewish and Italian refugees from fascism) congregated at Oak Ridge to create the atomic age in a life or death race against the Nazis. The winning edge was not the brains, for the Nazis themselves boasted famous scientists, but the vast quantity of electrical power available because of the "make work" project of the TVA. It is no accident that Oak Ridge was in Tennessee, and no accident that the electricity necessary to produce fissionable uranium was there, waiting, courtesy of the Tennessee Valley Authority.

After the war, during the prosperity of the 1950s economic boom which, for a while, made the United States the premier power of the West, "free enterprise" industrialists cheerfully forgot that their prosperity depended on the interstate highways and surplus power provided by the "socialist" Roosevelt. And, perhaps, the American people cheerfully forgot, in their 1950s materialist frenzy, that the real foundation of freedom is not free enterprise sloganeering, but a concrete determination to alleviate unnecessary human suffering and despair so that human energy, hope and courage are able to produce and create.

Deanna and I would speak of the equally inconsistent personalities around FDR. Why did Roosevelt have such regard for the mystic architect, Frank Lloyd Wright? Why did the super-wealthy Jewish industrialist and financier, Bernard Baruch, become a personal ambassador for Roosevelt's "socialist" policies both in America and abroad. Baruch, the Jew, endorsed FDR's revolutionary plan to rebuild *all* of war-torn Europe... *even Western Germany and Austria*... through the Marshall Plan. This was definitely a departure from normal European practice where the tradition had always been to ravage and rape the defeated enemy, not to help the enemy back to dignity. Selling this concept to America's allies, even Britain, proved difficult. Just as America's own "free enterprise" industrialists had branded FDR a socialist during the Dirty Thirties, so America's allies branded FDR's rebuilding scheme as madness in the late Forties.[53]

In his autobiography, Bernard Baruch recounts an incident where a wealthy British industrialist Peer sarcastically compared Franklin Roosevelt with Columbus. As Baruch tells it:

> One gentleman decided to amuse the company by asking me the riddle — why were Roosevelt and Columbus alike? His answer was that, like Columbus, Roosevelt did not know where he was going or where he was when he got there, or where he had been when he got back.
>
> Rising, I replied, "Perhaps it is true that Roosevelt and Columbus were alike, since both explored new frontiers and new horizons and both brought a new world into existance to redress the troubles of the old world". Churchill banged the table in approval, crying, "Hear, hear!"[40]

I wondered if Baruch knew that Columbus had very probably been a Jew or a Cathar heretic, as heretical as Roosevelt, and that Columbus's lifelong dream was to "recapture Jerusalem."

This has just been seized upon by some modern scholars who believe it was a ploy Columbus used to flatter Their Most Catholic Majesties, Ferdinand and Isabella, with the sponsorship of another crusade. Indeed, Delno West, chairman of the History Department at Northern Arizona University, plans to write a book on this theme based on a supposedly untranslated Latin work by Columbus recently discovered in Spain. And it is probably no accident that Dr. West's plan was leaked to the press just in time to drum up publisher interest with the 500th anniversary of the

1492 voyage just five years away . . . But readers of this book will suspect that Columbus's dream to "recapture Jerusalem" may have another meaning. He had hoped to create a New Jerusalem across the Atlantic where the Jews, heretics (Cathars) and Moors, who were all at higher intellectual levels difficult to distinguish because of their common bond in Albigensianism's secret, could live in religious tolerance and security.

Did Baruch know of this heretical dream of Columbus? Perhaps, because Baruch had been a disciple of George Gurdjieff, a Cathar-like mystic who had founded the "Institute for the Harmonious Development of Man" in Fontainbleu, France during the 1920s and 1930s. French author, Louis Pauwels, had also been a follower of Gurdjieff and reports the presence of Bernard Baruch at the Institute over a number of months in the mid-1920s. Perhaps understandably, Baruch skips over this part of his life in his autobiography intended for American readers, but Baruch's studies under Gurdjieff are documented by Pauwels in *The Morning of the Magicians*.

Deanna could offer some first-hand insight into Gurdjieff teaching and training. She, too, had been a student of the mystic — not of Gurdjieff personally, because he died the year after Deanna was born, but of people who had known Gurdjieff and continued "the work", as it was called. What were these teachings? That there was a true history of humanity that differed greatly from the history offered in conventional textbooks. That to become cognizant of both true history, and true evolution, of mankind the student had to "awaken" to consciousness and not remain in the dreamy illusion of "reality" that is supported mostly by intellectual fear and laziness, laced with materialism carried to extremes. Perhaps it is true that the "Jerusalem" that Columbus hoped to recapture was not the old city in the Holy Land, but a new order to be established in a new world. That is, in fact, the meaning of the Latin on the American Great Seal. "A new order of the ages".

I could not speak of Gurdjieff's neo-Catharism, having no first-hand experience of it myself, although I was aware that Roosevelt, Baruch and Frank Lloyd Wright seemed motivated by some hidden commitment, and secret knowledge, that directed their unusual lives.

But I could speak personally of something similar. I had been privileged to know Tommy Douglas during the 1960s. I worked, in minor ways, to help build the New Democratic Party of which Tommy Douglas was the first leader. Although Tommy Douglas is a household word in

Canada, he's virtually unknown in the United States so I will tell his story briefly for American readers. Douglas was a Scottish immigrant to Canada whose family settled on the Canadian prairies just after World War I. He was a young man in the Depression, a minister, and he was appalled at the deprivations suffered by farm families, particularly, during this time. Tommy Douglas saw the Canadian version of America's "Dust Bowl"tragedy. He decided to do something about it and, in company with some other prairie personalities, founded a political party called the Co-operative Commonwealth Foundation, or CCF.

Douglas and the CCF basically did only what Franklin Delano Roosevelt's "New Deal" did in America. In fact, there can be little doubt that the CCF was greatly influenced in its policies by aspects of Roosevelt's "New Deal". Naturally, like FDR himself, Tommy Douglas and his colleagues in the new party were branded "socialists"and worse by Canada's "Eastern Establishment" which very much reflected America's. Nonetheless, because of the appalling economic conditions and human suffering, the CCF gained swift support. Farmers, unemployed urban workers and humanistic intellectuals voted for it.

Enough people voted for it, in fact, that the party eventually came to power in Saskatchewan and other western Canadian provinces. In the 1940s it threatened to win in Ontario, and even seemed capable of winning a Federal election, which corresponds, more or less, to an American Presidential Election. The two "Eastern Establishment" parties in Canada, the Liberals and the Conservatives, warned voters of the "socialist scourge" coming from the west and managed to defeat the CCF at the polls by fielding joint candidates, rather than competing with each other and splitting the vote, in crucial electoral districts.

The "socialist scourge" of Tommy Douglas and the CCF proved to have some disconcerting elements for both "capitalists" and Canada's Marxists when it came to power in Saskatchewan. Douglas introduced a form of social security in Saskatchewan and this was later adopted by Canada as a whole because of fear that the CCF would win a Federal election if the Liberals and Conservatives didn't "borrow" this "socialist" idea. Then, just like Franklin D. Roosevelt, Douglas embarked on a series of "make work" projects in Saskatchewan, not only to employ people, but also to increase the capital assets of the province. Partly using government money, but seeking always partnerships with private enterprise, within ten years "socialist" Saskatchewan had more capital investment than any other province of Canada! Alone of all Canadian provinces, Saskatchewan was able to pay off with interest (not "repudiate") its massive debt. That was the shock for the "free enterprise" critics of the Eastern Establishment. Marxists got their shock a bit later. Douglas vowed to bring electrification to all of Saskatchewan, even to remote farm communities and even to individual isolated farms. He had seen, first hand, the miseries of subsistence living on Dust Bowl farms and realized that electrification would not only decrease human drudgery, but would increase farm productivity. But the powerful utility workers' union, a truly "socialist" and Marxist-dominated organization, decided that the cost of rural electrification could better be spent by increasing their own salaries. Without hesitation, Douglas threatened to legislate the union out of existence if it didn't back down. Marxists were appalled, but rural electrification continued according to Douglas's plan.

Douglas went a bit further than Franklin Roosevelt in that he also thought that people should have a medical insurance plan just like a social security plan. This is, in fact, something that Americans might consider for themselves which would alleviate a great deal of unnecessary human suffering among impoverished minorities. When Douglas tried to introduce "medicare" into Saskatchewan, the doctors who had favoured it in the 1930s in order to assure payment of their fees, opposed it vehemently in the prosperous 1950s. Douglas treated the doctors exactly as he'd treated the selfish Marxist-dominated utility worker's union — he threatened to "disband" them, not by an act of legislation, but by the simple expedient of flying over from Britain many young doctors who were quite happy to work with guaranteed fees under medicare. Douglas and the CCF made it clear that this might not be a temporary measure (the Saskatchewan doctors were on strike), since some of the Brits seemed to like Saskatchewan and might settle there . . . The Medical Association got the message, and accepted medicare. In one way or another, medicare is established in all Canadian provinces, another policy "borrowed" quickly from the CCF by the Liberals and Conservatives.

In the 1960s there was a desire to "update" the old Co-operative Commonwealth Foundation, and also to change the name of the party since the name really had no translation into French. This desire to make the old CCF more modern also disguised neo-Marxist plans to bring organized labour directly into the political party in a controlling position. The "new"party was called the New Democratic Party, or NDP, and its name was translatable into French. Incongruously, although Eastern neo-Marxists engineered this transformation, they could find no one with a track record of winning elections except the aging prairie preacher, Tommy Douglas. With misgivings, Douglas agreed to lead the NDP into the 1960s, although the conflict between the "religiously motivated" Douglas and the "neo-Marxist motivated" urban intellectuals was never far beneath the surface of outward party cohesion.

Canada's CCF and later NDP were, naturally, modelled to some extent after Britain's Labour Party. And Clement Atlee once sagely observed that the British Labour Party "owes more to Methodism than to Marxism", meaning that the leaders were often ministers of Protestant denominations and the followers mostly committed Christians. Their goal was to form a national community which reflected values of Christian compassion. Only sometimes did this goal dovetail with Marxist ideas of wealth redistribution, and never comfortably, since the "Methodists" distrusted the Marxists' materialist orientation, while the Marxists distrusted their colleagues' religious orientation. Nonetheless, during the Depression, human misery and economic inequality made the Methodists and Marxists the strangest of political bedfellows in Britain's and Canada's fledging "socialist" parties.

When I knew Tommy Douglas in the 1960s, the basic incompatibility of "Marxist" and "Methodist" was becoming more apparent and more acute. The Marxist and neo-Marxist urban intellectuals who virtually controlled the NDP by this time were often puzzled and impatient with Tommy Douglas's campaign tactics. At whistle stops, and rural barbeques, Tommy would often lead NDP supporters in a battle hymn he'd picked up from the British Labour Party and had adapted for Canadian usage. The song was based on Blake's poem, *The New Jerusalem*.

> I shall not cease from mortal strife,
> Nor shall my sword rest in my hand,
> Till we have built Jerusalem
> In this green and pleasant land.

By now, we know what this means. Jerusalem was not a place, it is an ideal. A society in which there can be freedom of the individual tempered by responsibility and compassion.

In her biography of Tommy Douglas, Doris French Shackleton writes of an experience in the life of the young Tommy Douglas:

Annie Douglas was the religious influence in the home and it was she who took most pride in Tommy's growing interest in the church. His father had become cynical of the Christian offices performed by chaplains at the fighting front. He donated money to the Salvation Army and stayed away from the church.

The earliest occasion Douglas speaks of, when his platform skill evoked a profound audience response, involved a sympathetic moment shared by father and son. Tom Douglas (the father) had shown an interest in the Masonic Order, but it was Tommy who involved himself deeply in the junior Order of De Molay. This youth organization had spread widely through the United States after the First World War. A chapter was formed in Winnipeg. One of its high moments was a dramatic production before a convention of Masons held in the old Board of Trade building at the corner of Portage and Main. The play concerned the life and death of the patron of the junior order, Jacques De Molay, the fourteenth century knight-at-arms who led expeditions against the Saracens, and was put to death as a heretic by Philip the Fair of France. Tommy took the title role and threw himself heroically into the part. He spoke of that evening:

> "My father was there and he was sparing of praise as in most things. When we came out he said, 'Let's walk' which we did, for a distance of about four miles. I knew he had been deeply moved. There was never a word. We walked in silence. Going up the front steps he tapped me on the shoulder and said, 'you did no bad' ".

Douglas is reluctant to talk about experiencing a "call". He is more apt to joke about impromptu prayers at De Molay meetings.[41]

It is clear that Doris French Shackleton does not know the significance of the Masons or of Jacques de Molay. We will remember that Jacques de Molay was the last Grand Master of the Knights Templar, who was roasted to death over a slow fire in an attempt to extract from him the secret of the Cathars. He did not reveal it.

Shackleton does not appreciate the significance of the "dramatic production" in which the young Tommy Douglas took the title role. It was not just a play to entertain Masonic dads. It was a ritual in which Tommy Douglas pledged to *become* Jacques de Molay and to dedicate himself to that secret commitment to human progress that we have traced in this book. Like all of the other heroes and heroines we have dealt with in this book, Tommy Douglas pledged to preserve, protect and represent

the Holy Grail. *This is literally, no more and no less, what he vowed to do.*
And that forced him to become a minister in the Dirty Thirties in
Canada's Dust Bowl. That forced him to take humanistic action to
alleviate human suffering. That forced him to become involved in politics to achieve more compassionate welfare policies. That, one suspects,
allowed him to tolerate the Marxist intellectuals clinging to his party
with some degree of humour. And that commitment compelled a sense of
integrity in Tommy Douglas that was recognized by political opponents
and supporters alike, an honesty that forced millions of Canadians to love
him whether they voted for him or not. A political critic of Douglas, Jack
Scott of the Vancouver *Sun,* wrote just after the 1960 election in
Saskatchewan:

> This man Douglas — well, how'll I put it? He's a good deed in a
> naughty world. He's a breath of clean, prairie air in a stifling climate
> of payola and chicanery and double-talk and pretence, global and
> local.
>
> Forget the politics. Here's a man who wanted to do something
> for the human race. He chose the method that seemed best to him,
> quarrel with it if you will. He was motivated by an ideal.
>
> To call him a politician, as you'd call Bennett or Diefenbaker a
> politician, is to insult him. He was and is a dreamer and a human-
> itarian, incorruptible, genuine and intellectually honest.[42]

Understandably, while active as a politician Douglas never mentioned his pledge of commitment to the Holy Grail. As Shackleton
wrote, he was more apt to "joke" about the De Molay society if anyone
referred to it. Yet it was anything but a joke. Tommy Douglas died in 1986.
I spoke with him during his last illness, not directly but through a lifelong
companion who was with him, and Douglas confirmed that the experience of the Order of de Molay directed the future course of his life.

Douglas, no less than de Molay himself, Arthur, Sinclair and Champlain had become part of the "Grail Complex".

The Holy Grail had crossed the Atlantic, not just to find a refuge
from the Inquisition raging in Europe, but also to exercise its ancient
powers in the formation of new social structures in a New World.

*   *   *

As darkness deepened, like other pilgrims on other hilltops we found
our thoughts drawn to the memory of all the knights and heroines who

had defended now-fallen ramparts in the service of the Grail Dynasty. And especially we often thought of King Arthur with whom the Grail first emerged into the light of history. He focused our attention, just as he had haunted the minds of the troubadours. We now had an inkling of what had inspired Arthurian courage, we suspected what could have kindled Arthurian chivalry. We knew what force could have transformed the all-too-human passions of Uther Pendragon and Ygerne into something a little more than human, we knew what had created Arthur.

Although we were three thousand miles from Camelot, it was easy to imagine the jingling of chain-mail armor and horse-trappings as the dying Arthur was borne up the hill under the defiant, snapping dragon-banner of Wales. The banner, like the name of his father, were clues to the real nature of the Holy Grail.

Human will. Animated by love. Tempered with compassion. *Guided by knowledge,* the dragon, that much-maligned "Serpent" in the Garden of Eden. Human will animated by love, tempered with compassion and guided by knowledge finds itself obligated to take action that people recognize as "courageous". Armed with love, compassion and knowledge, the human will can transcend the stigma of birth, as Arthur had done, to lead knights of light into a gathering darkness. It can impell an individual to overcome the social parochialisms and cultural expectations that he or she may have inherited from birth, to create and defend new and more humane communities. Armed with love, compassion and knowledge, one can cast off the cumbersome and crippling armor of religious dogma or political and economic dialectics to carve out, with supple and determined strokes, more appropriate social structures and a more rewarding human environment, using equally sharp edges of intellect and heart. That is what knights and heroines of the Grail have always done. That has been their job. It still is, and anyone with a properly molded will can join the elite company of the Grail because the battles, and the ramparts, are all around us.

We would usually leave the hilltop of The Cross by the time that night had truly fallen, by the time starlight flashed coded messages off the mica flakes in the ruined walls, by the time the chill wind began to whisper secrets to the grass. And we left with the faith and confidence that the Grail would not abandon the Western World in the crisis years of our immediate future. There would be enough knights and heroines to battle for humane solutions to our contemporary problems.

So, on our long night-time drive back home to Kentville and Minas Basin we enjoyed the smell of apples and woodsmoke in the dells, assured that some "once and future king (or queen)" would appear to offer leadership in our time of converging crises.

Notes

Chapter One
The Christmas King of Camelot

1. Bearing in mind that there is no absolute proof of King Arthur's existence, all dates for his life must be considered conjecture. The span from about 470 A.D. to about 550 A.D. simply reflects Geoffrey of Monmouth's *History*, but this cannot be relied upon. Geoffrey Ashe, for example, author of a number of books on Arthur, originally agreed with this span but later revised his opinion with the 1985 publication of *The Discovery of King Arthur* and identifies Arthur with Rhiothamus who was defeated in Gaul and disappeared in 470 A.D. In this opinion, Ashe is in agreement with Sharon Turner (*The History of the Anglo-Saxons*, Vol. 1., Paris, 1840) that Arthur may have been a British chieftain named, or titled, Rhiothamus who led 12,000 troops into southern Gaul to oppose the Visigoths according to Sidonius Apolinaris (Book III, Chapter 9). However, both Sidonius Apolinaris and Sharon Turner agree that Rhiothamus was defeated and disappeared in 437 A.D. John Morris (*The Age of Arthur*, New York, 1973) revised the Turner/Sidonius Apolinaris date of the defeat of Rhiothamus to 469-470 A.D., and this is accepted by Geoffrey Ashe. Therefore Ashe would have Arthur's life span the years 420 A.D. to 470 A.D. roughly. Obviously, the span of Arthur's life remains uncertain, as does the date for Rhiothamus' defeat ... and Arthur may, or may not, have been "Rhiothamus" in any case. Therefore, about the most that can be said is that King Arthur lived "sometime" between about 420 A.D. and about 550 A.D.
2. Here I follow Ashe's spelling of Camlann. Other authorities spell it "Camlan".
3. Unfortunately, there seem to have been a succession of wounded and crippled "Fisher Kings" in the Grail Castle of the romances. All of these cannot have been the one King Arthur. It seems that with the "Fisher Kings" we have the historical King Arthur confused with, and melded into, a cycle of much earlier Celtic myth.

4. Geoffrey's *History* proved so popular that no less than 191 handwritten copies of it still survive. There must have been hundreds of copies in circulation by the year 1200 A.D.

5. There are two major branches of the Celtic (Gaelic) languages: P-Celtic and Q-Celtic. P-Celtic is today represented by modern Welsh, while Q-Celtic is represented by Irish and Manx which are nearly extinct as spoken languages and, in any case, have evolved greatly since the Dark Ages. In Arthur's time, four tribes spoke P-Celtic in distinctive dialects amounting to languages: the Votadini, the Selgovae, the Novantae and the Damnoni (as the Romans distinguished them), besides several dialects/languages spoken in Wales. Of the Q-Celt group, there was Manx, Cornish and Irish and several other dialects/languages in Brittany and Gaul. Therefore, although Caradoc spoke both P-Celt and Q-Celt in the form of 12th Century Welsh and Irish respectively, Geoffrey's old Gaelic-language source book could have been written in any one, or several, of antiquated or extinct dialects or languages. See *King Arthur* by Norma Lorre Goodrich (Franklin Watts, New York and Toronto, 1986) pages 24-25 for a discussion of the Celtic languages. See also Robert Graves, *The White Goddess* (Faber and Faber, London, 1961) pages 245-271 for a more detailed discussion of the same linguistic material. The P-Celt and Q-Celt languages are thought to represent vestiges of two distinct Celtic migrations into Western Europe and the British Isles, the earlier migration originating from the Balkan area with a language more closely related to Greek (P-Celtic) and the later migration originating from Central Europe with a language (Q-Celt) more closely related to the Italic languages.

6. *History of the Kings of Britain* by Geoffrey of Monmouth, translated by Sebastian Stevens, London, 1944, but quoted here from *The Quest for Arthur's Britain* (Granada, London, 1971) edited by Geoffrey Ashe.

7. As many scholars have pointed out, the Arthurian material has been woven into a much older corpus of Celtic myth. Arthur, in being born around the time of the winter solstice, takes his place as a "hero of the waxing year", just one more seasonal sun god in a tradition reaching back to the Neolithic.

8. According to Goodrich (*King Arthur*, page 360), there was another British appeal for Roman military assistance in the year 446 A.D., but Rome did not respond.

9. Both Geoffrey of Monmouth and the Nennius Compilation agree on the number of battles (12), but not on their location or name.

10. Some romances also say that Arthur and Guinevere had a son named Lohot and a second son named Amhar (Amr), but there is disagreement and confusion about the number and names of the sons. Some sources do not mention offspring at all. During this period of military stability in Arthur's kingdom, he undertook a military campaign on the continent, but whether into "Germany" or Gaul is disputed.

11. Goodrich identifies "Lancelot" as Agnuselus, King of Scotland, although tradition has him coming from Gaul or Brittany.

12. That is, Arthur's illegitimate son. Some sources identify Mordred as

Arthur's nephew, son of Arthur's sister Anna, who married King Loth "of the northerners". But other traditions give Arthur no sister at all, or, alternatively, identify her as Morgan. The only agreement seems to be that "Mordred" opposed "Arthur" at Camlann.

13. Quoted from *King Arthur*, Goodrich, page 45.

14. Quoted from *King Arthur*, Goodrich, page 45. Strangely enough, although some modern scholars may doubt that there was such a book, it is mentioned as early as 718 A.D. Helinand de Froidmont's *Chronicle* mentions a history of the Grail, but says "This history I have not been able to find in Latin, but so far witten in French only, and in the possession of certain chieftains, and, as they say, not even then in a complete text." This "French" language as opposed to Latin, would, of course, have been some form of Gaulish or Celtic language in 718 A.D. and particularly if it was composed earlier than 718 A.D. and held by the chieftains as a relic of past times. Although there is no proof, this book mentioned by Helinand de Froidment may be the same source that later came into the hands of Walter, who then passed it to Geoffrey.

15. See, for example, the genealogy of the Campbells and MacArthurs in George Crawford's *Peerage of Scotland* where there are no less than 6 separate Arthurs in 11 generations of one family.

16. Katherine E. Maltwood, for example, claimed that the land around Glaston-bury had been artificially formed into a giant topographical Zodiac about 10 miles in diameter (*Guide to Glastonbury's Temple of the Stars*, London, 1934, 1964). Glastonbury Tor is mostly a natural formation, a conical spur of Jurassic limestone that has been eroded into its present shape. However, Geoffrey Ashe found evidence that the natural shape had been artificially altered by man, probably in the Bronze Age, to form a maze or "Troy Dance" around the cone . . . It can only be said that the geography around Glaston-bury is disconcerting.

17. The Glastonbury Thorn sometimes also blooms at Christmas as well as Easter. The type of thorn indigenous to Britain and northern Europe is *Crataegus oxyacantha*. However, the Glastonbury Thorn is a specimen of *Crataegus praecox* which is native to the eastern Mediterranean area . . . see *Pursuit*, Vol. 6, No. 1, January 1973, "'Yesu' Of The Druids", by biologist Ivan T. Sanderson, pages 18-19. Sanderson points out that there is not just *one* Glastonbury Thorn. Several other small trees, apparently seeded over the centuries from the original one, are growing in the immediate area of Glastonbury but nowhere else in all of Europe.

18. This quote and all subsequent information about the Cadbury Hill excava-tion from *The Quest for Arthur's Britain* by Geoffrey Ashe, Leslie Alcock (Professor of Archeology at the University of Glasgow), C.A. Ralegh Rad-ford (Former President of the Royal Archeological Institute), and Philip Rahtz (Head of the Archeology Department at the University of York), edited by Geoffrey Ashe.

19. For a detailed discussion of Late Roman cavalry, particularly the *cataphracti*,

see A *History of the Art of War in the Middle Ages* by Sir Charles W.C. Oman (Methuen, 2 Vols., London, 1924).

20. For instance, King Cerdic of Wessex ruled from Winchester about 480 A.D. or around the time of Arthur's birth. Cerdic was a Saxon. All of "Anglia" was in the hands of the Angles by the time of Arthur's birth. Northern Scotland was controlled by Picts, while some of eastern Scotland was settled by Saxons. The Irish were enemies of the Britons. In actual fact, therefore, "Arthur's Britons" held less than half the total land area of the British Isles. Quite obviously, it was too late to "defend Britain by controlling the sea".

21. British forces were traditionally foot soldiers and Macsen's army, a century before Arthur, would have been predominantly infantry. Cavalry was rare in British warfare until the "unexpected bands of cavalry" mentioned by Gildas in the Roman campaign of 418-425 A.D. Arthur's very success was probably due mostly to his innovative use of heavy cavalry against the infantry of Angles, Saxons, Jutes and Picts. It was not until the advent of the longbow and the pike that infantry evolved tactics to withstand the charge of heavy cavalry . . . see Oman's *A History of the Art of War in the Middle Ages* for a very detailed study of the cavalry vs. infantry situation from Roman times until the 16th Century.

22. It has always been the position of Arthurian and Grail Literature experts that Chrétien de Troyes first mentioned the Holy Grail. However, it appears the the Grail was mentioned almost 500 years earlier by Helinand de Froidmont who calls it a "gradale" in Latin but explains that it is a vessel of some sort connected with Joseph of Arimathaea . . . see *King Arthur*, Goodrich, pages 356-357 for the original Latin and Goodrich's translation of this intriguing document. However, elsewhere in *Holy Grail Across The Atlantic* I have held to the "orthodox" opinion that Chrétien de Troyes was the first romancer to mention the Grail pending confirmation of the accuracy of Goodrich's translation.

23. For a full discussion of Grail linguistics, see Jean-Michel Angebert's *The Occult and the Third Reich*, pages 56-88.

Chapter Two
The Castle at The Cross

1. "The Cross" is not the real name of this Nova Scotia village, although it was the village's official designation up to the 1930s. I have been asked to conceal the modern name of the village to prevent amateur "investigation" of the ruins and to prevent possible vandalism.

2. John and Jeanne McKay are pseudonyms I invented for the owners of the site. Their real names are known to the Nova Scotia Ministry of Culture, Recreation and Fitness, of course, and to my publisher.

3. *The Black Discovery of America* (Personal Library, Toronto, 1981) has just been re-published in a revised edition entitled *Dawn Voyage* (Summerhill Press, Toronto, 1987).

4. See Robert Graves, *The White Goddess*, pages 66, 229, 230 and 284.

5. Petromantic sculpture is a style of sculpture that uses the natural form of stone as much as possible, with the sculptor chipping and polishing the stone minimally in order to "suggest" the subject in an almost abstract manner. Striking and vital works of art can result from the petromantic style. This style was favoured by the Celts when they did stone sculpture at all, apparently from a belief that working stone destroyed the power in it. So Celtic sculptors worked stone as little as possible. It is interesting that the taboo against working stone seems to have been shared by the megalith builders of Britain who preceded the Celts. Although Dr. Alexander Thom of Oxford, among others, has demonstrated a high degree of engineering and astronomical/ mathematical knowledge among these ancient people in the construction of their numerous stone circles, the stones themselves which compose the circles (and also free-standing menhirs) are all worked as little as possible. Perhaps the best and most obvious example of this is Stonehenge where, although the stones have obviously been shaped to the same size and configuration with great skill, they were not finished to a smooth surface and no attempt was made to render them absolutely identical. They retain a primitive and un-finished appearance which greatly contributes to the monument's powerful character.

6. This historical plaque can be seen by any visitor to "The Ovens" southeast of Chester, Nova Scotia on the shore of Mahone Bay.

7. Measurements of an ancient structure can sometimes suggest a convenient unit-of-measure which the builders probably used. As early as 1884, C.S. Pierce painstakingly measured the Newport Tower and suggested that the builders had used a basic unit of measure that was 12.31 English inches . . . that is, slightly longer than a standard English foot. Professor Kenneth J. Conant ("Newport Tower or Mill", *Rhode Island History,* January 1948, pages 2-7) was puzzled that the structure had not, apparently, been built using the standard English foot and inches of British colonists. Conant suggested that the tower, which predates the settlement of Newport itself, might have been built prior to 1632 by "the windmill building Dutch of New Netherlands." But Conant either forgot, or did not bother to find out, that the old Netherlandic *voet* ("foot") was *smaller* than the standard English foot, amounting to only 11.14 English inches. The next Netherlandic unit of measure, the *el*, is 27.08 English inches, approximating the English "yard". However, the Norse foot, or *fet* in Icelandic, was 12.3543 English inches. It is worth noting, too, that the English inch, and foot, have been standardized within 1/30th of an inch since 1490 . . .

Standard Yard of	Year	Inches
Henry VII	1490	35.924
Elizabeth I	1588	36.015

Guildhall	1660	36.032
Clockmaker's Company	1671	35.972
Rowley's Tower Standard	1720	36.004

This being the case, since the very standardized measures covered the time of settlement and building of Newport, it seems obvious that the mysterious "Newport Tower" was built with some non-English unit of measure, particularly since the structure was in existence for at least 44 years before Newport town was founded (it was mentioned in a document as existing as of 1588). The closest unit of measure to that which the original builders used was apparently the Icelandic *fet* of 12.3543 English inches. This unit was used all over Scandinavia (except Denmark) in the 14th Century. Architecturally, the Newport Tower is in the style of 14th Century Scandinavia. See Frederick J. Pohl, *The Lost Discovery* (W.W. Norton, New York, 1952) pages 174-194 for a detailed discussion of the problem. See also Hjalmar Ruud Holand's article "The Age of the Newport Tower", *Archeology*, Autumn 1951, pages 155-158, who concludes that the tower is a 14th Century structure of Scandinavian origin.

8. Although Champlain said this in his journal, it is difficult to decide what part of "Fundy" he is referring to. He may be writing about oaks in Passamaquoddy Bay area. As we will note later, Champlain's journal is always "vague" when referring to the Fundy region.

9. The Celts, both before and after King Arthur's time, had an alphabet in which the letters were designated by the names of trees. Although it is an over-simplification, it is enough to say that as the various Celtic alphabets evolved and changed, the process was poetically called "The Battle of the Trees", meaning which letters should be added, left out, or changed in the order of the alphabet. But I should add that most of the alphabet changes apparently took place because of religious and mystical reasons, since the "trees" (or letters) also had mythical and seasonal importance attached to them. The oak tree was deemed to have certain associations as the letter "D". Taliesin was a Welsh bard who was apparently also familiar with Irish (Q-Celt) alphabetic tree lore, and who wrote a poem called "Câd Goddeu" ("The Battle of the Trees") in a collection called *The Book of Taliesin* dating from the 12th Century, but containing lore compiled as early as the 6th. In the Câd Goddeu we read, (translated by Robert Graves):

> The alders in the front line
>   Began the affray.
> Willow and rowan-tree
>   Were tardy in array.
>
> The holly, dark green,
>   Made a resolute stand;

He is armed with many spear points,
  Wounding the hand.

With foot-beats of swift oak
  Heaven and earth rung;
'Stout Guardian of the Door',
  His name in every tongue.

And so on. From this we learn that "oak" was *duir* ("door") and represented the letter "D" in every tongue . . . in all Celtic languages, that is. To make it clear that this "Battle of the Trees" was actually an evolution of the alphabet, Taliesin's sense of humour compelled him to add a final verse:

Under the tongue root
  A fight most dread,
And another raging behind,
  In the head!

The Celts considered that the oak (*duir*) was the most divine of all trees since it attracted both lightening and mistletoe, which the Celts called "all-heal". Being the "king" or "god" of the trees, it was only proper that the oak should be chosen as the weapon of divine heroes. Hercules, for instance, is always pictured with an oak club, and naturally it is in his *right* hand since most people (then as now) were right-handed. Therefore, the oak is associated in Celtic lore with doors, divinity, and right-handedness, etc. Such verses may seem like light-hearted nonsense, but, in fact, Welsh and Irish bards trained in ancient lore communicated both forbidden Celtic history and heretical religious notions through this sort of poetry.

Curiously enough, even this Câd Goddeu of Taliesin is one tiny thread connecting King Arthur with Franklin Delano Roosevelt and the rebuilding of post-World War II Europe. Perhaps this connection is worth explaining. It is at least intriguing.

The 12th Century Taliesin, author of Câd Goddeu, claimed great learning and had pretentiously named himself after a famous and legendary bard of the 6th Century, an earlier "Taliesin", who also claimed great knowledge and the possession of a momentous secret. The "bards", or *ollaves*, were the historians of the Celts.

This much earlier Taliesin had confronted and defied King Maelgwn Gwynedd of North Wales. According to tradition, this King Maelgwn Gwynedd had been an ally of King Arthur, but betrayed his trust and joined forces with Mordred at Camlann. Because of the weakening of the Arthurian kingdom after Camlann, Maelgwn Gwynedd was able to establish an independent realm of his own in North Wales . . . see Goodrich's *King Arthur*, pages 63 and 264.

However, the bard Taliesin taunted Maelgwn Gwynedd that what he had won was worth much less than what he had lost as King Arthur's ally.

Maelgwn Gwynedd would have won immortal fame in song and history had he remained loyal, but won merely obscure independence by his treason. Taliesin claimed to know a great truth and secret connected with King Arthur and he offered to tell it in a riddle. If Maelgwn Gwynedd's 26 learned bards could guess the answer, then Taliesin was willing to forfeit his head. But if the learned men could not guess the answer, then Taliesin would be free to go in spite of his impertinence to the king. Maelgwn Gwynedd agreed to this and Taliesin forthwith started the *Hanes Taliesin* ("Song of Taliesin"), a long and complex riddle. The 26 bards could not guess the answer, and Taliesin went free . . . see Robert Graves, *The White Goddess*, pages 74-96 where Graves gives the *Hanes Taliesin* in both Lady Charlotte Guest's translation and in the translation of D.W. Nash as published in *Myvyrian Archeology*.

Robert Graves himself tried to answer Taliesin's riddle, which no one had been able to do for almost 1500 years, and came close to the answer . . . but missed the mark, in my opinion, because of his obsession with moon and fertility goddesses. Answering this riddle is what *The White Goddess* is all about.

The correct answer to Taliesin's riddle might simply be "San Graal" since answers to his verses are all personalities related to, or connected with, the same lineage from Abraham to Arthur.

Now, it is widely known that the famous architect, Frank Lloyd Wright, was also a serious student of "cryptohistory", or what established historians would prefer to call "the occult" and "myth". Sara Lee Stadelman of Ottawa knew Frank Lloyd Wright, stayed at his estate for some time, and has personally confirmed his interest in ancient lore to me. And it is at least intriguing that, of all the names he could have chosen for his estate, Wright named it "Taliesin" in honour of the Celtic bard who knew a great secret connected with King Arthur and who confronted the traitor, Maelgwn Gwynedd.

Frank Lloyd Wright was one of two personal representatives chosen by Franklin Delano Roosevelt to attend post-war negotiations for the reconstruction of Europe. The other was the financier, Bernard Baruch, who had also been a student of ancient lore under the famous mystic, George Gurdjieff. The significance of these two men, and one of the Frenchmen they met at Lake Geneva, will be discussed further in the text and notes.

Chapter Three
The Knights of the Temple

1. It does not seem, however, that Godfroi de Bouillon, actually accepted the kingship although he was offered the crown. Nonetheless, he was king in all but title and is even identified as King of Jerusalem in the genealogy compiled by Henri Lobineau which is reproduced in *Holy Blood, Holy Grail* although the authors of the book (Michael Baigent, Richard Leigh and

Henry Lincoln) explain that the only real title apparently held by de Bouillon was "Protector of the Holy Sepulchre." However, Edward Burman writing in *The Templars, Knights of God* seems to accept Godfroi de Bouillon as the first King of Jerusalem when he notes (page 13): "When Baldwin I became the titular King of Jerusalem on 18 July 1100, after the death of his brother, Godfrey of Bouillon, he inherited an unstable and precarious kingdom." It is evident that Godfroi de Bouillon was king in fact, if not in title. Baigent, Leigh and Lincoln were able to establish that Godfroi apparently did found the Order of Sion, which was very probably located in the Abbey of Notre Dame du Mont Sion (pages 110-113 of *Holy Blood, Holy Grail*). This substantiates the curious remark made by René Grousset in his monumental multi-volume work on the crusades (*Histoire des croisades et du royaume franc de Jérusalem*, Paris, 1934-1936) that de Bouillon's kingdom was founded on "the rock of Sion." (Vol. III, page xiv.). Baigent, Leigh and Lincoln accept the premise that de Bouillon's Order of Sion apprently had the power to confer the Kingship of Jerusalem. One might therefore term Godfroi de Bouillon as a sort of "king of kings," or at least a maker of kings, since he founded the Order of Sion that could crown Kings of Jerusalem.

2. *Holy Blood, Holy Grail*, page 67. But see also Burman's *Templars*, pages 13-25.
3. *Holy Blood, Holy Grail*, page 66. *The Templars*, page 20.
4. Burman, in *The Templars* gives a detailed and documented account of the Templars' banking and fiscal activities (Chapter 5., "International Financiers," pages 74-97), while the same material is covered more briefly in *Holy Blood, Holy Grail*, page 71.
5. *Holy Blood, Holy Grail*, page 76. But see also Malcolm Barber's *The Trial of the Templars* (Cambridge University Press, Cambridge 1978) for mention of this fleet.
6. This Templar and Christian contact with Moorish and Jewish savants seems to have been concentrated on the island of Sicily where it was easier to hide and disguise the contact from Rome. Roger II of Sicily (1130-1154) welcomed to his court at Palermo the Arab geographer Ibn Idrisi and together they produced *Al Rojari*. This was a geographical treatise incorporating all the knowledge of the age, a combination of Norse and Arabic explorations. Idrisi also made a sphere and a disc representing the known world while at the court of Roger II. See Paul Hermann's *Conquest By Man* (Harper & Brothers, New York, 1954, pages 318-320) for details of this unorthodox co-operation.
7. R. A. Schwaller de Lubicz in *The Temple in Man* (Autumn Press, Brookline, 1977, pages 35-37) emphasizes that the Gothic cathedrals all conformed to "an exact canon: two towers; a narthex; a nave — triple and with seven windows, as a rule — on the walls of which the stations of the Cross are later drawn. Then comes the transept, and then the entrance proper to the Sanctuary, the remainder being reserved for the faithful." De Lubicz points out that this Gothic canon was a departure from earlier European church construction and seems to have been inspired by temples in the Middle East.

He writes "In the Temple of Luxor we find an identical layout." Now, it has been surmised that the original Temple of Solomon itself was designed after Egyptian models, such as the Temple of Luxor. De Lubicz also emphasizes that the Gothic canon, no less than the Temple of Luxor, also accurately represented a reclining human figure using the so-called "Golden Section" to achieve correct proportions, the number designated as φ by mathematicians (1.61803395 . . . etc.). In a Gothic cathedral, the congregation sat in the area corresponding to the Peristyle Court in the Temple of Luxor, which is to say, within the "womb" of a reclining female figure. After Communion and in the act of leaving the cathedral, the faithful passed through the doorway of the building that corresponded to the pubis in the Egyptian/ Gothic canon and were thus symbolically and spiritually "reborn." This is probably where the idea of "born again Christians" comes from, based on the injunction of Jesus that "ye must be born again." Louis Charpentier, in his *The Mystery of Cathedrals*, explores the use of the Golden Section and other mathematical relationships in Gothic cathedrals, speculating that both secular and spiritual knowledge are embodied in the mathematical proportions of the churches. *All* Gothic cathedrals are designated as "Notre Dames," "Our Lady," and the obvious lady would be the Virgin Mary. But, as the argument of this book (and others) is unfolded, it is quite possible that the "Mary" intended to be honored in Gothic cathedrals is, perhaps, Mary Magdalene who may have been the wife of Jesus. Thus, Gothic cathedrals built during the time of Templar ascendancy and while the de Bouillons held Jerusalem may well have been monuments to Mary Magdalene. However, it is clear that the name "Mary" has deeper significance still since it means "of the sea" and, within a Gothic cathedral, the faithful could be said to be "born again of Mary" which would symbolically mean that they renewed their communion with whatever came "from the sea" to create humanity. Naturally, these deeper and more esoteric notions were unsuspected by the great majority of cathedral-goers, but it seems clear that the symbolism was known, and intended, by the designers and master masons who actually constructed the Gothic cathedrals.

8. De Rougement, *Love in the Western World*, London, 1956, page 78, but quoted here from *Holy Blood, Holy Grail* page 56. For a general overview of Cathar religion see: *The Treasure of Montségur* by Walter Birks and R. A. Gilbert (Thorsons Publishing Group, 1987); *Les Cathares de Montségur* by Fernand Niel (Paris, 1973).

9. Baigent, et al seem both intrigued and puzzled by references to "Ormus" in documents relating to Templars and Cathars. They note that "orm" means "elm" in French and this leads them into a bemused chase for the relevance of "Ormus" and a curious event known as "the cutting of the elm" which took place at Gisors in 1188. Readers are referred to *Holy Blood, Holy Grail* pages 121-125. However, it may be relevant that "orm" is Norse for "worm", or "dragon". The de Bouillons no less than other prominent French aristocracy were intermarried into "Norman" bloodlines which were Norse. Like

the word "Graal" itself, this puzzling "ormus" may have been a symbolic pun used for security reasons since it could mean both the nonsensical "elm" and also the more relevant "dragon."

10. *The Sufis* by Idries Shah (Anchor Books, New York, 1971, pages 197-203).

11. Sir Steven Runciman, *A History of the Crusades* (Hammondsworth, 1978, Vol. 2. page 477). But see also Idries Shah, *The Sufis*, page 203. While some see the Cathars as being "Buddhist" and immigrating into Europe via the Balkans and the so-called "Bogomil" sect (see Runciman's *The Medieval Manichee*, Cambridge University Press, 1969, page 117). Others think that the Cathars were related to the "Sufi" Islamic gnostics. Perhaps the simplest explanation is that the Cathars merely preserved aspects of early Christianity later abandoned by Rome. This, in fact, is the view expressed by Walter Birks and R. A. Gilbert in *The Treasure of Montségur* pages 101-102.

12. Meg Bogin, *The Women Troubadours* (W. W. Norton, New York, 1976, pages 37-61).

13. *The Women Troubadours*, pages 54-55 particularly.

14. *The Women Troubadours*, pages 22-24, 35-36, 57.

15. *Holy Blood, Holy Grail*, page 62. Although Wolfram's "Munsalvaesch" could be a Germanic corruption of the French *Montsalvat*, with Wolfram actually referring to a "mountain" of salvation, the pronunciation of the time leads me to believe that Wolfram used the Germanic *Mund* ("World") on purpose. If so, he ascribed to the Cathars and the "treasure of Montségur" greater importance than many of his contemporaries.

16. The four knights are named in Fernand Niel's *Les Cathares de Montségur*, page 291ff, and referred to in *Holy Blood, Holy Grail* pages 61-62.

17. The Templar dispersal is covered in *The Templars* (pages 172-175) and also in *Holy Blood, Holy Grail* (pages 78-80). Both of these sources and many others agree in linking the Templars with various secret societies that emerged after the Templars were disbanded.

18. Michael Bradley, *The Iceman Inheritance* (Dorset Publishing Inc., Toronto, 1978, page 145.)

19. *The Iceman Inheritance*, page 145.

20. General information concerning portolan charts relies on *Maps Of The Ancient Sea Kings* by Professor Charles Hapgood (Chilton Books, Radnor, 1966).

21. *Maps Of The Ancient Sea Kings*, page 170.

22. *Maps Of The Ancient Sea Kings*, page 41.

23. *Admiral Of The Ocean Sea: The Life of Christopher Columbus*, by Samuel Eliot Morison (Little, Brown, New York, 1942, page 186.)

24. Fernandao Pigafetta, *A Report On The Kingdom of Congo, Etc.*, London 1881, page 137.

25. Frederick Pohl, *The Lost Discovery* (W. W. Norton & Company, New York, 1952, page 242.

26. The popular story that Queen Isabella pawned her jewels to pay for Columbus's epic voyage of 1492 is, as might be expected, a myth. Money for the

372 HOLY GRAIL ACROSS THE ATLANTIC

expedition was raised by Luis de Santangel, Alonso de Harana, Alonso de Carvajal and Diego de Harana. All of these men were *conversos*, or Jews who had voluntarily accepted the Roman Catholic faith. See Morison's *Admiral Of The Ocean Sea*, pages 275-298.

27. Stan Steiner, *Dark and Dashing Horsemen* (Harper & Row, San Francisco, 1981, pages 92-109).

28. I prefer my own idiosyncratic *Judaeism* to the dictionary's *Judaism* to designate the Jewish corpus of religion and tradition as it has existed since the rebuilding of the Temple in 516 B.C. after the Babylonian Captivity. *Judaism* is derived from the name of Judah, son of Jacob, and the traditional ancestor of one of the 12 tribes which settled in southern Palestine. As such, then, *Judaism* refers to the ancient pre-Babylonian Captivity complex of Jewishness which incorporated strong traditions of kingship, deep belief in the Messiah and awe of inspired prophecy. I have coined *Judaeism* from the Greco-Roman word "Judea", the Hellenistic name for southern Palestine that was ruled by the puppet kings of the Herod dynasty at the time of Christ. The older *Judaism* might well have accepted Christ as the Messiah and king, but *Judaeism* rejected his claims because Hellenistic influences during and after the Babylonian Captivity had undermined the older Jewish beliefs in kingship, the Messiah and prophecy. During the Babylonian Captivity and afterwards, it was rabbis, not kings and prophets, who molded Jewishness and this new Hellenistic-influenced Judaeism retained only much-diluted "lip service" loyalties to the notions of a revived kingship, the coming of a Messiah and it was frankly suspicious of prophecy. Judaeism had become a more modern and sophisticated religion because of exposure to Greek and Persian culture. Jesus in many ways represented what might be called a "fundamentalist reform" movement within Jewishness which, at the same time, offered some new concepts. Christ and his teachings might well have enjoyed acceptance among pre-Babylonian Captivity Jews, but was considered a dangerous and irrelevant anachronism in the view of the new rabbis of the Sanhedrin: dangerous because Christ's claims of kingship would offend Rome and its puppet Herod dynasty; irrelevant, because Christ's fundamentalist Jewishness had little to do with the realities of day-to-day living in the Greco-Roman world. So, I prefer to designate this evolved Jewishness which confronted Christ, and which has existed since, as "Judaeism". I reserved "Judaism" for the older Hebrew religion and social traditions that flourished before the Babylonian Captivity. It is "Judaeism" that is relevant to the theme of this book.

29. According to Frederick Pohl, author of *Prince Henry Sinclair*, the name has been spelled some 91 different ways in the available historical documents. But the two most common spellings are "Saint-Clair" and "Sinclair".

Chapter 4
The Sea-Chieftain

1. Quoted here from *Prince Henry Sinclair*, Clarkson N.Potter Inc., New York, 1974, page 173.
2. William Peace & Son, Kirkwall (Orkney), Scotland, 1901, page 98.
3. In fact, all references in this chapter originate from Pohl's book, although I have independently checked some sources where indicated. I have sometimes wondered whether Pohl would have connected Henry Sinclair with the de Bouillon complex if he had read the French authors I have referred to, or if *Holy Blood, Holy Grail* had been published a decade earlier and had made the original French research available in English. Pohl must also have wondered at Sinclair's motivation for undertaking the transatlantic voyage, given the insecurity of the Orkney Earldom. Pohl concedes the title of "Prince" ("principe") which occurs in *The Zeno Narrative*, although Henry Sinclair's actual titles appear to have been Earl of Orkney and Baron of Rosslyn.
4. "The honesty of the Zeno narrative has been sufficiently well established, but whether or not the fisherman had the experiences he narrated on Drogio, and whether that may be identified with North America, are questions that have been much debated," *Encyclopedia Americana*, 1951 edition. In 1982 the Nova Scotia Museum had a panorama of Henry Sinclair stepping ashore in Nova Scotia. This has since been replaced by another exhibit.
5. *Holy Blood, Holy Grail*, page 183.
6. G. T. Stevenson, Edinburgh, 1835, page 42.
7. Balfour and Jack, Edinburgh, 1837, page 71.
8. The *Hauksbók* (Hauk's Book) was commissioned by an Icelandic lawyer named Hauk who claimed descent from Thorfinn Karlsefni and so concentrated on Karsefni's relatively large expedition to North America circa 1010 to 1020. The *Flateyjarbók* (Flat Island Book) is a source for Karlsefni and Lief Ericsson. The *Landnámabók* ("The Taking of the Land Book" about Icelandic settlement) is another source for the voyages of Eric the Red. These three "sagas," plus the *Eriks Saga Rauda* ("Eric the Red's Saga") are the sources for Viking voyages to North America.
9. Although the Greenland Vikings eventually died out due to isolation and a climatic deterioration, they lingered until approximately 1450. Greenland graves show that these Norse people, although stunted in stature by malnutrition, continued to follow European fashions to the end. This indicates at least sporadic contact between Greenland and Europe until the time that the Greenlanders perished. As late as 1327 Peter's pence representing 6,912 persons was sent to Rome from Greenland although, as Dr. Luka Jelic pointed out in 1894 "this payment may have covered two or more years" and the number, 6,912, should not be taken as the population of Greenland in 1327. See Pohl's *Prince Henry Sinclair*, pages 92-104 and notes on page 197;

see also Paul Hermann's *Conquest By Man*, pages 219-299 for a very complete description of Greenland's contacts with Europe.

10. *Prince Henry Sinclair*, page 63.
11. *Prince Henry Sinclair*, page 63.
12. *Prince Henry Sinclair*, page 65.
13. *Prince Henry Sinclair*, pages 74-76. Pohl discusses the possibility that Nicolo Zeno may have arrived in 1390, but prefers the 1391 date.
14. Nicolo Zeno died in the service of Sinclair, probably in 1394. Nicolo's brother, Antonio Zeno, served Sinclair until Henry's death in 1400.
15. Translation taken from *Prince Henry Sinclair*, pages 110-115. Perhaps the only implausible part of this narrative concerns the multi-lingual inhabitants of Icaria. However, if Icaria is taken to be Newfoundland, which seems almost certain, then it is interesting that several early explorers reported that the Beothuk Indians of Newfoundland were multi-lingual from contact with European fishermen. Robert LeFant of Bayonne, quoted by Bernard G. Hoffman in *Cabot to Cartier* page 146 says: "the Indians understood any language, French, English, Gascon and their own tongue." In and around Newfoundland, Cartier picked up words "derived from various seafaring groups (that is, Old French, Breton and Norman, West Coast, Catalan and Italian)" (Hoffman, page 151). But it would be absolutely justifiable to add Basque, Portuguese, Spanish, Norse and Celtic to this list. Therefore the inhabitants of Newfoundland at this period *were* multi-lingual because of contact with all manner of European seamen. Certainly, they could not have been accomplished linguists in all these languages, but probably spoke a crude "pidgin" based on each. But we cannot ignore the possibility of castaways from European vessels living among the Beothuks, just as the narrative describes. It is also possible that some Celtic king of Scotland did, at one time, found a settlement in Newfoundland which susbequently "went native" by intermarriage with the Beothuks, leaving only oral traditions and "laws." Regarded objectively, the Zeno description of Icaria is not really implausible at all. In fact, it merely represents a 14th-century and Newfoundland version of the alleged Celtic (and other) influences in New England argued by Drs. Barry Fell, George Carter, etc.
16. Hay, *Genealogy*, page 18.
17. Hobbs, William Herbert. "The Fourteenth-Century Discovery of America by Antonio Zeno," *Scientific Monthly*, Vol. 72 (January, 1951), pages 24-31. Hobbs pointed out that the only other open pitch deposit on the western side of the Atlantic is in Trinidad off the coast of South America, and then there are the tar pits of Le Brea in Hollywood, California.
18. *Prince Henry Sinclair*, page 136.
19. *Prince Henry Sinclair*, page 137.
20. *Prince Henry Sinclair*, page 143.
21. *Prince Henry Sinclair*, page 154.
22. *Prince Henry Sinclair*, page 152.
23. *Prince Henry Sinclair*, page 152.

24. *Prince Henry Sinclair*, page 139.
25. Dr. William S. Fowler, *Bulletin* of the Massechusetts Archeological Society, July 1954, pages 78-80. Fowler states: "Line sinkers are found all the way up from the lowest strata, while the net sinkers first appear much later at the Green Point site . . . a date of 1343 A.D. for the origin of the pit, of the net sinker, and presumably of net fishing. However, since this is subject to error, add or subtract 50 years" . . . Fowler did not use Carbon 14 for his dating of the Green Point Abenaki Indian site, but used soil accumulation measurement. His date of 1343 ± 50 years might be subject to some greater error since soil accumulation dating is not so accurate as C14. Nonetheless, the correlation with the time of Sinclair's voyage is remarkable, giving an estimate of 1393 for the introduction of net fishing while Sinclair must have come in 1398.
26. *Prince Henry Sinclair*, page 149-150.
27. Aside from the Zeno Map of the North, which shows one city in mid-peninsular Nova Scotia and another city in the northern part of the province, the Mercator Map of 1577 shows a city in the same mid-peninsular location and names it "Norumbega."
28. Leland, Charles Godfrey and Prince, John Dynely. *Kulóskap The Master and Other Algonkin Poems*, Funk and Wagnalls, New York, 1902, page 133.
29. *Prince Henry Sinclair*, page 158.
30. Clarkson N. Potter, Inc., New York, 1967, page 161.

Chapter Five
Doors

1. D'Arcy O'Connor, *The Money Pit*, Coward, McCann & Geoghegan, New York, 1978, page 30.
2. All quotes and general references to the Oak Island pit have been taken from O'Connor's *The Money Pit* since this fairly recent book is the most detailed, in my opinion, and also very objective, but written in a popular style. However, another book on Oak Island is *The Money Pit Mystery* by Rupert Ferneaux (T. Stacey, London, 1972) and there are several others that can be found in all major libraries.
3. I first verified these dates with Geochron Labs in Cambridge, Massachusetts back in 1982. More recently, in July 1987 I verified them again with Mr. Charles Sullivan of Geochron and requested a letter which is reproduced in the text.
4. In a number of papers, Professor J. Norman Emerson demonstrated the value of using psychics in archeological research: "Further Note on the McDonald Site", *Ontario History*, Volume 52, March 1960, pages 60-61; "New Pages of Prehistory," *Ontario History*, Volume 52, March 1960, pages 53-76;

"Puckasaw pits and the Religious Alternative," *Ontario History,* Volume 52, March 1960, pages 71-72. These three papers, all from the same issue of *Ontario History* illustrate the prolific output of Emerson. To some degree, his inordinate success in finding and surveying Indian sites in Ontario was due to his use of psychics.

5. O'Connor, *The Money Pit,* page 168.
6. O'Connor, *The Money Pit,* page 161.
7. Father Eugene Vetromile, *The Abnakis,* New York, 1866, page 43.
8. Vetromile, *The Abnakis,* page 44.
9. Barry Fell, America B.C., New York Times Book Co., New York, 1976, page 239.
10. *Fell, America B.C.,* page 240.
11. Fell, *America B.C.,* pages 1-12.
12. Fell, *America B.C.,* page 256-257.
13. Pohl, *The Lost Discovery,* page 144.
14. Pohl, page 261-262.
15. Canadian writer/researcher John Robert Colombo, volunteered to help me with this question of apples. After consulting numerous books, Colombo reported that no apples are native to North America. From what I have been able to gather from various sources, apples are a part of the rose family and originated in Central Asia. Edible fruit, however, appears to originate from the eastern shores of the Black Sea where there are still believed to be some wild groves of these earliest apples. It is thought that early Greek mariners in the Black Sea, circa 1200 B.C., brought the fruit to Europe where it spread rapidly in a semi-domesticated and domesticated form. Robert Graves in *The White Goddess* discusses these botanical aspects of the apple, pages 251-261.

Chapter 6
The French Connection

1. Gérard de Sède, *L'Or de Rennes,* Robert Charroux, Tresors du Monde, Paris, 1962, page 247 ff.
2. Ibid, pages 246-251.
3. Ibid, pages 246-251.
4. Baigent, Leigh and Lincoln, *Holy Blood, Holy Grail,* pages 262-263, 264-265.
5. All of the material about the life of Bérenger Saunière derived originally from Gérard de Sède's *L'Or de Rennes,* but is also covered, in English, in *Holy Blood, Holy Grail,* pages 31-38.
6. Again, Gérard de Sède in *L'Or de Rennes,* was the first to come to this conclusion, one now shared by Fernand Niel (*Albigeois et cathares*), Maurice Magré (*Le Trésor des albigeois*), Pierre Belperron *La croisade contre les albigeois*

et l'union du Languedoc à la France), Pierre Durban (*L'Actualité du catharisme*) and many others. *Holy Blood, Holy Grail*, presented, in English, a compendium of this French research.

7. Baigent, Leigh and Lincoln, *Holy Blood, Holy Grail*, pages 245-250. But see also Gérard de Sède's *La Race fabuleuse*, Robert Charroux, Paris, 1973, page 112-118.

8. Geoffrey Ashe, ed., *The Quest for Arthur's Britain*, pages 73-82.

9. Baigent, Leigh and Lincoln, *Holy Blood, Holy Grail*, pages 245-253

10. Baigent, Leigh and Lincoln, *Holy Blood, Holy Grail*, pages 245-253. But also de Sède, *La Race fabuleuse*, pages 85-91.

11. de Sède, *La Race fabuleuse*, page 16.

12. Baigent, Leigh and Lincoln, *Holy Blood, Holy Grail*, illustration 32.

13. de Sède, *La Race fabuleuse*, page 36.

14. Baigent, Leigh and Lincoln, *Holy Blood, Holy Grail*, illustration 29.

15. J.M. Wallace-Hadrill, *The Long Haired Kings*, London, 1962, page 238.

16. Baigent, Leigh and Lincoln, *Holy Blood, Holy Grail*, page 246. But see also Wallace-Hadrill, *The Long Haired Kings*, page 239-141.

17. Baigent, Leigh and Lincoln, *Holy Blood, Holy Grail*, pages 266-267 reproduction of genealogies prepared by Henri Lobineau.

18. Charles Davis writing in *The Observer*, London, March 28, 1971, page 25.

19. Baigent, Leigh and Lincoln, *Holy Blood, Holy Grail*, page 332.

20. Ibid, page 333.

21. Ibid, pages 336-337

22. Ibid, page 354.

23. Ibid, page 365.

24. Victor Gollancz, London, 1962, page 124.

25. Baigent, Leigh and Lincoln, *Holy Blood, Holy Grail*, pages 285-304.

26. Robert Graves gives evidence for a connection between "Arimathaea" and "Amalthea", *The White Goddess*, pages 51, 85, 195, 218, 319, 355 and 437. See also the derivation of Math ap Mathonwy, *The White Goddess*, pages 303-304.

Chapter Seven
Map Memorials

1. Four metal artifacts have already been recovered from the ruins by the McKays and these objects are illustrated in this book. However, our metal detector indicated a great deal of metal in the rubble. In fact, the detector responded so emphatically that I became suspicious. I also noticed that some of the stones in the ruins seemed very heavy for their size, while others seemed to be of normal weight. I tested the heavy rocks with the metal detector and got an strong response. All of these inordinately heavy stones

were alike: a buff outer color, but when broken they were a deep black inside. I began to suspect some variety of metallic ore in the heavy rocks used by the builders of the apparent castle. Dalhousie University's geology department identified a sample of heavy rock as being titanium ore. Therefore, since these unusually heavy rocks were distributed all through the ruins, the metal detector was not necessarily responding to metal artifacts. Nonetheless, based on the four metal artifacts that have so far been recovered from the site, there's no reason to doubt that systematic excavation would be rewarded with more artifacts.

2. Excavation at Cadbury Hill, the supposed site of Camelot, revealed the castle's walls to have been earthworks reinforced by a core of stone rubblework. Camelot was an earthwork palisade, probably with a wooden barricade erected on top of the earthen walls. Henry Sinclair's castle, which he built in Kirkwall (Orkney), was of mortared rubblework and its walls were so thick that soldiers barracked within them. It was called "one of the strongest houses in Britain" and its final destruction, long after Henry Sinclair's time, required the use of huge cannon. The story of Sinclair's Kirkwall castle is told, in various places, in Pohl's *Prince Henry Sinclair*. The castle at The Cross, if the ruins are genuine, would have been a "barbaric" construction similar to the real Camelot and to Henry's Kirkwall castle.

3. The accuracy of longitude demonstrates that this map did not *originate* in the 14th Century. Hapgood says that the Zeno Map of the North *as it comes down to us* had been drawn by Nicolo Zeno around 1380. Hapgood is of this opinion because it is known that Nicolo made a voyage to Greenland in the service of Sinclair. Certainly, Nicolo *contributed* to this map and probably drew in details relating to the east and west coasts of Greenland. But neither he nor any other European of the time could have drawn northern Greenland since perpetual pack ice around northern Greenland makes navigation impossible near the pole. In attributing the map to Nicolo in the year 1380, Hapgood has made a minor slip. Nicolo died in the service of Sinclair, probably in 1394, or four years before the transatlantic voyage, leaving only Antonio to carry on *The Zeno Narrative*. Only Antonio could have known about Estotiland, Icaria and Drogio, and it must have been Antonio who drew these features on the map. Since the Sinclair expedition has been dated satisfactorily as taking place in 1398, and Sinclair seems to have returned home in the summer of 1399 (or, less likely, in the summer of 1400 in time to be killed in August of that year), the map in its final form was the handiwork of Antonio Zeno and was probably drawn in 1399 or 1400 because it shows details that only Sinclair would have known and could have communicated to Antonio upon his eventual return to Orkney.

4. Readers are referred to *Crucial Maps* by William Francis Ganong, published by the University of Toronto Press in co-opertion with the Royal Society of Canada in 1964. Ganong and Theodore E. Layng offer interesting personal backgrounds of some of the early cartographers, and also present interpretations of geographic features depicted by these early maps.

5. I am assuming, here, that Jacques Cartier undertook his 1534 voyage in the service of the Holy Bloodline. Cartier is the first known European to have reached the future site of Montreal which was then called (by the Hurons) "Hochelaga"and is shown as "Chilaga" and other variants on many early maps.

6. It was often the practice of Protestants to give their children Christian names from the Old Testament, in contradistinction to Roman Catholics who took names mostly from the New Testament. It is on the basis of his Christian name, Samuel, that some scholars are willing to grant that Champlain may have been born into a Protestant family. For the same reason, some historians are open to the idea that Champlain's wife may have come from a Protestant family as well. However that may be, Champlain converted to Catholicism and has been described as "an ardent Catholic" by Francis Parkman, *Pioneers of France in the New World*, Musson, London, 1885, page 231; and by Edward Robert Adair in "Evolution of Montreal Under the French Regime", *Canadian Historical Association Annual Report*, 1942, page 23. See also Bishop Morris, *Champlain, The Life of Fortitude*, Macdonald & Co., London, 1949, pages 9 and 10.

7. Champlain, *Works*, page xv (Editors' Introduction)

8. Champlain, *Works*, Vol. I, pages 233-236.

9. Champlain, *Works*, Vol. I, page 235.

10. Champlain, *Works*, Vol. I, page 236, Note 3.

11. Champlain, *Works*, Vol. I, pages 237-239.

12. Champlain, *Works*, Vol. I, page 460.

13. Champlain, *Works*, Vol. I, page 460.

14. Champlain, *Works*, Vol. I, pages 461-462.

15. Unfortunately, I can cite no authority for this. In 1984 while writing the second draft of this book I contacted several people in the French departments of both York University and the University of Toronto who gave me this surprising information about Sesambre and the origin of the "cesser" words. Subsequently, all of my notes were lost in a 1986 relocation to Ottawa. Attempts to contact these professors before this book went to press in the summer of 1987 met with failure because the professors were on vacation.

16. Champlain, *Works*, Vol. I, pages 253-254.

17. Champlain, *Works*, Vol. I, page 245.

18. Champlain, *Works*, Vol. I, page 254.

19. Champlain, *Works*, Vol. I, page 255, Note 2.

20. Assuming that this method was used, and assuming that Aubry was accurate in taking his sightings, my calculations indicate that he would have arrived at a point approximately two miles east of The Cross. But his course would not actually have been a straight line due east, but a series of straight-line daily marches that, together, formed a curve from St. Mary's Bay to near The Cross. The sun rises in a slightly different position each day, and from June 15 to June 21 rises a little more to the north. After June 21, the sun begins to retreat toward the south, rising a little further south each day.

21. Champlain, *Works*, Vol. I, pages 255-256.
22. This is just another (of many) indications that Europeans were active in North America before the official discoverers and explorers.
23. Champlain, *Works*, Vol. I, pages 454-455.
24. Champlain, *Works*, Vol. I, page xvi (Editors' Introduction).
25. Adair, "Evolution of Montreal Under The French Regime", page 26.
26. Adair, "Evolution of Montreal Under The French Regime", page 26.
27. Champlain, *Works*, Vol. II, pages 303-304. See also the same pages for identification of the "rapids of St. Louis" with the Lachine rapids.
28. Champlain, *Works*, Vol. I, page 10.
29. Thomas Henry Gilmour, *Knights of Malta, Ancient and Modern*, Kennedy, Roberton Co. Ltd., Glasgow, 1903, page 231.
30. William Inglis Morse, *Pierre du Gua, Sieur de Monts: records: colonial and (saintongeois)*, B. Quaritch Ltd., London, 1939, page 12.
31. Adair, "Evolution of Montreal Under the French Regime", page 36.
32. Florian de la Horbe, *L'Incroyable Secret de Champlain*, Editions du Mont Pagnote, Paris, 1958.
33. However, Joe C.W. Armstrong, author of *Champlain* (MacMillan of Canada, Toronto, 1987, pages 274-278) has reproduced documentary evidence that Champlain's uncle called "le Provençal" did exist and was, indeed, named Guillaume Hélaine (or, in Spanish, "Guillermo Elano"). This document is an affidavit executed by Guillaume Hélaine on June 26, 1601 which also refers to the ship, the *St. Julien*. This affidavit, which is something in the nature of a Will, partly nullifies at least one charge of "disinformation" levelled against Champlain by Florian de la Horbe. But, at the same time, this document, which was found in the Archivo Historico Provincial in Cadiz in the 1950s and forwarded to the Public Archives of Canada in 1975, raises some questions. As a Will, the affidavit specifies Champlain as the beneficiary, but the context makes it clear that this Will supercedes a previous one which had named another beneficiary ... Guy Eder de la Fontenelle? Property and wealth left to Champlain under the terms of this Will were located in the old Templar port of La Rochelle and, besides houses and vinyards, included "le Provinçal's" one-eighth share in the *St. Julien's* cargoes. This Will makes Champlain a potentially wealthy burgher of La Rochelle and one wonders, therefore, why he chose to undertake explorations in Arcadia and New France that risked his life. Perhaps Champlain was simply adventurous, but before this Will was discovered the traditional view was that Champlain's adventurousness was at least partly dictated by his poverty and that he chose to be the king's explorer and cartographer in order to make a living. This affidavit of 1601, as interesting as it is, does not contradict the many *other* aspects of de la Horbe's research which indicates much purposeful "disinformation" on Champlain's part.
34. de la Horbe, *L'Incroyable Secret de Champlain*, page 83.

Chapter Eight
The Shepherds of Arcadia

1. Pohl, *Prince Henry Sinclair,* page 201 (note 4. to Chapter Eleven), where he mentions the buffalo hides supposedly circulating in Florence before 1492. Previously I have read, but do not remember the source, that a German church dating from the 13th Century incorporated a decorative mural of birds in which an American turkey was depicted. Eben Norton Horsford in his *The Landfall of Lief Erikson, AD 1000, and the Site of his Houses in Vinland* (Boston, 1892) suggests that one of the major exports from North America eventually became sacremental dishes made of Mösur wood (bird's eye maple) which were highly prized by churches in Europe (pages 233-256).
2. Paul Hermann, *Conquest By Man,* page 292-294.
3. In the South Atlantic, Cape Sao Roque in Brazil is only about 475 miles west of the meridian of Fogo, the westernmost of the Cape Verde Islands. This is only about 158 leagues (of 2.72 miles), and therefore Brazil is Portuguese-speaking to this day. The revised boundary of 370 leagues, about 1005 miles west of Fogo, cuts deep into the Brazilian interior. However, contradicting the expectations of the time, the Line of Demarcation inter-sects with the North American coast at about 60 degrees west longitude, cutting Cape Breton in half and leaving all of Newfoundland and Labrador to the Portuguese. However, at the time, everyone underestimated the distance across the Atlantic, and also had a distorted idea of the trend of the coast, and so it was believed that the Line of Demarcation would cut the Atlantic seaboard near present-day Delaware.
4. Gonzalo Fernando de Oviedo y Valdes, or simply "Oviedo" to historians, is the major source for information on the voyage of Estevan Gomez which is mentioned in both the *Sumario* of 1526 and Oviedo's *Historia General y Natural de las Indias* of 1537 (but not published until 1852). Gomez did not say that he visited "Norumbega," but only that he took captives in the north where early maps and explorers indicated the existence of Norumbega. Oviedo describes these captives as "Indians" but this may have been to disguise Spanish embarrassment at discovering a heretical community in Portuguese territory. See *Historia,* Vol. II, page 147.
5. The original manuscript version of Polydore Vergil's *History of England* written in 1512 contains a mention of John Cabot and his voyages. Similarly, Pasqualigo, the Venetian ambassador in London, spoke with Cabot and wrote a 1497 letter to his family describing Cabot's discoveries. But the major source is the report of Pedro de Ayala, a Spanish envoy in London, who also spoke with Cabot about the voyage. See Hermann, *Conquest by Man,* page 294, for a partial reproduction of the Pasqualigo letter. See Ganong, *Crucial Maps,* pages 8-13, where he discusses the Spanish report without, however, naming the envoy, Pedro de Ayala. Thus we have three second hand reports of Cabot's supposed first voyage of 1497, but no ship's log or record that has survived. Ganong notes that the evidence for Cabot's

supposed *second* voyage in 1498 "are scant and dubious". It seems to me that Cabot's supposed *first* voyage is also fairly dubious for he merely *told* people what he had discovered, wrote no report that has survived, and *returned with nothing that could prove the crossing*, not even an Indian artifact, although Pasqualigo's letter says that Cabot met a savage king and gave him presents (several traps for catching wild beasts, and a needle for making nets). Surely, Cabot could have received something in return? See a popular update on the Cabot situation, "Historians tackle trail of elusive John Cabot" by Donald Jones, *The Toronto Star*, June 27, 1987, page M3. To put Cabot in perspective, it should be said that Bristol had been sending ships annually in search of land to the west since at least 1480 when the 80-ton *Jon Jay Junior* spent nine fruitless weeks on the North Atlantic being buffeted by storms. Cabot was involved in this effort and his turn to command a ship came in 1497, the little *Matthew* of about the same size as the *Jon Jay Junior* with a crew of eighteen. So, Cabot was just one sailor among many involved in Bristol's westward search. The only difference between Cabot's voyage and previous Bristol ones was that Cabot claimed success (at last) while offering no shred of proof.

6. Pohl, *The Lost Discovery*, page 231.
7. Morison, *Christopher Columbus, Mariner*, pages 147-153 for a general discussion of westward variation.
8. Ganong, *Crucial Maps*, page 10.
9. Ganong, pages 8-32.
10. Adair, "Evolution of Montreal Under the French Regime", page 20.
11. Adair, page 21.
12. Adair, page 27.
13. Gustave Lanctot, *Montreal Under Maisonneuve*, Clarke Irwin & Company Limited, Toronto/Vancouver, 1969, page 14.
14. Joseph Kearney Foran, *Jeanne Mance, The Angel of the Colony*, The Religious Hospitallers of St. Joseph, Hotel-Dieu, Montreal, 1931, page 10.
15. Marie-Clair Daveluy, *Jeanne Mance 1606-1673*, Fides, Montreal, 1962, pages 161-163.
16. Foran, *Jeanne Mance*, pages 17-18.
17. Foran, page 22.
18. Foran, pages 22-23.
19. William Inglis Morse, *Pierre du Gua, Sieur de Monts*, Author's Foreword.
20. Lanctot, *Montreal Under Maisonneuve*, pages 19-20.
21. Francis Parkman, *Pioneers of France in the New World*, Musson, London, 1885, page 273.
22. Foran, *Jeanne Mance*, page 161.
23. Foran, page 51.
24. Baigent, Leigh and Lincoln, *Holy Blood, Holy Grail*, 133-164.
25. Josephy, Alvin M. J., *The Indian Heritage of America*, Alfred A. Knopf Inc., New York 1966, pages 47-48, 85-87.

Chapter Nine
The Bees of Childeric

1. David G. Chandler, *The Campaigns of Napoleon*, Macmillan, New York, pages 533-541.
2. Chandler, *The Campaigns of Napoleon*, page 42.
3. Chandler, *The Campaigns of Napoleon*, page 43.
4. Chandler, *The Campaigns of Napoleon*, pages 44-45. It has often been stated that the "wily Talleyrand" had no deep loyalties at all which accounted for his success in serving revolutionary and royalist regimes in France. However, it maybe that Tallyrand's apparent behaviour was dictated by a commitment to another royalty more legitimate than the Bourbons and of which both the revolution and Napoleon's empire were expressions.
5. Chandler, *The Campaigns of Napoleon*, page 47.
6. Chandler, *The Campaigns of Napoleon*, pages 223-261.
7. R. Descardeillas, *Rennes et ses derniers seigneurs*, Toulouse, 1964, page 34.
8. Baigent, Leigh and Lincoln, *Holy Blood, Holy Grail*, page 467, Note 3 to Chapter 9; but see also Philippe de Cherisey's *L'Or de Rennes pour un Napoleon*.
9. Chandler, *The Campaigns of Napoleon*, page 126.
10. Chandler, *The Campaigns of Napoleon*, page 126.
11. Although Europe had previously sent out purely scientific expeditions such as the voyages of Captain Cook no earlier scientific enterprise could compare with the 150 scientists and artists that Napoleon incorporated into his Army of Egypt, considering that he specified that they were to have no military role whatsoever, even in battle.
12. Chandler, *The Campaigns of Napoleon*, page 332.
13. Las Cases, *Memoirs of the Emperor Napoleon*, Paris, 1841, page 341.
14. Chandler, *The Campaigns of Napoleon*, page 286.
15. Chandler, *The Campaigns of Napoleon*, page 623
16. Chandler, *The Campaigns of Napoleon*, page 621-622.
17. Peter Tompkins, *The Magic of Obelisks*, Harper & Row, New York, 1981, pages 309-339 for these facts about Masonic influence in the birth of the American republic (and many other facts). Tompkins, using the recovery of Egyptian obelisks as a foil, reconstructs the connection between the medieval Templars and later esoteric orders like the Masons and the Rose-Cross. In this extremely detailed work, Tompkins anticipated the same arguments of a Templar-Masonic connection as are offered in *Holy Blood, Holy Grail*.
18. Baigent, Leigh and Lincoln, *Holy Blood, Holy Grail*, page 183.
19. John G. Bennett, *Gurdjieff: The Making of A New World*, Turnstone Books, London, 1973, pages 68-69.

Chapter Ten
The Dynasty in the 20th Century

1. Walter Birks and R.A. Gilbrt, *The Treasure of Montségur*, Thorsons Publishing Group, London, 1987, pages 38-40; but see also Jean-Michel Angebert's *The Occult and the Third Reich* for a much more detailed account of Otto Rahn's activities, pages 42-68.
2. Rahn steadfastly insisted that the Grail was an *object*, or, rather *the* object called "Solomon's Jewel Case" which was supposed to have been made of stone, mentioned in Iberian-Moorish sources, but supposed to have been lost since A.D. 711. Personally, I think that Rahn did this only to "create" a Grail corresponding to *one* of Wolfram von Eschenbach's descriptions of it . . . "a stone from the sky", since Wolfram was a "German" author of a Grail Romance. Otto Rahn's 20th Century SS recruits could not be expected to know that Wolfram was indulging in a religious pun and joke which is described in the text. If "Solomon's Jewel Case" existed it was probably exactly that. A jewel case. It has nothing to do with the Holy Grail.
3. Jean-Michel Angebert, *The Occult and the Third Reich* reproduces photographs of Nazi signposts declaring (in German and French) that Montségur was part of Germany and off-limits to the French.
4. Jean-Michel Angebert, *The Occult and the Third Reich*, page 73.
5. Quoted and translated from Jean-Michel Angebert's *The Occult and the Third Reich*, but they do not name the poem or the author, page 75. The language is, however, Provençal of the 13th Century.
6. Quoted from Rauschning's *Hitler m'a dit (Hitler Told Me)* by Jean-Michel Angebert in *The Occult and the Third Reich*, page 77.
7. Quoted in Jean-Michel Angebert's *The Occult and the Third Reich*, page 147.
8. Quoted from Baigent, Leigh and Lincoln, *Hold Blood, Holy Grail* pages 287-288.
9. Baigent, Leigh and Lincoln, *Holy Blood, Holy Grail*, page 288.
10. Baigent, Leigh and Lincoln, *Holy Blood, Holy Grail*, pages 288-289.
11. *Perlesvaus*, page 89.
12. *Perlesvaus*, page 268.
13. Baigent, Leigh and Lincoln, *Holy Blood, Holy Grail*, page 291.
14. *Perlesvaus*, page 199ff.
15. Helen M. Mustard and Charles E. Passage, editors and translators of *Parzival* by Wolfram von Eschenbach, Random House ("Vintage editions"), New York, 1961, from Editor/Translator Introduction, page i.
16. Baigent, Leigh and Lincoln, *Holy Blood, Holy Grail*, pages 294-295.
17. Wolfram von Eschenbach, *Parzival*, page 244ff.
18. Wolfram von Eschenbach, *Parzival*, page 244.
19. Wolfram von Eschenbach, *Parzival*, page 244.
20. Wolfram von Eschenbach, *Parzival*, page 129.
21. Wolfram von Eschenbach, *Parzival*, page 130.
22. Wolfram von Eschenbach, *Parzival*, page 251.

23. Wolfram von Eschenbach, *Parzival*, page 264.
24. Wolfram von Eschenbach, *Parzival*, Editor/Translator Introduction, Vintage edition cited above (15), page xi-xii.
25. This leads us back to the "Rhiothamus" chronology covered in the notes to Chapter one.
26. Wolfram von Eschenbach, *Parzival*, Editor/Translator Introduction cited above (15), page xvi.
27. Wolfram von Eschenbach, *Parzival*, page 130.
28. Wolfram von Eschenbach, *Parzival*, page 129.
29. Wolfram von Eschenbach, *Parzival*, page 244.
30. Baigent, Leigh and Lincoln, *Holy Blood, Holy Grail*, page 288. But before leaving Wolfram von Eschenbach I would like to comment on his reference to "Greenland knights". These "Greenland knights" take a prominent place in his romance, and the first thing that springs to mind is how Wolfram could have heard of Greenland. Eric the Red discovered Greenland in the year 984 and rounded up colonists in 986. It was a very obscure Viking colonization attempt. Greenland did not come to the attention of the European nobility until the publication of Frederick II's book about falconry *(De arte venandi cum avibus . . .* "On the Art of Falconry") which was written in 1250 extolling the virtues of Greenland gyrfalcons, or, about thirty years after Wolfram von Eschenbach wrote *Parzival*. That being the case, I consulted original German versions of *Parzival* in various libraries to determine whether, in translation, careless editors might have substituted some other known land (such as Iceland) for Greenland. But no, the word used in the German versions of *Parzival* was "Engroneland", the name for Greenland in the very early times of European exploration. This still remains a mystery for me, unless Greenland has some significance for Wolfram that has escaped everyone's attention. The only thing that I can think of is that Wolfram was aware of Roger II of Sicily (1130-1154) who was a real Scandinavian, and possible a Templar, and who, in any case, could know of Greenland before that place came into common European knowledge because of the falcons bred there. Possibly supportive of this idea is the fact that these "Greenland knights" came into romantic (and otherwise) contact with some dark-skinned queens. Is this a reference to the Norse conquest of Sicily? If so, then Wolfram was remarkably well informed. Or was he told that "Greenland knights" (ie. Norse, Norwegian) "knights" would carry the Grail to safety? The reference to Greenland knights in *Parzival* is something that has escaped the attention of both literary and historical scholars.
31. Baigent, Leigh and Lincoln, *Holy Blood, Holy Grail*, pages 214-226.
32. Mattieu Paoli, *Les Dessous d'une ambition politique*, Nyon (France), 1973.
33. This was first presented by Gérard de Sède in his *La Race fabuleuse*, Paris, 1973.
34. Baigent, Leigh and Lincoln, *Holy Blood, Holy Grail*, pages 220-221, but quoted here from *Le Charivari* No. 18, page 55.
35. *Le Charivari*, No. 18, page 53.

36. Baigent, Leigh and Lincoln, *Holy Blood, Holy Grail*, page 222.
37. Baigent, Leigh and Lincoln, *Holy Blood, Holy Grail*, page 204.
38. Jean-Michel Angebert, *The Occult and the Third Reich*, page 196.
39. Poem by Charles Peguy, "La Tapisserie de Sainte Genevieve", *Oeuvres poétiques complètes*, Paris, 1957, page 849.
40. Bernard Baruch, *My Story*, Pocket Books, New York, 1958, page 286.
41. Doris French Shackleton, *Tommy Douglas*, McClelland and Stewart, Toronto, 1975, pages 28-30.
42. Quoted from *Tommy Douglas* by Doris French Shackleton, pages 290-291.

Selected Bibliography

King Arthur and Celtic Lore.

Alcock, Leslie, "By South Cadbury is that Camelot . . . ", *Antiquity*, Vol. XLI, March 1967, pages 50-53.

Ashe, Geoffrey (Ed.), *The Quest For Arthur's Britain*, Granada Publishing Limited, London, 1968.

Geoffrey of Monmouth, *History of the Kings of Britain*, ed. and trans. Lewis Thorpe, Penguin, Harmondsworth and Baltimore, 1966.

Goodrich, Norma Lorre, *King Arthur*, Franklin Watts, Danbury, 1986.

Graves, Robert, *The White Goddess*, Faber and Faber, London, 1961.

Hermann, Paul, *Conquest By Man*, Harper & Brothers, New York, 1954.

Henry Sinclair, Transatlantic Voyages and Old Maps

Ganong, William Francis, *Crucial Maps*, University of Toronto Press, Toronto, 1964.

Hapgood, Charles, *Maps Of The Ancient Sea Kings*, Chilton Book Company, Radnor, 1968.

Pohl, Frederick, *Prince Henry Sinclair*, Clarkson N. Potter, New York, 1974.

Pohl, Frederick, *The Lost Discovery*, W.W. Norton, New York, 1952.

Templars, Cathars and the Holy Grail

Angebert, Jean-Michel, *The Occult and The Third Reich*, McGraw-Hill, Toronto, 1975.

Baigent, Michael; Leigh, Richard and Lincoln, Henry, *The Holy Blood and the Holy Grail*, Jonathan Cape, London, 1982.

Barber, Malcolm, "The Origins of the Order of the Temple", *Studia Monastica*, XII (1970), pages 219-240.

Birks, Walter and Gilbert, R.A., *The Treasure of Montségur*, Thorsons Publishing Group, London, 1987.

Burman, Edward, *The Templars, Knights of God*, Thorsons Publishing Group, London, 1986.

Eschenbach, Wolfram von, *Parzival*, trans. Helen M. Mustard and Charles E. Passage, Vintage, New York, 1961.

Guirdham, A., *Catharism, The Medieval Resurgence of Primitive Christianity*. St. Helier, Paris, 1969.

Magre, Maurice, *The Return of the Magi* (English translation of *Magiciens et Illuminés*), London, 1931.

Runciman, Steven, *A History of the Crusades*, Peregrine Books, Harmondsworth, 1978 (3 vols.).

Sède, Gérard de, *L'Or de Rennes*, Paris, 1967.

Sède, Gérard de, *La Race Fabuleuse*, Paris. 1973.

Tompkins, Peter, *The Magic of Obelisks*, Harper & Row, New York, 1981.

Champlain, Acadia and Montreal

Adair, Edward Robert, "Evolution of Montreal Under The French Regime", Canadian Historical Association, *Annual Report*, 1942, pages 20-41.

Champlain, Samuel de, *The Works of Samuel De Champlain* (6 Vols. & Folio), ed. H.P. Biggar, University of Toronto Press, Toronto, 1971.

Fell, Barry, *America B.C.*, Pocket Books, New York, 1979.

Foran, Joseph Kearney, *Jeanne Mance, The Angel of the Colony*, Montreal 1931.

Furneaux, Rupert, *The Money Pit Mystery*, T. Stacey, London, 1972.

Lanctot, Gustave, *Montreal Under Maisonneuve*, Clarke Irwin, Toronto, 1969.

Morris, Bishop, *Champlain, The Life of Fortitude*, MacDonald & Co., London, 1949.

Morse, William Inglis, *Pierre du Gua, Sieur de Monts*, B. Quaritch Ltd., London, 1939.

O'Connor, D'Arcy, *The Money Pit*, Coward, McCann and Geoghegan, New York, 1976.

Parkman, Francis, *Pioneers of France in the New World*, Musson, London, 1885.

General Reference

Bennett, John G., Gurdjieff, *The Making of a New World*, Turnstone books, London, 1973.

Bradley, Michael, *Dawn Voyage*, Summerhill Press, Toronto, 1987.

Chandler, David G., *The Campaigns of Napoleon*, Macmillan, New York, 1966.

Gilmour, Thomas Henry, *Knights of Malta, Ancient and Modern*, Kennedy, Robert Co. Ltd., Glasgow, 1903.

Horbe, Florian de la, *L'Incroyable Secret de Champlain*, Editions du Mont Pagnote, Paris, 1959.

Jones, Donald, "Historians tackle trail of elusive John Cabot", *Toronto Star*, June 27, 1987, page M3.

O'Connor, D'Arcy, "Treasure hunters continue their search but Oak Island still winning", *Wall Street Journal*, but reprinted in *The Globe and Mail*, Toronto, July 27, 1987, pages B1-B9.

Sanderson, Ivan T., "Yesu Of The Druids", *Pursuit* Vol. 6, No. I., January 1973, pages 18-19.

Saunders, A. E., *Small Craft Piloting and Coastal Navigation*, Van Nostrand Reinhold, New York and Toronto, 1982.

Shah, Idries, *The Sufis*, Anchor Books, New York, 1971.

Singer, Jon Douglas, "The Quest for Norumbega: Ancients Civilizations in New England" in three parts *Pursuit* Vol. 12, No. 1, Winter 1979, pages 13-20 (Part I); *Pursuit* Vol. 12, No. 1, Spring 1979, pages 63-67 (Part II); *Pursuit* Vol. 12, No. 4, Fall 1979, pages 179-187 (Part III).

Steiner, Stan, *Dark and Dashing Horsemen*, Harper & Row, San Francisco, 1981.

Tompkins, Peter, *Secrets of the Great Pyramid*, Harper & Row, New York, 1971.

Vermes, Geza, *The Dead Sea Scrolls in English*, Pelican Books, Harmondsworth, 1962.